B.O.D.Y.

Vol. 3

Story & Art by
Ao Mimori

Contents

The Story Thus Far...

Ryoko falls hard for Ryunosuke, the quiet, bespectacled cutie who sits next to her in class. Then she learns that he moonlights as a host—a guy who dates women for money! Soft-spoken bookworm by day, aggressive ladies' man by night, Ryu may be more than the inexperienced Ryoko can handle. But she can't seem to get him out of her head...or her heart...

Ryu wants to quit working as a host and become a one-Ryoko man, but Jin, the sleazy president of his host club, has other ideas. To buy Ryu's freedom, Ryoko agrees to take his place... and work as a hostess! But on her first night at a hostess bar, she's forced to make a run for it when a client gets too hot and heavy. Then Ryu catches her talking to Jin and demands to know what's going on...

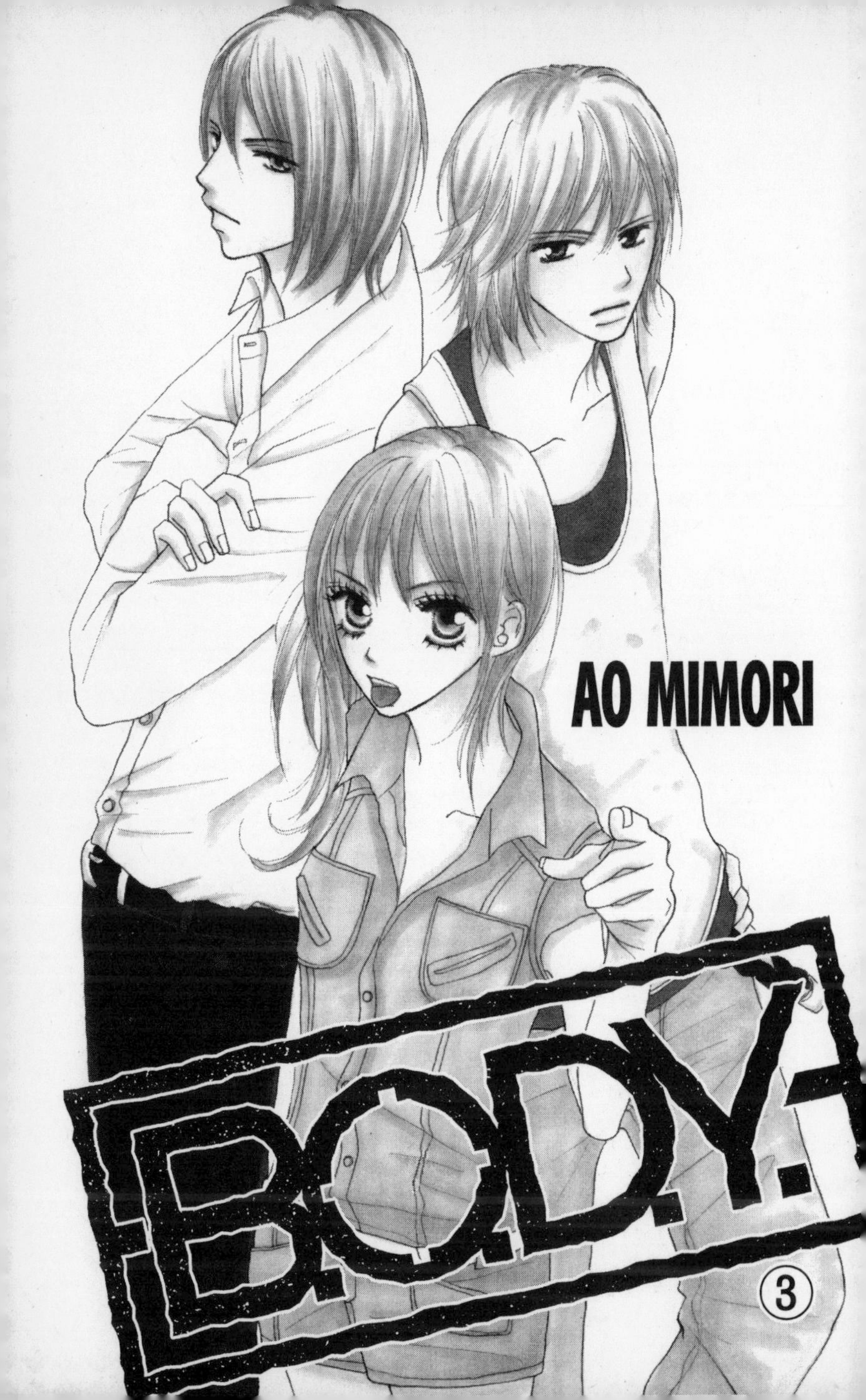
AO MIMORI
B.O.D.Y.
3

Welcome to...

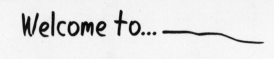 Volume 3!!

Hey guys!!

Ao "Goes-to-the-Bookstore-in-her-Pajamas" Mimori here.

B.O.D.Y.'s finally reached its third volume, and since the story's not over yet, it looks like we're going on to a fourth!

It's only the bookstore, what do I care?

TWIRL

TWIRL

PLAY-TYPHOON

I can't believe this is really happening to me. I'm scared that I'm going to find out it's all a big joke at my expense. I mean, I'm living my dream! Anyway, this is all thanks to you, my readers. By way of saying thank you, I added a little something for your pleasure to the end of the book.

I'm writing this stream of consciousness, so this is probably too much information, huh?

Let's get on with the story, then...

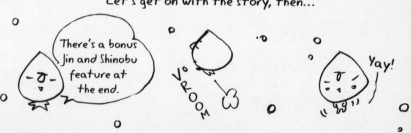

There's a bonus Jin and Shinobu feature at the end.

VROOM

Yay!

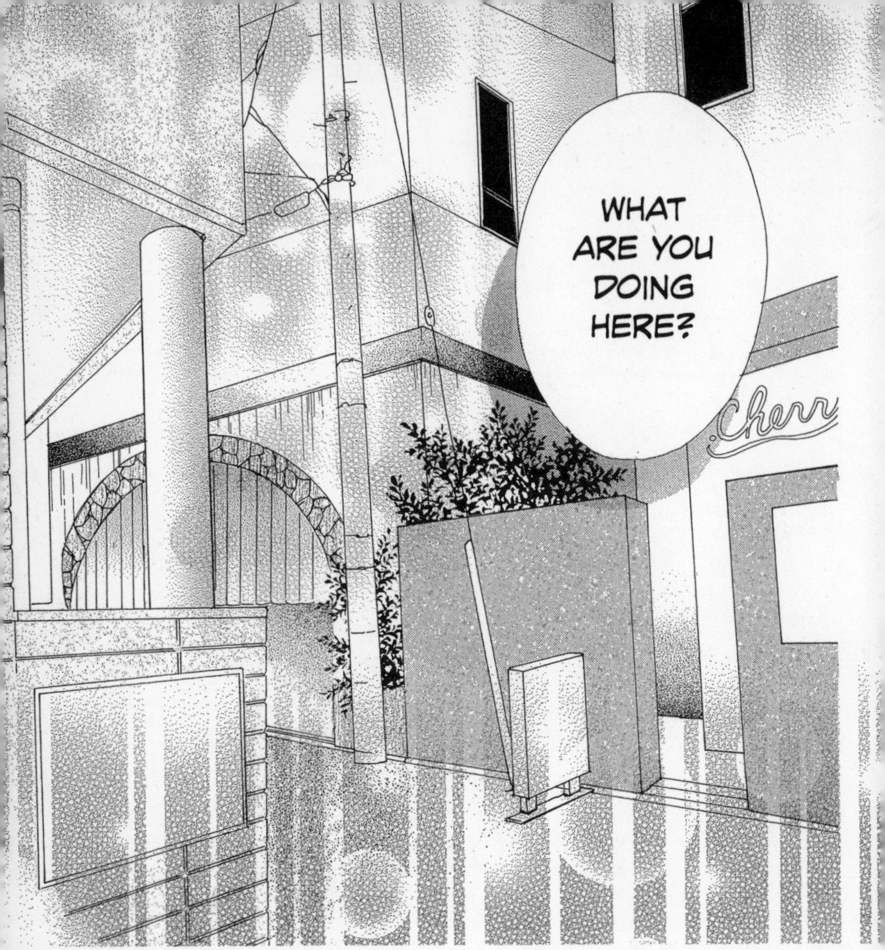
WHAT ARE YOU DOING HERE?

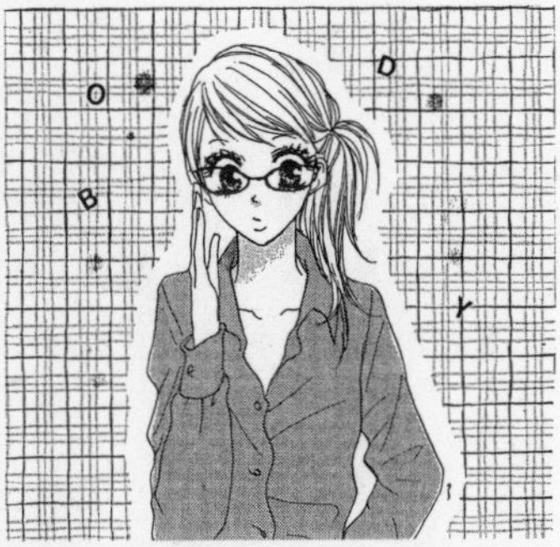

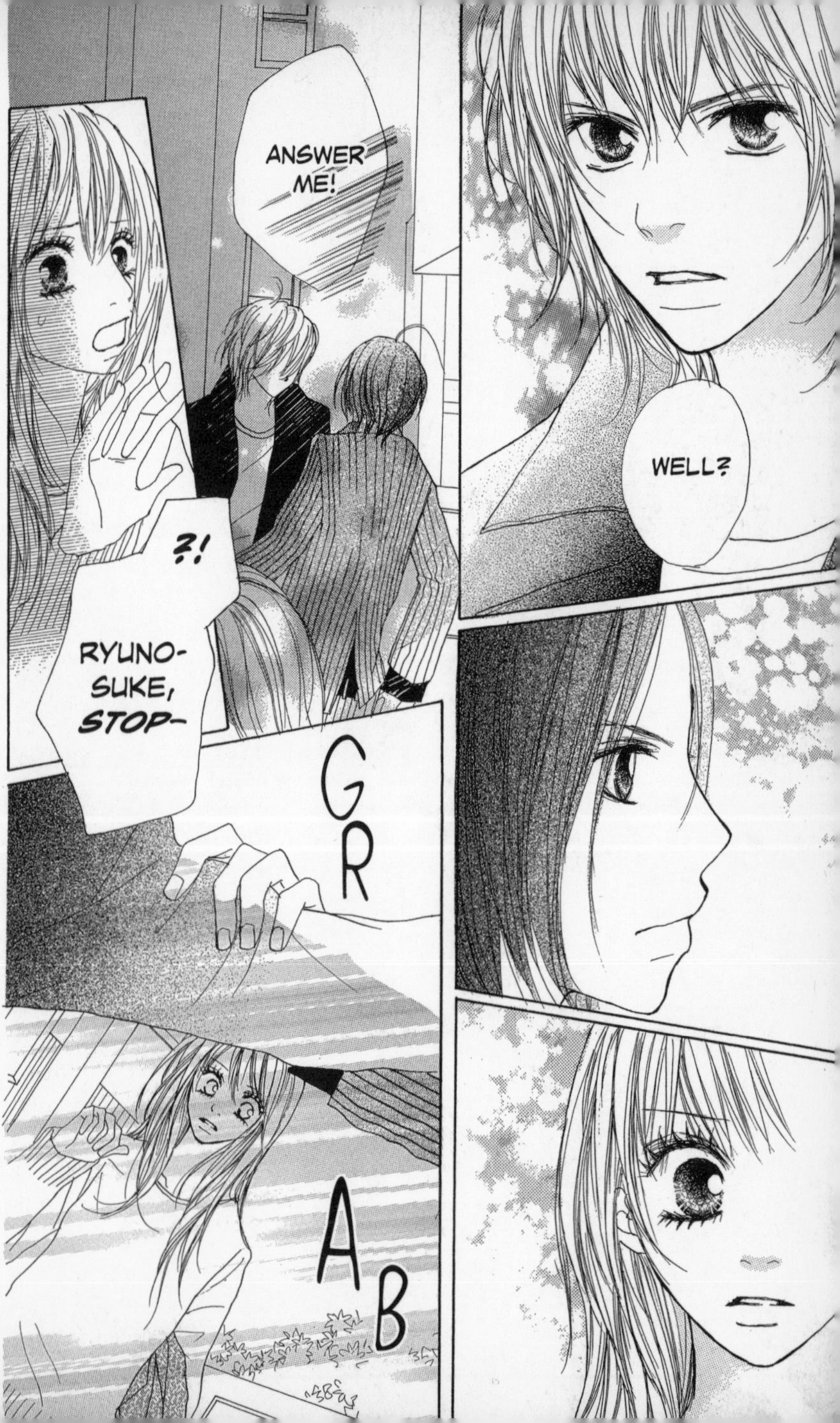
WELL?
ANSWER ME!
?!
RYUNO-SUKE, STOP-
GRAB

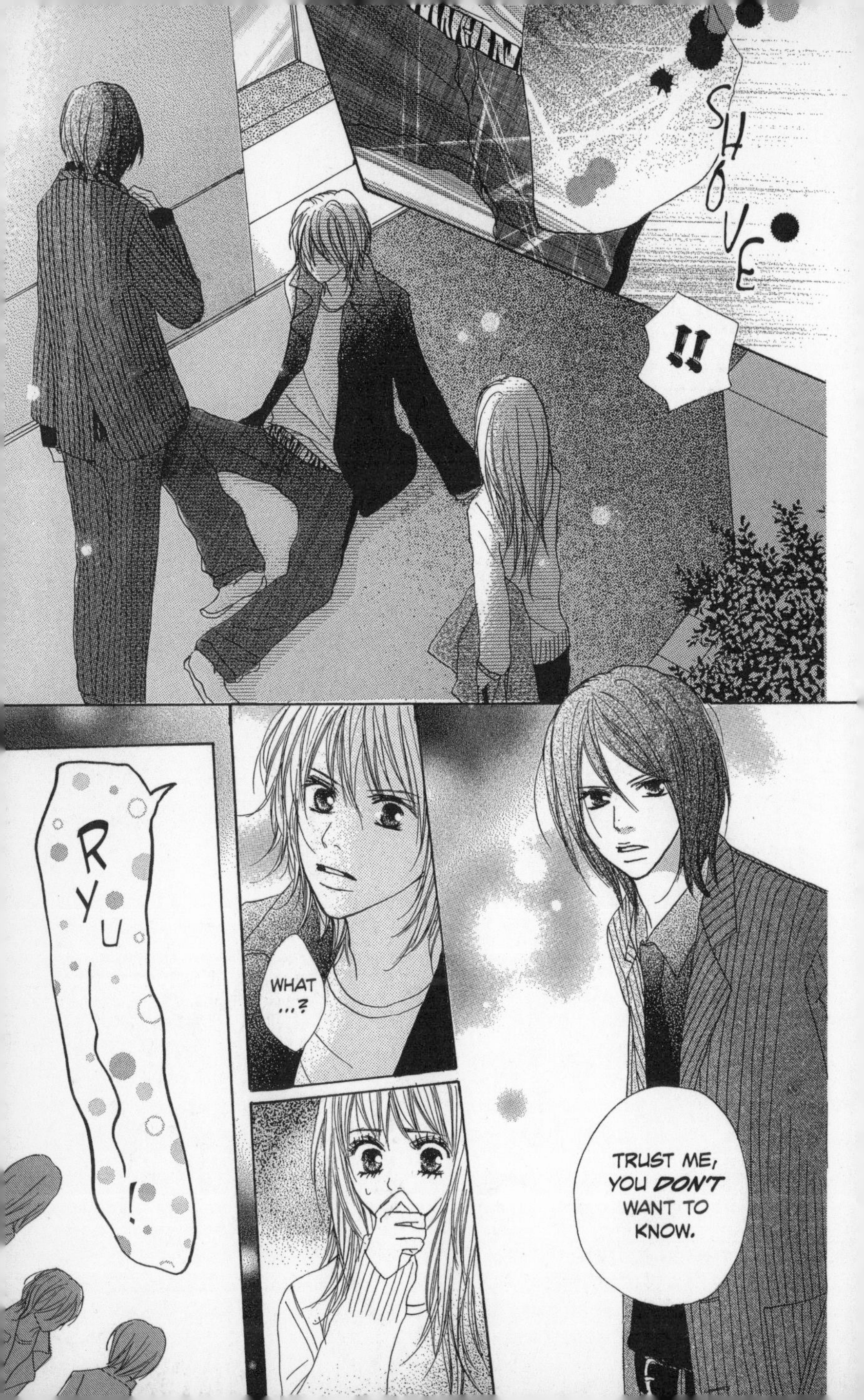
SHOVE
!!
TRUST ME, YOU DON'T WANT TO KNOW.
WHAT ...?
RYU!

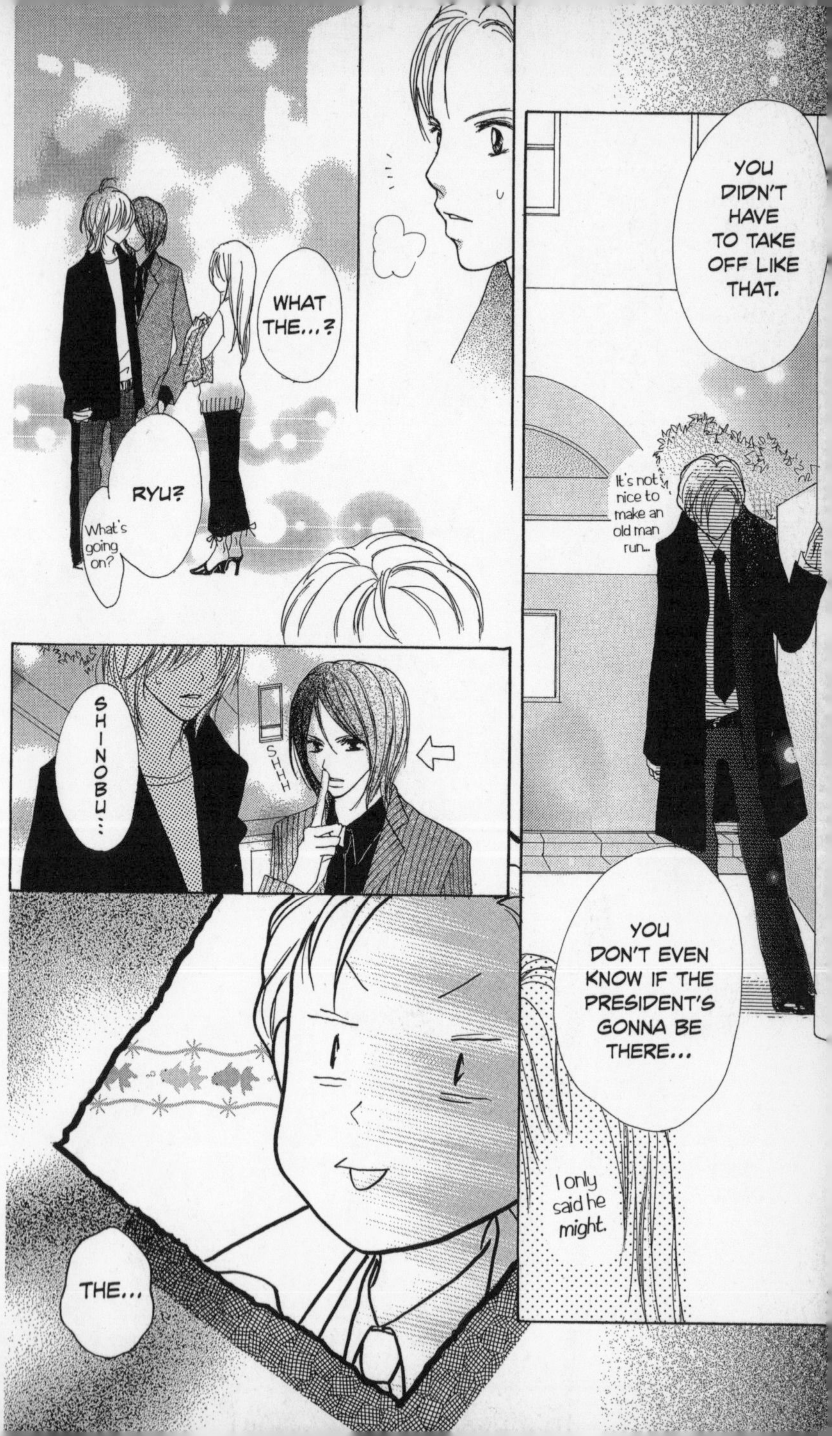

YOU DIDN'T HAVE TO TAKE OFF LIKE THAT.
It's not nice to make an old man run...
YOU DON'T EVEN KNOW IF THE PRESIDENT'S GONNA BE THERE...
I only said he might.
WHAT THE...?
RYU?
What's going on?
SHINOBU...
SHHH
THE...

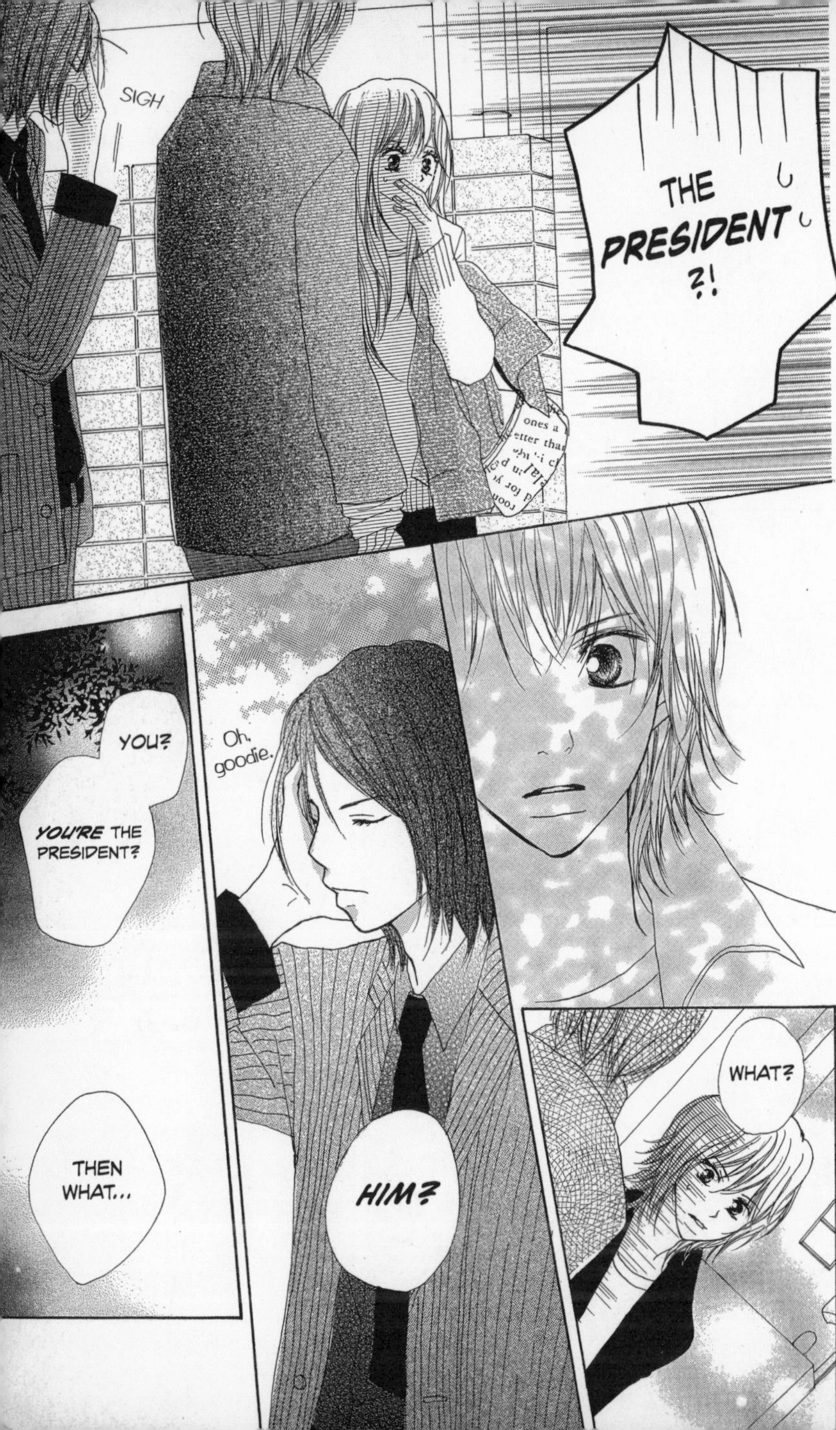
THE PRESIDENT ?!
SIGH
WHAT?
Oh, goodie.
HIM?
YOU?
YOU'RE THE PRESIDENT?
THEN WHAT...

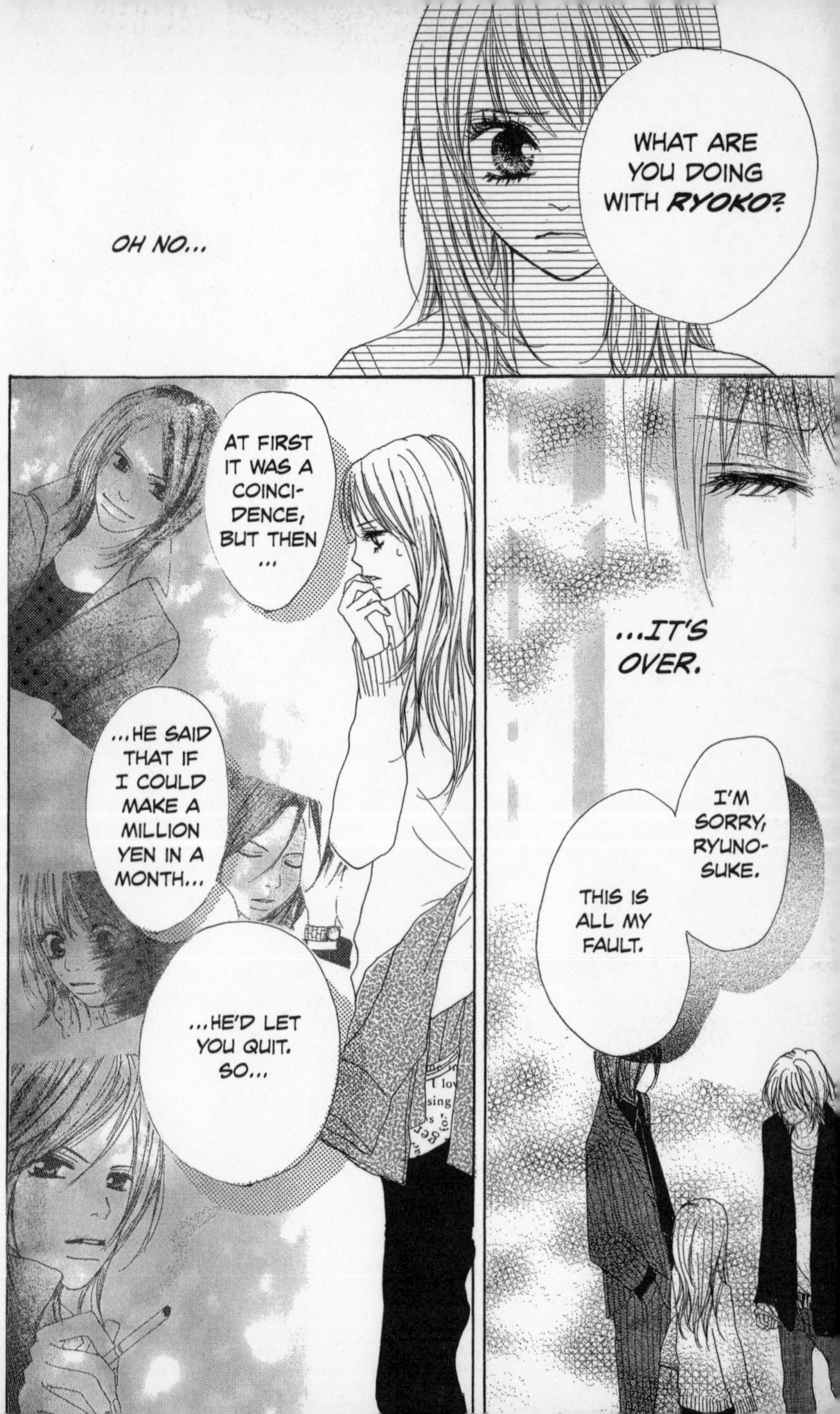
WHAT ARE YOU DOING WITH RYOKO?
OH NO...
...IT'S OVER.
I'M SORRY, RYUNOSUKE.
THIS IS ALL MY FAULT.
AT FIRST IT WAS A COINCIDENCE, BUT THEN ...
...HE SAID THAT IF I COULD MAKE A MILLION YEN IN A MONTH...
...HE'D LET YOU QUIT. SO...

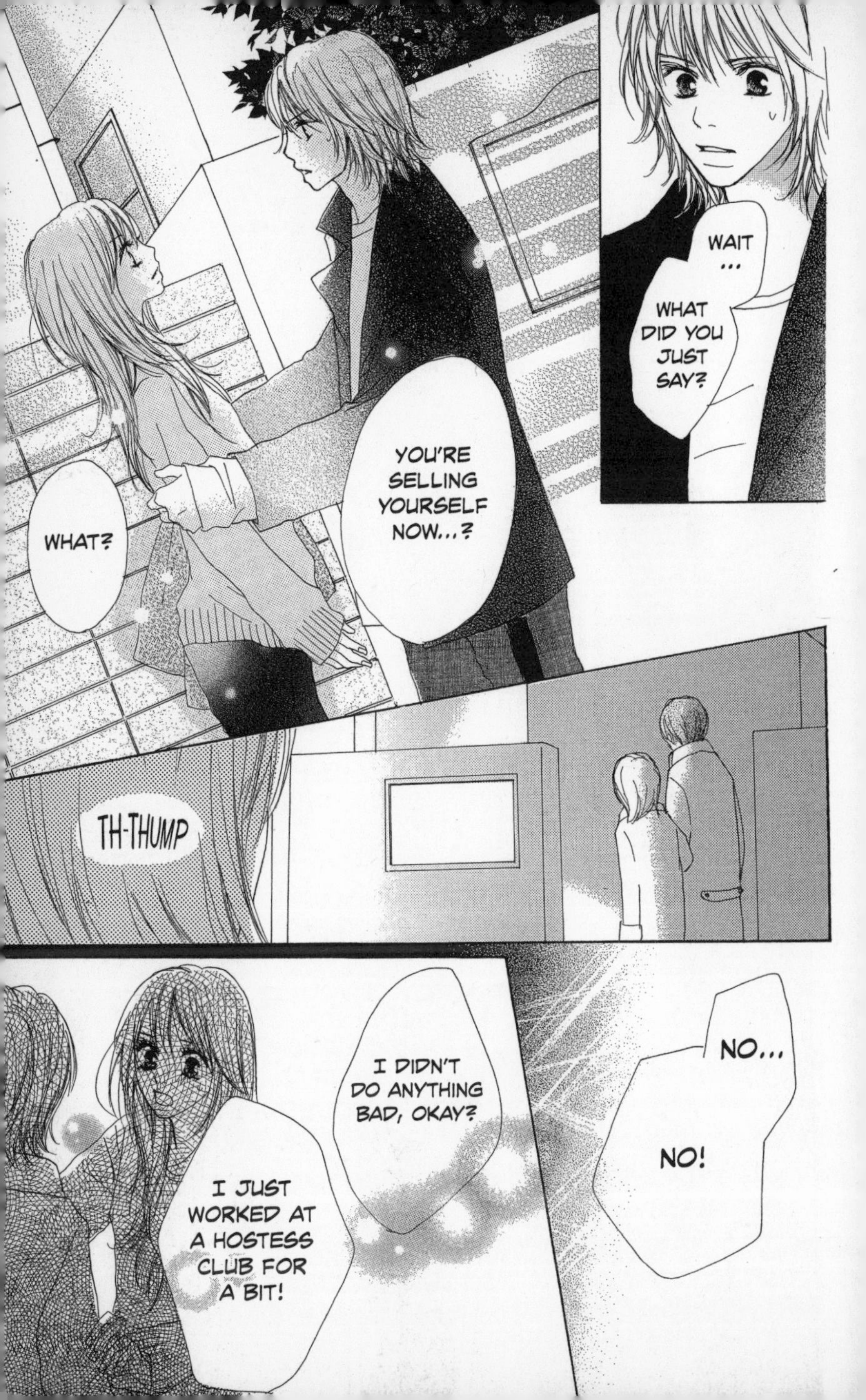
WAIT ...
WHAT DID YOU JUST SAY?
YOU'RE SELLING YOURSELF NOW...?
WHAT?
TH-THUMP
NO...
NO!
I DIDN'T DO ANYTHING BAD, OKAY?
I JUST WORKED AT A HOSTESS CLUB FOR A BIT!

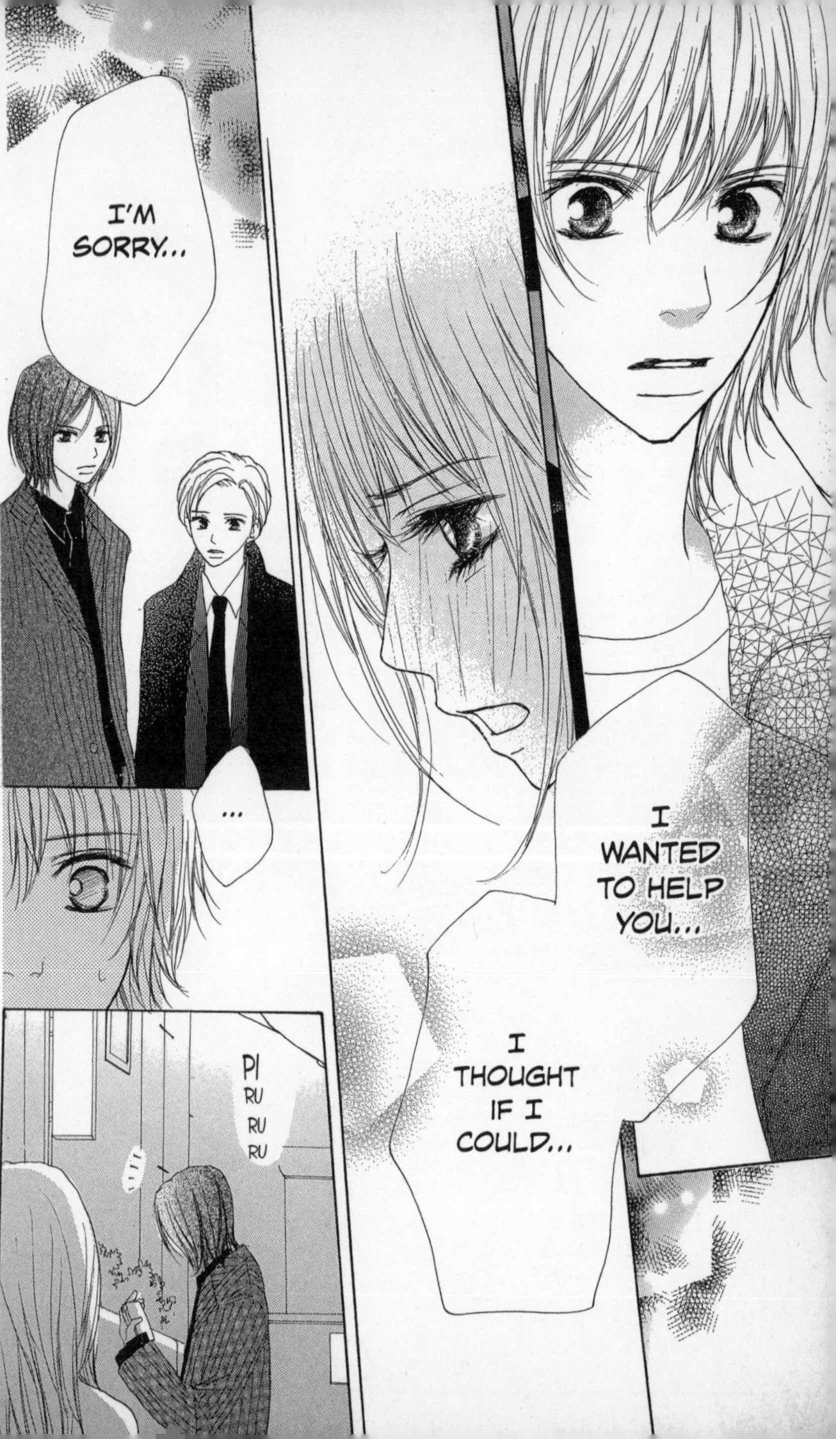
I WANTED TO HELP YOU...
I THOUGHT IF I COULD...
I'M SORRY...
...
PI RU RU RU
!

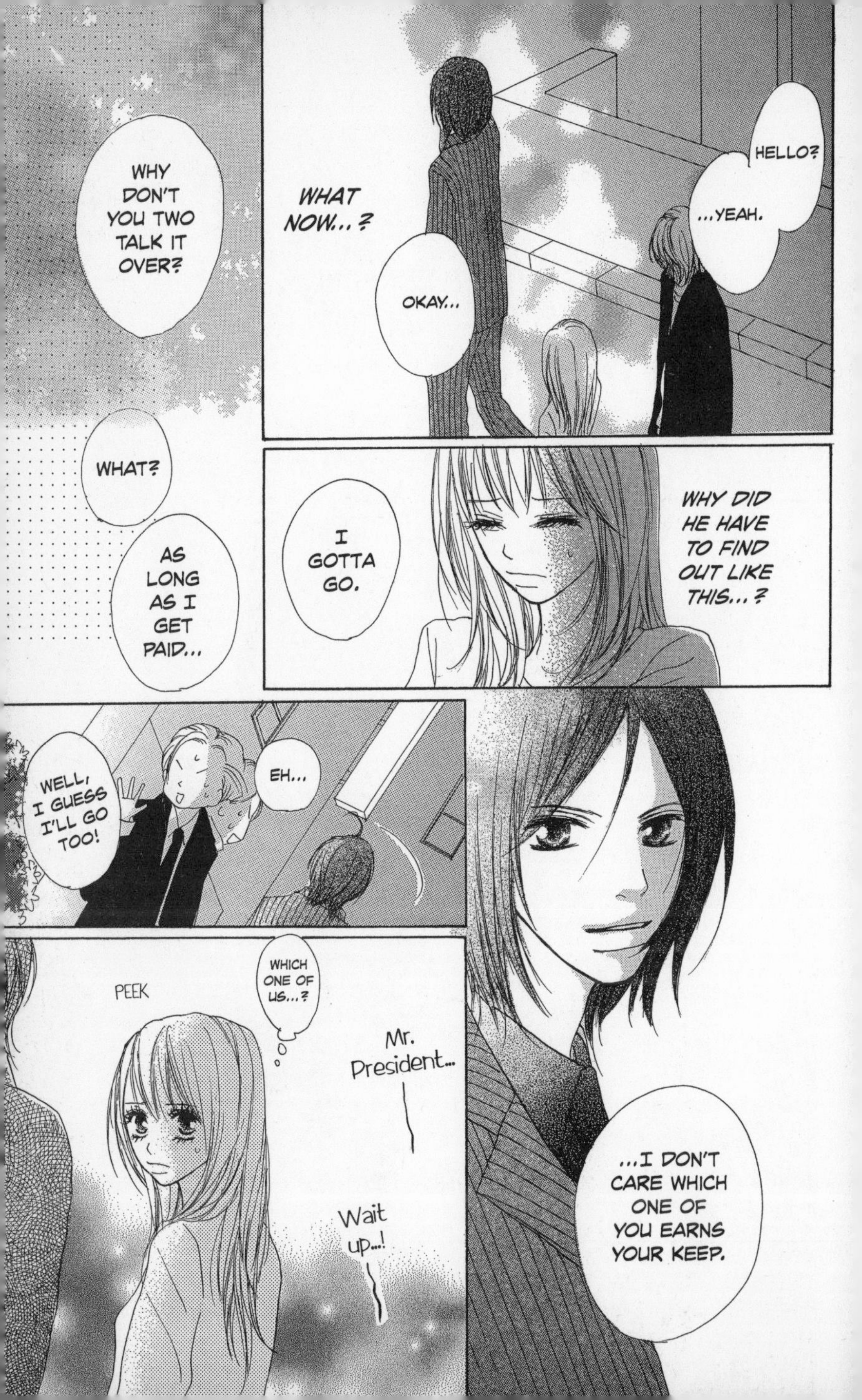
HELLO?
...YEAH.
WHAT NOW...?
OKAY...
WHY DID HE HAVE TO FIND OUT LIKE THIS...?
I GOTTA GO.
WHY DON'T YOU TWO TALK IT OVER?
WHAT?
AS LONG AS I GET PAID...
...I DON'T CARE WHICH ONE OF YOU EARNS YOUR KEEP.
EH...
WELL, I GUESS I'LL GO TOO!
WHICH ONE OF US...?
PEEK
Mr. President...
Wait up...!

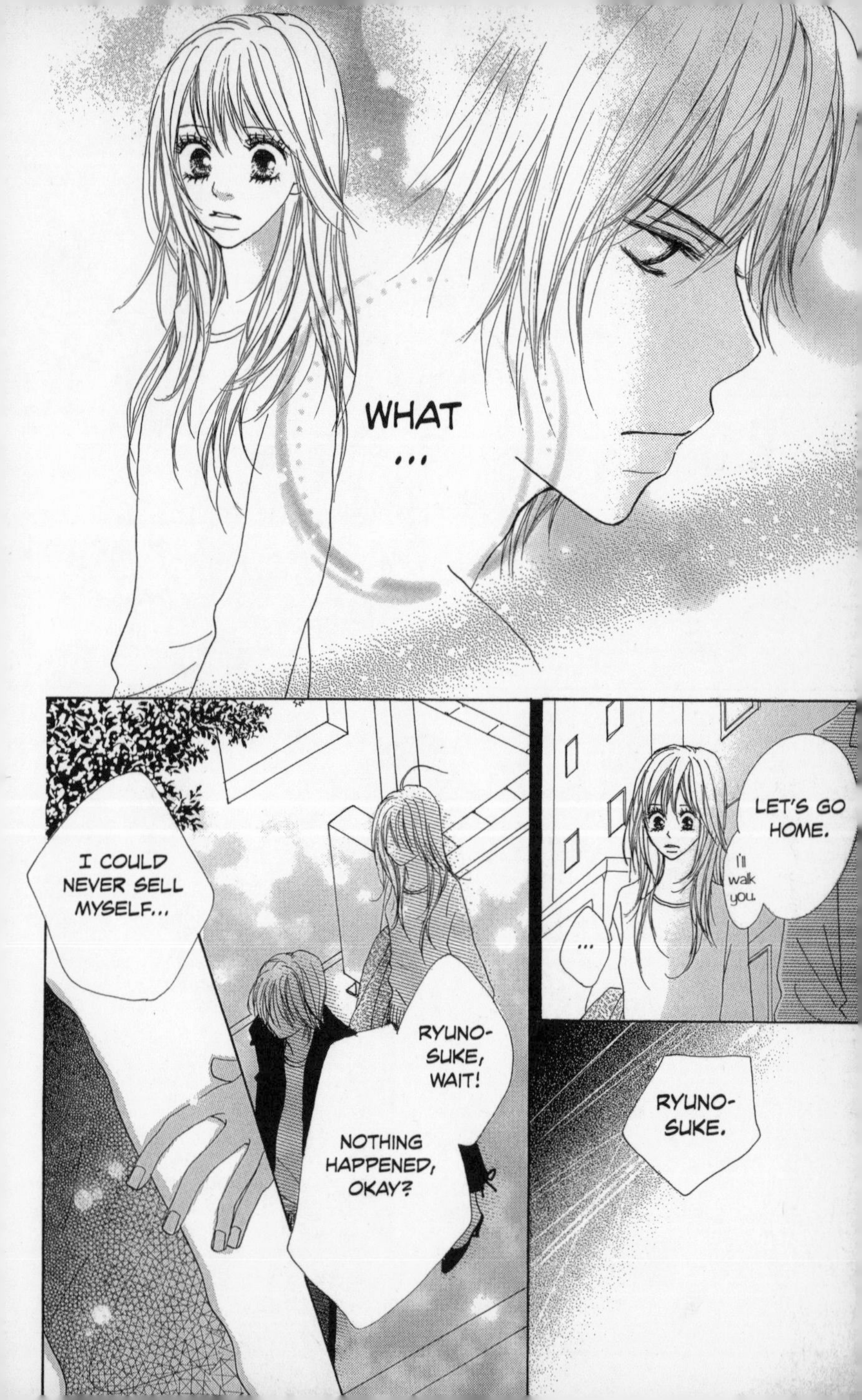
WHAT ...
LET'S GO HOME.
I'll walk you.
...
RYUNO-SUKE.
RYUNO-SUKE, WAIT!
NOTHING HAPPENED, OKAY?
I COULD NEVER SELL MYSELF...

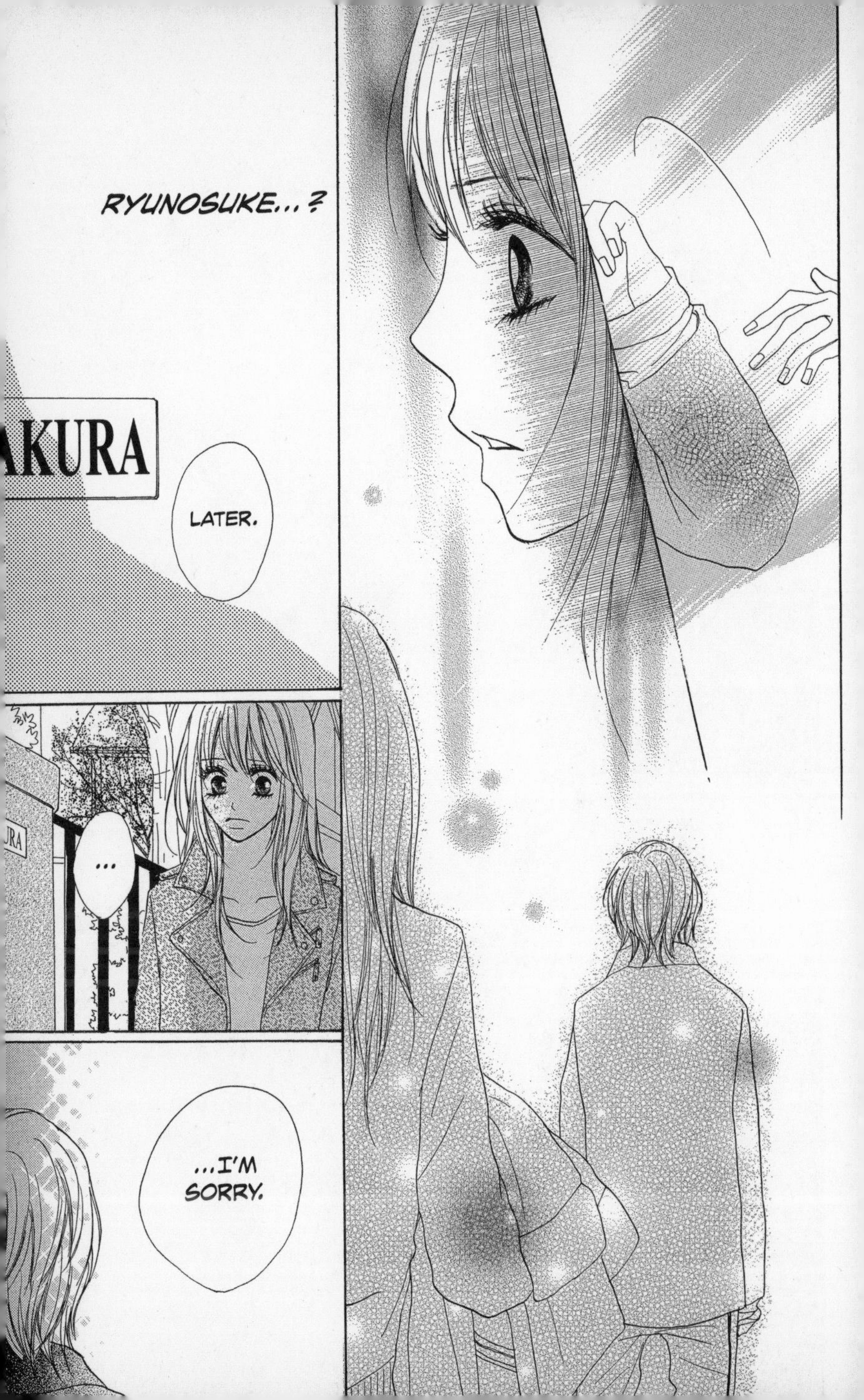
RYUNOSUKE...?
AKURA
LATER.
...
...I'M SORRY.

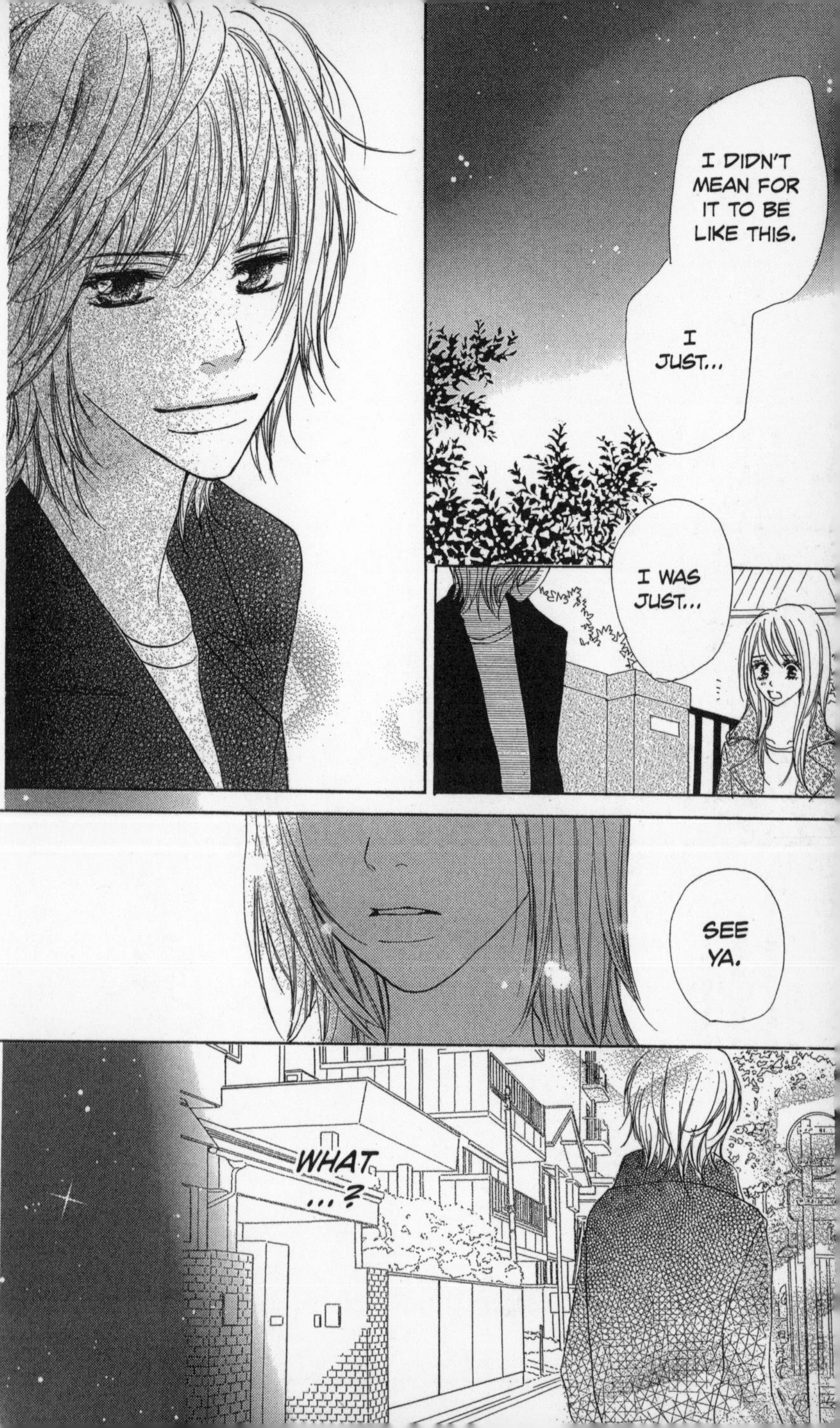
I DIDN'T MEAN FOR IT TO BE LIKE THIS.
I JUST...
I WAS JUST...
SEE YA.
WHAT ...?

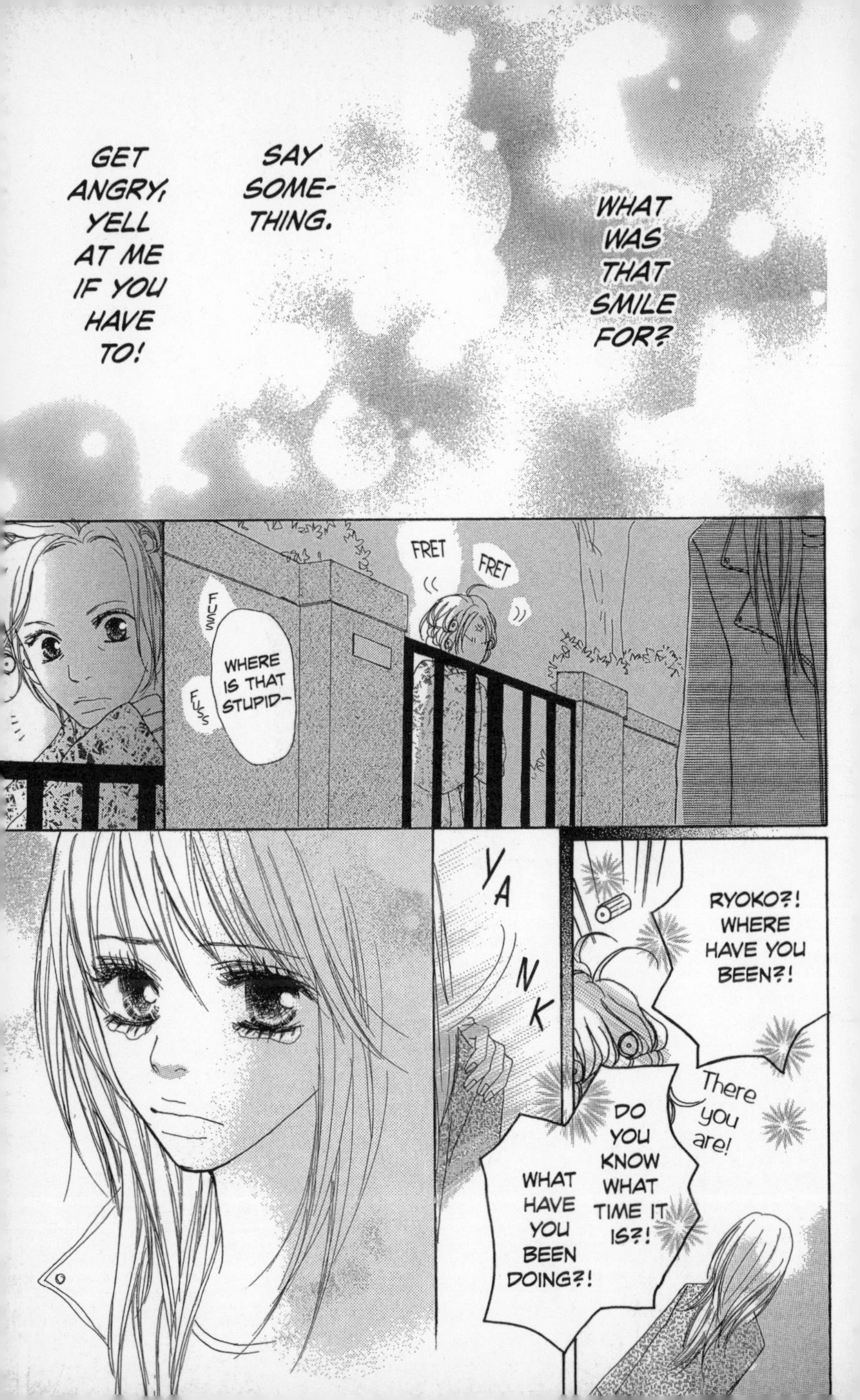
WHAT WAS THAT SMILE FOR?
SAY SOMETHING.
GET ANGRY, YELL AT ME IF YOU HAVE TO!
FRET
FRET
FUSS
WHERE IS THAT STUPID—
FUSS
RYOKO?! WHERE HAVE YOU BEEN?!
There you are!
DO YOU KNOW WHAT TIME IT IS?!
WHAT HAVE YOU BEEN DOING?!
YANK

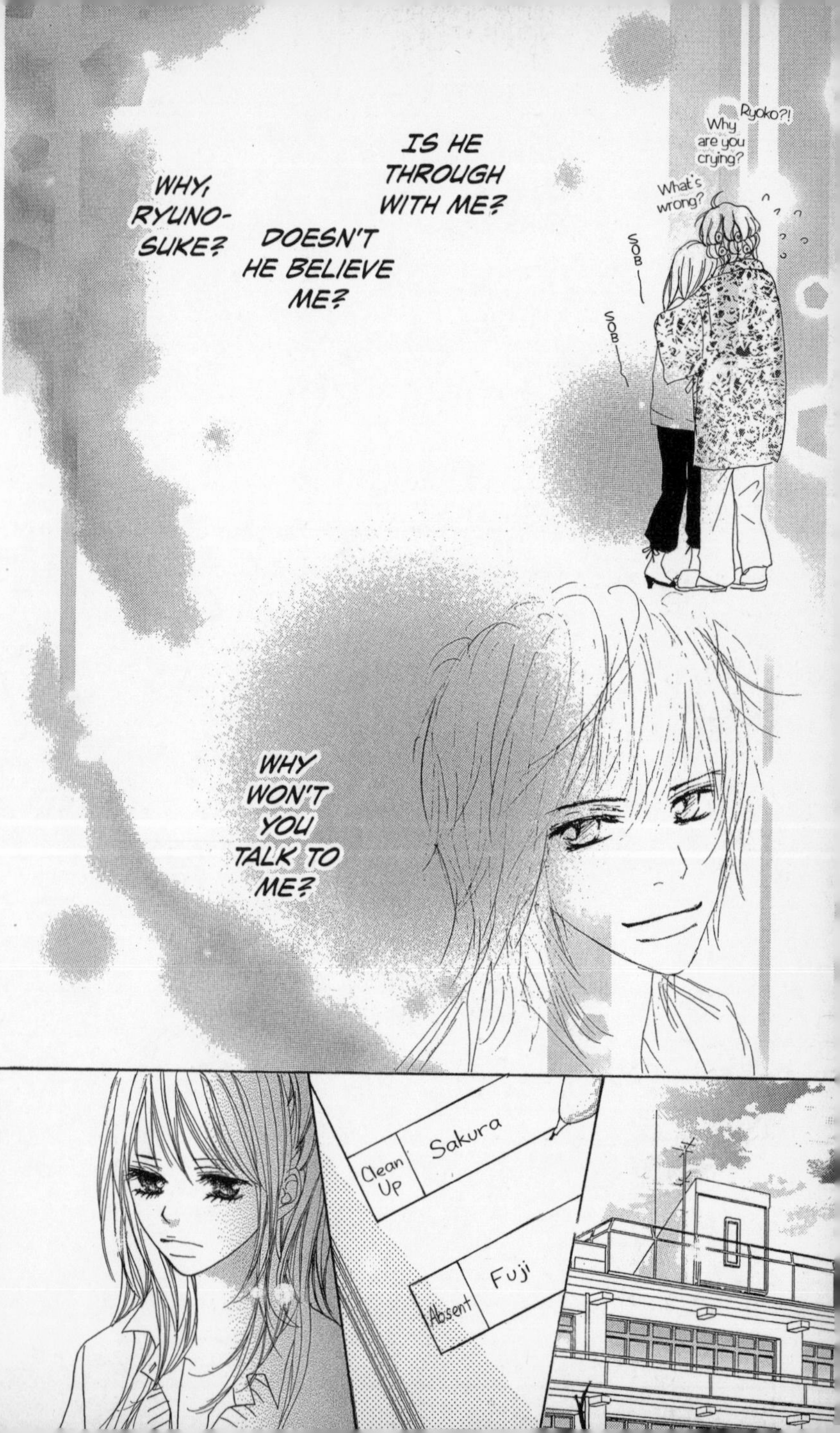
Ryoko?! Why are you crying?
What's wrong?
SOB
SOB
IS HE THROUGH WITH ME?
WHY, RYUNOSUKE?
DOESN'T HE BELIEVE ME?
WHY WON'T YOU TALK TO ME?
Clean Up
Sakura
Absent
Fuji

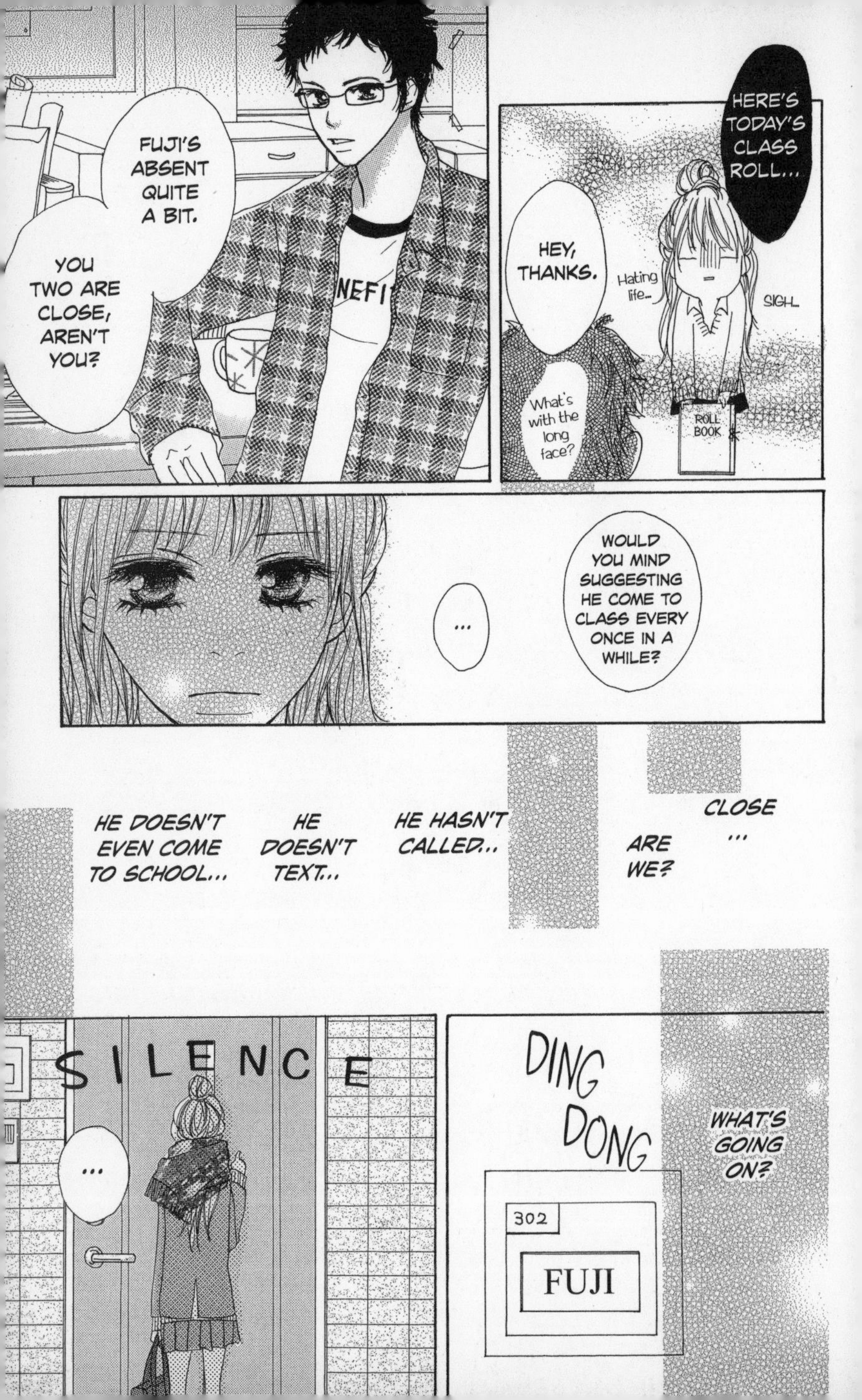
HERE'S TODAY'S CLASS ROLL...
Hating life...
SIGH...
ROLL BOOK
HEY, THANKS.
What's with the long face?
FUJI'S ABSENT QUITE A BIT.
YOU TWO ARE CLOSE, AREN'T YOU?
WOULD YOU MIND SUGGESTING HE COME TO CLASS EVERY ONCE IN A WHILE?
...
CLOSE...
ARE WE?
HE HASN'T CALLED...
HE DOESN'T TEXT...
HE DOESN'T EVEN COME TO SCHOOL...
DING DONG
WHAT'S GOING ON?
302
FUJI
SILENCE
...

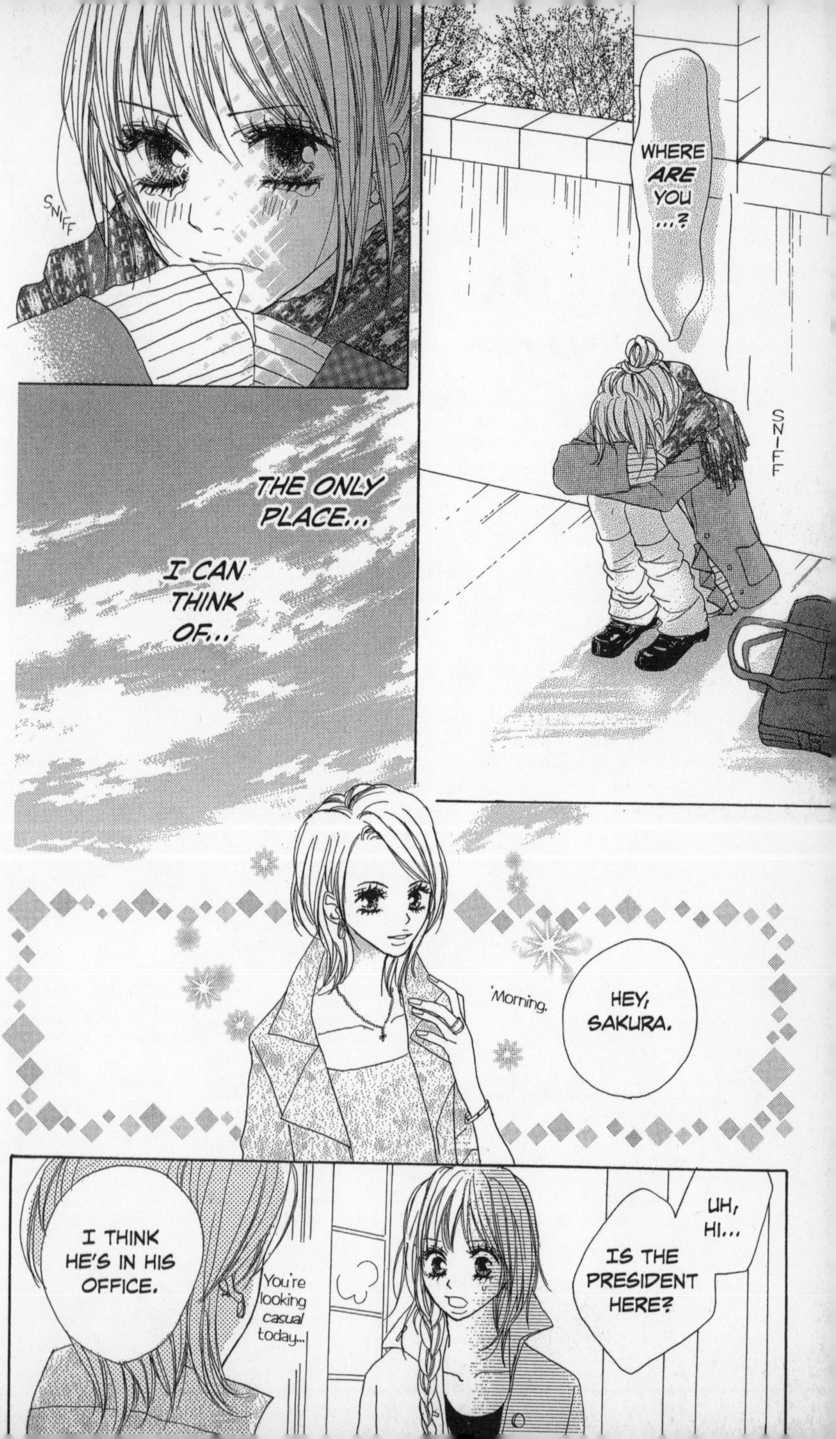
WHERE ARE YOU ...?
SNIFF
SNIFF
THE ONLY PLACE...
I CAN THINK OF...
'Morning.
HEY, SAKURA.
UH, HI...
IS THE PRESIDENT HERE?
You're looking casual today...
I THINK HE'S IN HIS OFFICE.

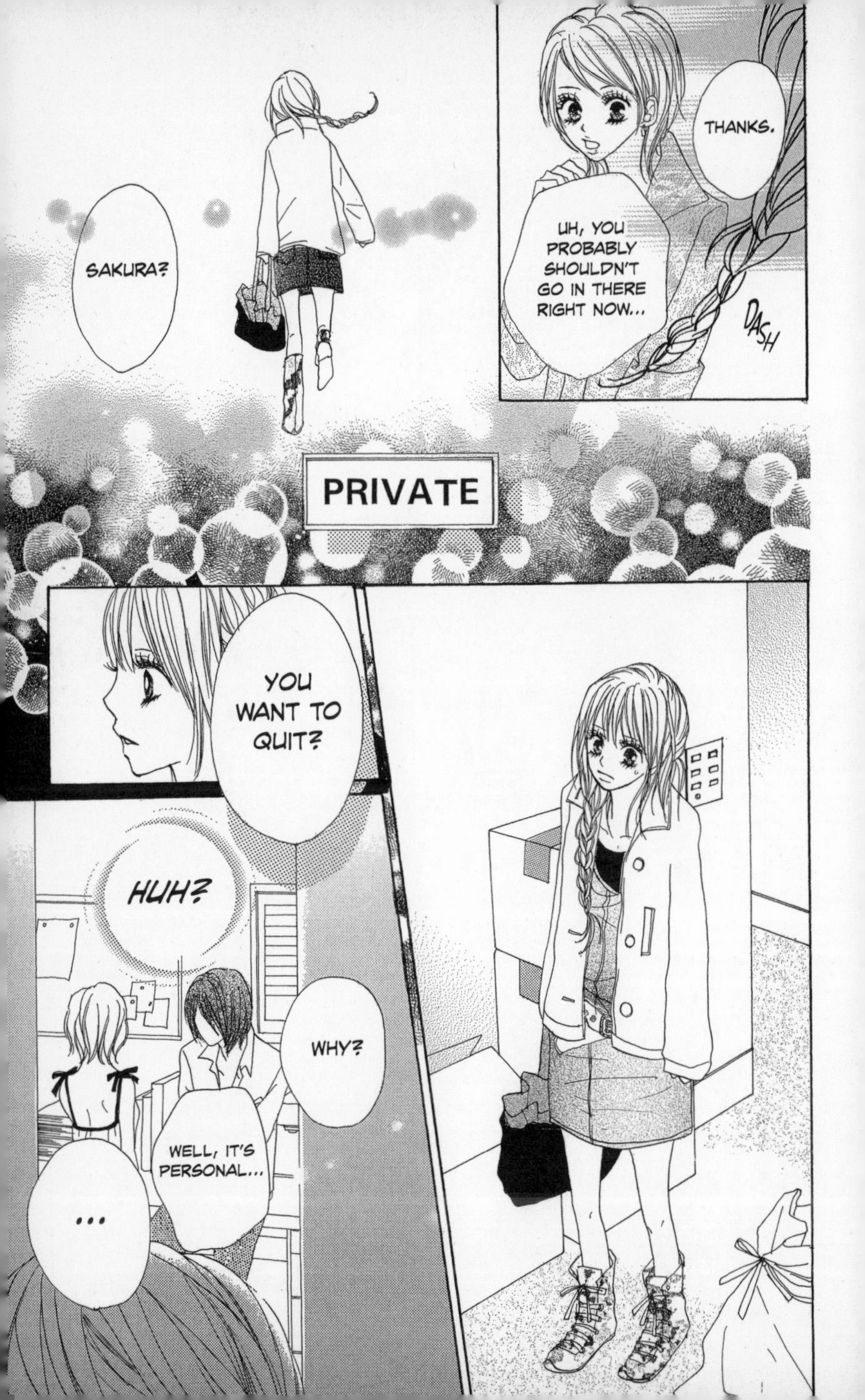
THANKS.
UH, YOU PROBABLY SHOULDN'T GO IN THERE RIGHT NOW...
DASH
SAKURA?
PRIVATE
YOU WANT TO QUIT?
HUH?
WHY?
WELL, IT'S PERSONAL...
...

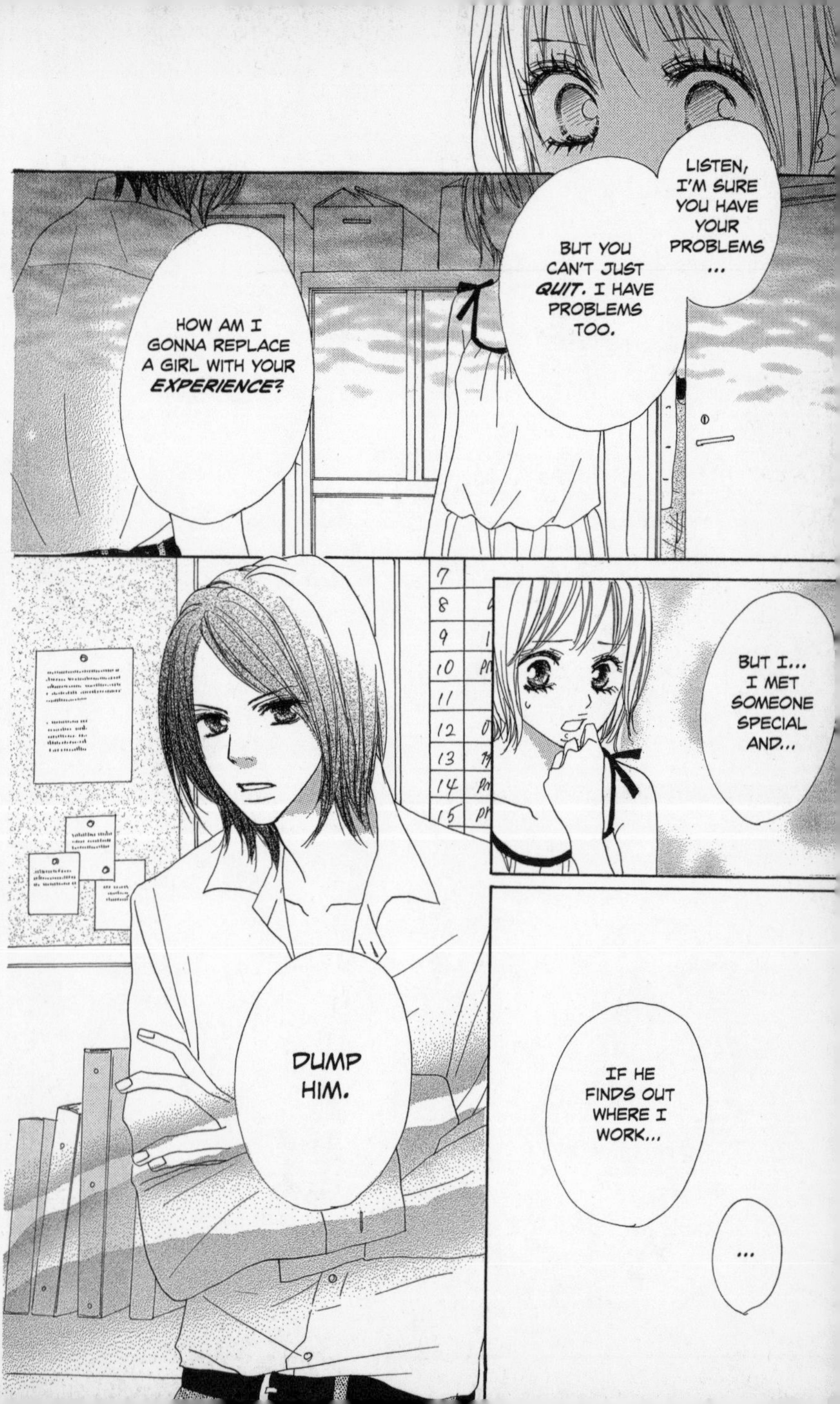
LISTEN, I'M SURE YOU HAVE YOUR PROBLEMS...
BUT YOU CAN'T JUST *QUIT*. I HAVE PROBLEMS TOO.
HOW AM I GONNA REPLACE A GIRL WITH YOUR *EXPERIENCE*?
BUT I... I MET SOMEONE SPECIAL AND...
IF HE FINDS OUT WHERE I WORK...
...
DUMP HIM.

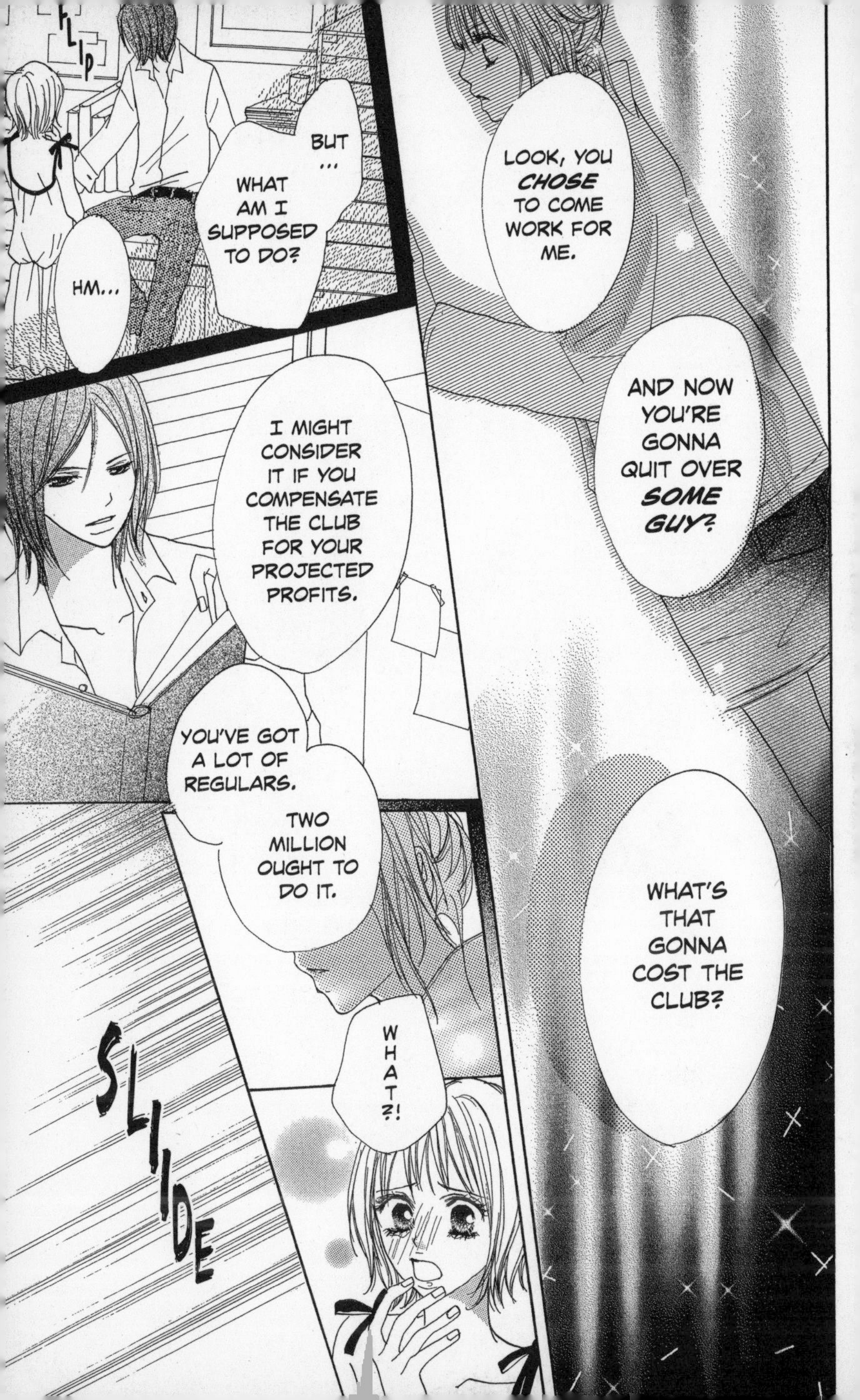
LOOK, YOU *CHOSE* TO COME WORK FOR ME.
AND NOW YOU'RE GONNA QUIT OVER *SOME GUY*?
WHAT'S THAT GONNA COST THE CLUB?
FLIP
BUT...
WHAT AM I SUPPOSED TO DO?
HM...
I MIGHT CONSIDER IT IF YOU COMPENSATE THE CLUB FOR YOUR PROJECTED PROFITS.
YOU'VE GOT A LOT OF REGULARS.
TWO MILLION OUGHT TO DO IT.
WHAT?!
SLIDE

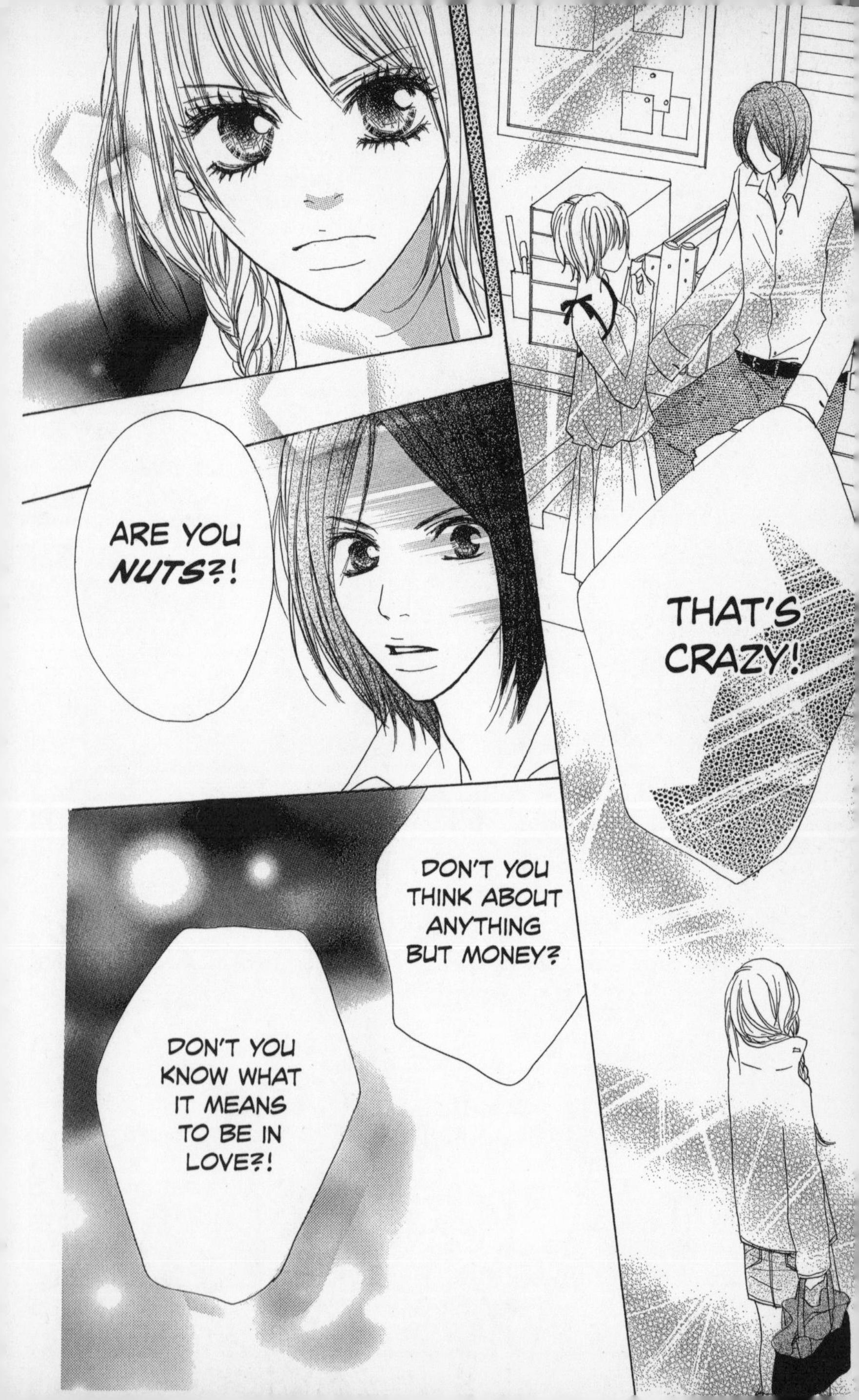
THAT'S CRAZY!
ARE YOU *NUTS*?!
DON'T YOU THINK ABOUT ANYTHING BUT MONEY?
DON'T YOU KNOW WHAT IT MEANS TO BE IN LOVE?!

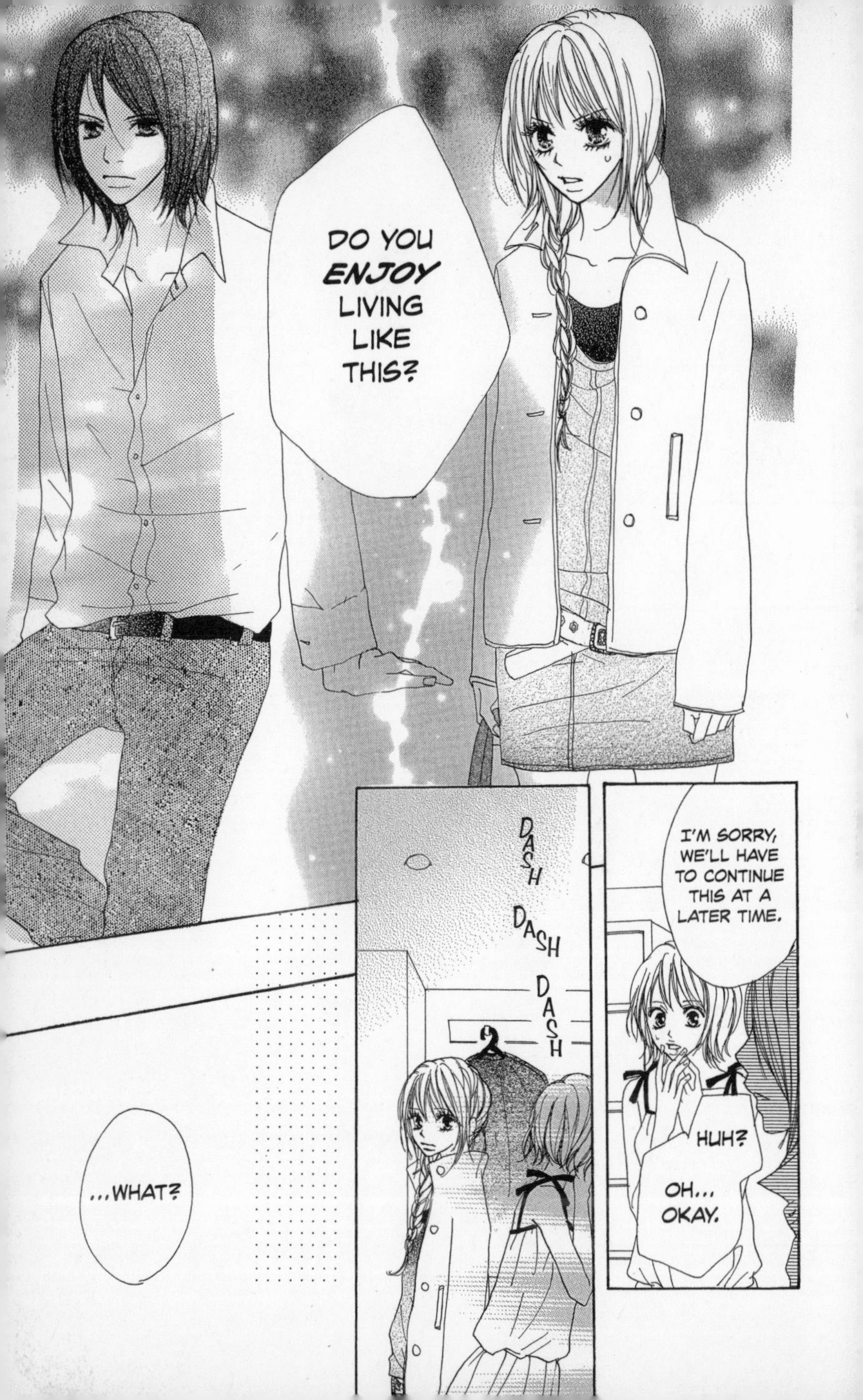
DO YOU *ENJOY* LIVING LIKE THIS?
I'M SORRY, WE'LL HAVE TO CONTINUE THIS AT A LATER TIME.
HUH?
OH... OKAY.
DASH
DASH
DASH
...WHAT?

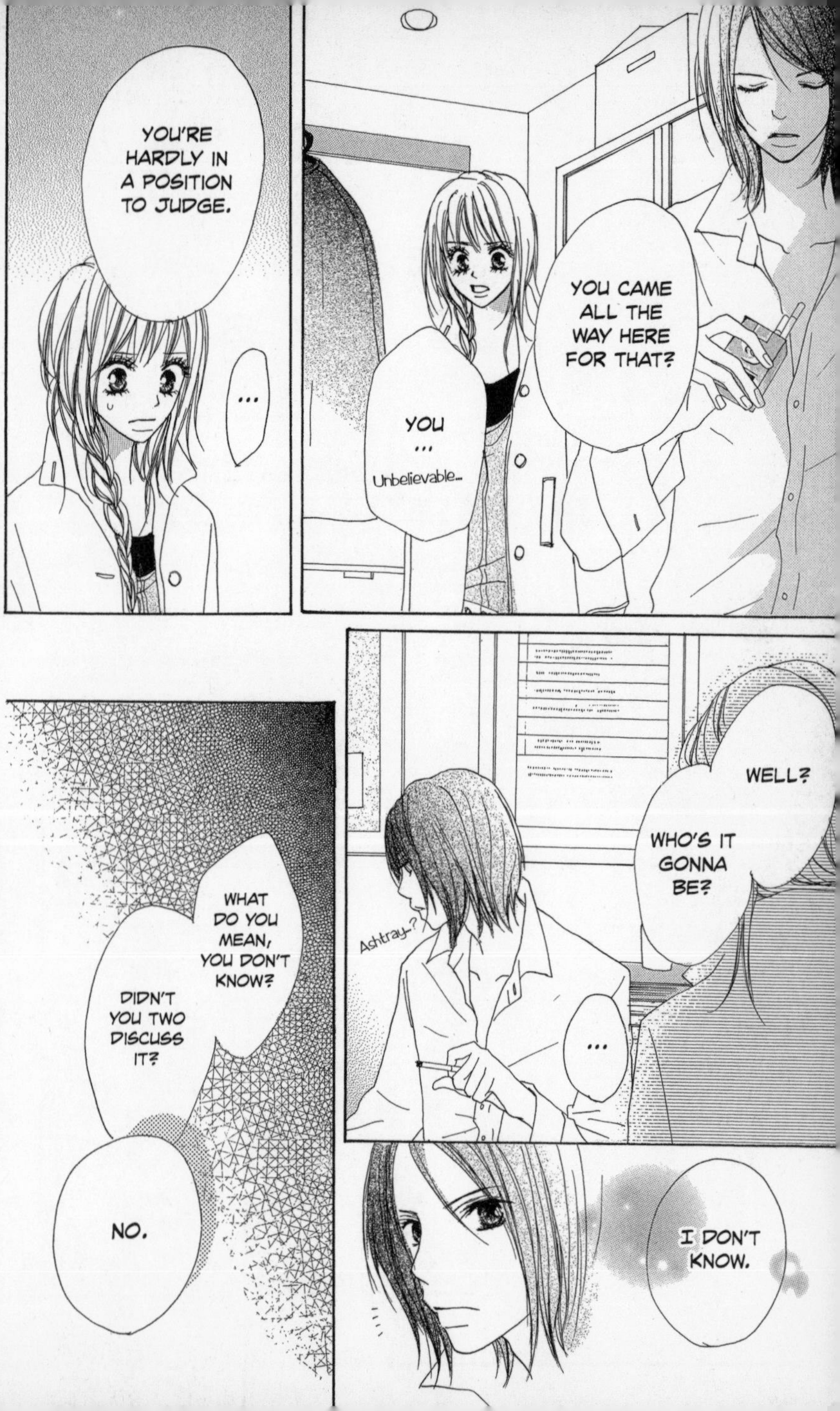
YOU CAME ALL THE WAY HERE FOR THAT?
YOU ... Unbelievable...
YOU'RE HARDLY IN A POSITION TO JUDGE.
...
WELL? WHO'S IT GONNA BE?
Ashtray...?
...
I DON'T KNOW.
WHAT DO YOU MEAN, YOU DON'T KNOW?
DIDN'T YOU TWO DISCUSS IT?
NO.

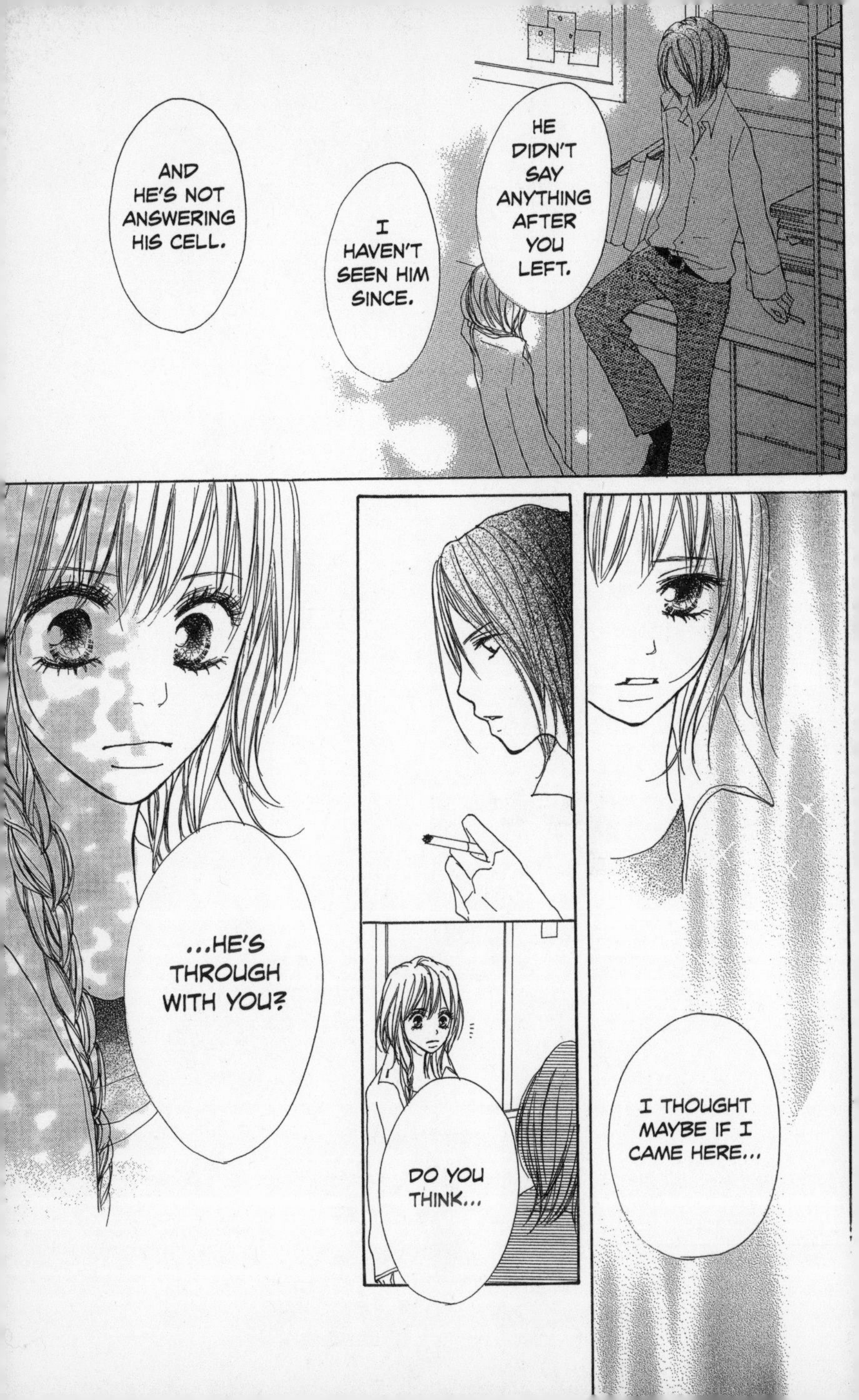
HE DIDN'T SAY ANYTHING AFTER YOU LEFT.
I HAVEN'T SEEN HIM SINCE.
AND HE'S NOT ANSWERING HIS CELL.
I THOUGHT MAYBE IF I CAME HERE...
DO YOU THINK...
...HE'S THROUGH WITH YOU?

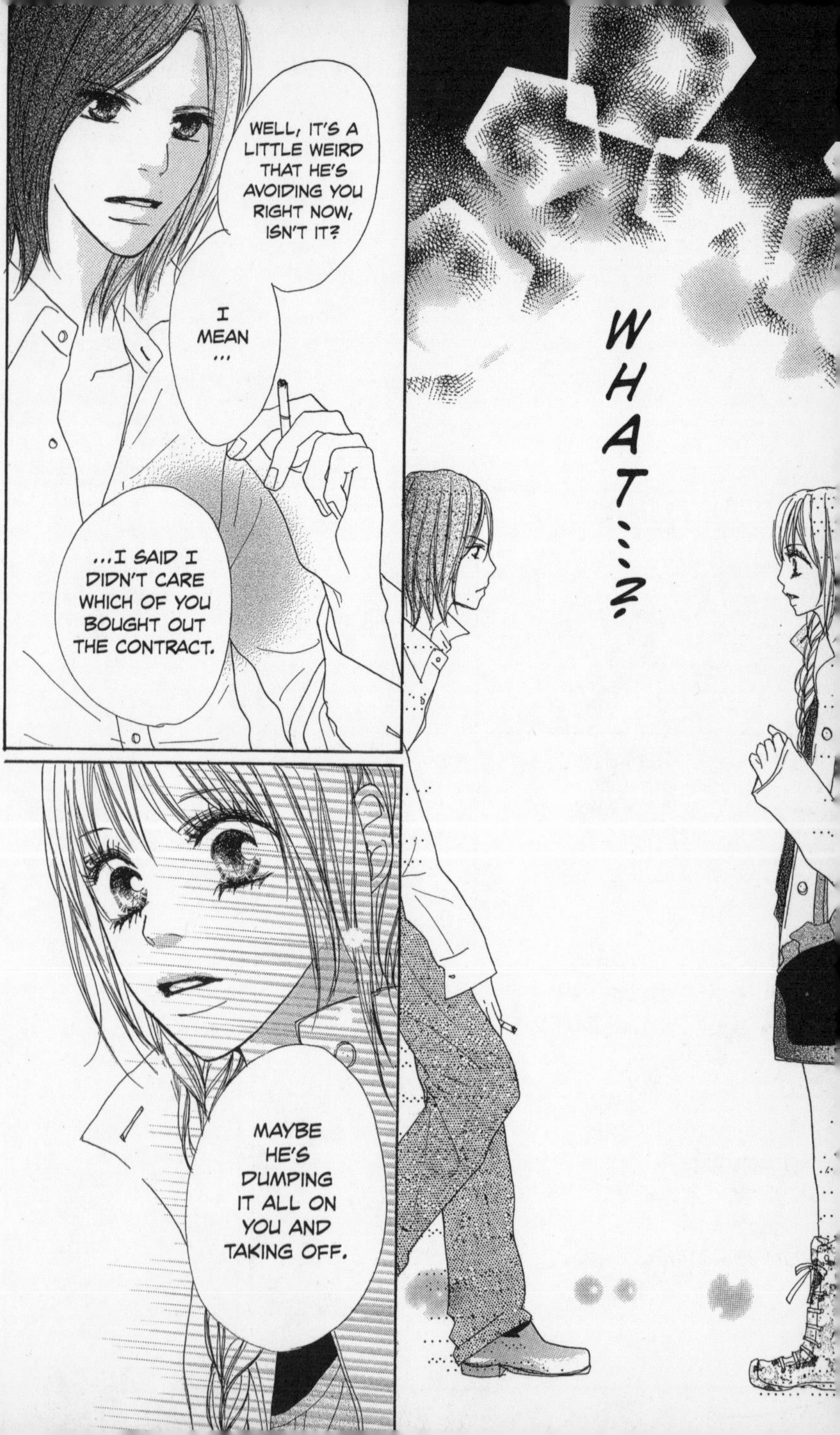
WHAT...?
WELL, IT'S A LITTLE WEIRD THAT HE'S AVOIDING YOU RIGHT NOW, ISN'T IT?
I MEAN ...
...I SAID I DIDN'T CARE WHICH OF YOU BOUGHT OUT THE CONTRACT.
MAYBE HE'S DUMPING IT ALL ON YOU AND TAKING OFF.

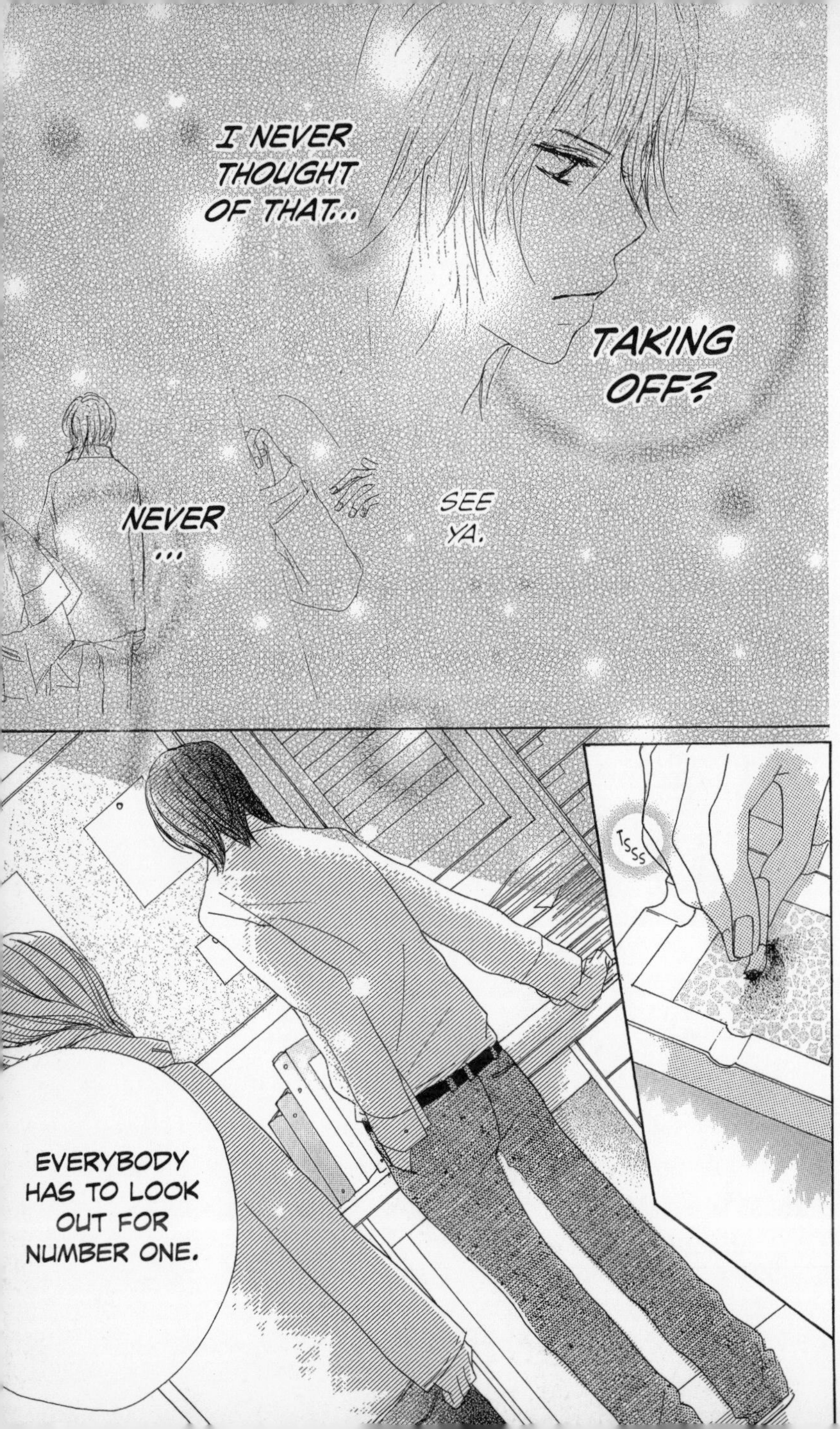
TAKING OFF?
I NEVER THOUGHT OF THAT...
SEE YA.
NEVER...
TSSS
EVERYBODY HAS TO LOOK OUT FOR NUMBER ONE.

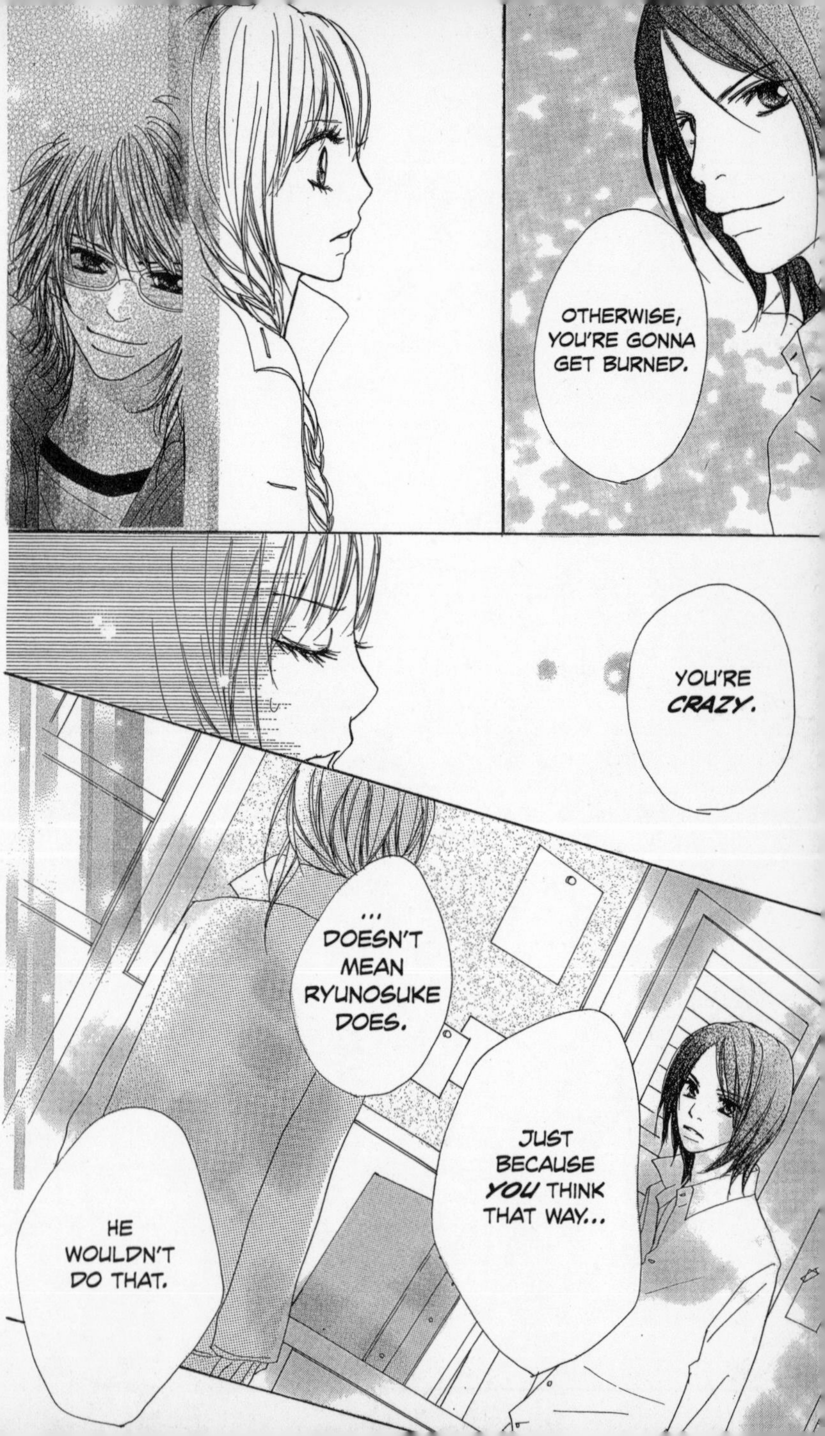
OTHERWISE, YOU'RE GONNA GET BURNED.
YOU'RE *CRAZY*.
JUST BECAUSE *YOU* THINK THAT WAY...
...DOESN'T MEAN RYUNOSUKE DOES.
HE WOULDN'T DO THAT.

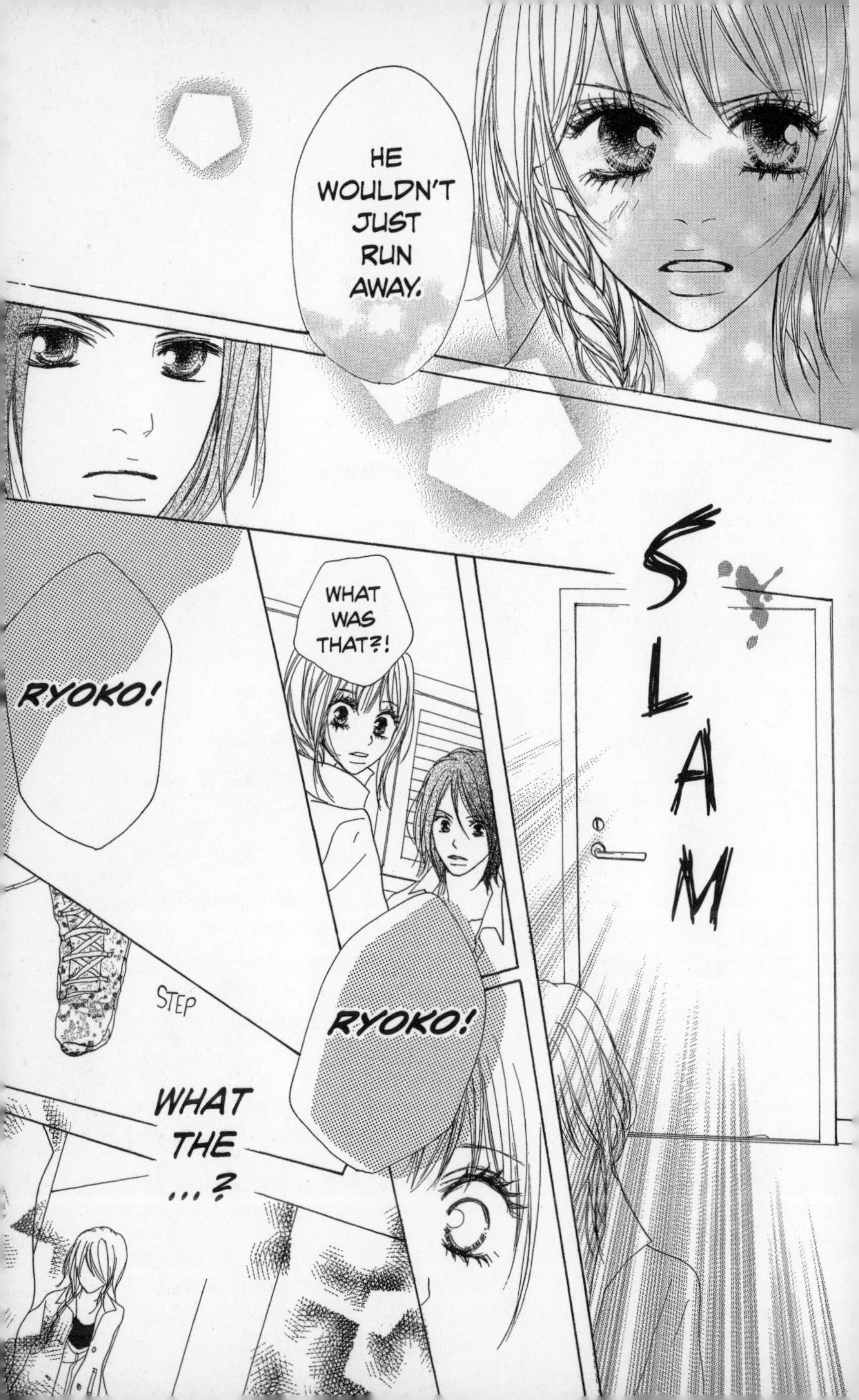
HE WOULDN'T JUST RUN AWAY.
SLAM
WHAT WAS THAT?!
RYOKO!
STEP
RYOKO!
WHAT THE ...?

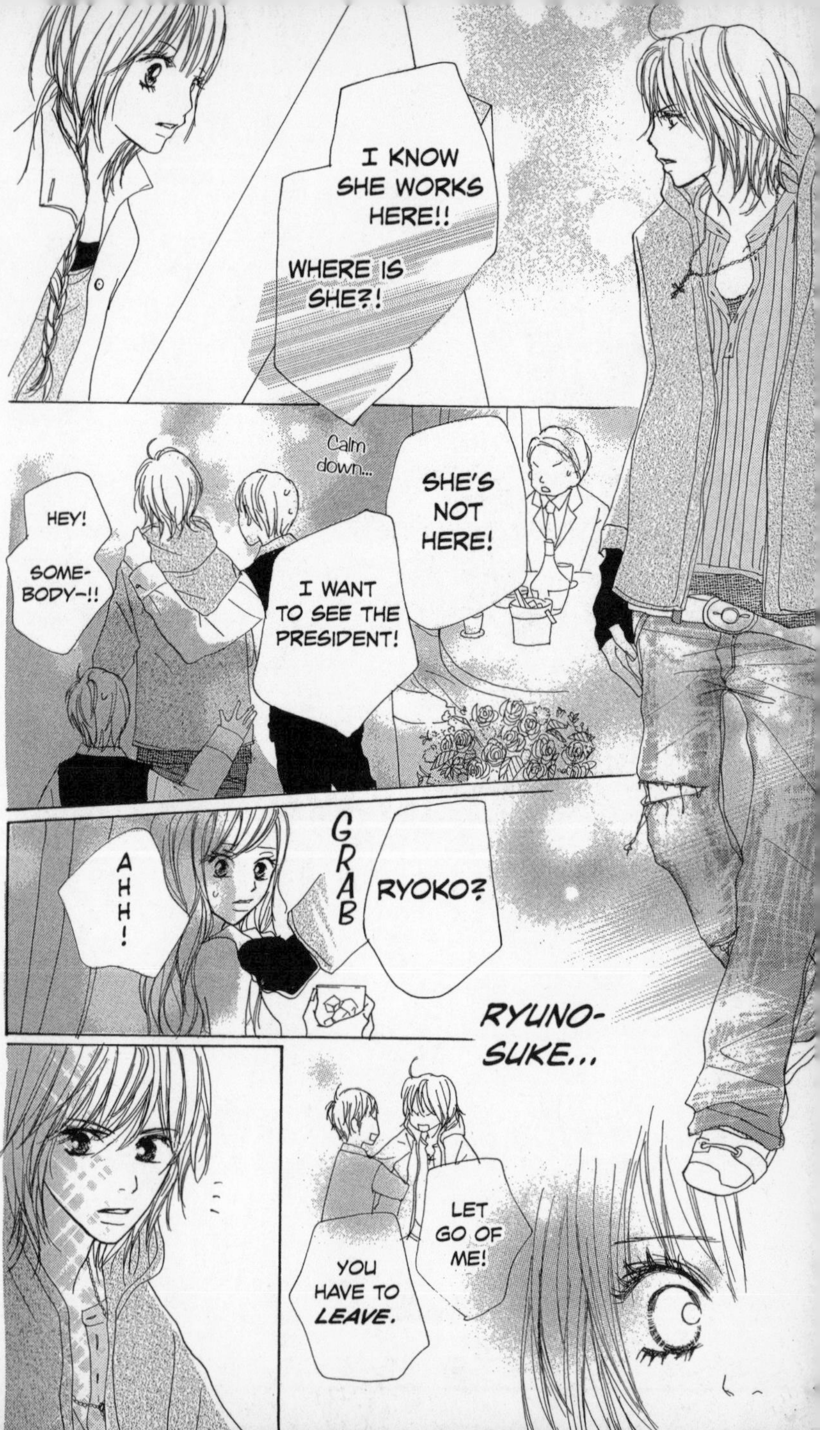
I KNOW SHE WORKS HERE!!
WHERE IS SHE?!
SHE'S NOT HERE!
Calm down...
I WANT TO SEE THE PRESIDENT!
HEY!
SOME-BODY—!!
RYOKO?
GRAB
AHH!
RYUNO-SUKE...
LET GO OF ME!
YOU HAVE TO *LEAVE*.

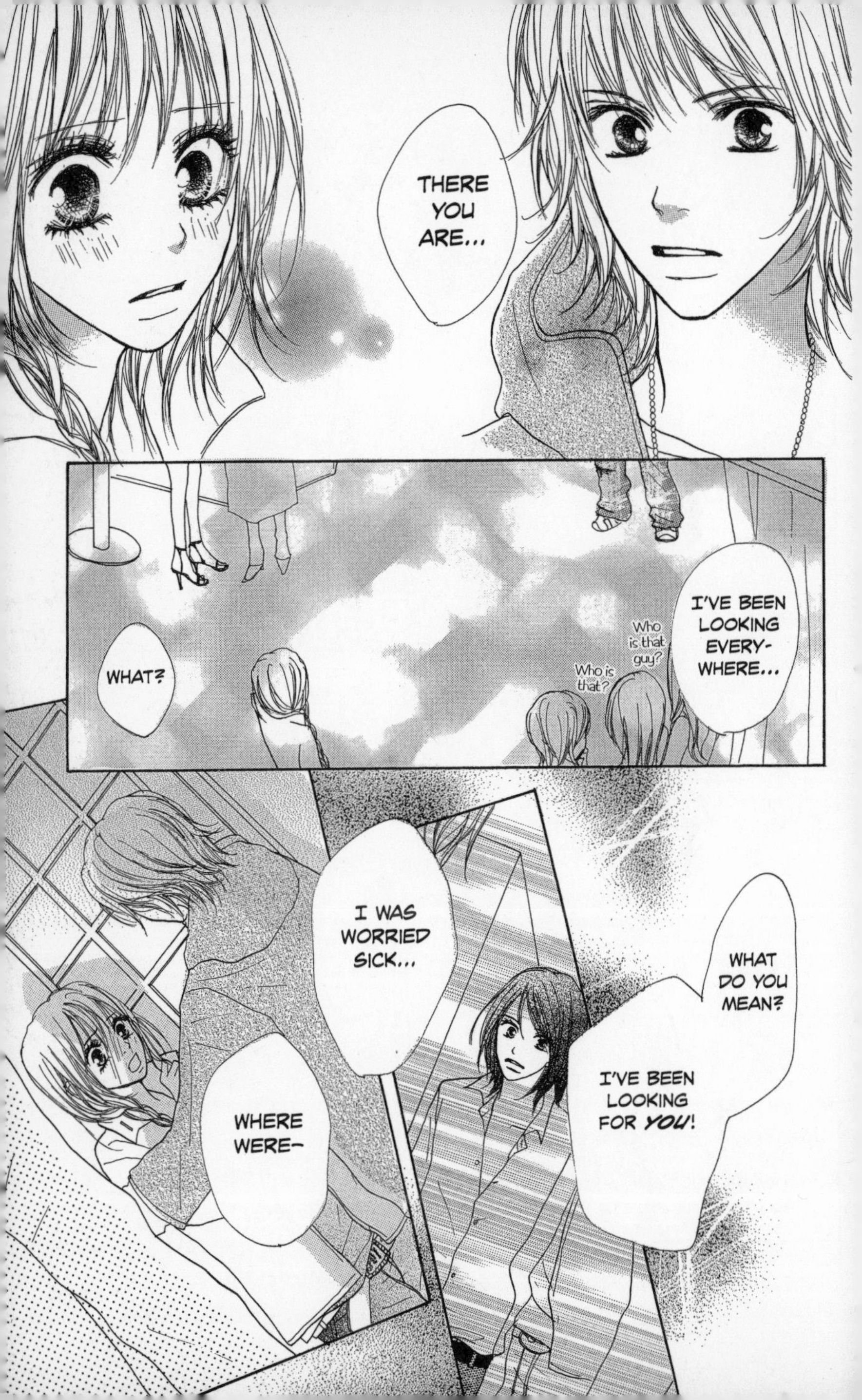
THERE YOU ARE...
I'VE BEEN LOOKING EVERY-WHERE...
Who is that guy?
Who is that?
WHAT?
I WAS WORRIED SICK...
WHERE WERE-
WHAT DO YOU MEAN?
I'VE BEEN LOOKING FOR *YOU*!

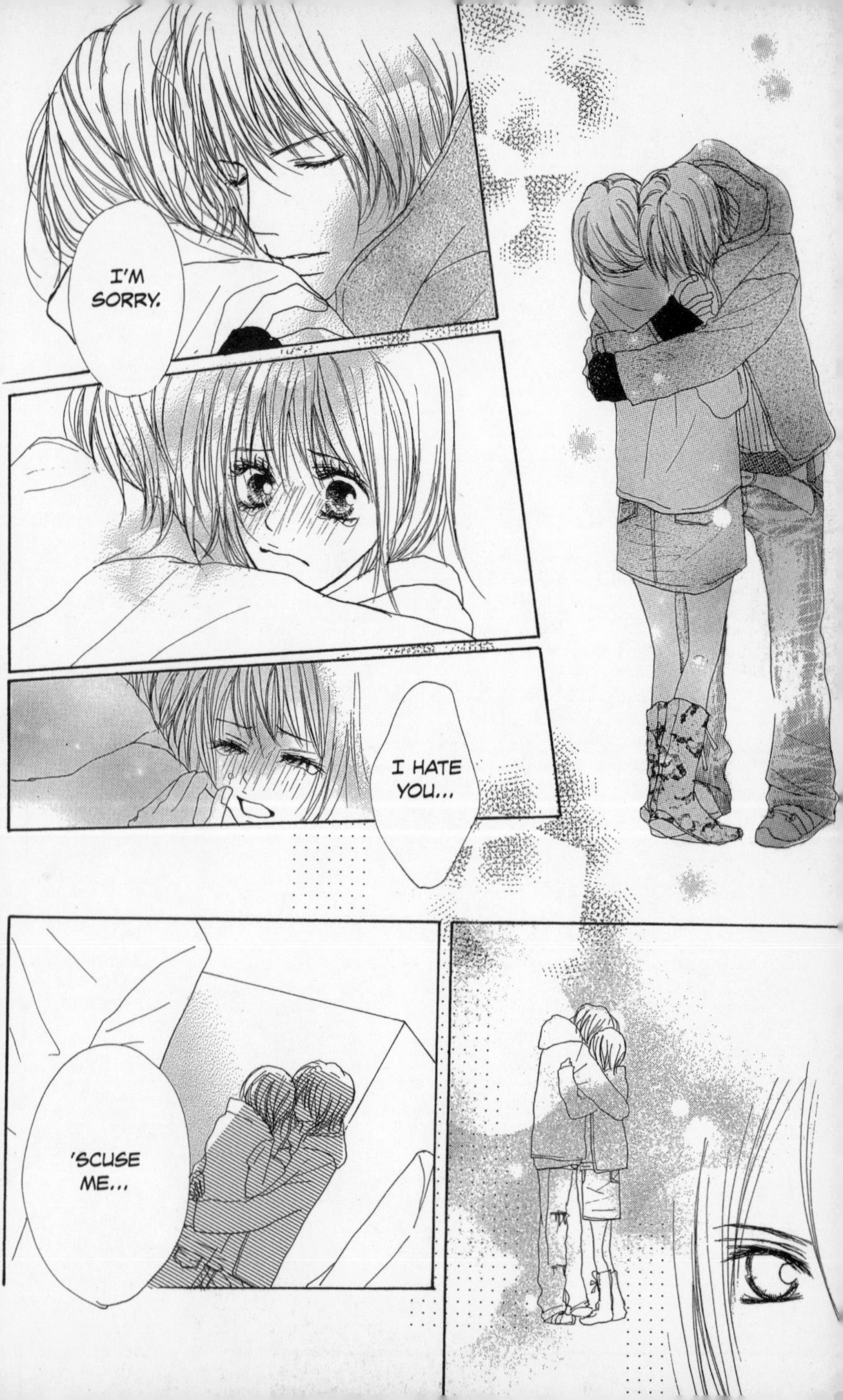
I'M SORRY.
I HATE YOU...
'SCUSE ME...

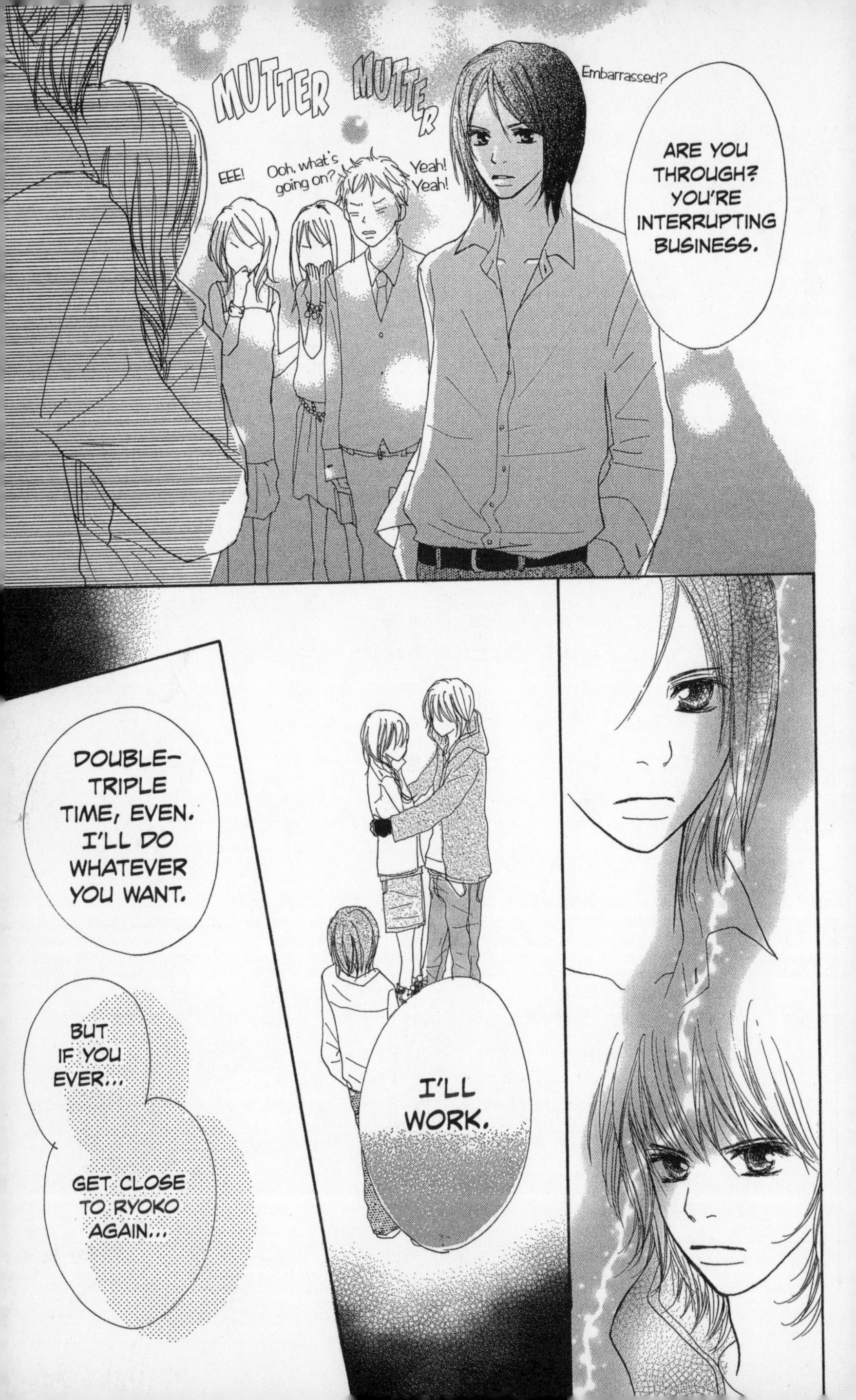
Embarrassed?
ARE YOU THROUGH? YOU'RE INTERRUPTING BUSINESS.
Yeah! Yeah!
Ooh, what's going on?
EEE!
MUTTER MUTTER
I'LL WORK.
DOUBLE-TRIPLE TIME, EVEN. I'LL DO WHATEVER YOU WANT.
BUT IF YOU EVER...
GET CLOSE TO RYOKO AGAIN...

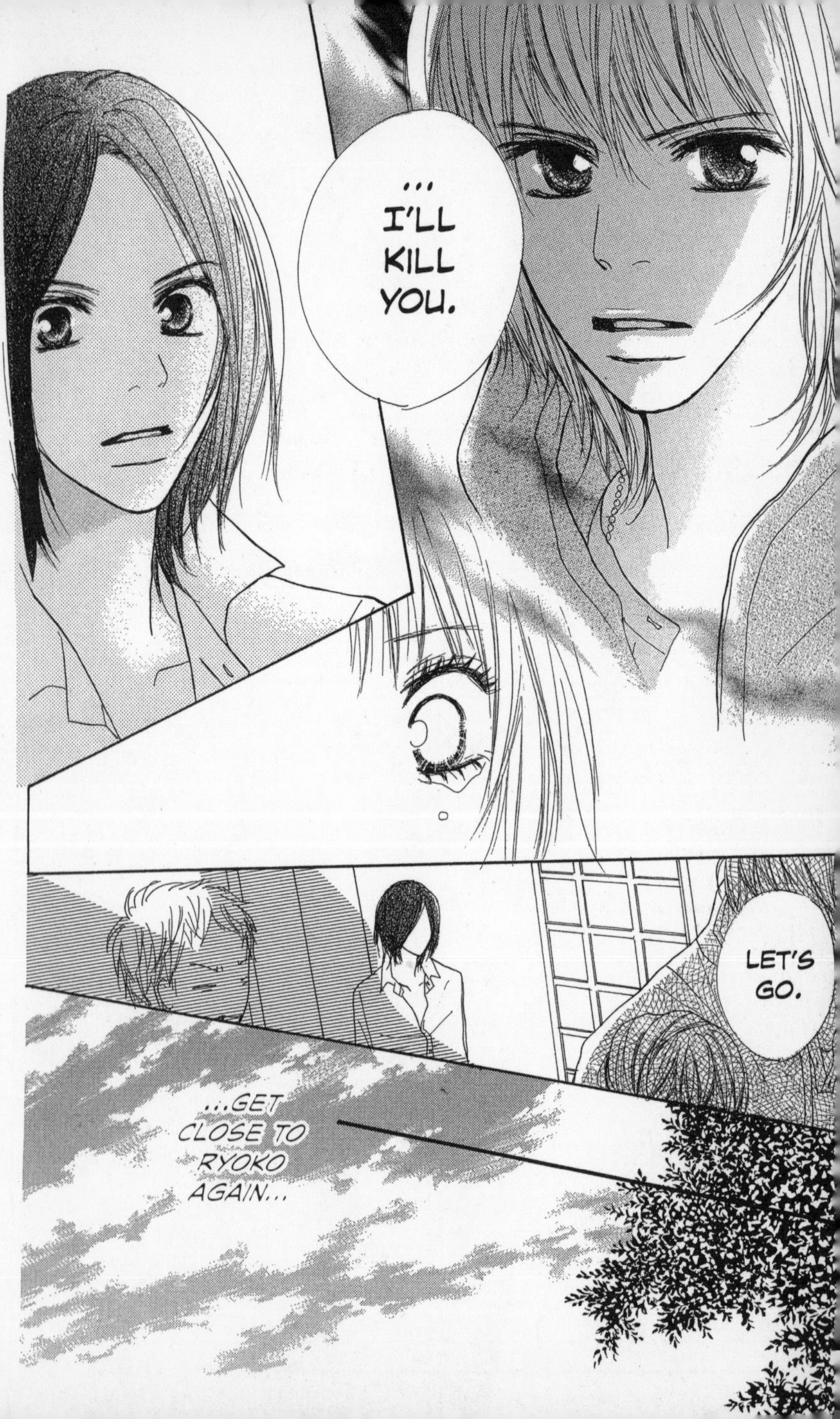
...
I'LL KILL YOU.
LET'S GO.
...GET CLOSE TO RYOKO AGAIN...

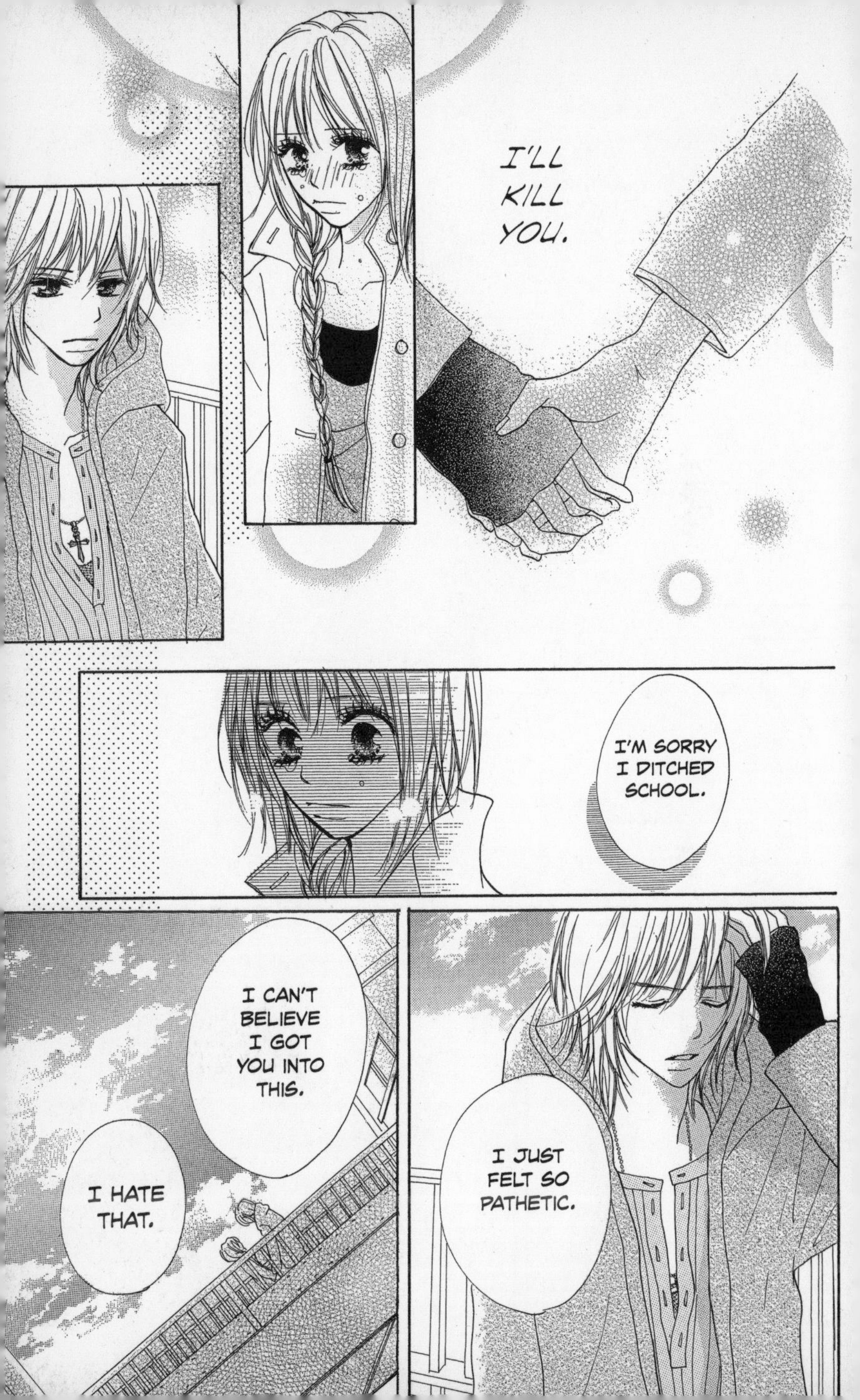
I'LL KILL YOU.
I'M SORRY I DITCHED SCHOOL.
I JUST FELT SO PATHETIC.
I CAN'T BELIEVE I GOT YOU INTO THIS.
I HATE THAT.

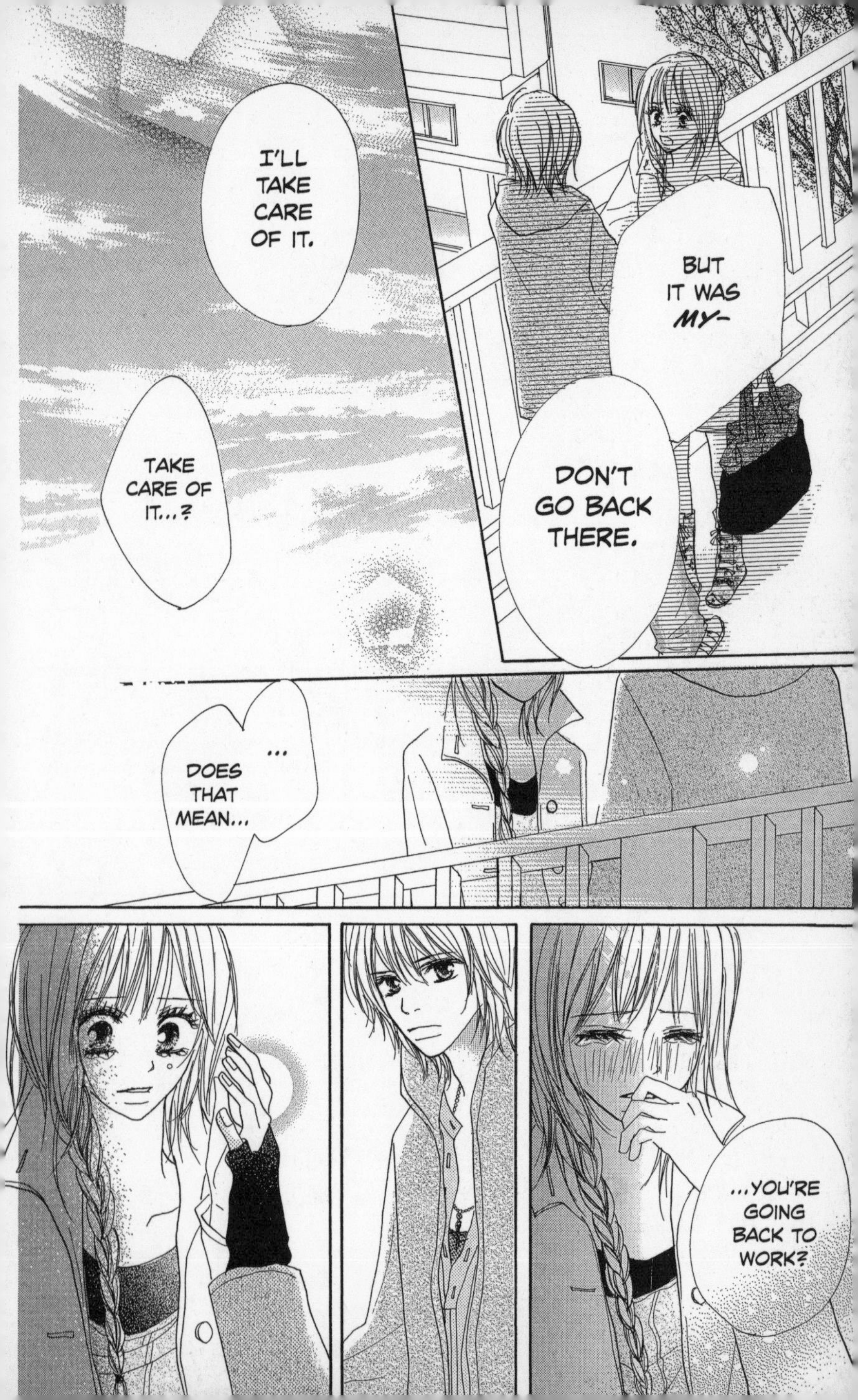
BUT IT WAS MY-
DON'T GO BACK THERE.
I'LL TAKE CARE OF IT.
TAKE CARE OF IT...?
... DOES THAT MEAN...
...YOU'RE GOING BACK TO WORK?

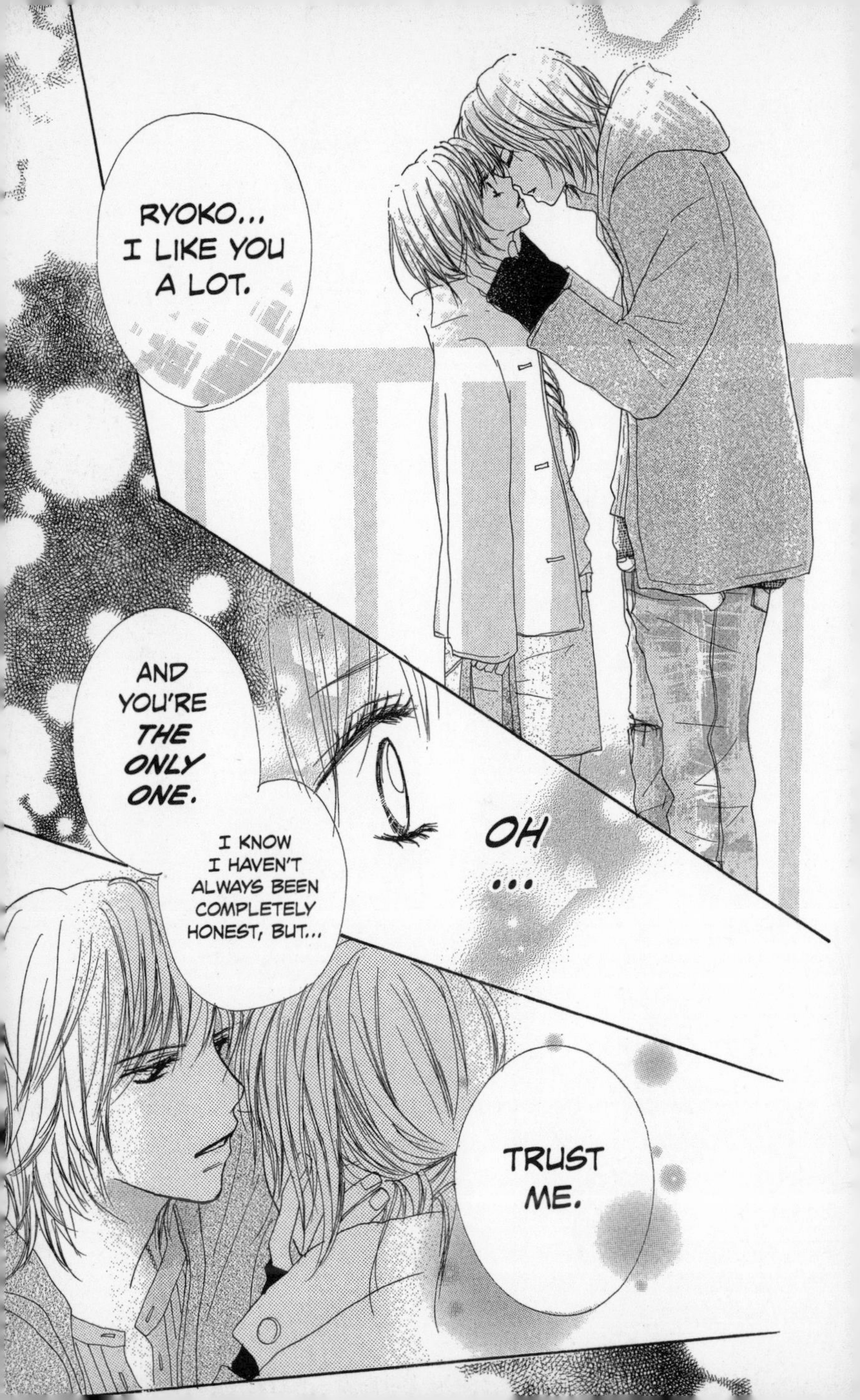
RYOKO... I LIKE YOU A LOT.
AND YOU'RE THE ONLY ONE.
OH...
I KNOW I HAVEN'T ALWAYS BEEN COMPLETELY HONEST, BUT...
TRUST ME.

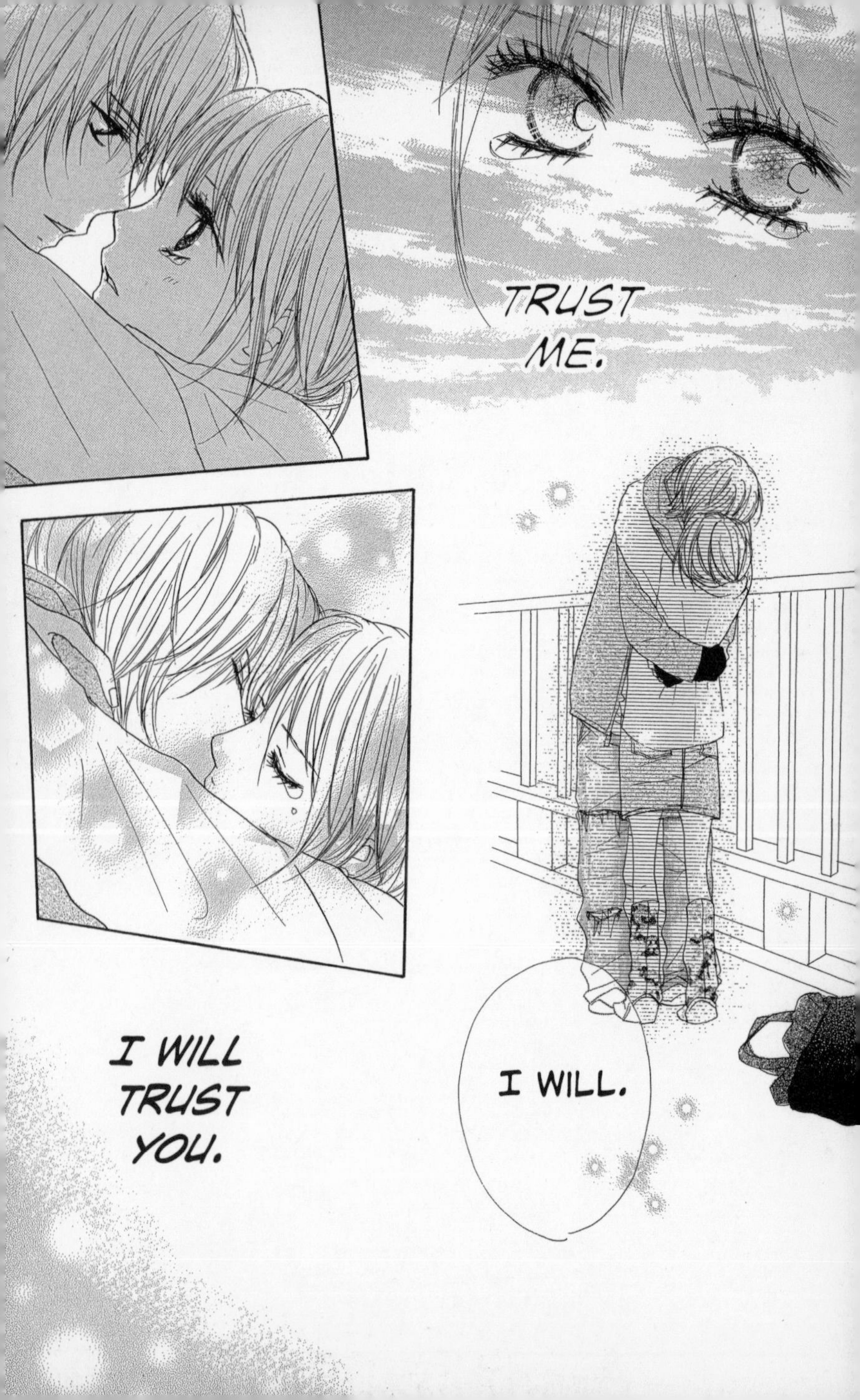
TRUST ME.
I WILL.
I WILL TRUST YOU.

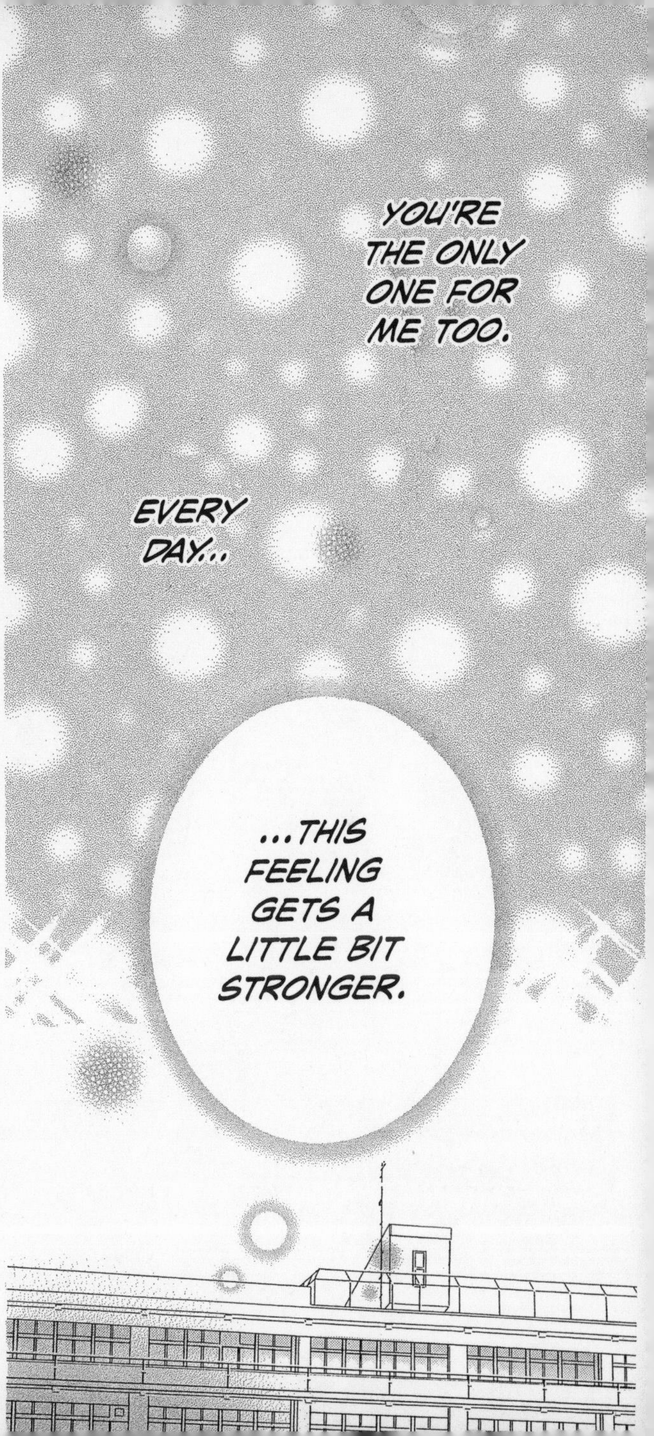
YOU'RE THE ONLY ONE FOR ME TOO.
EVERY DAY...
...THIS FEELING GETS A LITTLE BIT STRONGER.

1 About Jin

Hello again! Ao-pan here. Natsume Hirose's been calling me 'Panko' recently and I kind of like it. I've been playing it a lot for B.O.D.Y. Panko

So, anyway—Jin's story arc...it went on longer than I thought it would. I had to learn to draw neon lights and stuff, and I had a hard time with it at first. It wasn't exactly a world I was familiar with! But I did get it figured out, and now I'm having fun with it.

[At the beginning...]

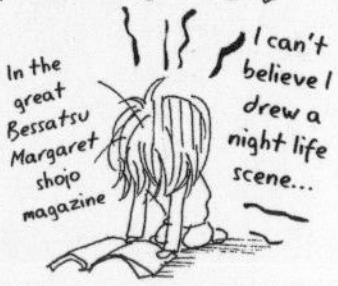
In the great Bessatsu Margaret shojo magazine
I can't believe I drew a night life scene...

I like Jin so I worked hard to get everything down properly... and this is how it turned out!

Continued...

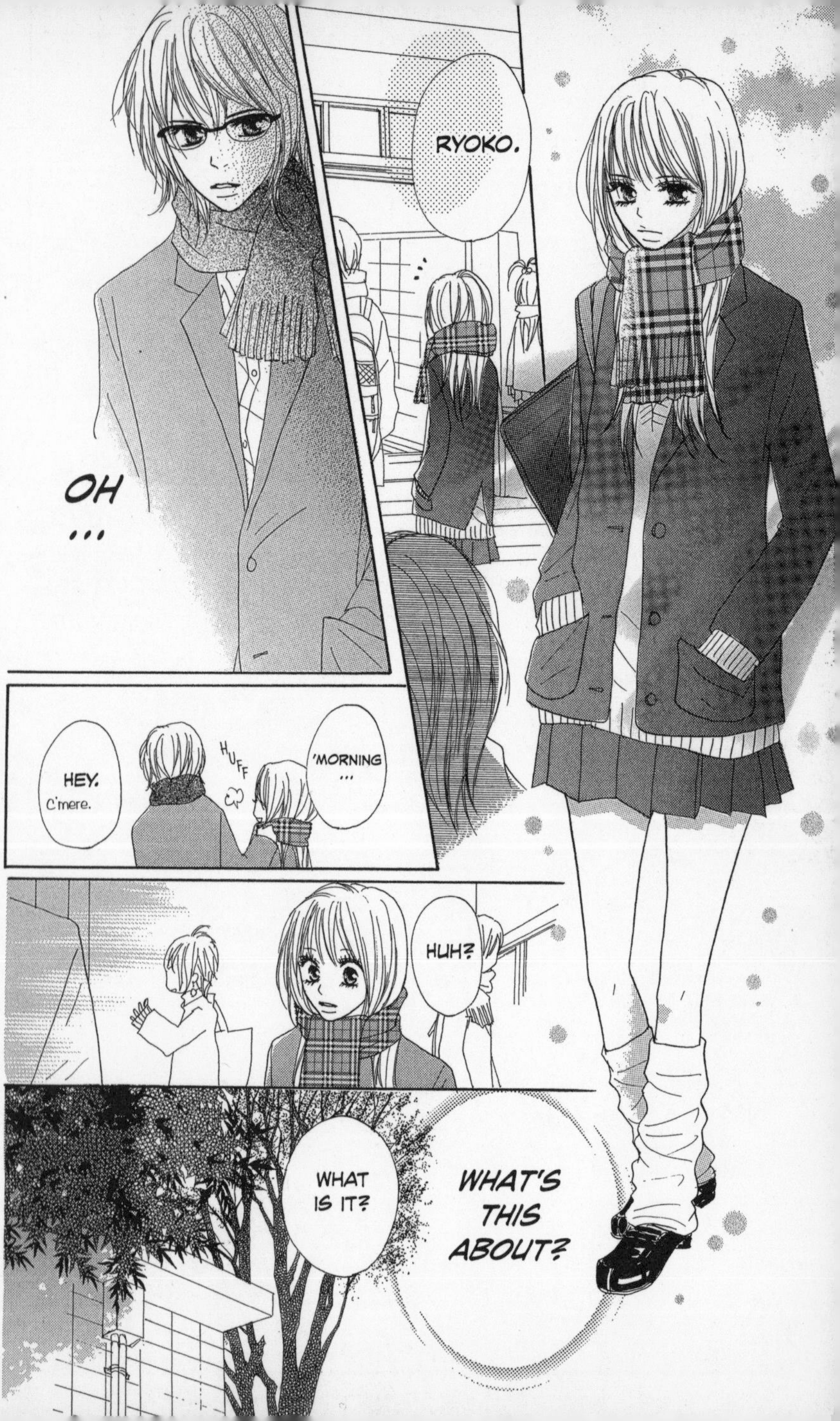

RYOKO.
OH ...
'MORNING ...
HUFF
HEY.
C'mere.
HUH?
WHAT IS IT?
WHAT'S THIS ABOUT?

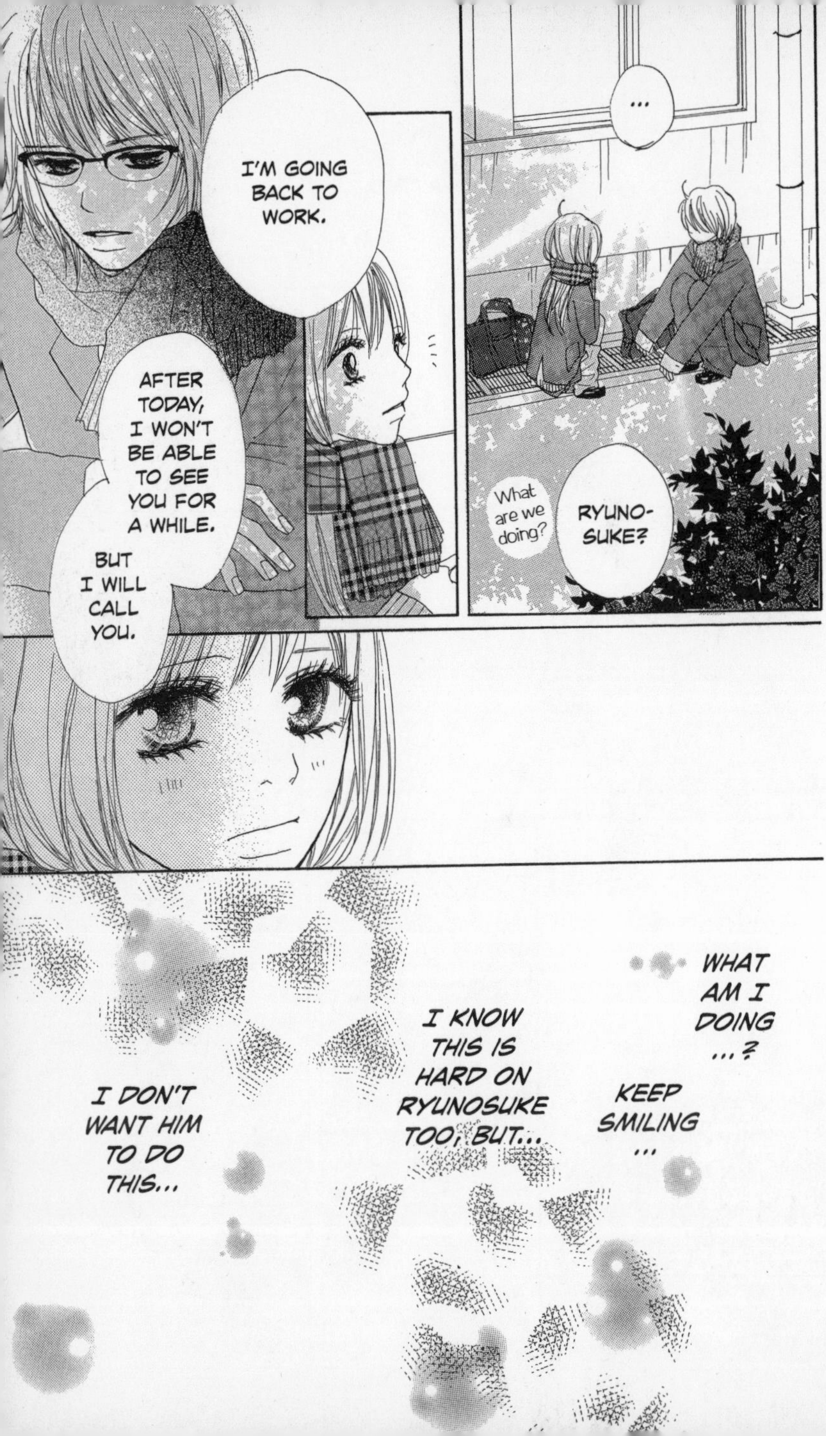
...
RYUNO-SUKE?
What are we doing?
I'M GOING BACK TO WORK.
AFTER TODAY, I WON'T BE ABLE TO SEE YOU FOR A WHILE.
BUT I WILL CALL YOU.
WHAT AM I DOING ...?
KEEP SMILING ...
I KNOW THIS IS HARD ON RYUNOSUKE TOO, BUT...
I DON'T WANT HIM TO DO THIS...

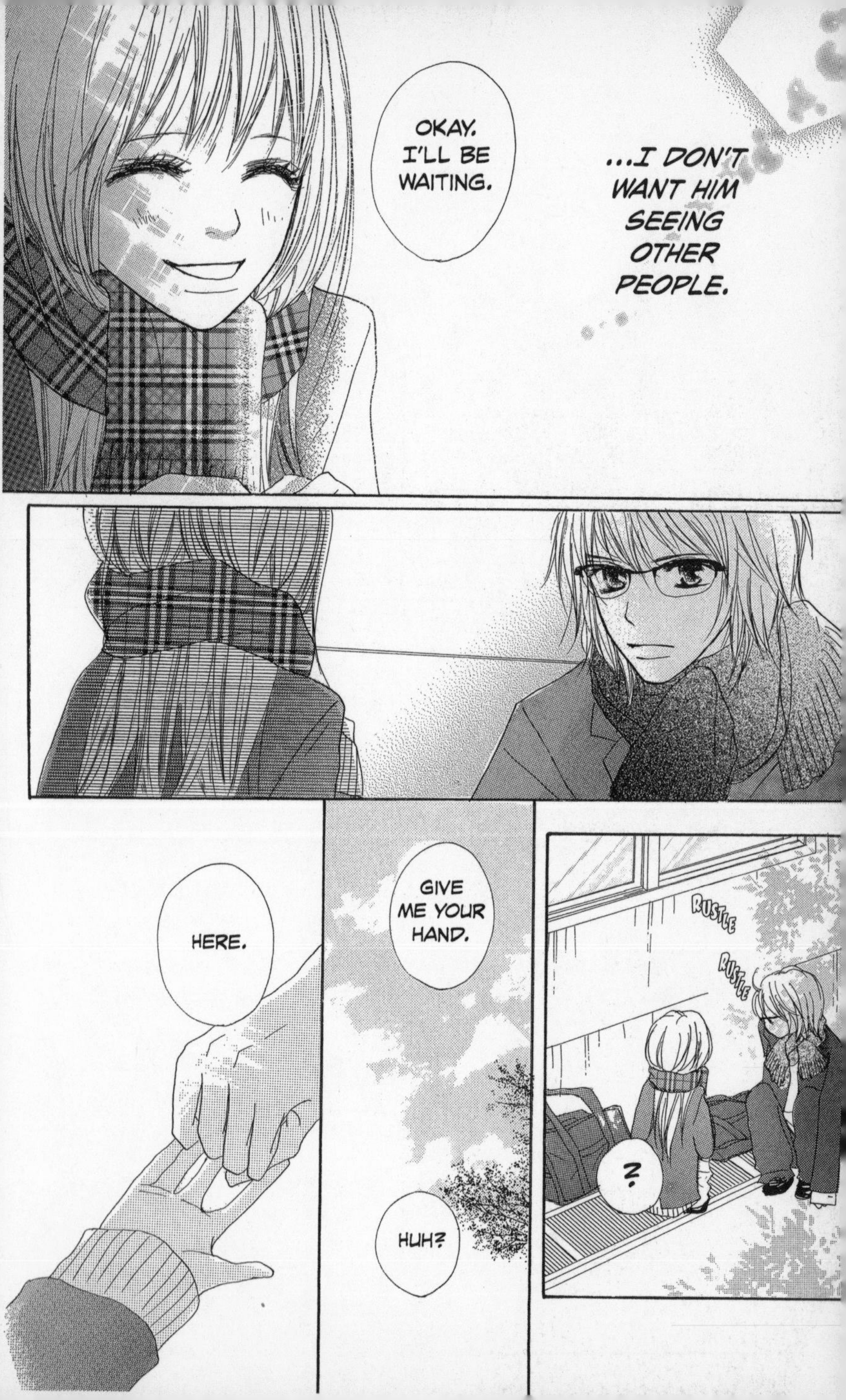
...I DON'T WANT HIM SEEING OTHER PEOPLE.
OKAY. I'LL BE WAITING.
RUSTLE
RUSTLE
?
GIVE ME YOUR HAND.
HUH?
HERE.

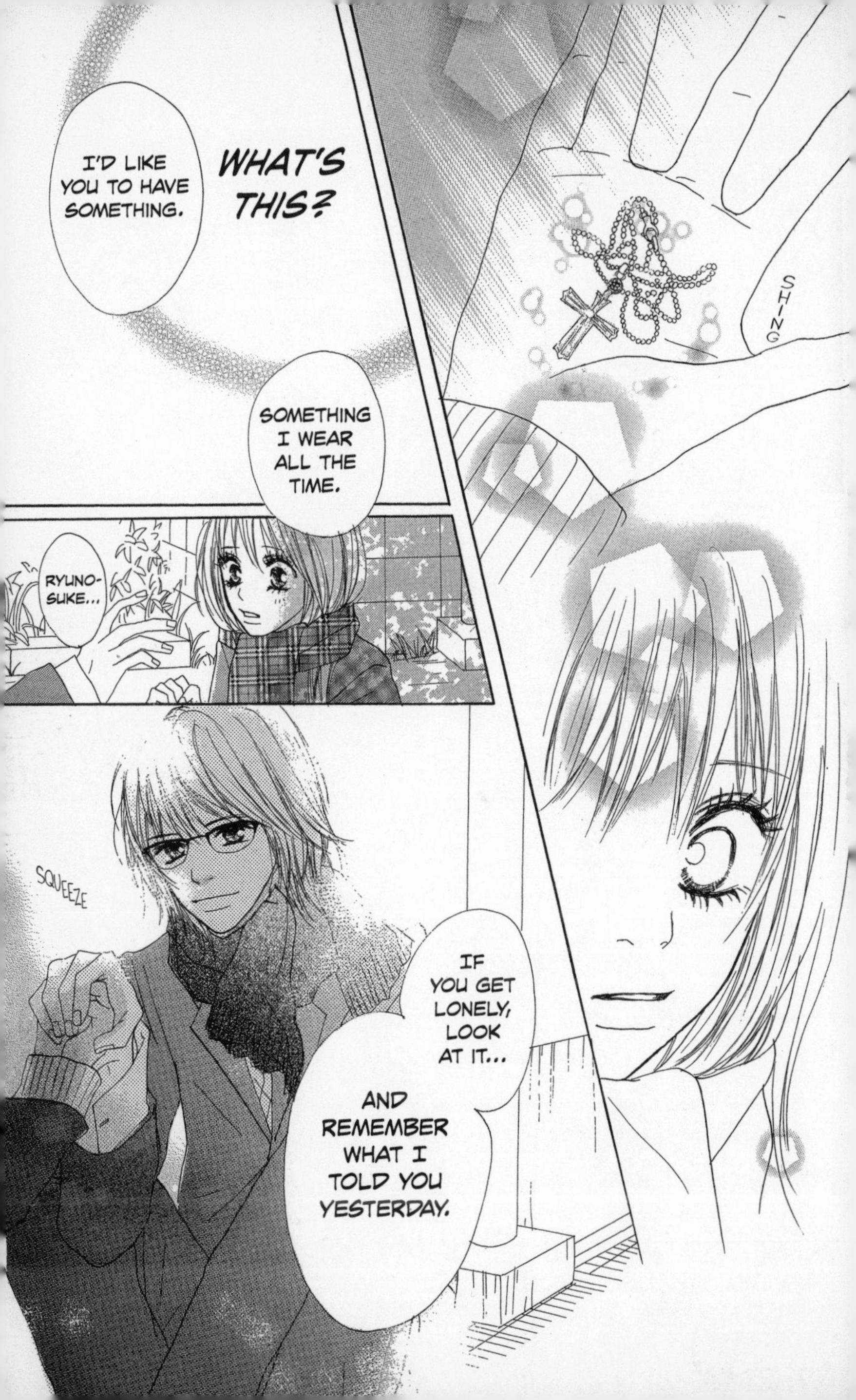
SHING
I'D LIKE YOU TO HAVE SOMETHING.
WHAT'S THIS?
SOMETHING I WEAR ALL THE TIME.
RYUNOSUKE...
SQUEEZE
IF YOU GET LONELY, LOOK AT IT...
AND REMEMBER WHAT I TOLD YOU YESTERDAY.

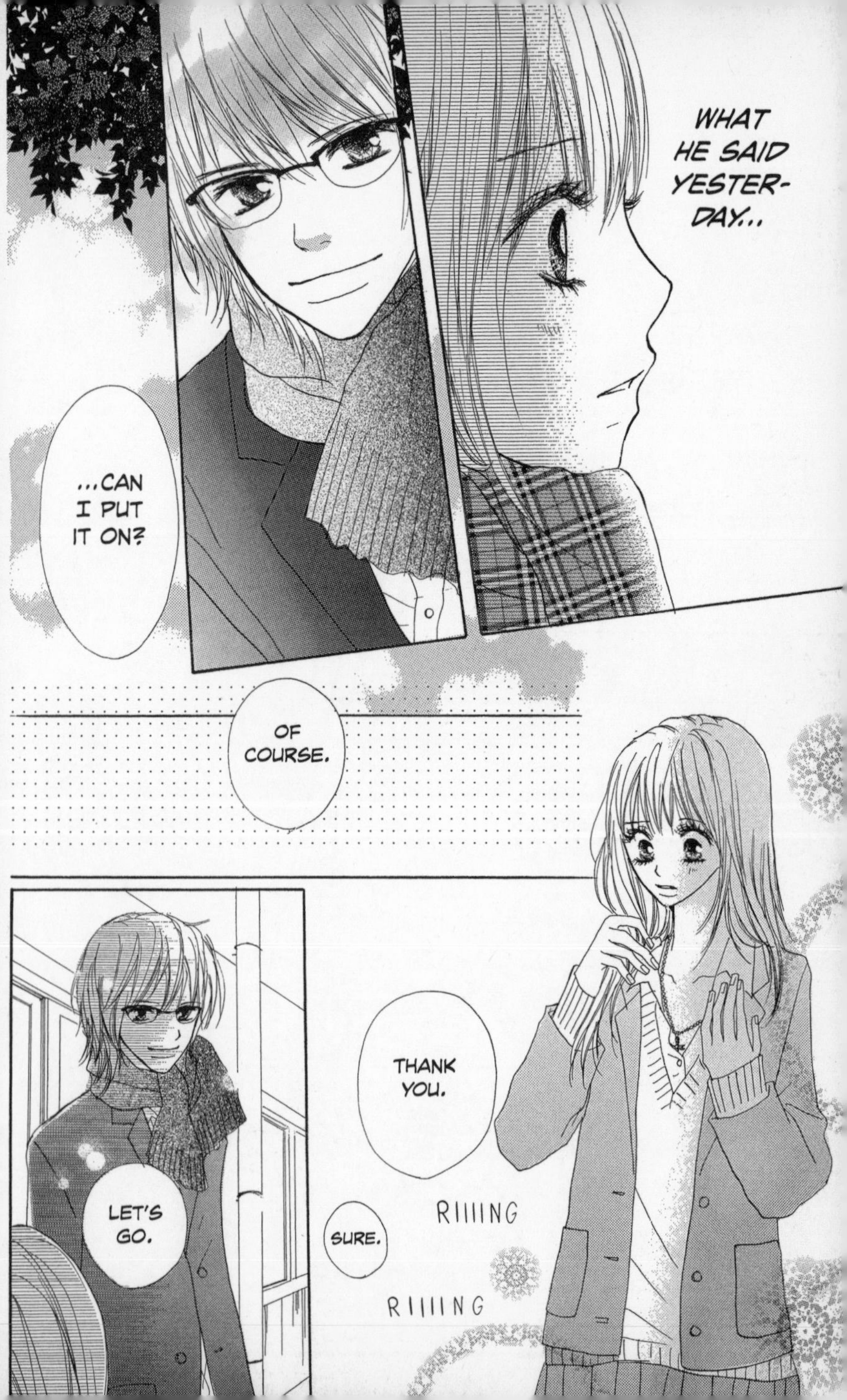
WHAT HE SAID YESTER-DAY...
...CAN I PUT IT ON?
OF COURSE.
THANK YOU.
RIIIING
RIIIING
LET'S GO.
SURE.

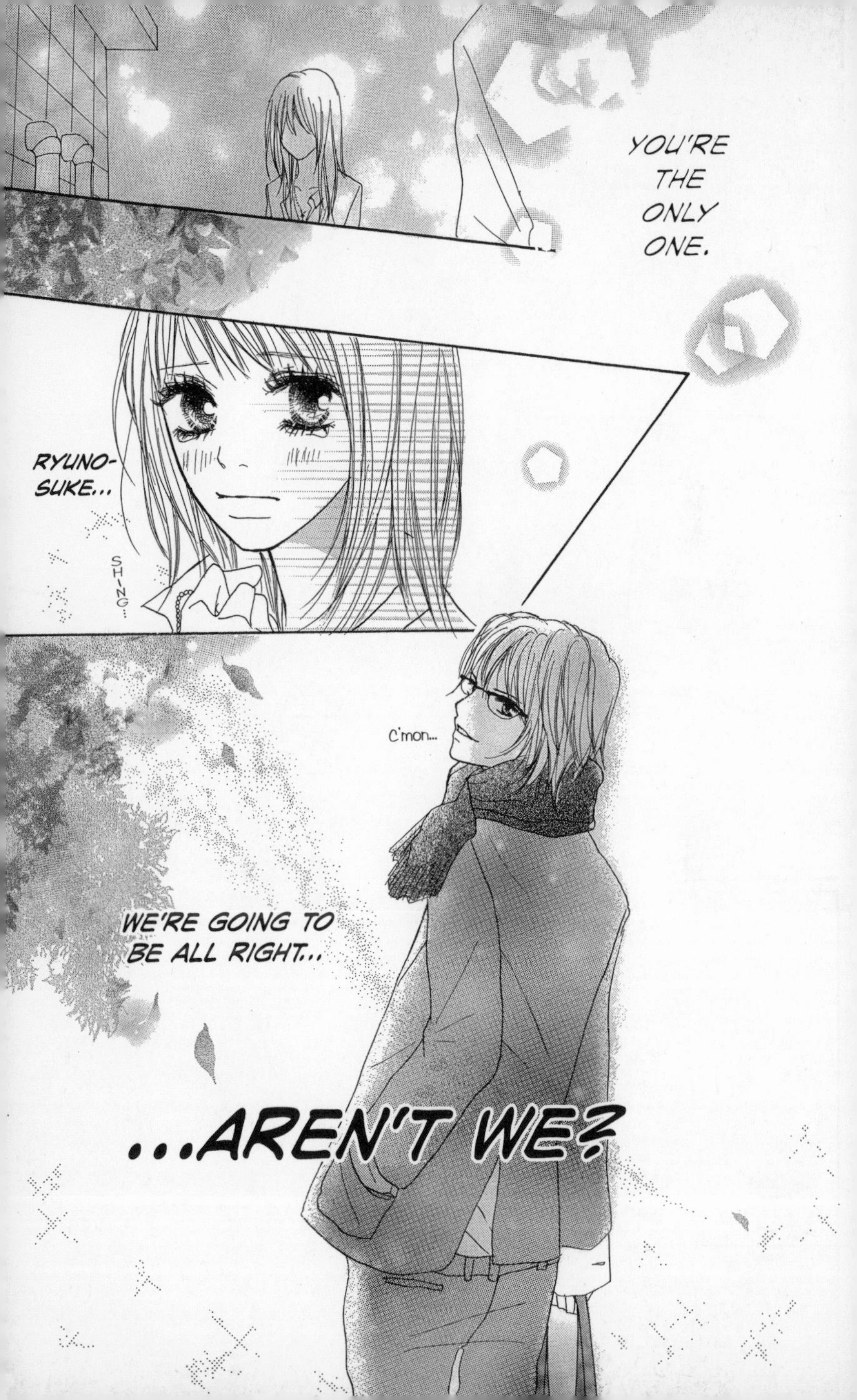
YOU'RE THE ONLY ONE.
RYUNOSUKE...
SHING...
C'mon...
WE'RE GOING TO BE ALL RIGHT...
...AREN'T WE?

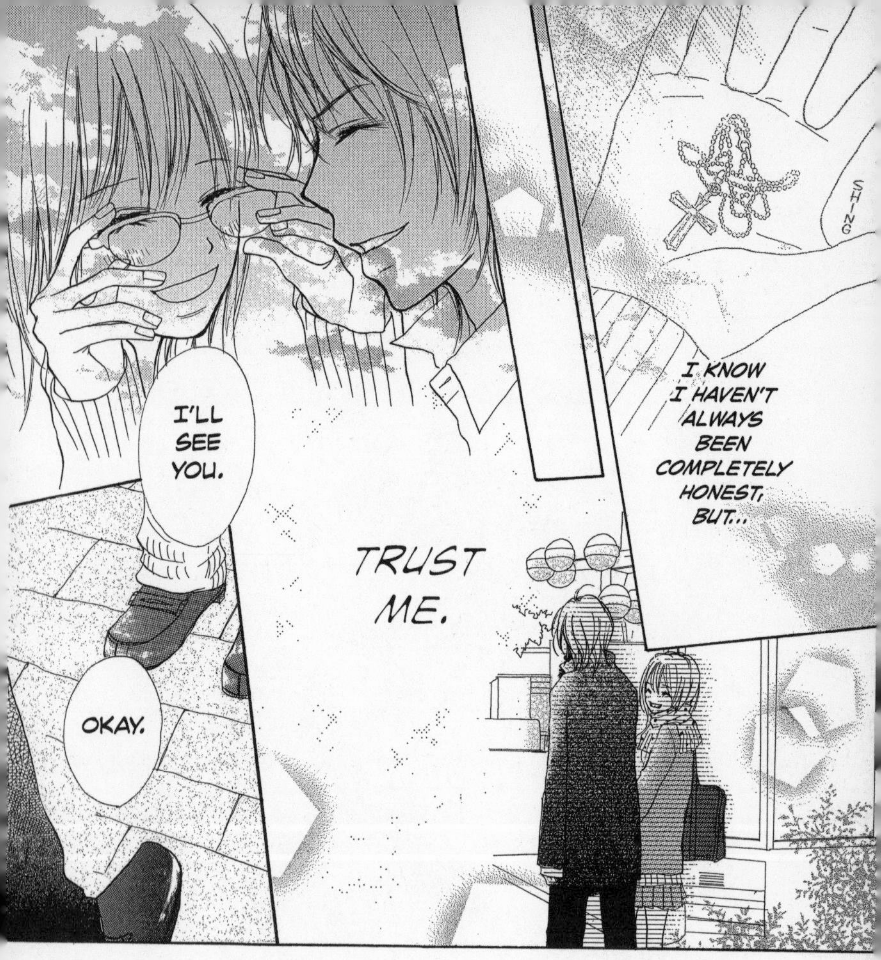
SHING
I KNOW I HAVEN'T ALWAYS BEEN COMPLETELY HONEST, BUT...
TRUST ME.
I'LL SEE YOU.
OKAY.

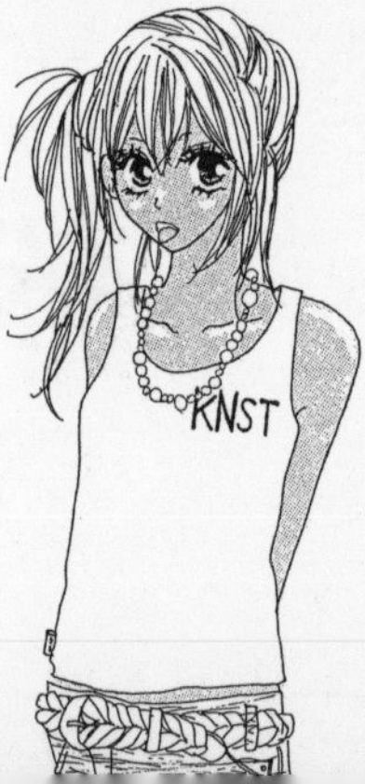
KNST

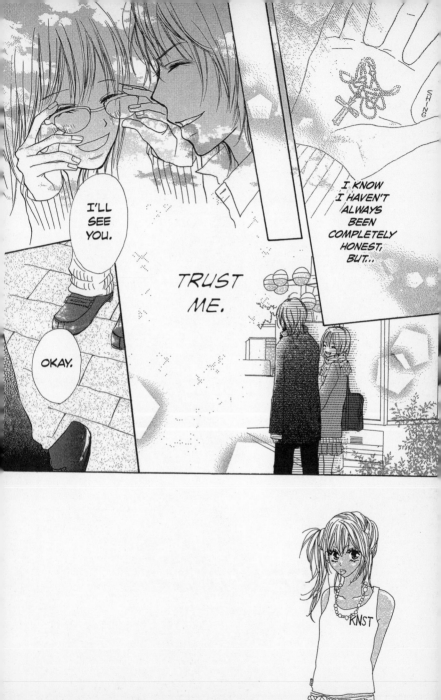

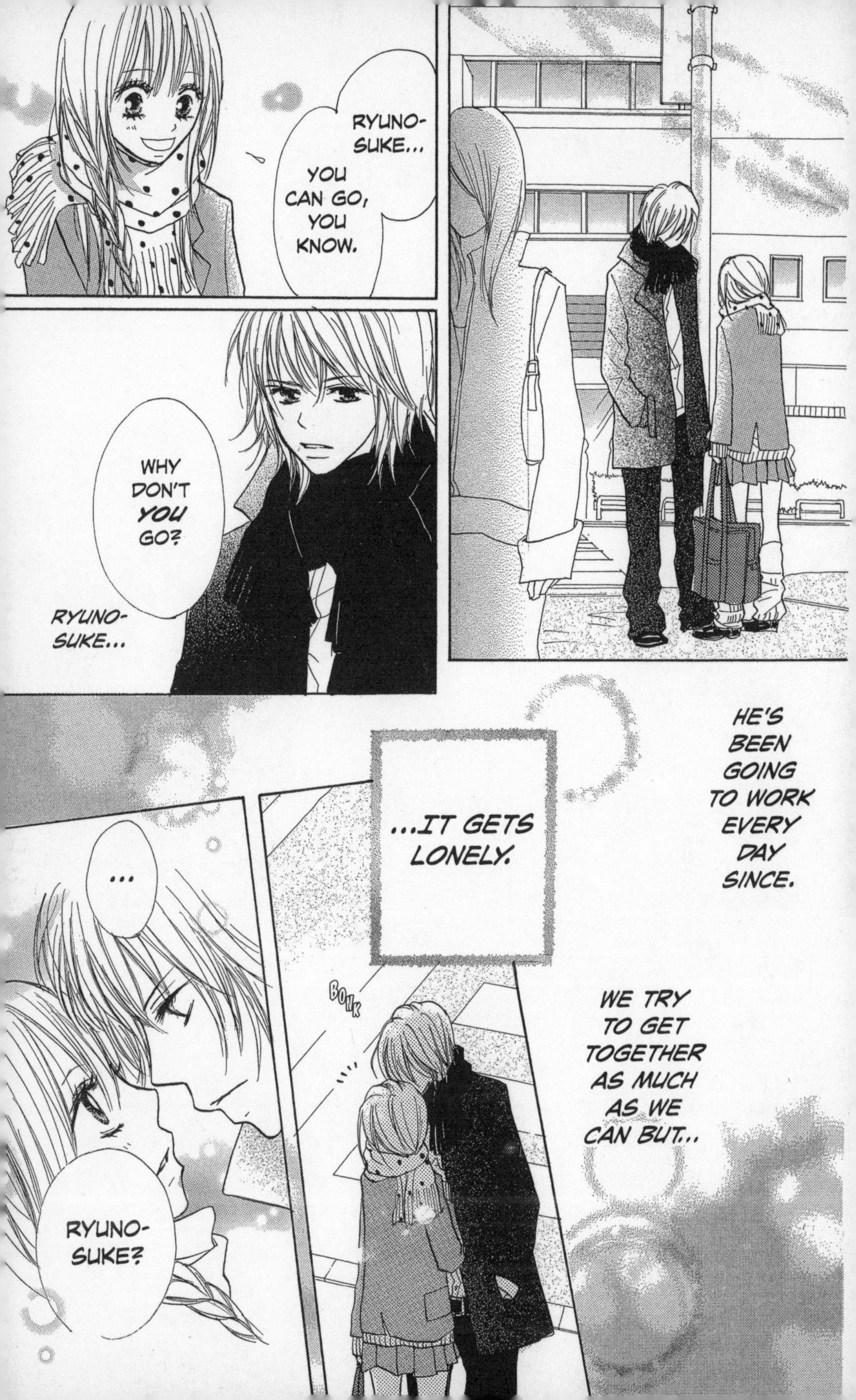
RYUNO-SUKE... YOU CAN GO, YOU KNOW.
WHY DON'T *YOU* GO?
RYUNO-SUKE...
HE'S BEEN GOING TO WORK EVERY DAY SINCE.
WE TRY TO GET TOGETHER AS MUCH AS WE CAN BUT...
...IT GETS LONELY.
BONK
...
RYUNO-SUKE?

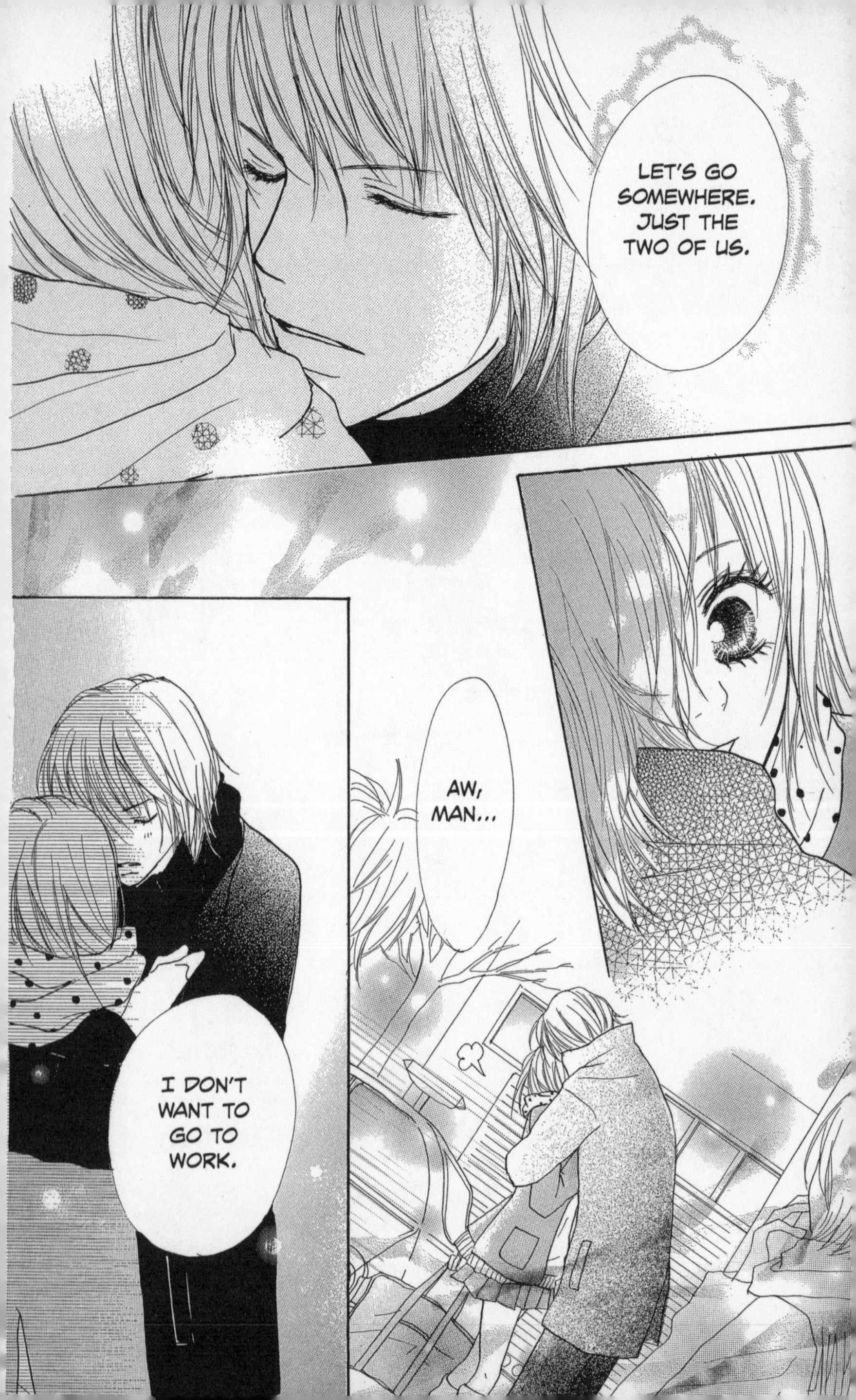
LET'S GO SOMEWHERE. JUST THE TWO OF US.
AW, MAN...
I DON'T WANT TO GO TO WORK.

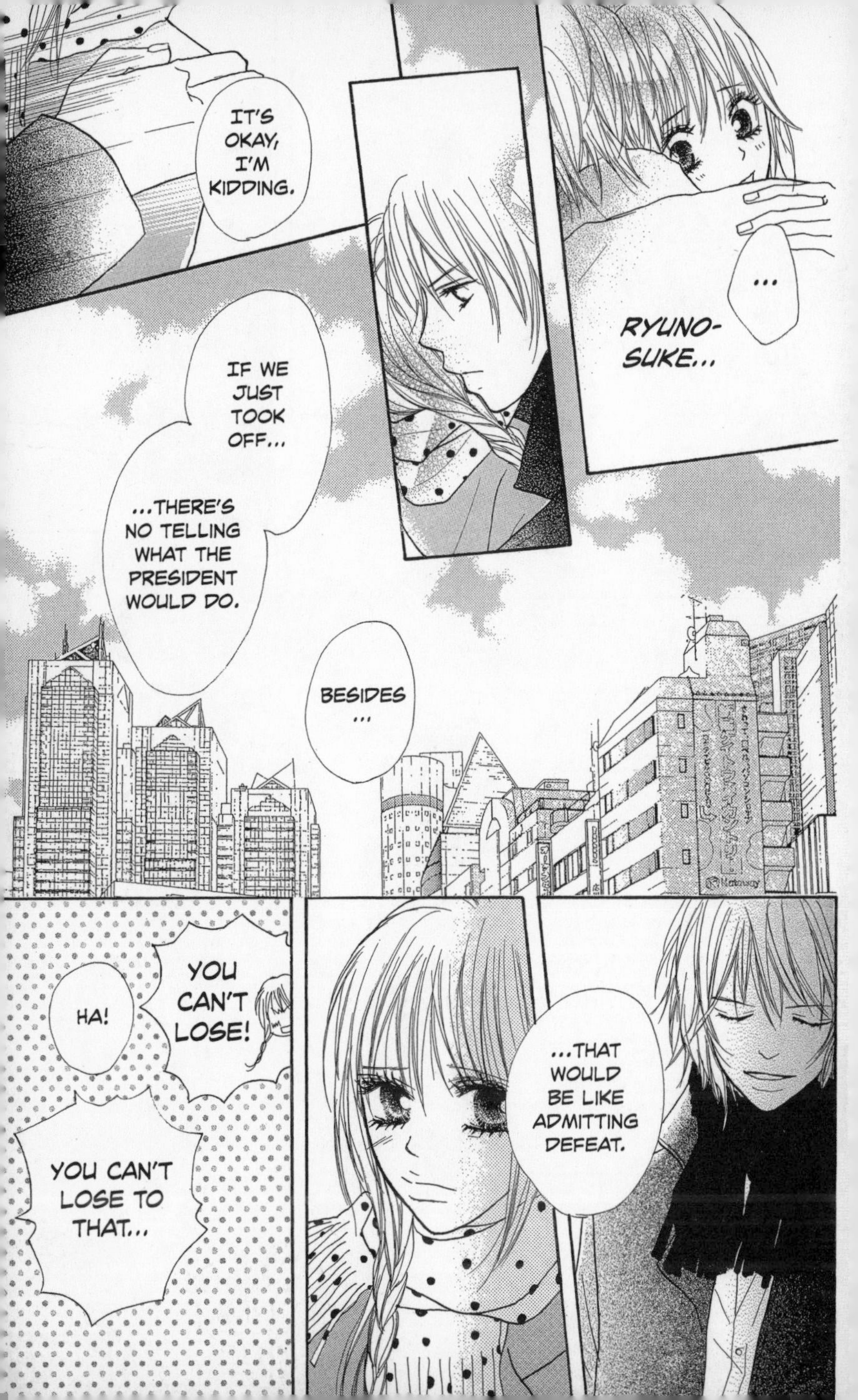
...
RYUNO-SUKE...
IT'S OKAY, I'M KIDDING.
IF WE JUST TOOK OFF...
...THERE'S NO TELLING WHAT THE PRESIDENT WOULD DO.
BESIDES...
...THAT WOULD BE LIKE ADMITTING DEFEAT.
YOU CAN'T LOSE!
HA!
YOU CAN'T LOSE TO THAT...

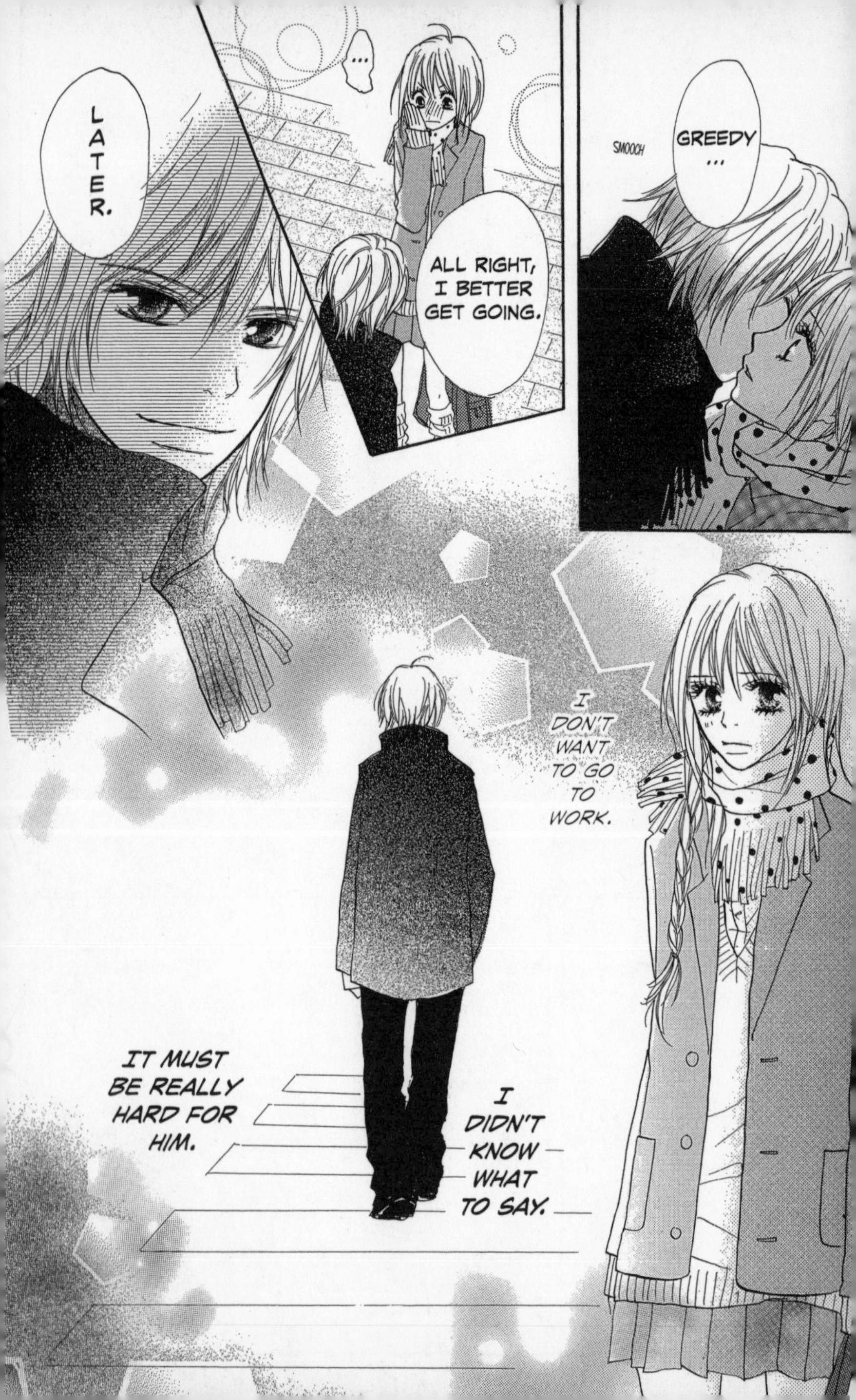
SMOOCH
GREEDY ...
...
ALL RIGHT, I BETTER GET GOING.
LATER.
I DON'T WANT TO GO TO WORK.
I DIDN'T KNOW WHAT TO SAY.
IT MUST BE REALLY HARD FOR HIM.

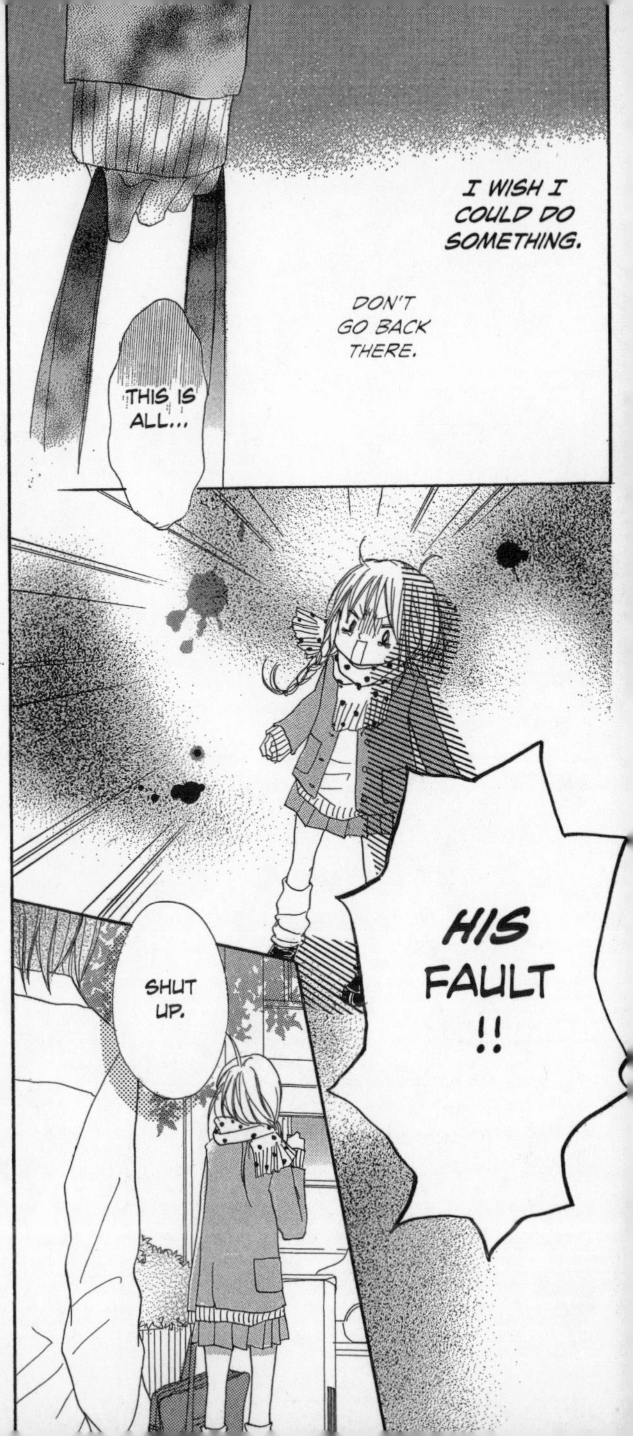
I WISH I COULD DO SOMETHING.
DON'T GO BACK THERE.
THIS IS ALL...
HIS FAULT !!
SHUT UP.

2 Continued...

The reference from my editors has gotten more and more hardcore...

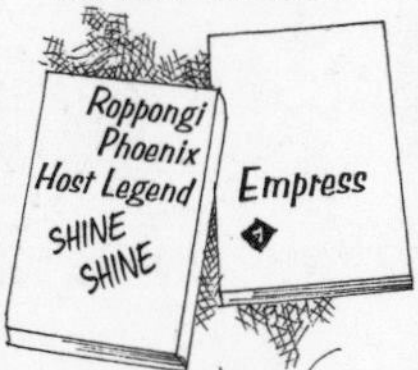
Roppongi Phoenix Host Legend
SHINE SHINE
Empress

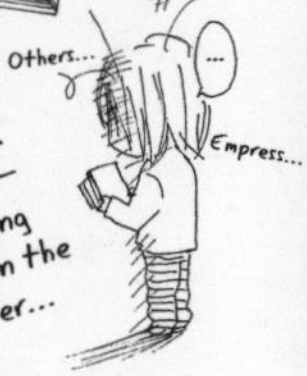
Others...
...
Empress...

A book with a fierce-looking host on the cover...

The thing is, they're awesome!! I even bought the sequels. I'm now a fan of a whole new genre...

• • • • •

Maybe someday they'll let me write what becomes of Jin and Shinobu in the future. Wishful thinking...?

The End

ORANGES

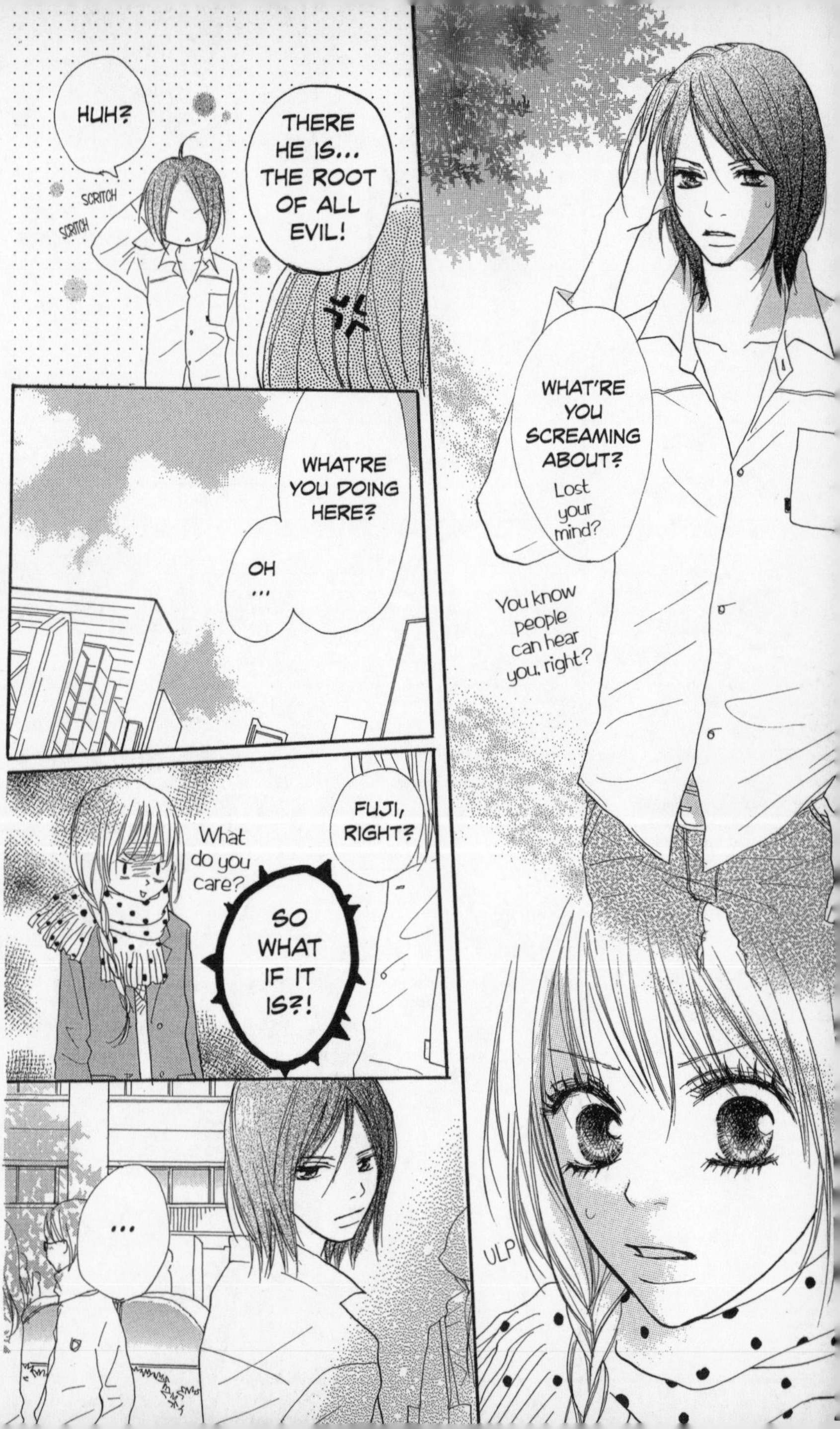
WHAT'RE YOU SCREAMING ABOUT?
Lost your mind?
You know people can hear you, right?
ULP
THERE HE IS... THE ROOT OF ALL EVIL!
HUH?
SCRITCH
SCRITCH
WHAT'RE YOU DOING HERE?
OH ...
FUJI, RIGHT?
SO WHAT IF IT IS?!
What do you care?
...

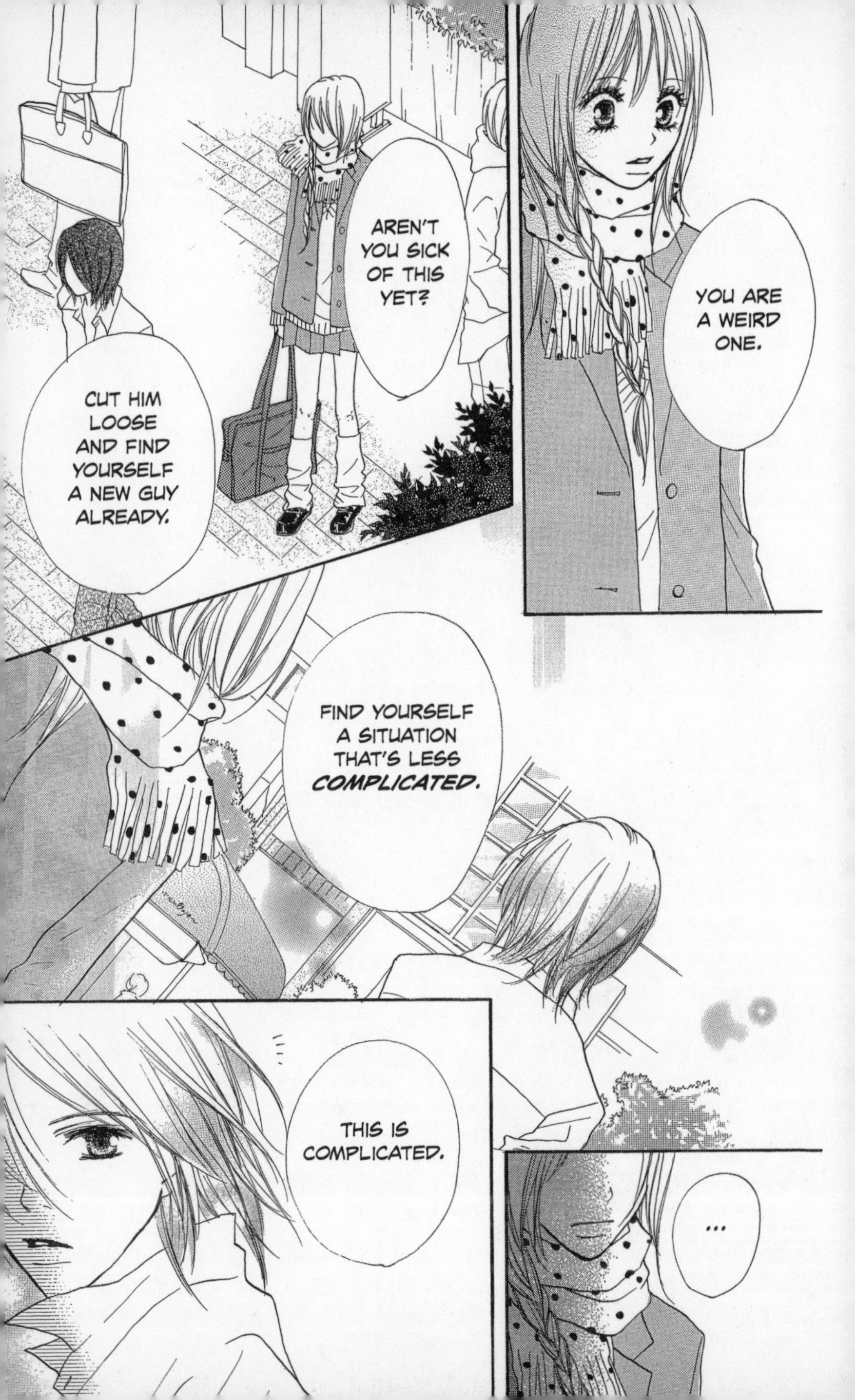
YOU ARE A WEIRD ONE.
AREN'T YOU SICK OF THIS YET?
CUT HIM LOOSE AND FIND YOURSELF A NEW GUY ALREADY.
FIND YOURSELF A SITUATION THAT'S LESS *COMPLICATED*.
THIS IS COMPLICATED.
...

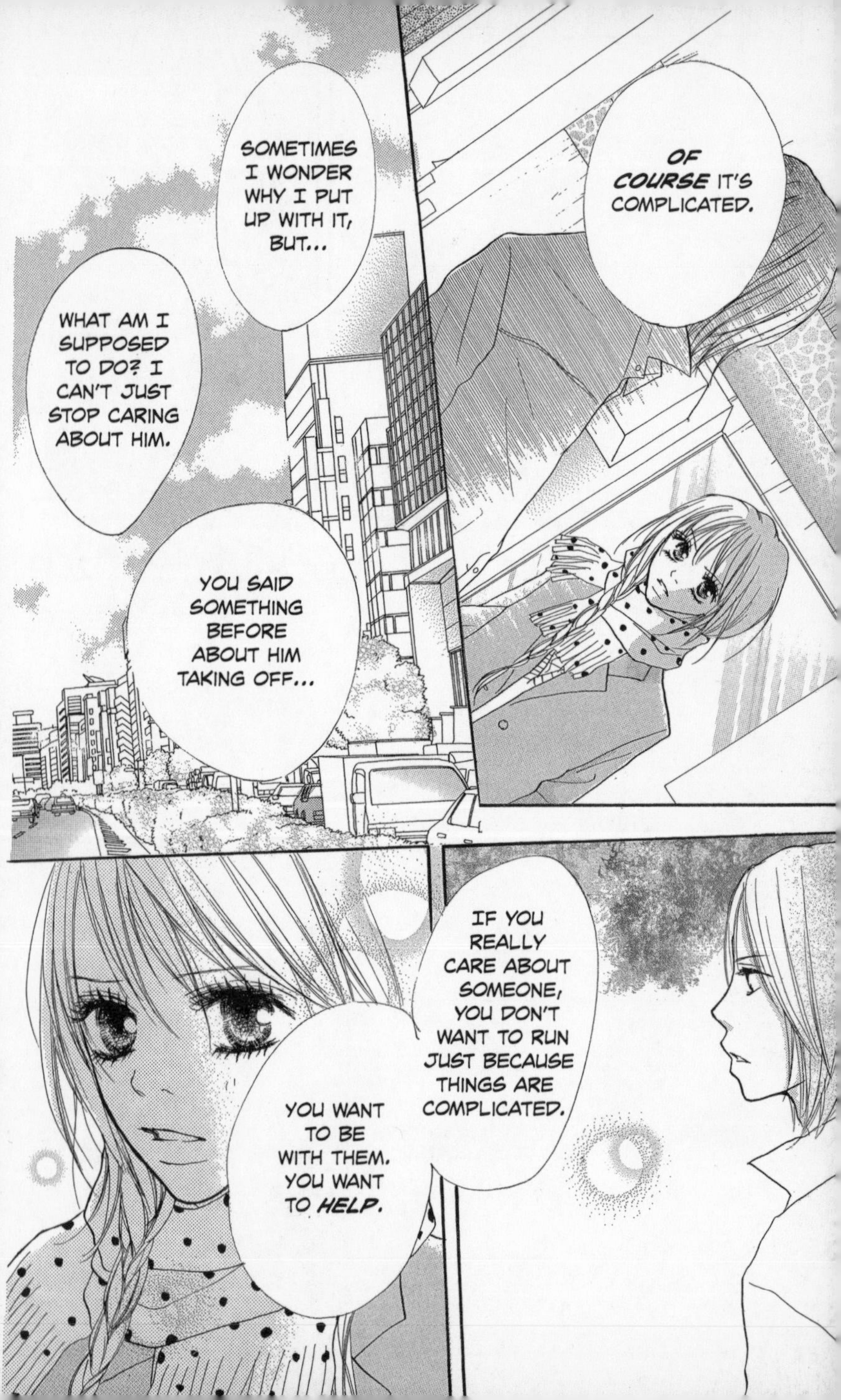
OF COURSE IT'S COMPLICATED.
SOMETIMES I WONDER WHY I PUT UP WITH IT, BUT...
WHAT AM I SUPPOSED TO DO? I CAN'T JUST STOP CARING ABOUT HIM.
YOU SAID SOMETHING BEFORE ABOUT HIM TAKING OFF...
IF YOU REALLY CARE ABOUT SOMEONE, YOU DON'T WANT TO RUN JUST BECAUSE THINGS ARE COMPLICATED.
YOU WANT TO BE WITH THEM. YOU WANT TO HELP.

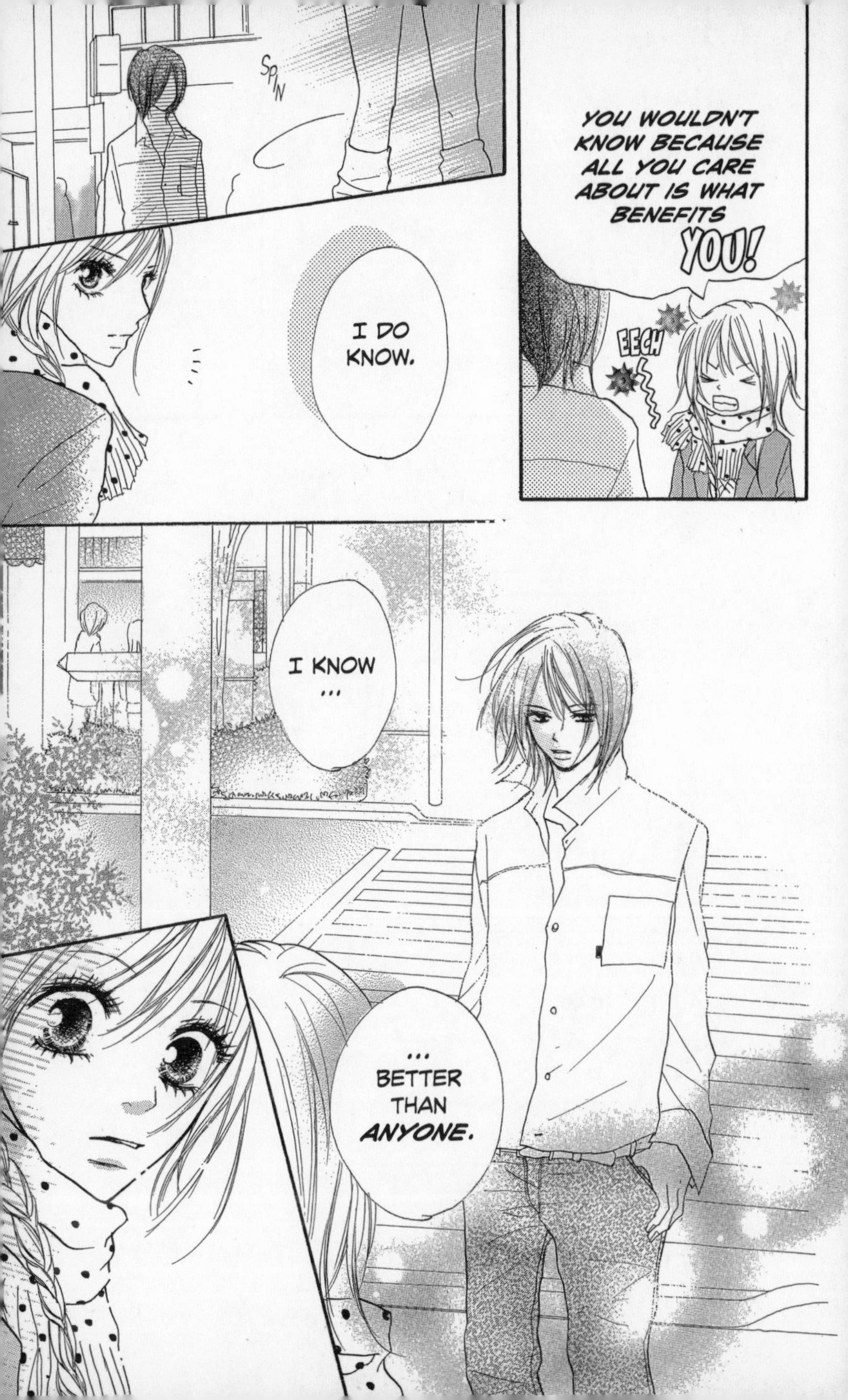
YOU WOULDN'T KNOW BECAUSE ALL YOU CARE ABOUT IS WHAT BENEFITS YOU!
EECH
SPIN
I DO KNOW.
I KNOW ...
... BETTER THAN ANYONE.

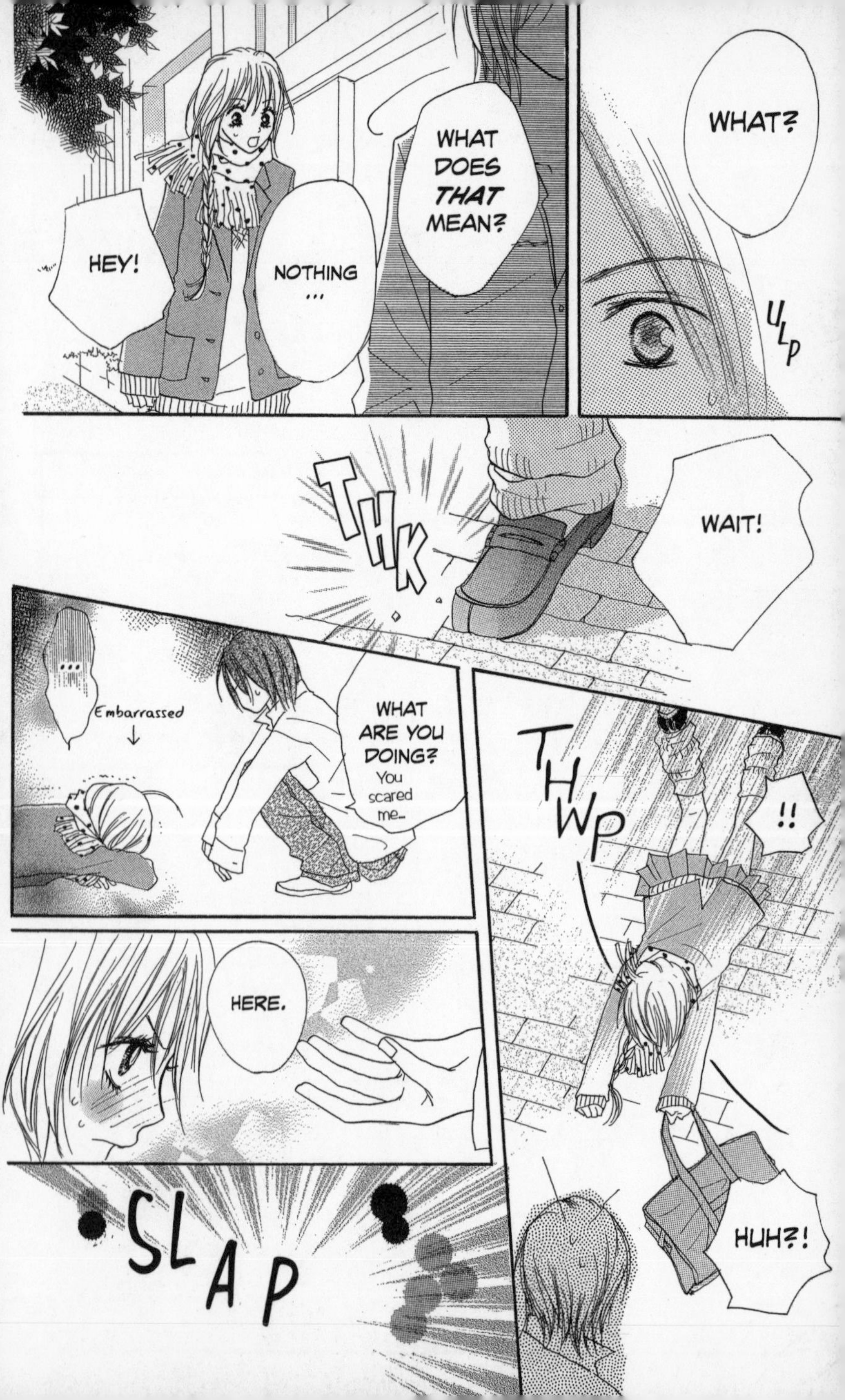
WHAT?
ULP
WHAT DOES *THAT* MEAN?
NOTHING ...
HEY!
WAIT!
THK
THWP
!!
HUH?!
WHAT ARE YOU DOING?
You scared me...
...
Embarrassed
HERE.
SLAP

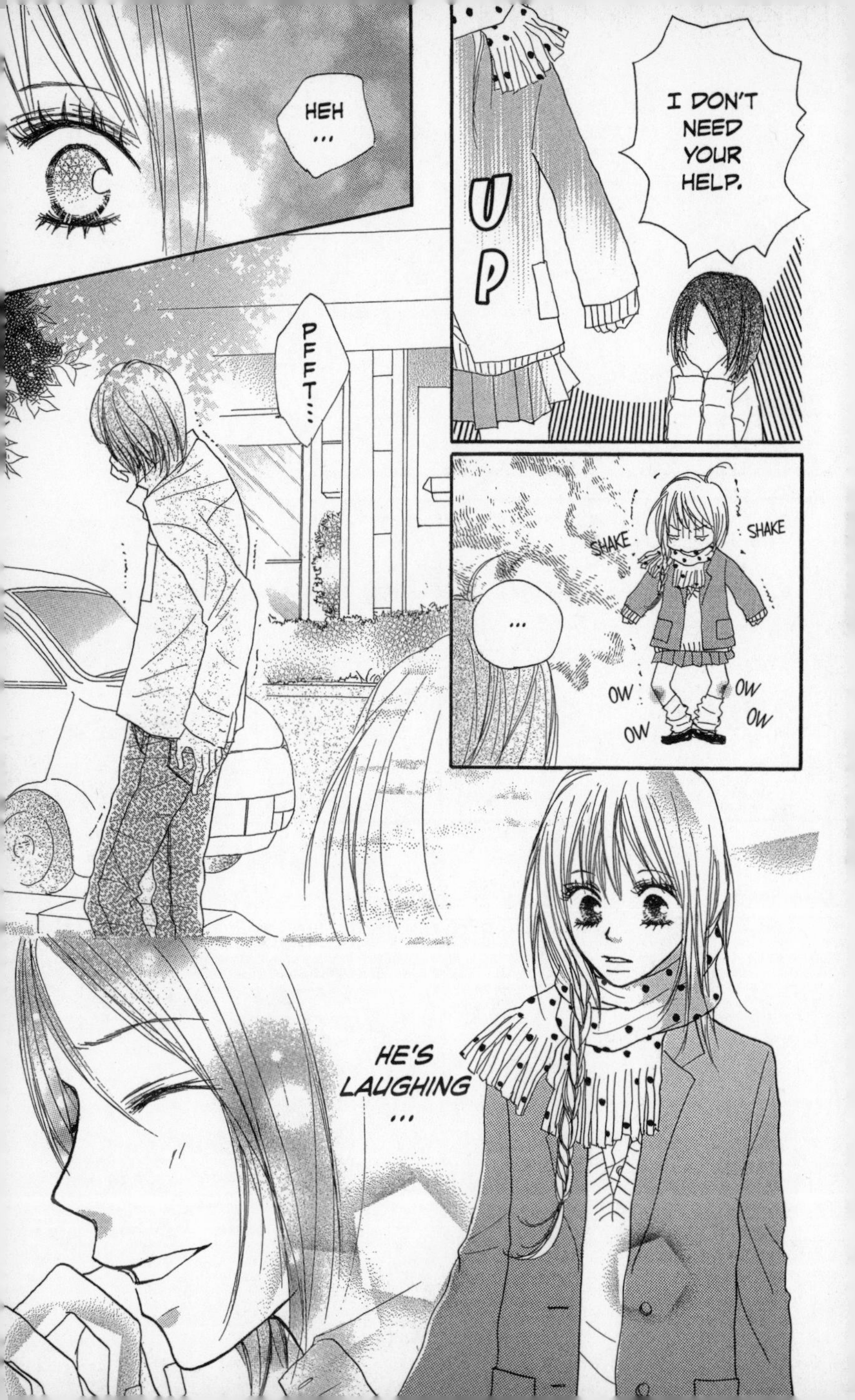
I DON'T NEED YOUR HELP.
UP
HEH ...
SHAKE
SHAKE
OW
OW
OW
OW
...
PFFT...
HE'S LAUGHING ...

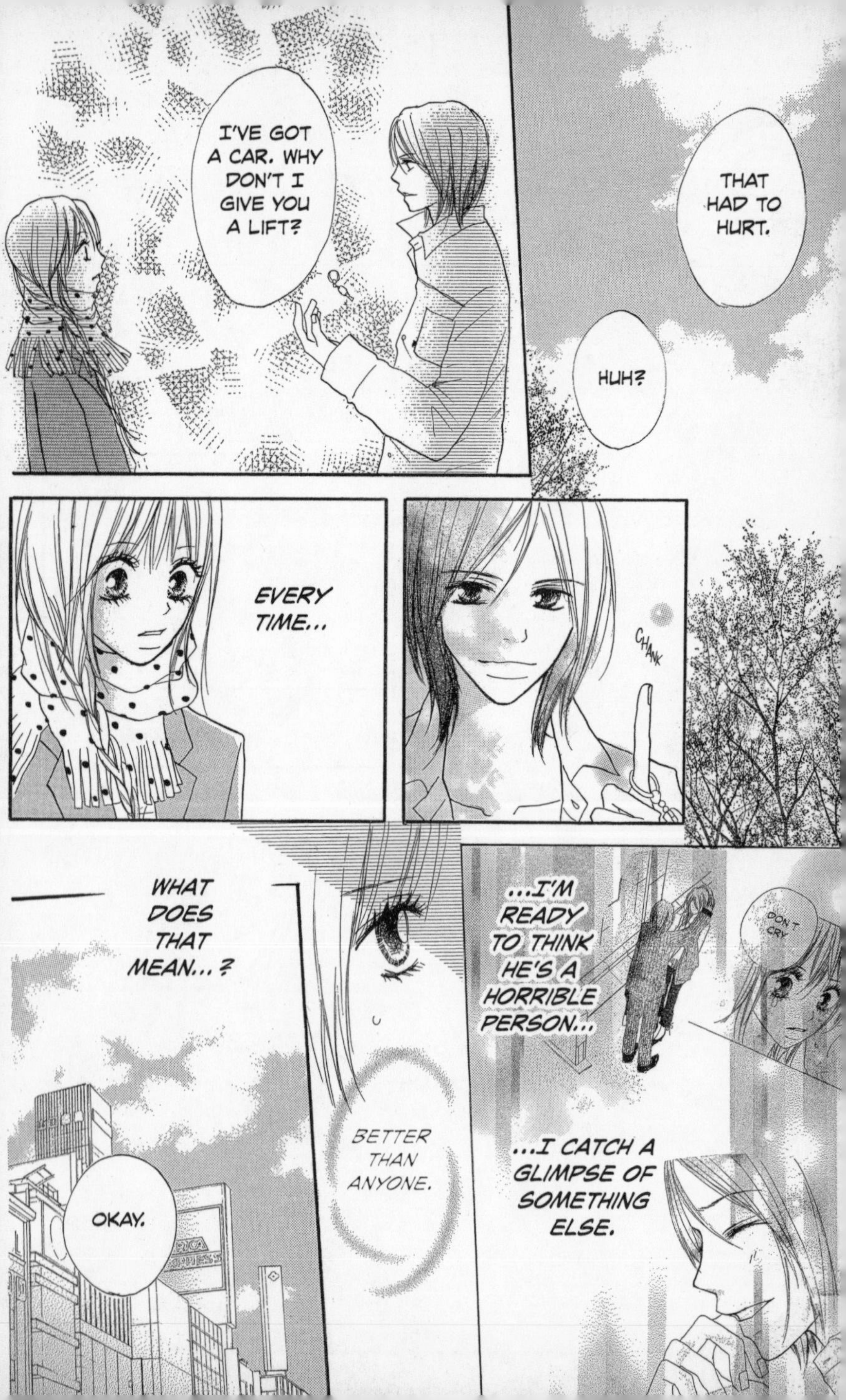
THAT HAD TO HURT.
HUH?
I'VE GOT A CAR. WHY DON'T I GIVE YOU A LIFT?
CHANK
EVERY TIME...
...I'M READY TO THINK HE'S A HORRIBLE PERSON...
DON'T CRY
...I CATCH A GLIMPSE OF SOMETHING ELSE.
BETTER THAN ANYONE.
WHAT DOES THAT MEAN...?
OKAY.

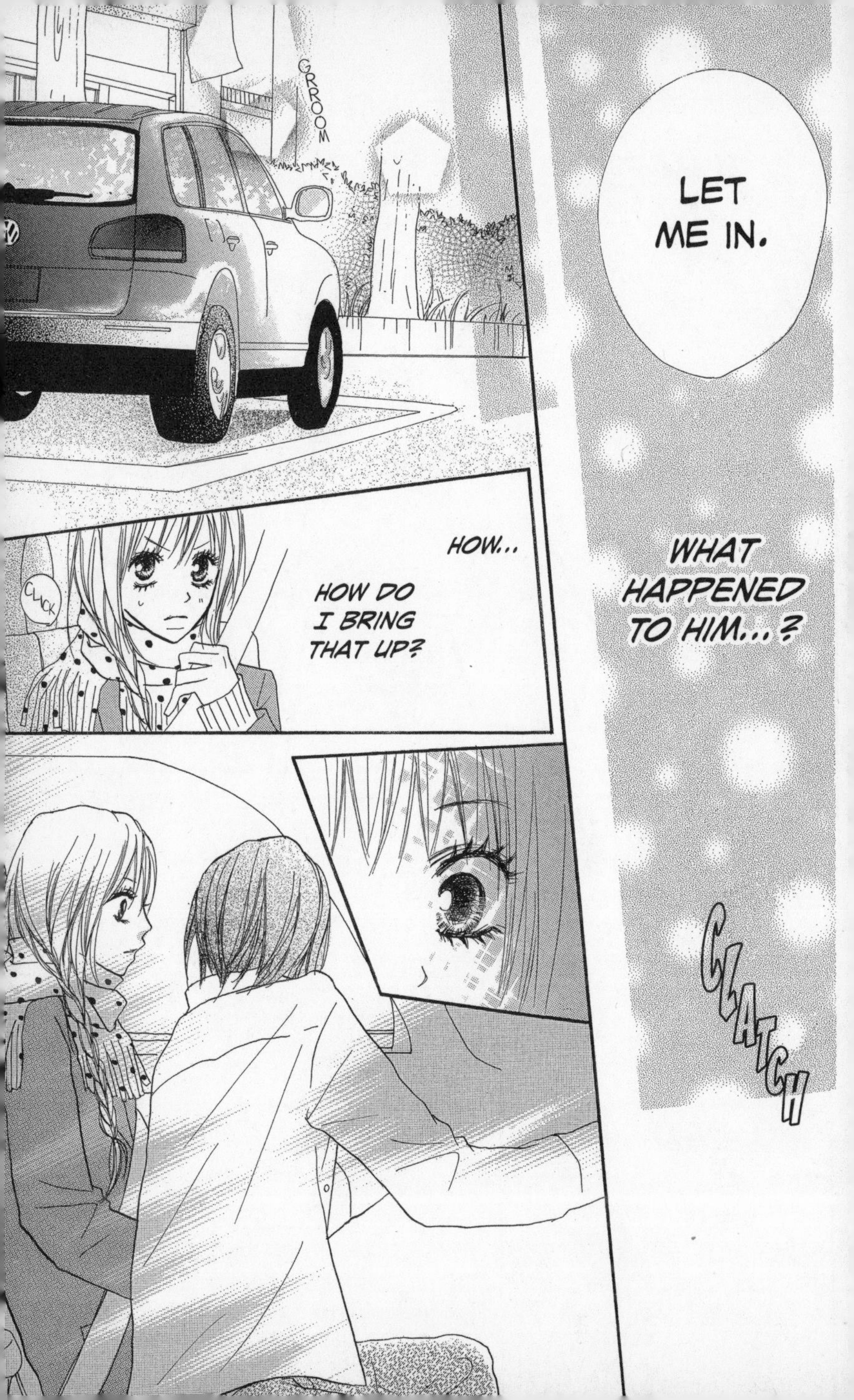
LET ME IN.
WHAT HAPPENED TO HIM...?
CLATCH
GRROOM
CLICK
HOW...
HOW DO I BRING THAT UP?

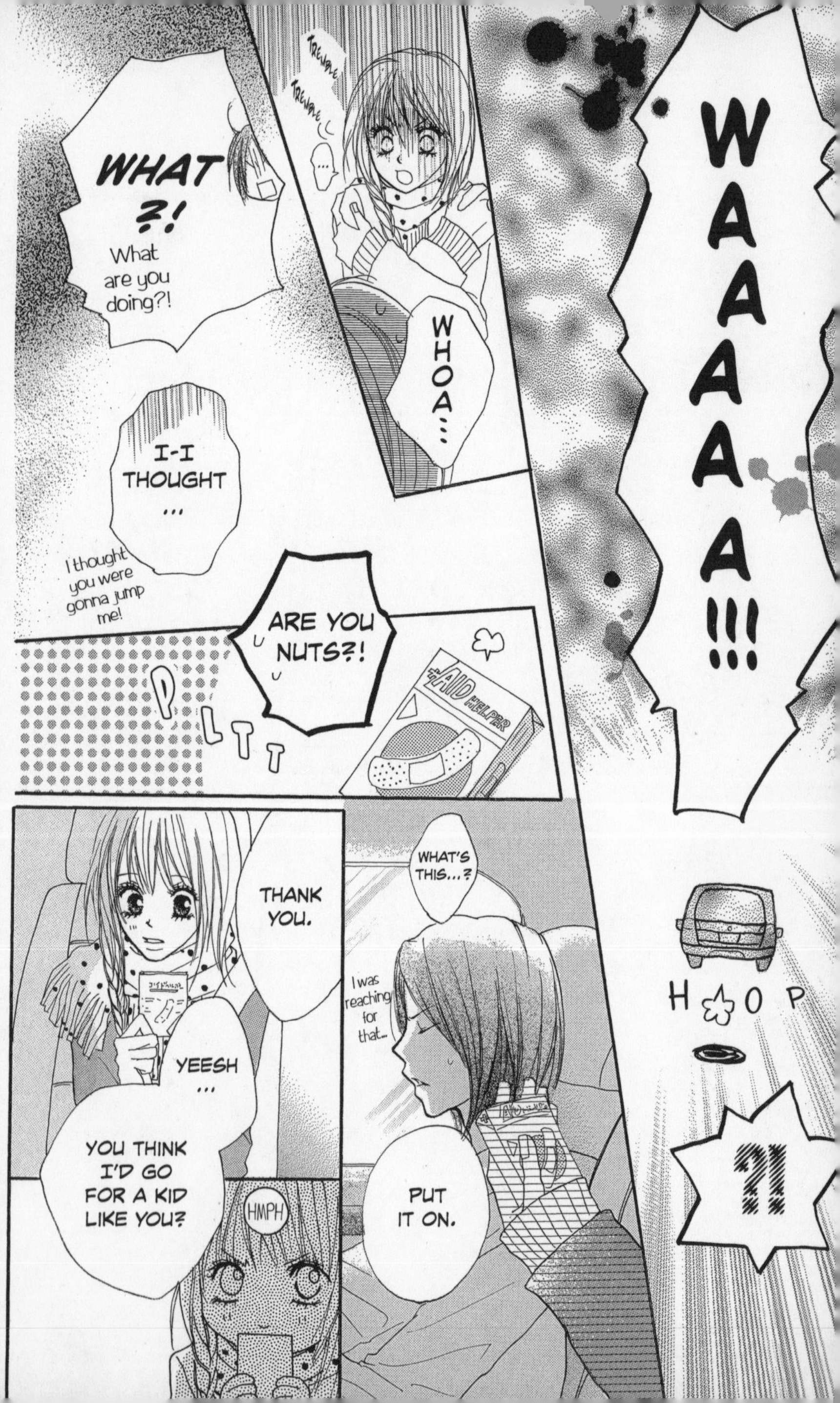
WAAAAA!!!
HOP
?!
TREMBLE TREMBLE
...
WHOA...
WHAT?!
What are you doing?!
I-I THOUGHT...
I thought you were gonna jump me!
ARE YOU NUTS?!
PLTTT
AID HELPER
WHAT'S THIS...?
I was reaching for that...
PUT IT ON.
THANK YOU.
YEESH...
YOU THINK I'D GO FOR A KID LIKE YOU?
HMPH

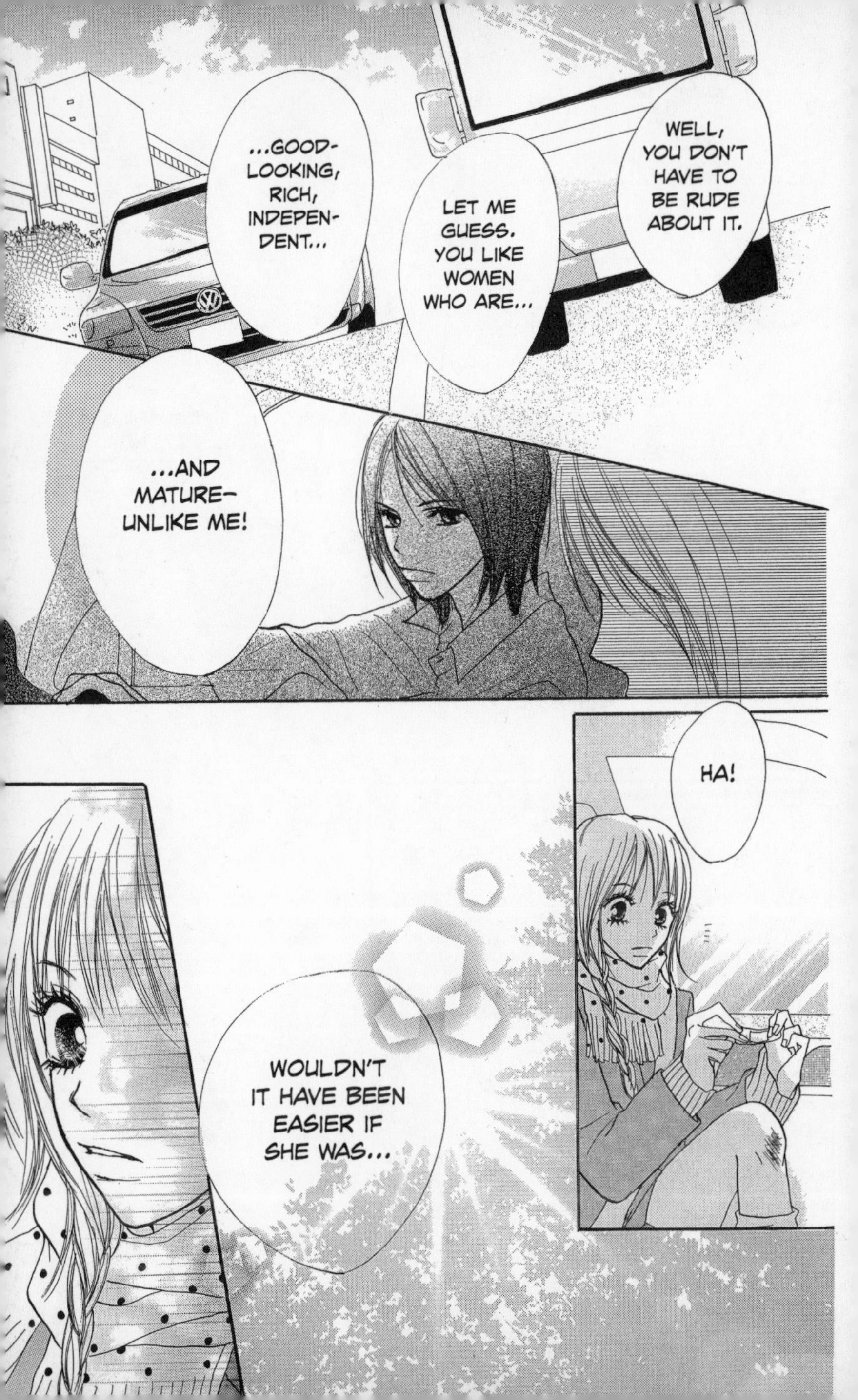

WELL, YOU DON'T HAVE TO BE RUDE ABOUT IT.
LET ME GUESS. YOU LIKE WOMEN WHO ARE...
...GOOD-LOOKING, RICH, INDEPEN-DENT...
...AND MATURE—UNLIKE ME!
HA!
WOULDN'T IT HAVE BEEN EASIER IF SHE WAS...

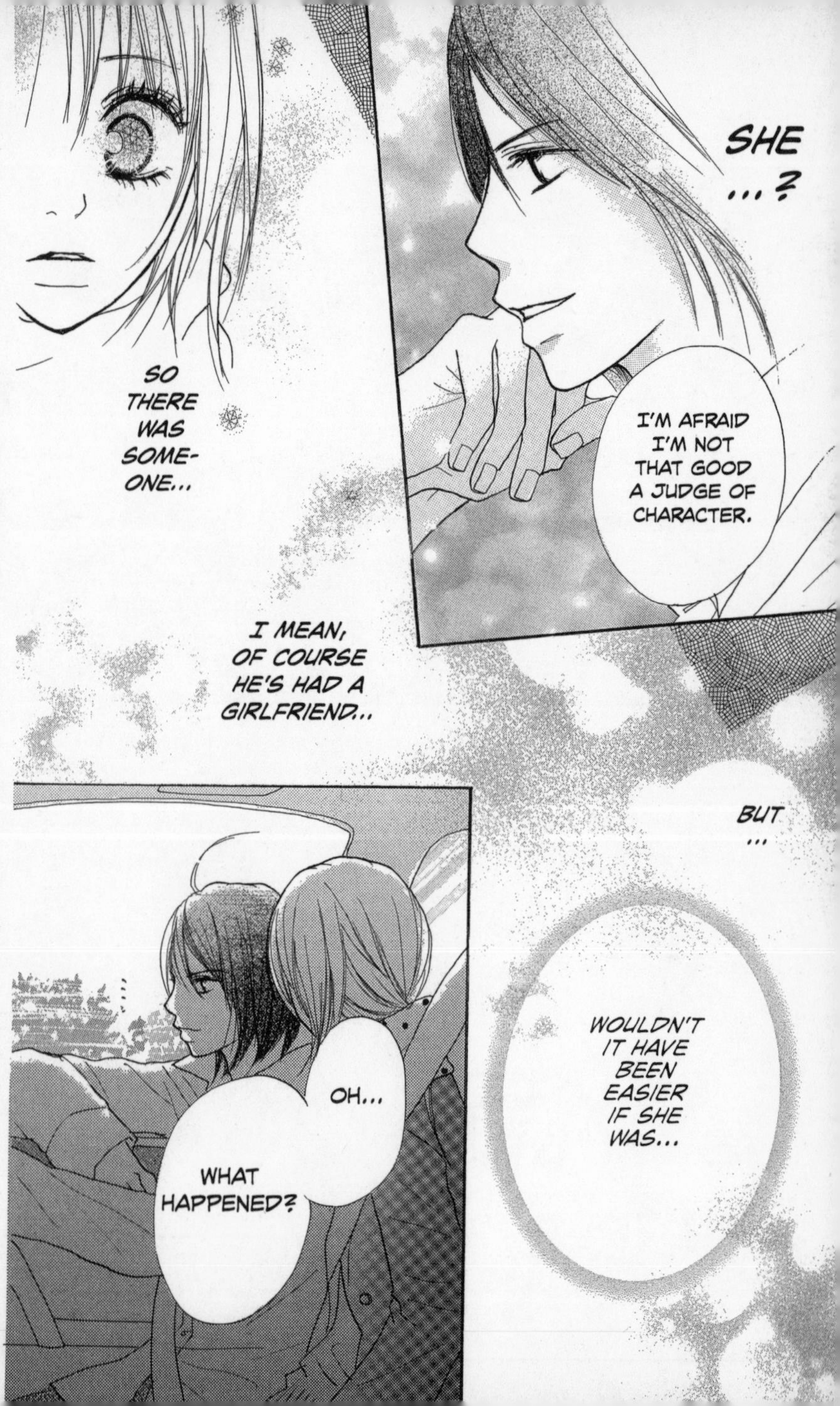
SHE ...?
I'M AFRAID I'M NOT THAT GOOD A JUDGE OF CHARACTER.
SO THERE WAS SOME-ONE...
I MEAN, OF COURSE HE'S HAD A GIRLFRIEND..
BUT ...
WOULDN'T IT HAVE BEEN EASIER IF SHE WAS...
OH...
WHAT HAPPENED?

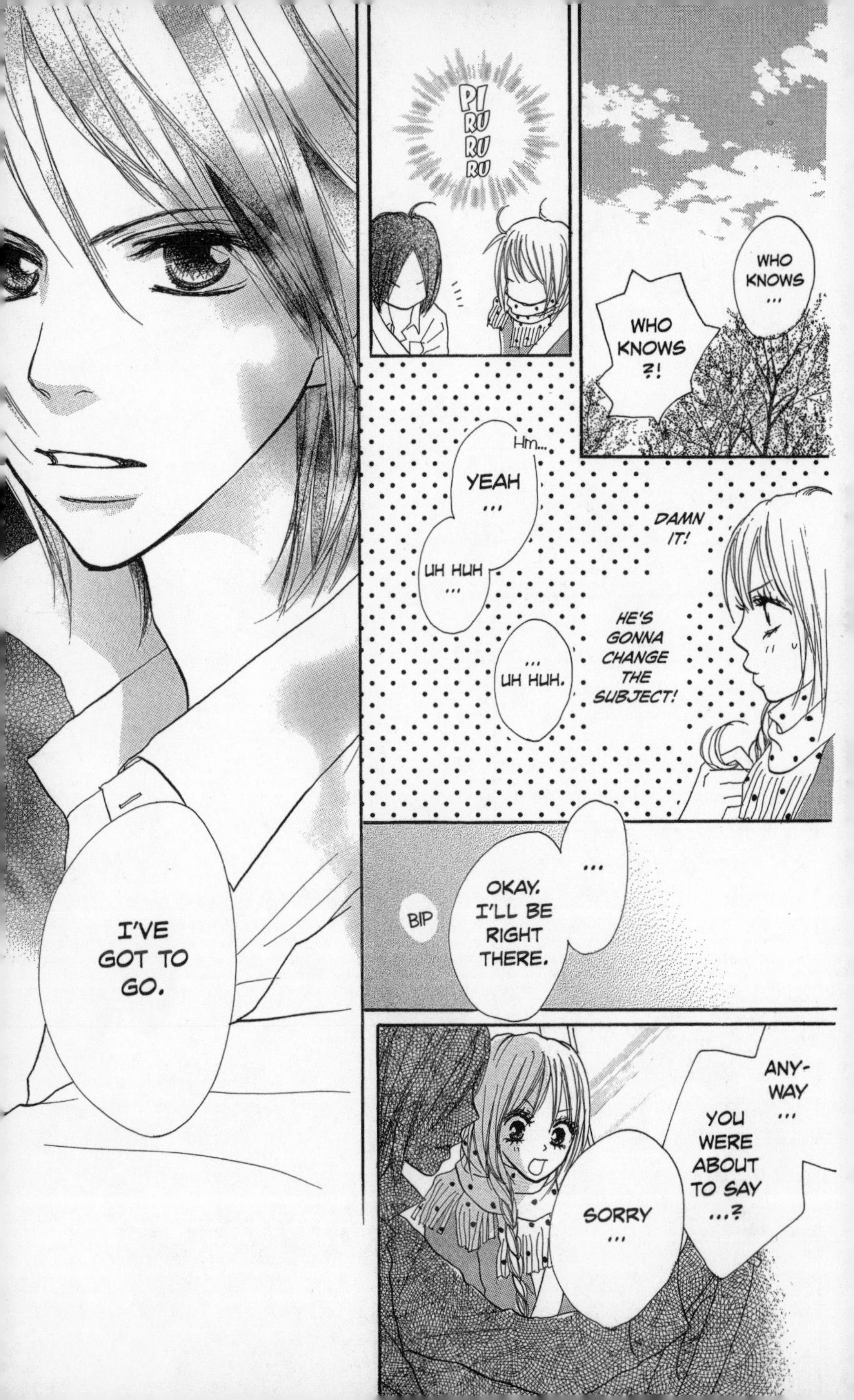
WHO KNOWS ...
WHO KNOWS ?!
PIRURURU
DAMN IT!
HE'S GONNA CHANGE THE SUBJECT!
Hm...
YEAH ...
UH HUH ...
... UH HUH.
...
OKAY. I'LL BE RIGHT THERE.
BIP
ANY-WAY ...
YOU WERE ABOUT TO SAY ...?
SORRY ...
I'VE GOT TO GO.

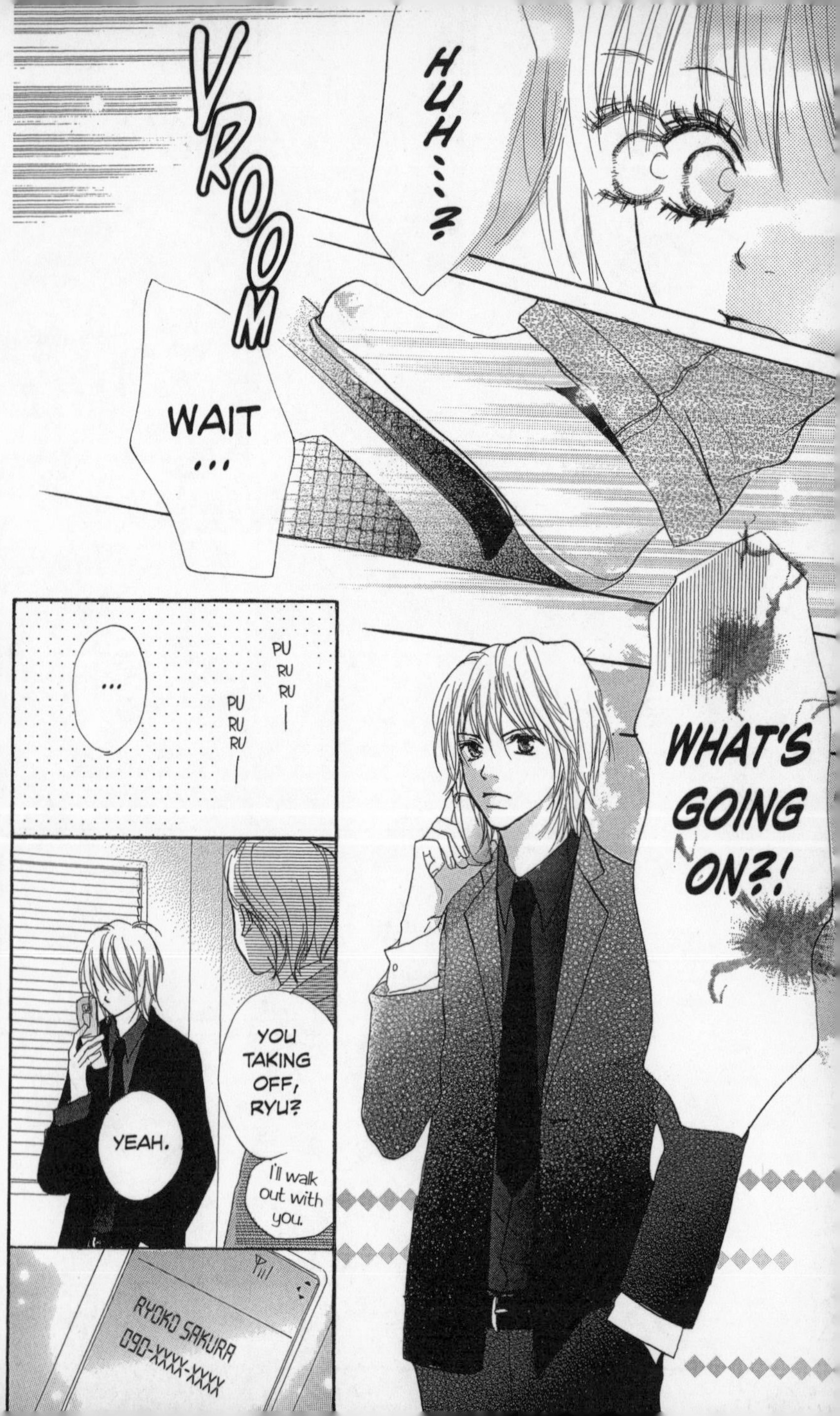
HUH...?
VROOM
WAIT...
WHAT'S GOING ON?!
PU RU RU —
PU RU RU —
...
YOU TAKING OFF, RYU?
YEAH.
I'll walk out with you.
RYOKO SAKURA
090-XXXX-XXXX

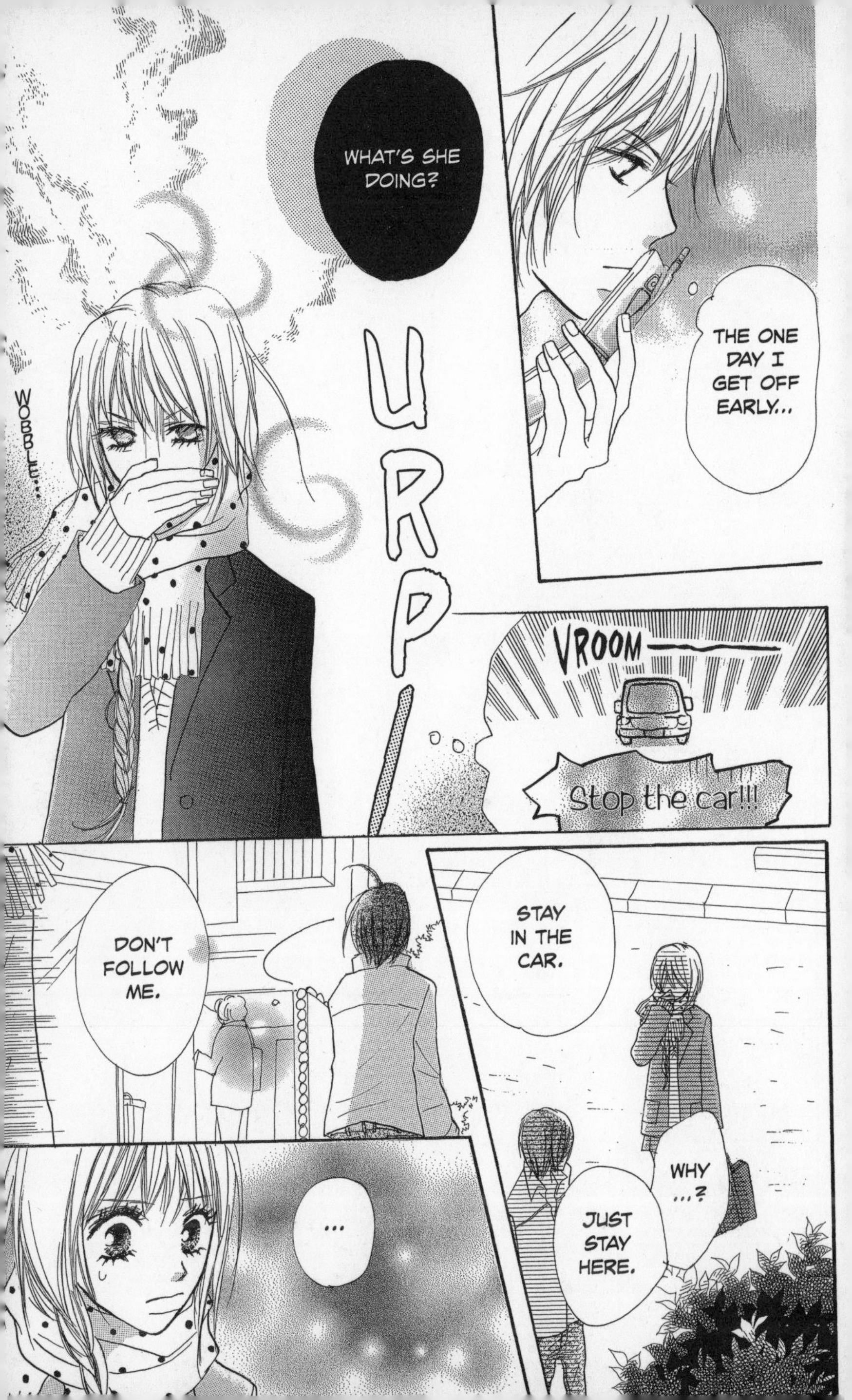
THE ONE DAY I GET OFF EARLY...
VROOM
Stop the car!!!
WHAT'S SHE DOING?
URP!
WOBBLE...
STAY IN THE CAR.
WHY...?
JUST STAY HERE.
DON'T FOLLOW ME.
...

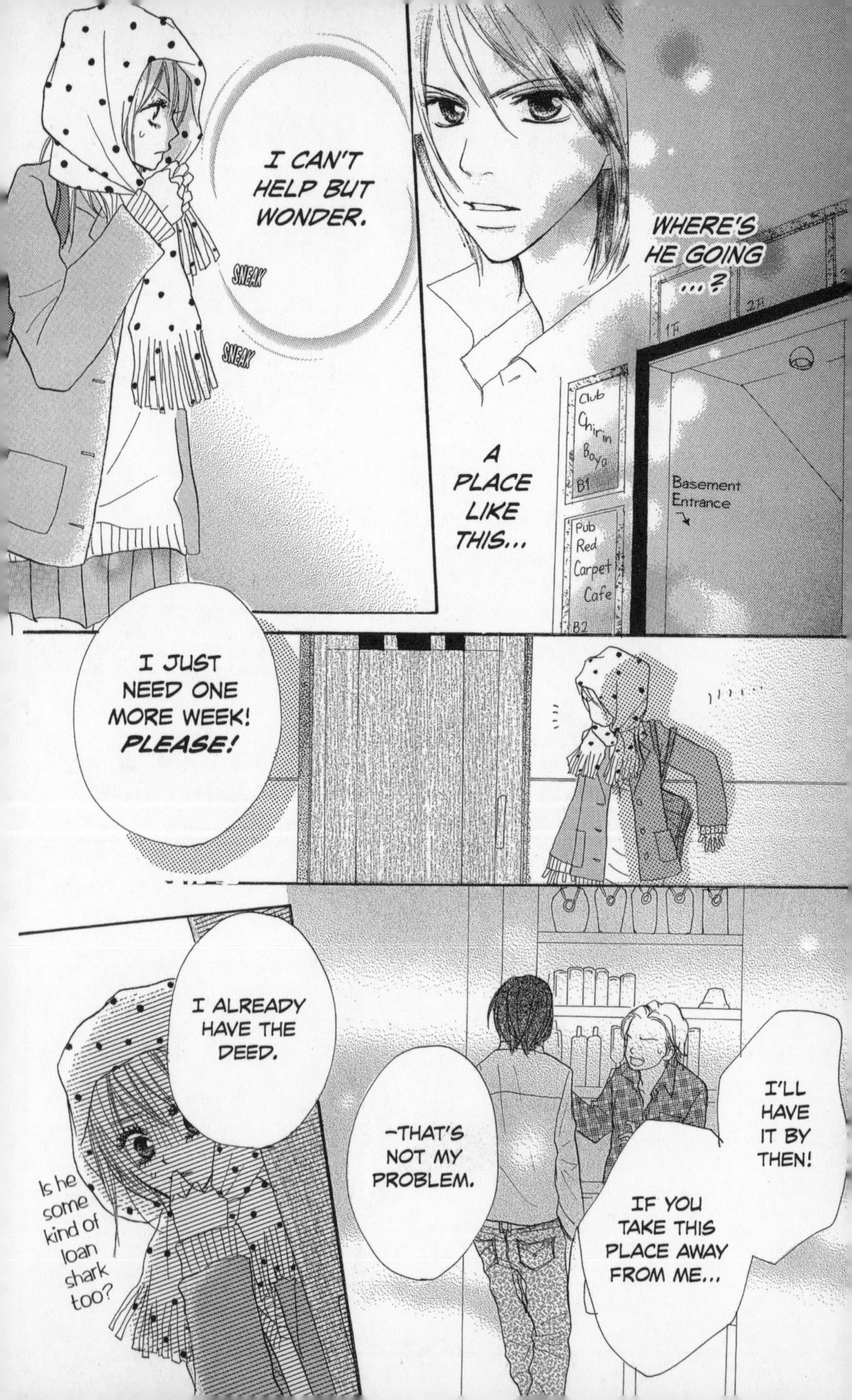
WHERE'S HE GOING ...?
A PLACE LIKE THIS...
Club Chirin Boya B1
Pub Red Carpet Cafe B2
Basement Entrance
I CAN'T HELP BUT WONDER.
SNEAK
SNEAK
I JUST NEED ONE MORE WEEK! PLEASE!
I'LL HAVE IT BY THEN!
IF YOU TAKE THIS PLACE AWAY FROM ME...
–THAT'S NOT MY PROBLEM.
I ALREADY HAVE THE DEED.
Is he some kind of loan shark too?

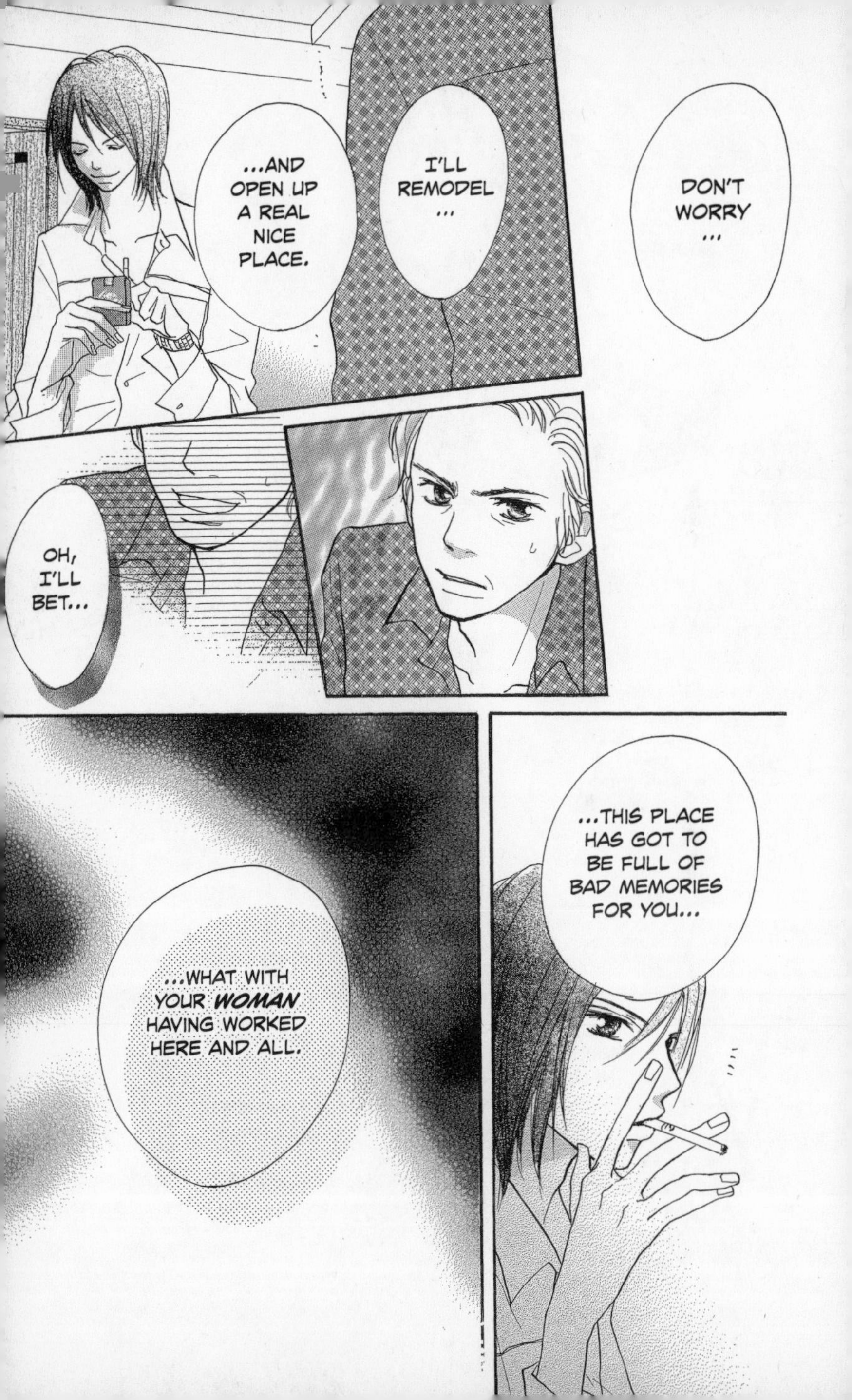
DON'T WORRY ...
I'LL REMODEL ...
...AND OPEN UP A REAL NICE PLACE.
OH, I'LL BET...
...THIS PLACE HAS GOT TO BE FULL OF BAD MEMORIES FOR YOU...
...WHAT WITH YOUR ***WOMAN*** HAVING WORKED HERE AND ALL.

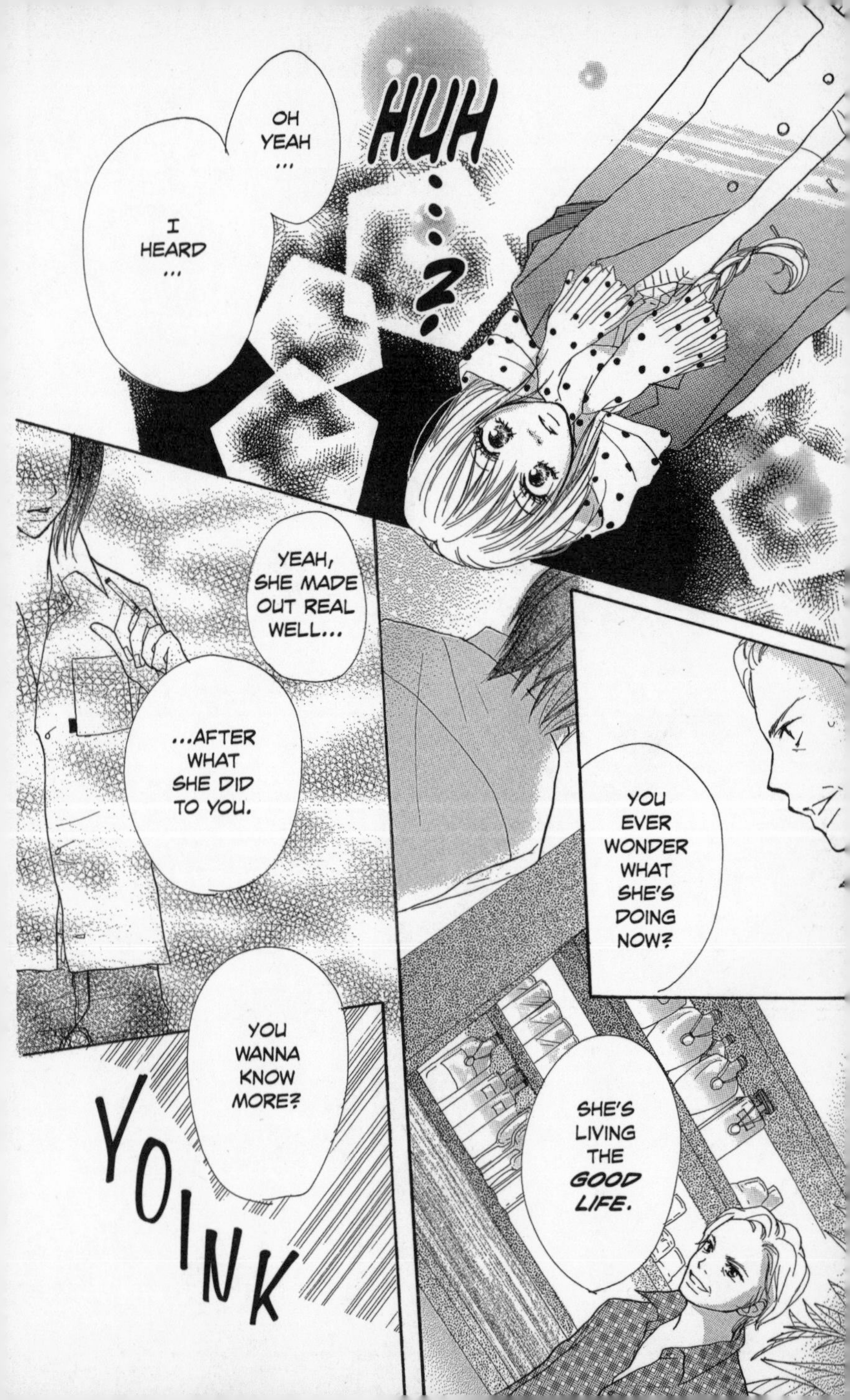
HUH...?
OH YEAH... I HEARD...
YOU EVER WONDER WHAT SHE'S DOING NOW?
SHE'S LIVING THE *GOOD LIFE*.
YEAH, SHE MADE OUT REAL WELL...
...AFTER WHAT SHE DID TO YOU.
YOU WANNA KNOW MORE?
YOINK

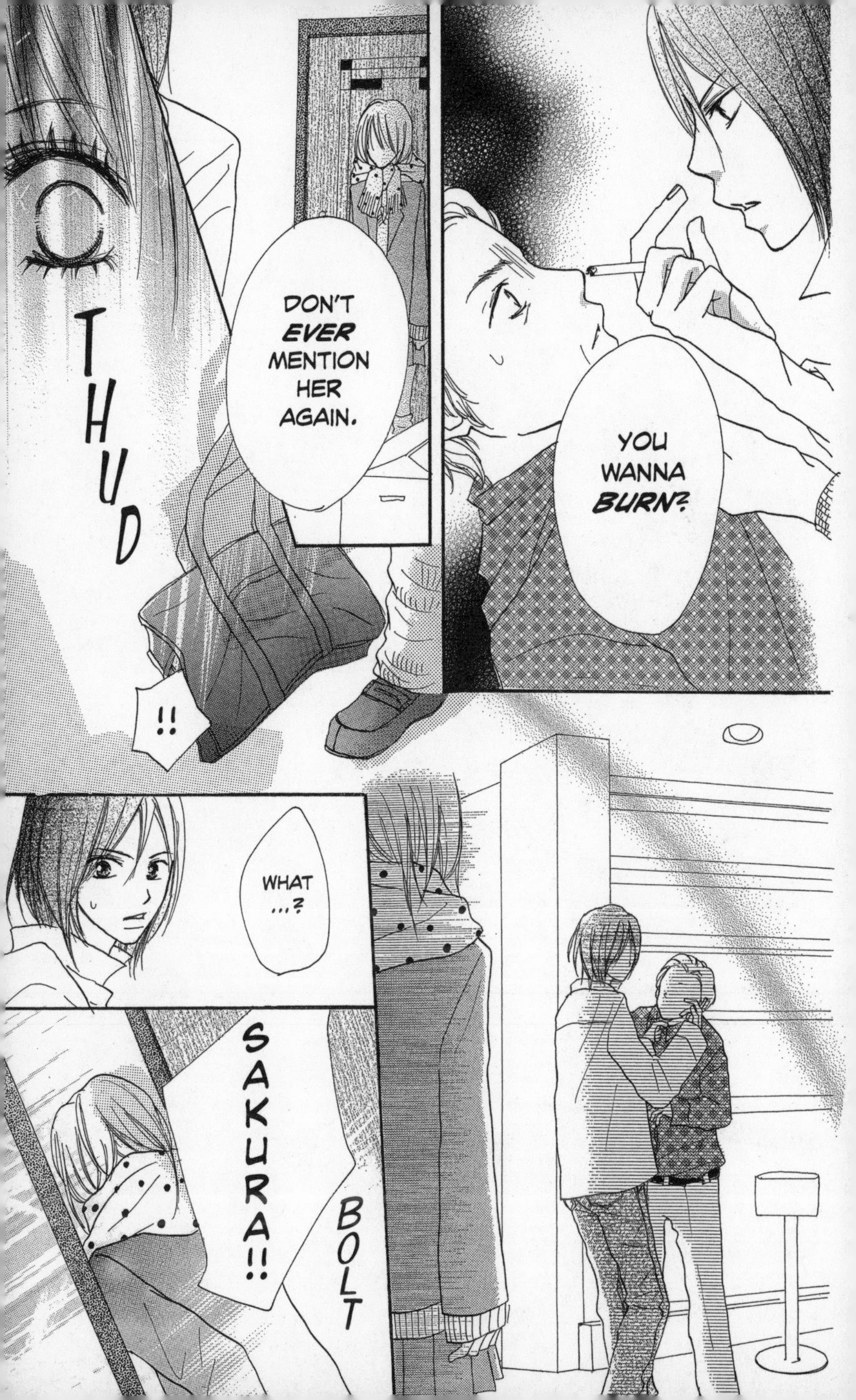
YOU WANNA BURN?
DON'T EVER MENTION HER AGAIN.
THUD
!!
WHAT ...?
SAKURA!!
BOLT

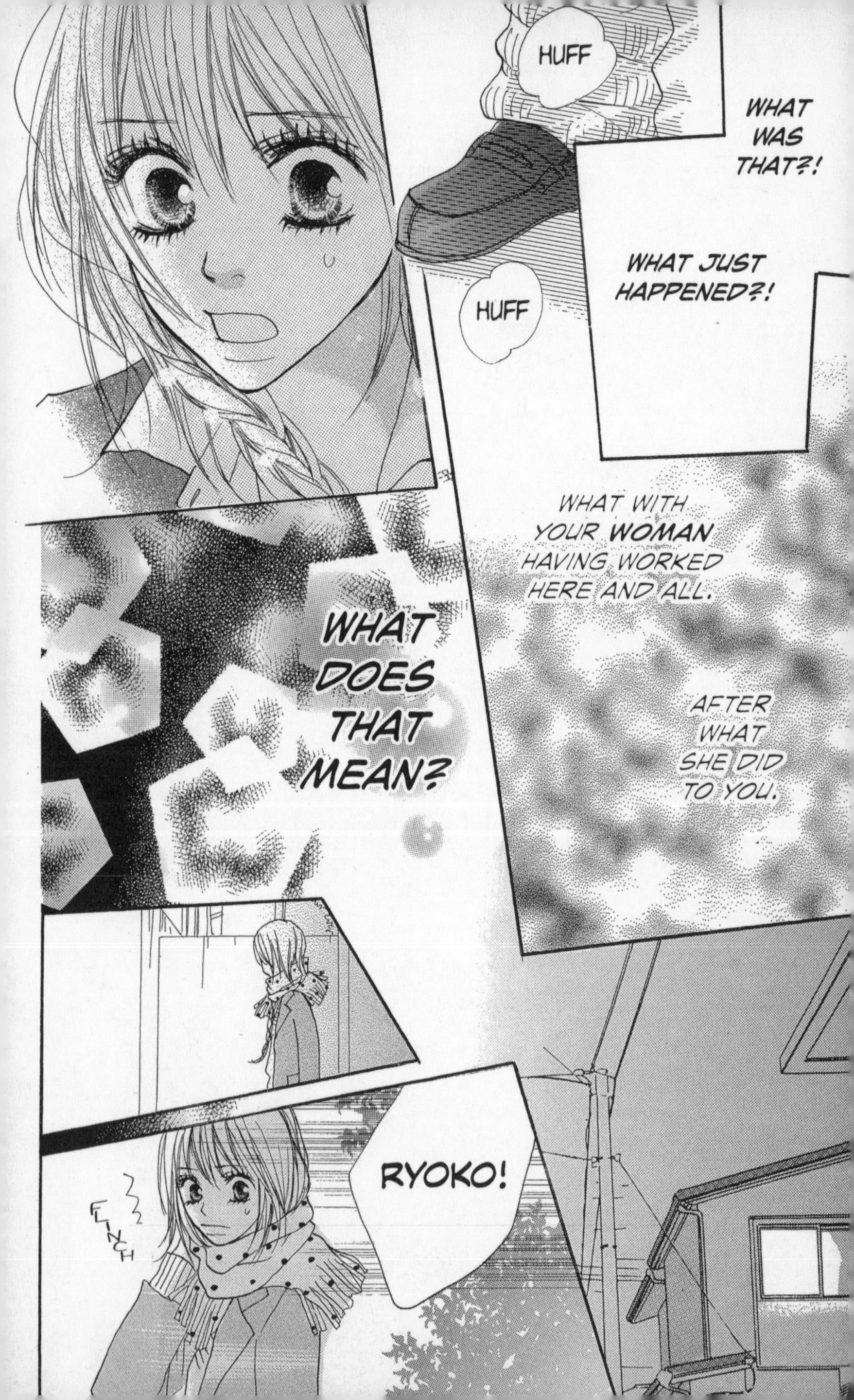
WHAT WAS THAT?!
WHAT JUST HAPPENED?!
HUFF
HUFF
WHAT WITH YOUR WOMAN HAVING WORKED HERE AND ALL.
AFTER WHAT SHE DID TO YOU.
WHAT DOES THAT MEAN?
RYOKO!
FLINCH

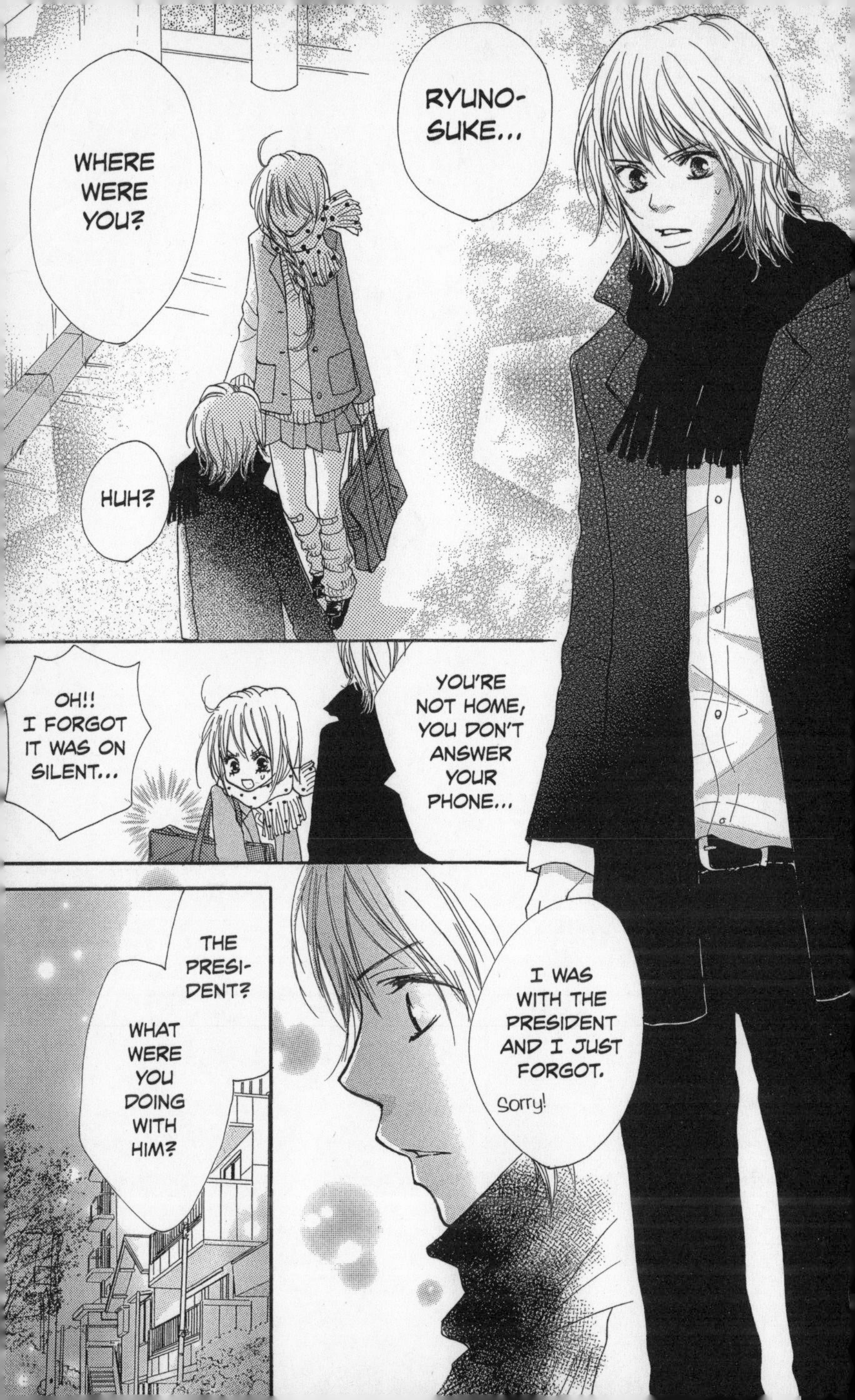
RYUNO-SUKE...
WHERE WERE YOU?
HUH?
YOU'RE NOT HOME, YOU DON'T ANSWER YOUR PHONE...
OH!! I FORGOT IT WAS ON SILENT...
I WAS WITH THE PRESIDENT AND I JUST FORGOT.
Sorry!
THE PRESI-DENT?
WHAT WERE YOU DOING WITH HIM?

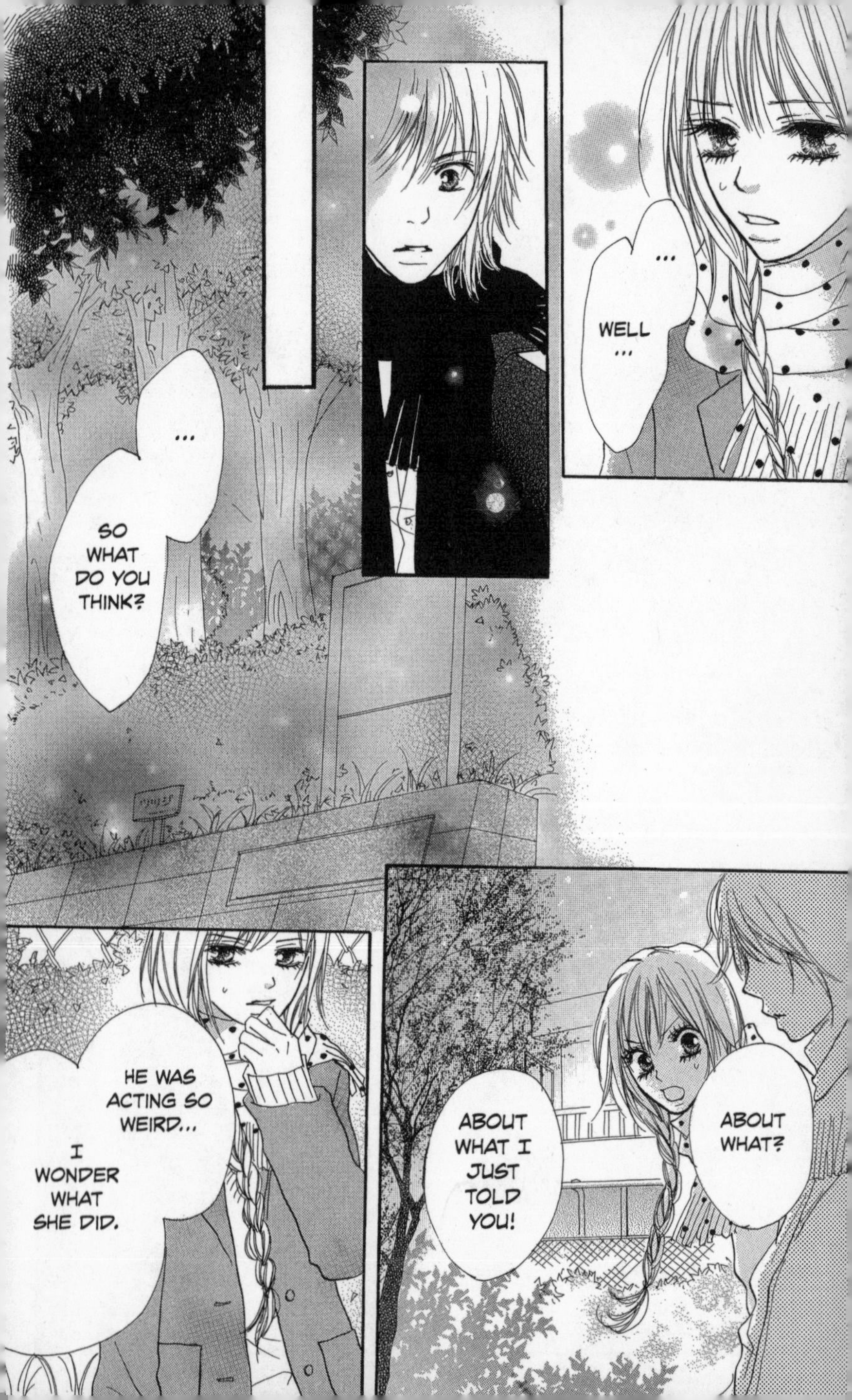
...
WELL ...
...
SO WHAT DO YOU THINK?
ABOUT WHAT?
ABOUT WHAT I JUST TOLD YOU!
HE WAS ACTING SO WEIRD...
I WONDER WHAT SHE DID.

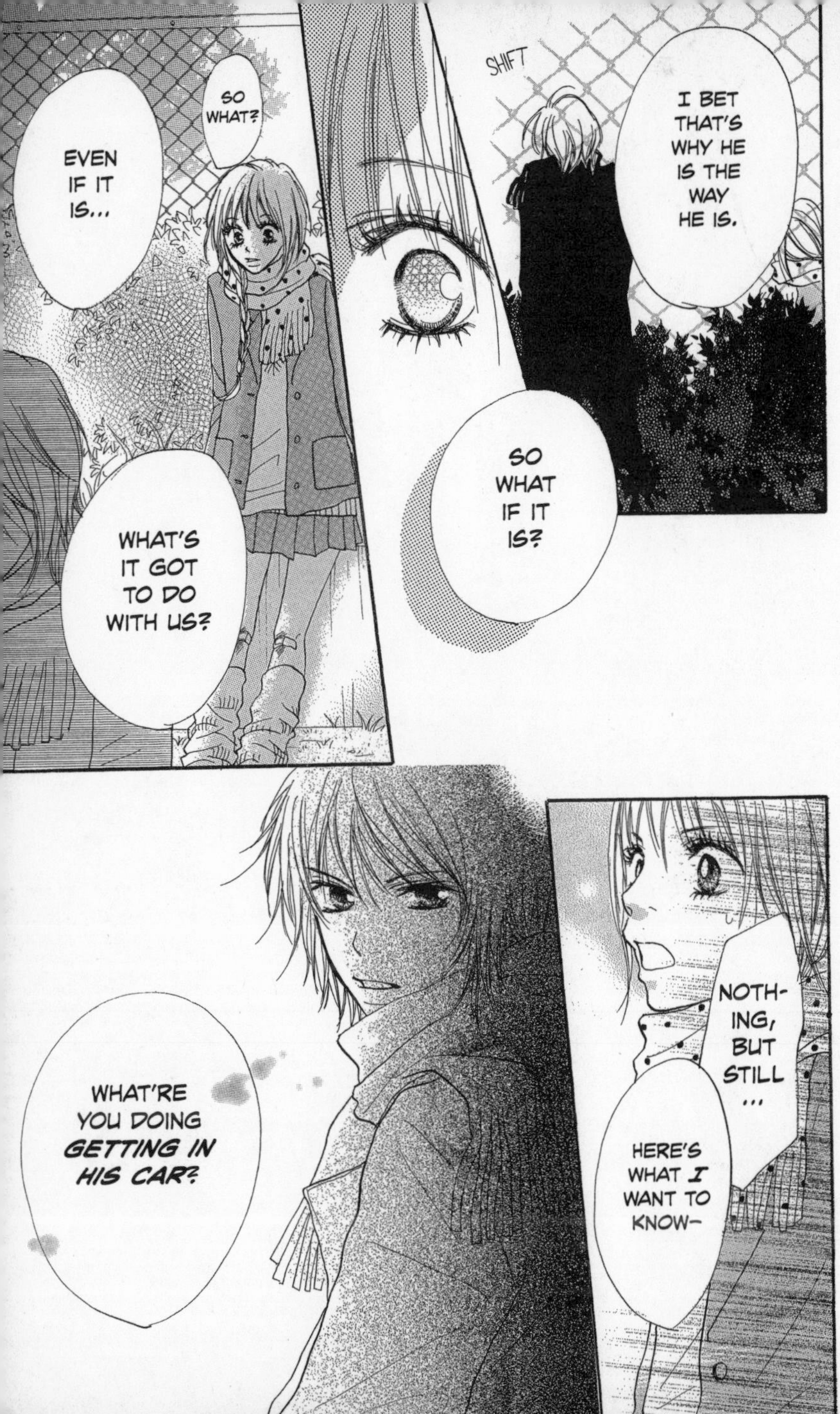
SHIFT
I BET THAT'S WHY HE IS THE WAY HE IS.
SO WHAT IF IT IS?
SO WHAT?
EVEN IF IT IS...
WHAT'S IT GOT TO DO WITH US?
NOTH-ING, BUT STILL ...
HERE'S WHAT *I* WANT TO KNOW—
WHAT'RE YOU DOING ***GETTING IN HIS CAR?***

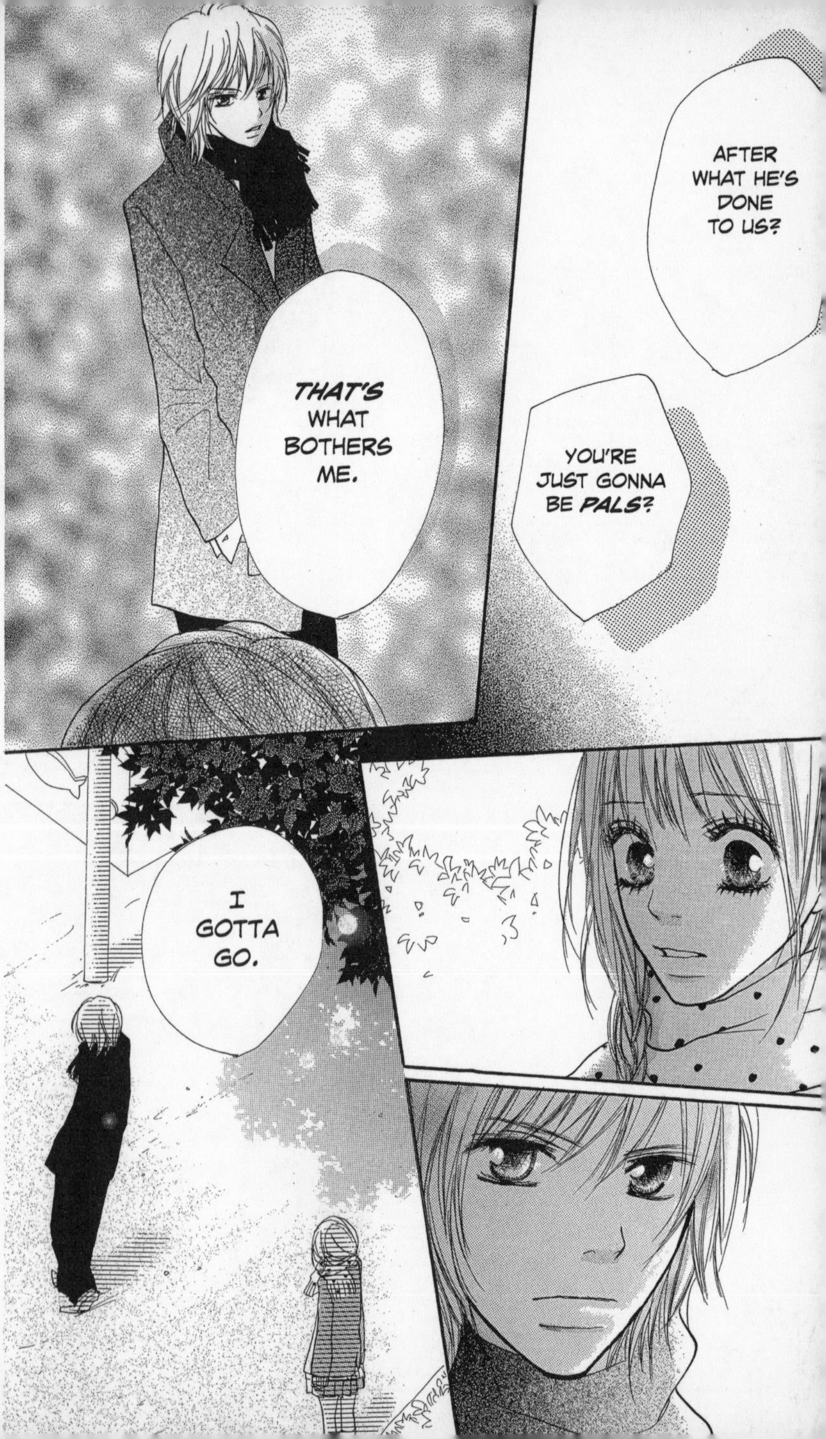
AFTER WHAT HE'S DONE TO US?
YOU'RE JUST GONNA BE PALS?
THAT'S WHAT BOTHERS ME.
I GOTTA GO.

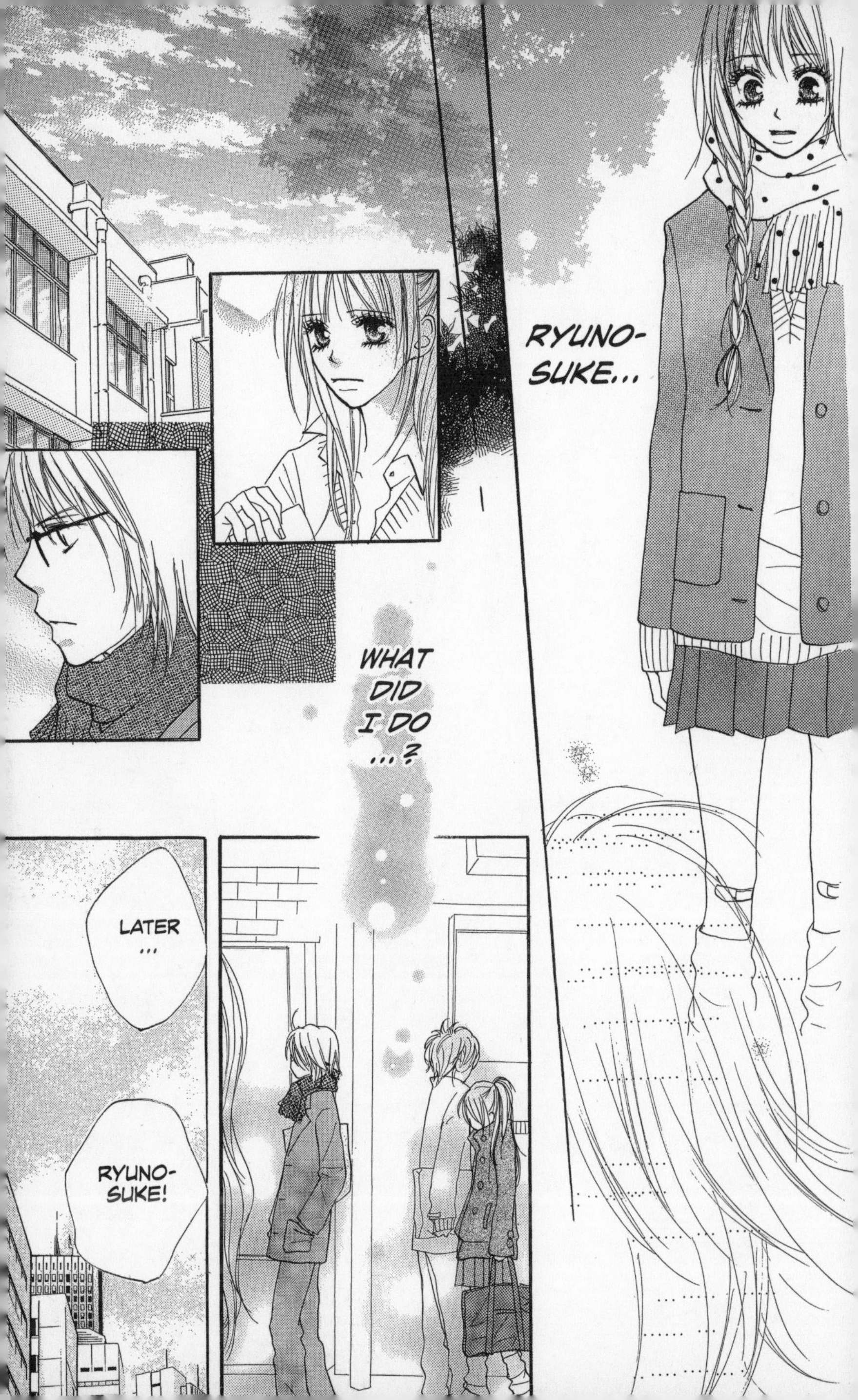
RYUNO-SUKE...
WHAT DID I DO ...?
LATER ...
RYUNO-SUKE!

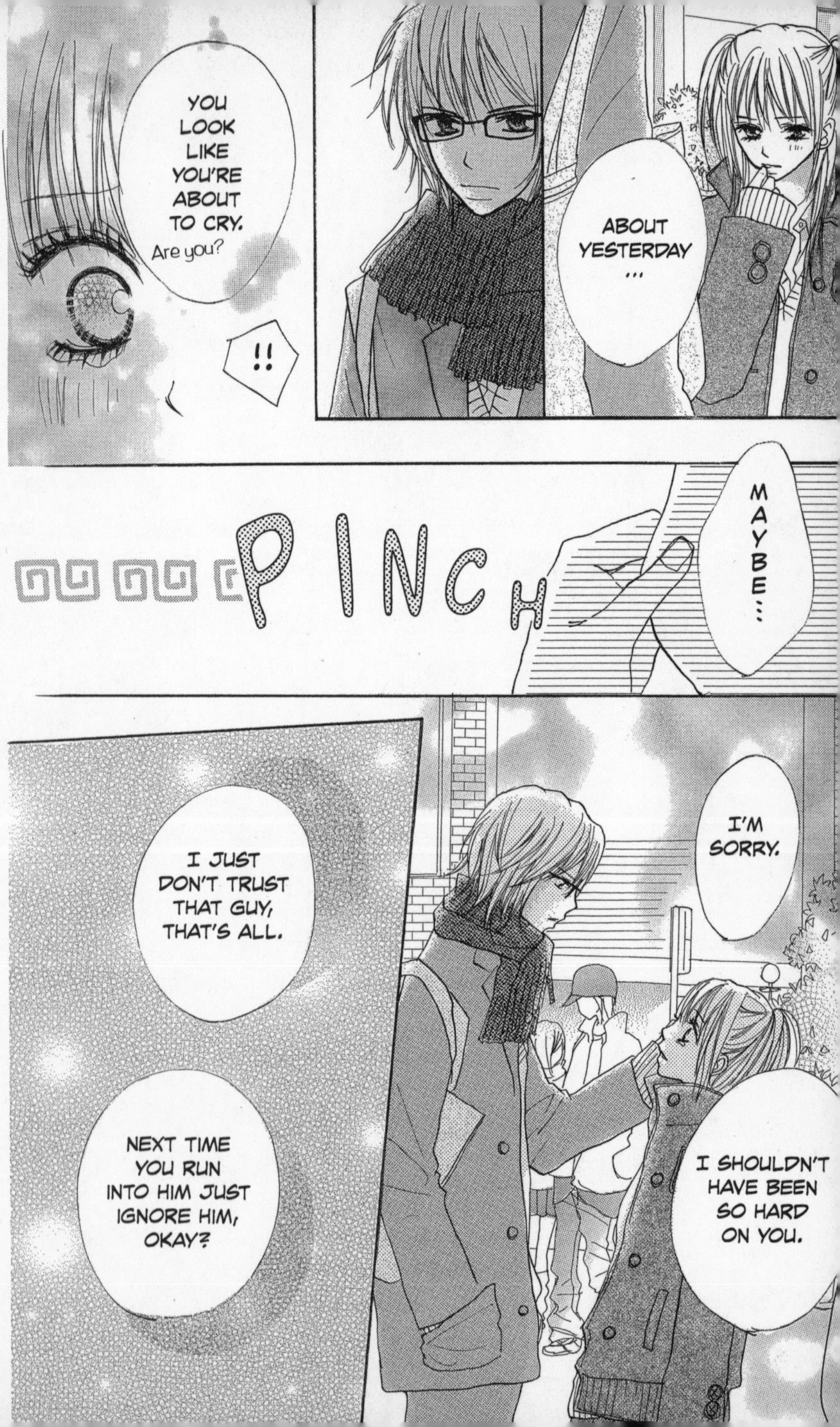
ABOUT YESTERDAY ...
YOU LOOK LIKE YOU'RE ABOUT TO CRY. Are you?
!!
MAYBE...
PINCH
I'M SORRY.
I SHOULDN'T HAVE BEEN SO HARD ON YOU.
I JUST DON'T TRUST THAT GUY, THAT'S ALL.
NEXT TIME YOU RUN INTO HIM JUST IGNORE HIM, OKAY?

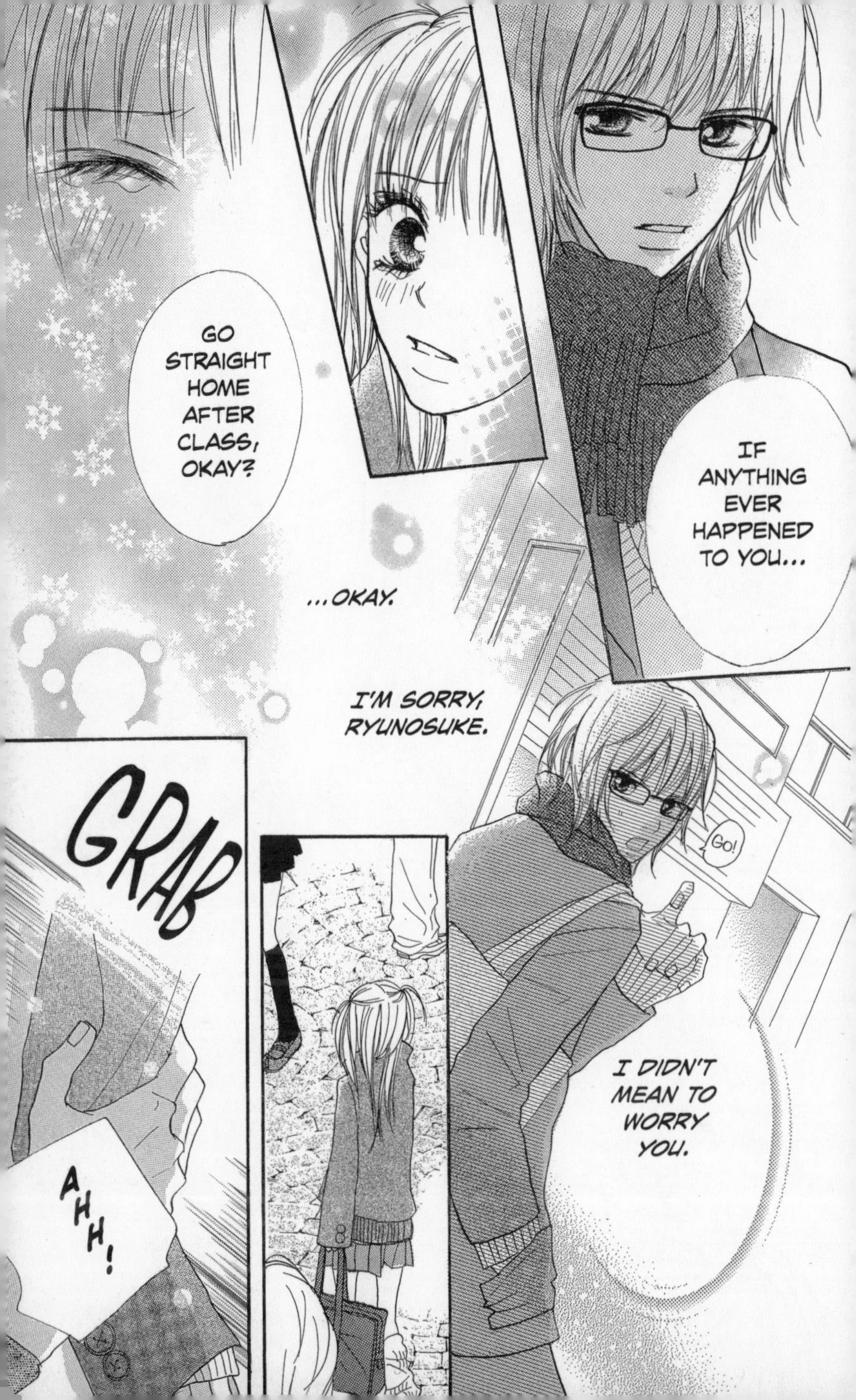
IF ANYTHING EVER HAPPENED TO YOU...
GO STRAIGHT HOME AFTER CLASS, OKAY?
...OKAY.
I'M SORRY, RYUNOSUKE.
GO!
I DIDN'T MEAN TO WORRY YOU.
GRAB
AHH!

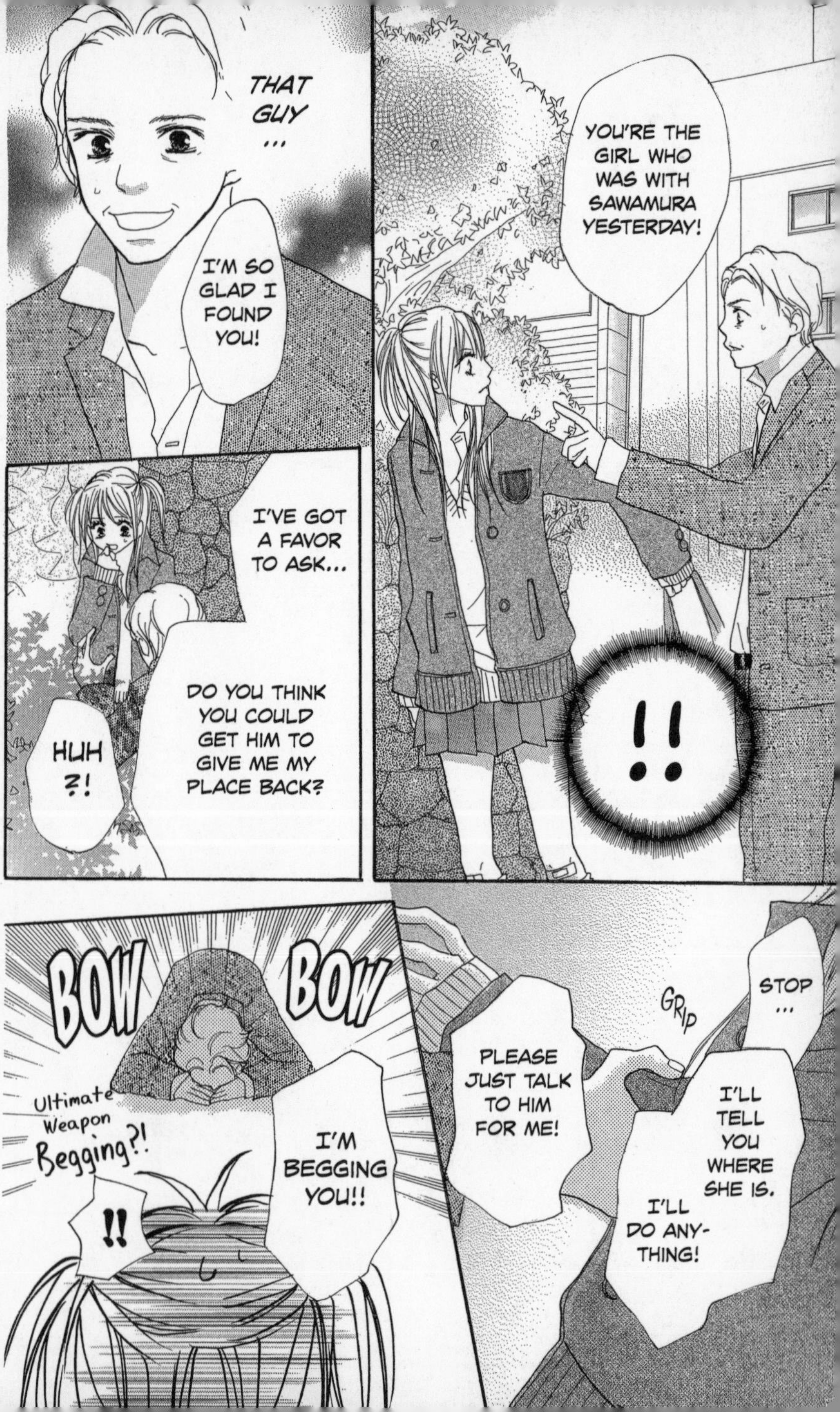
YOU'RE THE GIRL WHO WAS WITH SAWAMURA YESTERDAY!
!!
THAT GUY...
I'M SO GLAD I FOUND YOU!
I'VE GOT A FAVOR TO ASK...
DO YOU THINK YOU COULD GET HIM TO GIVE ME MY PLACE BACK?
HUH?!
STOP...
GRIP
PLEASE JUST TALK TO HIM FOR ME!
I'LL TELL YOU WHERE SHE IS.
I'LL DO ANYTHING!
BOW
BOW
I'M BEGGING YOU!!
Ultimate Weapon Begging?!
!!

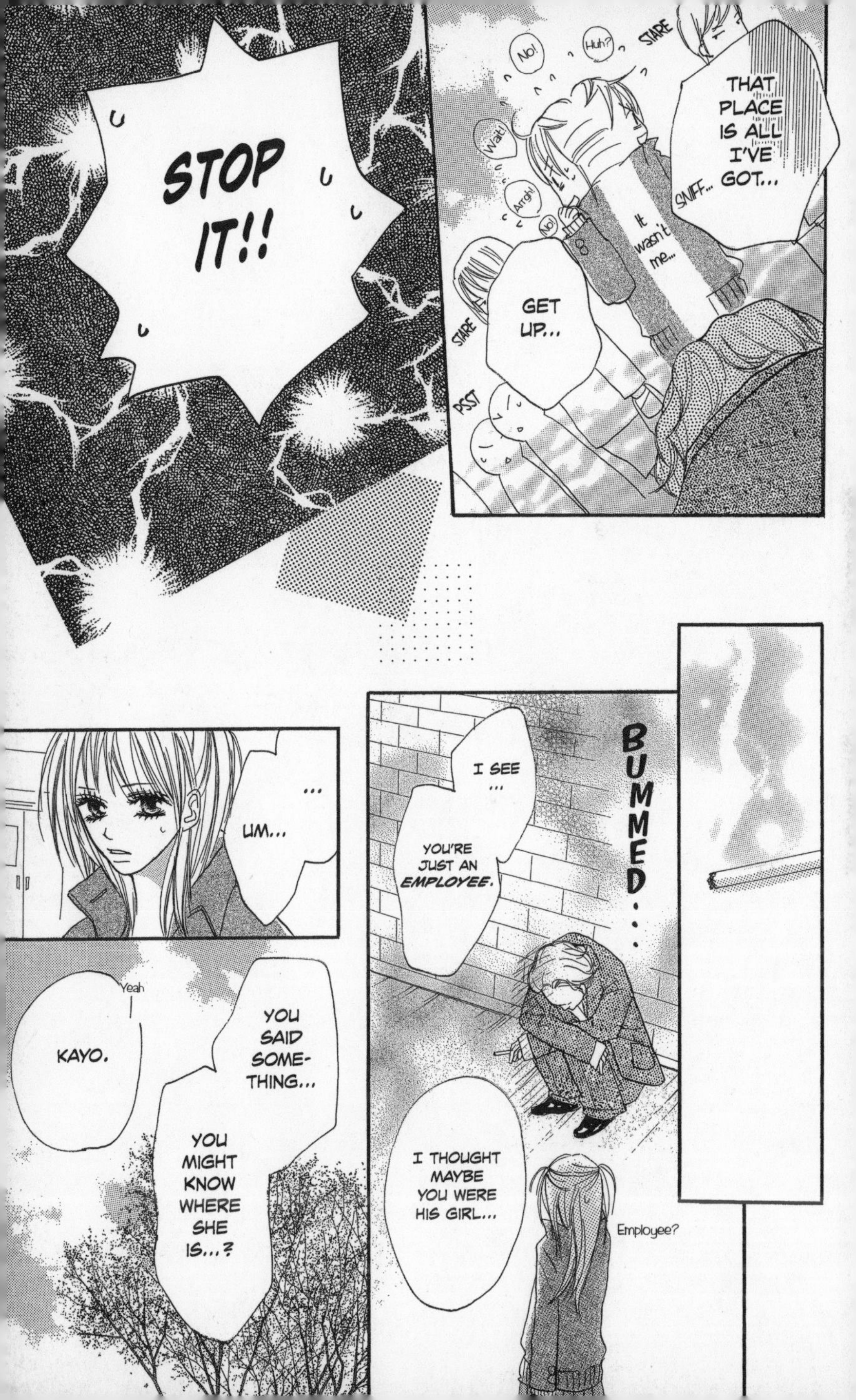
STARE
THAT PLACE IS ALL I'VE GOT...
SNIFF...
Huh?
No!
Wait!
Arrgh!
No!
It wasn't me...
GET UP...
STARE
PSST
STOP IT!!
BUMMED...
I SEE...
YOU'RE JUST AN EMPLOYEE.
I THOUGHT MAYBE YOU WERE HIS GIRL...
Employee?
...
UM...
YOU SAID SOME-THING...
YOU MIGHT KNOW WHERE SHE IS...?
KAYO.
Yeah

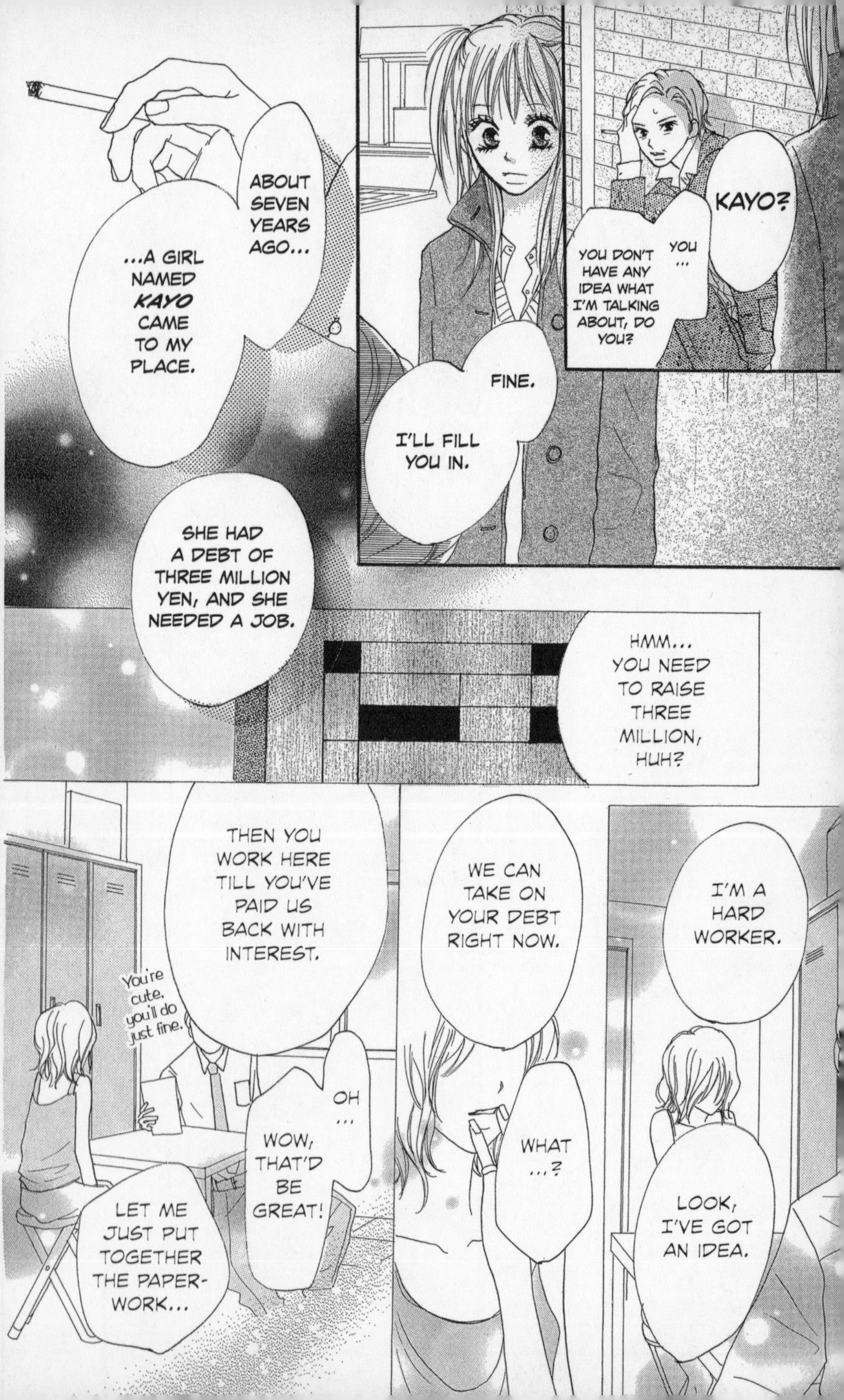
KAYO?
YOU ... YOU DON'T HAVE ANY IDEA WHAT I'M TALKING ABOUT, DO YOU?
FINE.
I'LL FILL YOU IN.
ABOUT SEVEN YEARS AGO...
...A GIRL NAMED *KAYO* CAME TO MY PLACE.
SHE HAD A DEBT OF THREE MILLION YEN, AND SHE NEEDED A JOB.
HMM... YOU NEED TO RAISE THREE MILLION, HUH?
I'M A HARD WORKER.
LOOK, I'VE GOT AN IDEA.
WE CAN TAKE ON YOUR DEBT RIGHT NOW.
WHAT ...?
THEN YOU WORK HERE TILL YOU'VE PAID US BACK WITH INTEREST.
OH ...
WOW, THAT'D BE GREAT!
You're cute, you'll do just fine.
LET ME JUST PUT TOGETHER THE PAPER-WORK...

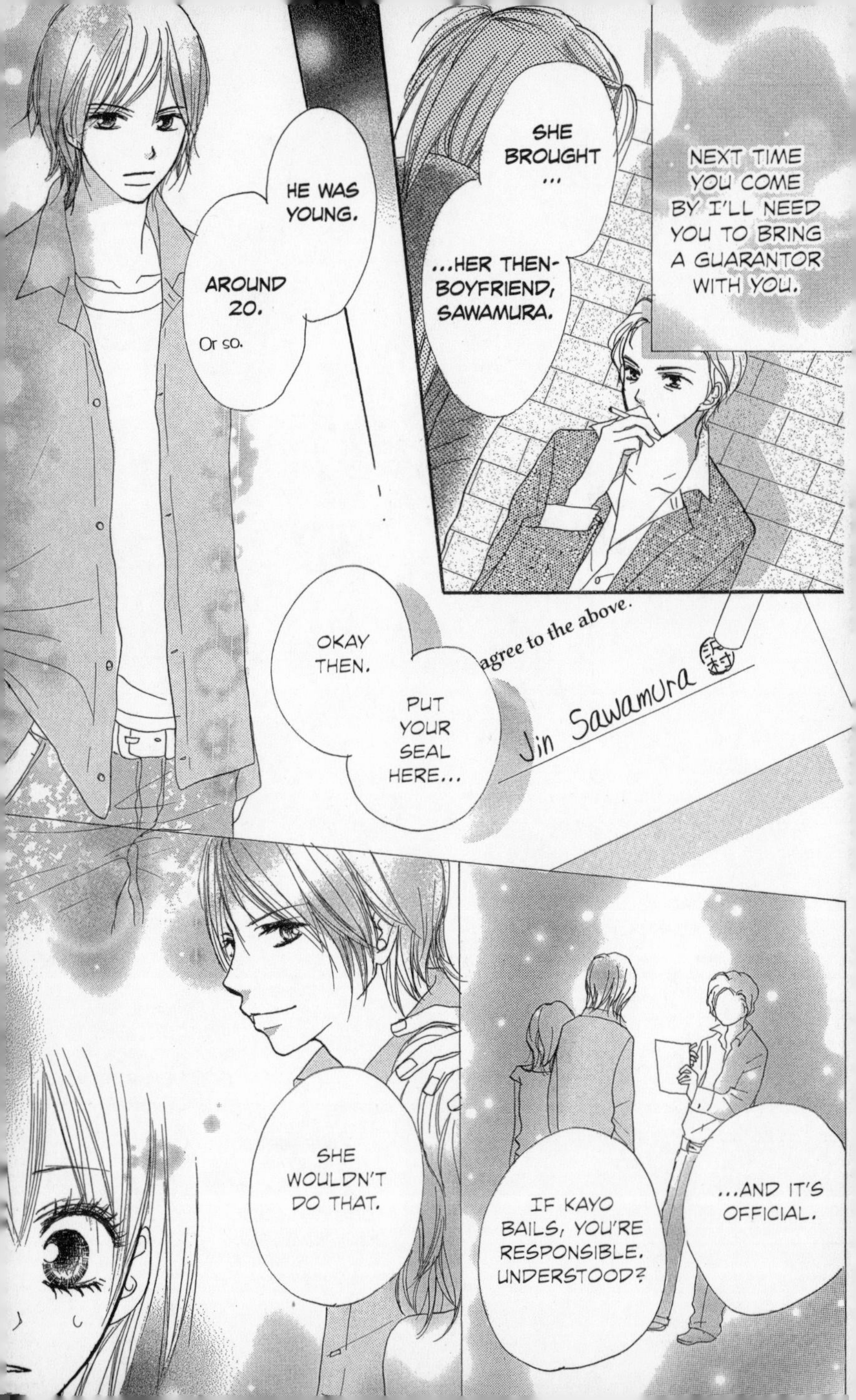
NEXT TIME YOU COME BY I'LL NEED YOU TO BRING A GUARANTOR WITH YOU.
SHE BROUGHT ...
...HER THEN-BOYFRIEND, SAWAMURA.
HE WAS YOUNG.
AROUND 20.
Or so.
OKAY THEN.
PUT YOUR SEAL HERE...
agree to the above.
Jin Sawamura
...AND IT'S OFFICIAL.
IF KAYO BAILS, YOU'RE RESPONSIBLE. UNDERSTOOD?
SHE WOULDN'T DO THAT.

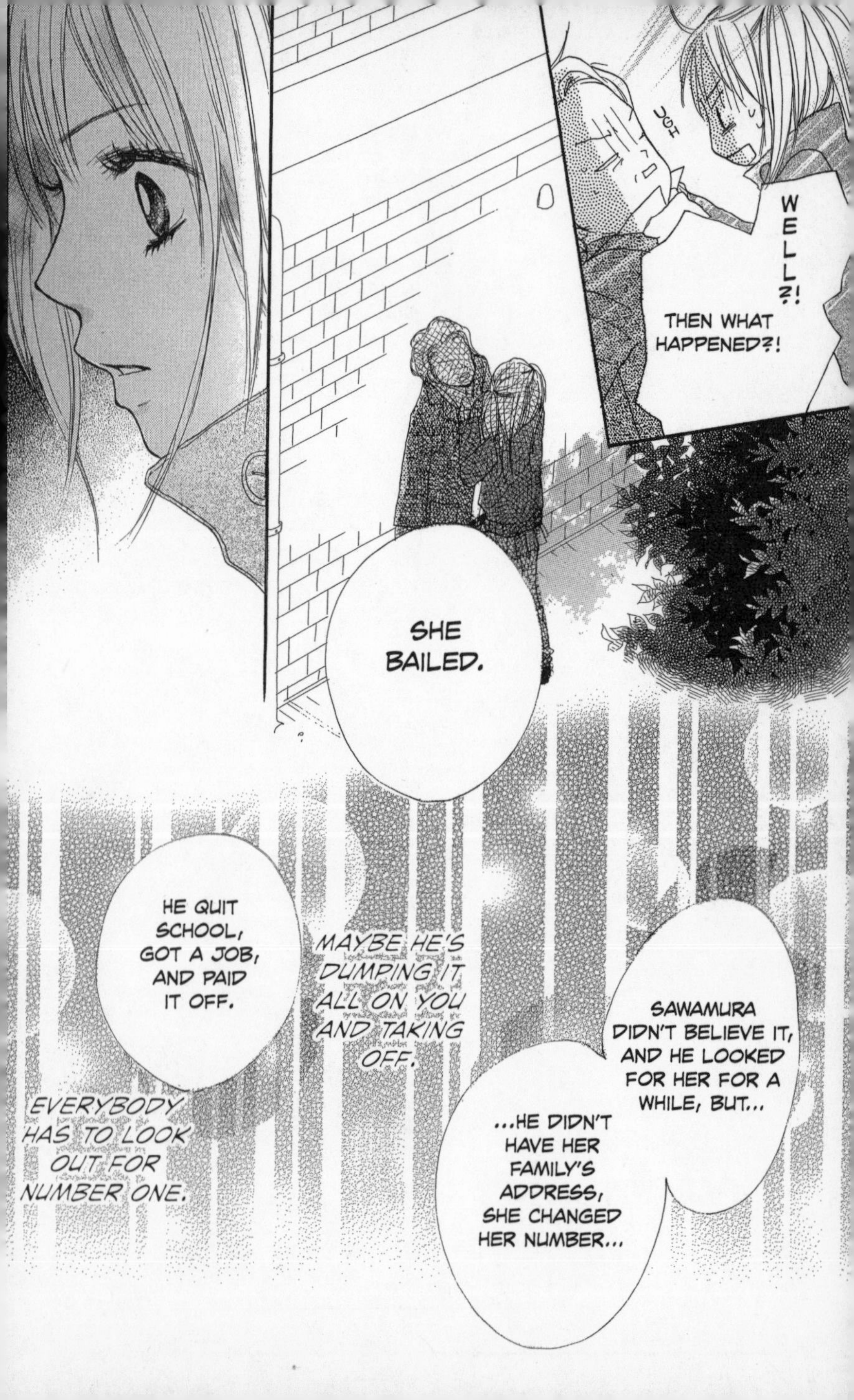
UGH
WELL?!
THEN WHAT HAPPENED?!
SHE BAILED.
SAWAMURA DIDN'T BELIEVE IT, AND HE LOOKED FOR HER FOR A WHILE, BUT...
...HE DIDN'T HAVE HER FAMILY'S ADDRESS, SHE CHANGED HER NUMBER...
MAYBE HE'S DUMPING IT ALL ON YOU AND TAKING OFF.
HE QUIT SCHOOL, GOT A JOB, AND PAID IT OFF.
EVERYBODY HAS TO LOOK OUT FOR NUMBER ONE.

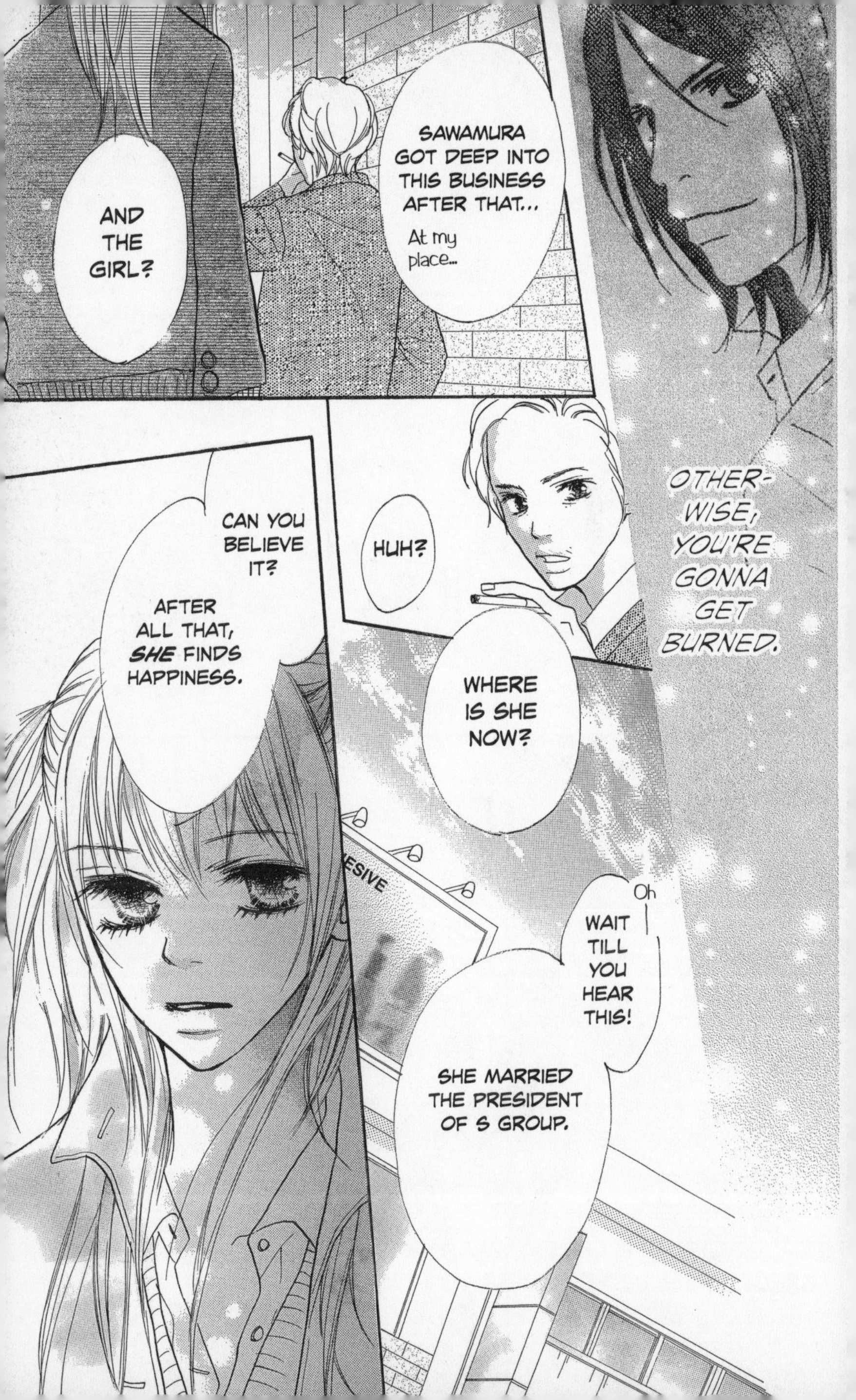
OTHER-WISE, YOU'RE GONNA GET BURNED.
SAWAMURA GOT DEEP INTO THIS BUSINESS AFTER THAT...
At my place...
AND THE GIRL?
HUH?
WHERE IS SHE NOW?
Oh
WAIT TILL YOU HEAR THIS!
SHE MARRIED THE PRESIDENT OF S GROUP.
CAN YOU BELIEVE IT?
AFTER ALL THAT, SHE FINDS HAPPINESS.

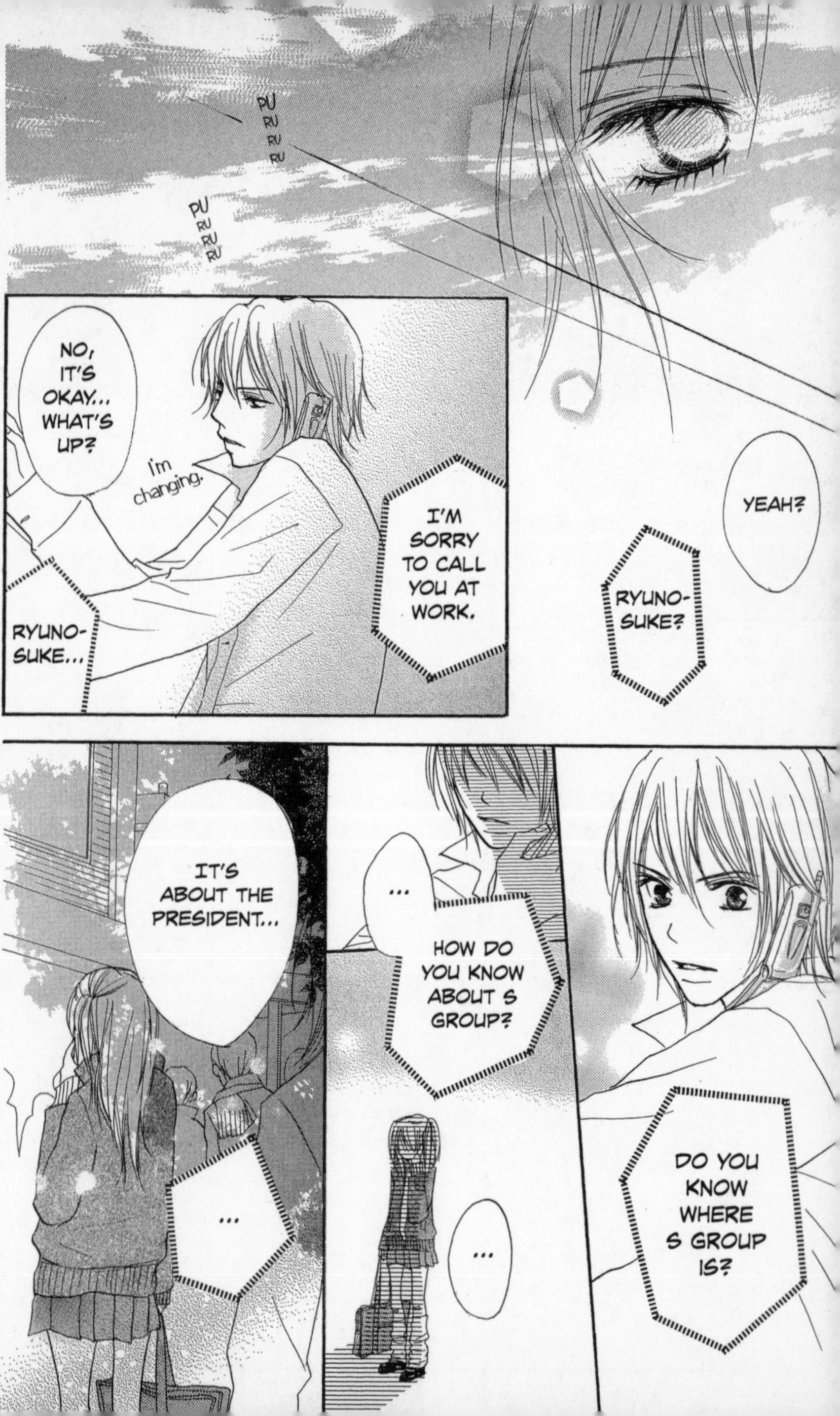
PU RU RU RU
PU RU RU RU
YEAH?
RYUNO-SUKE?
RYUNO-SUKE...
I'M SORRY TO CALL YOU AT WORK.
NO, IT'S OKAY... WHAT'S UP?
I'm changing.
DO YOU KNOW WHERE S GROUP IS?
...
HOW DO YOU KNOW ABOUT S GROUP?
...
IT'S ABOUT THE PRESIDENT...
...

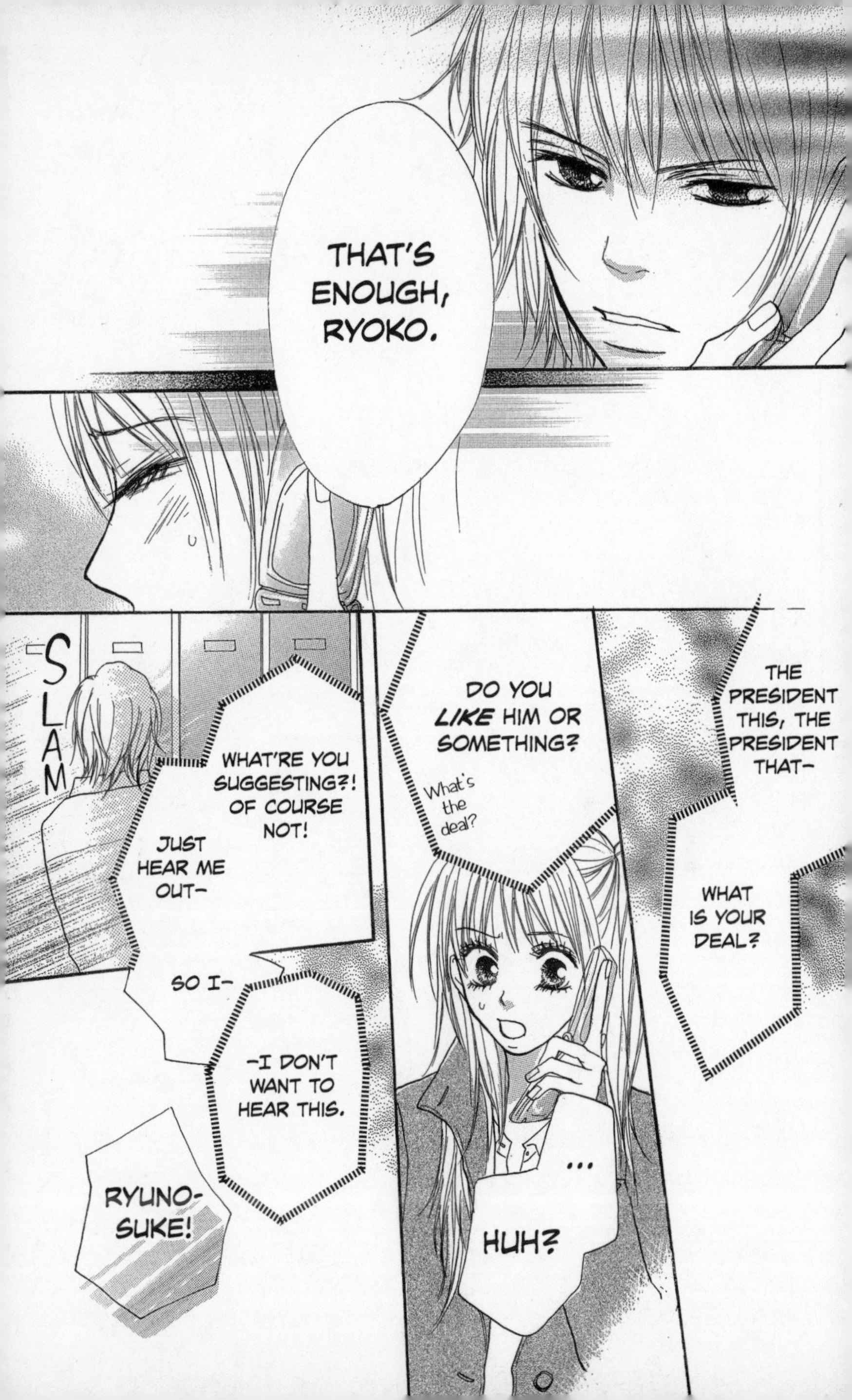
THAT'S ENOUGH, RYOKO.
THE PRESIDENT THIS, THE PRESIDENT THAT—
DO YOU *LIKE* HIM OR SOMETHING?
What's the deal?
WHAT IS YOUR DEAL?
...
HUH?
WHAT'RE YOU SUGGESTING?! OF COURSE NOT!
JUST HEAR ME OUT—
SO I—
—I DON'T WANT TO HEAR THIS.
SLAM
RYUNO-SUKE!

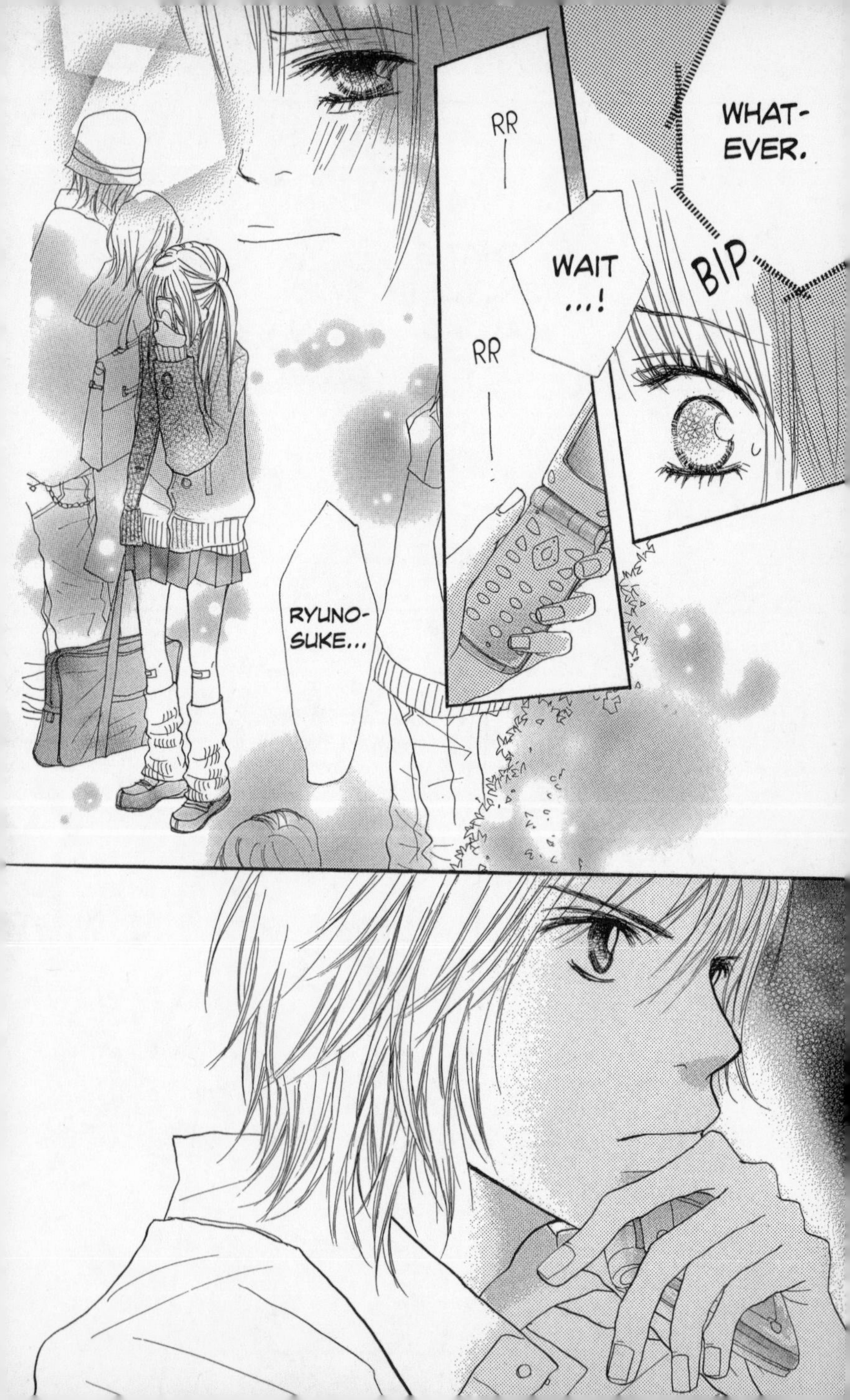
WHAT-EVER.
BIP
WAIT ...!
RR—
RR—!
RYUNO-SUKE...

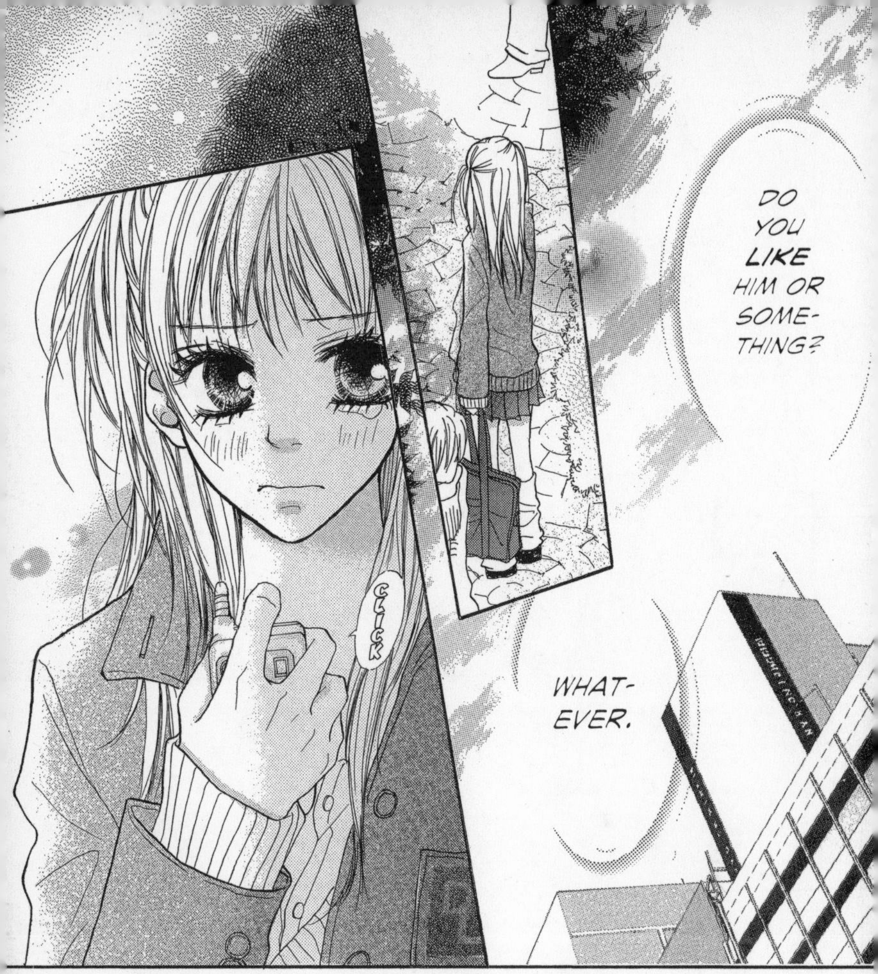
DO YOU LIKE HIM OR SOME-THING?
WHAT-EVER.
CLICK
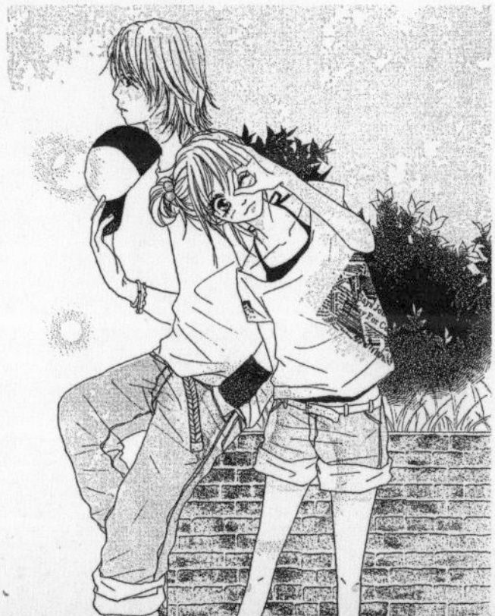

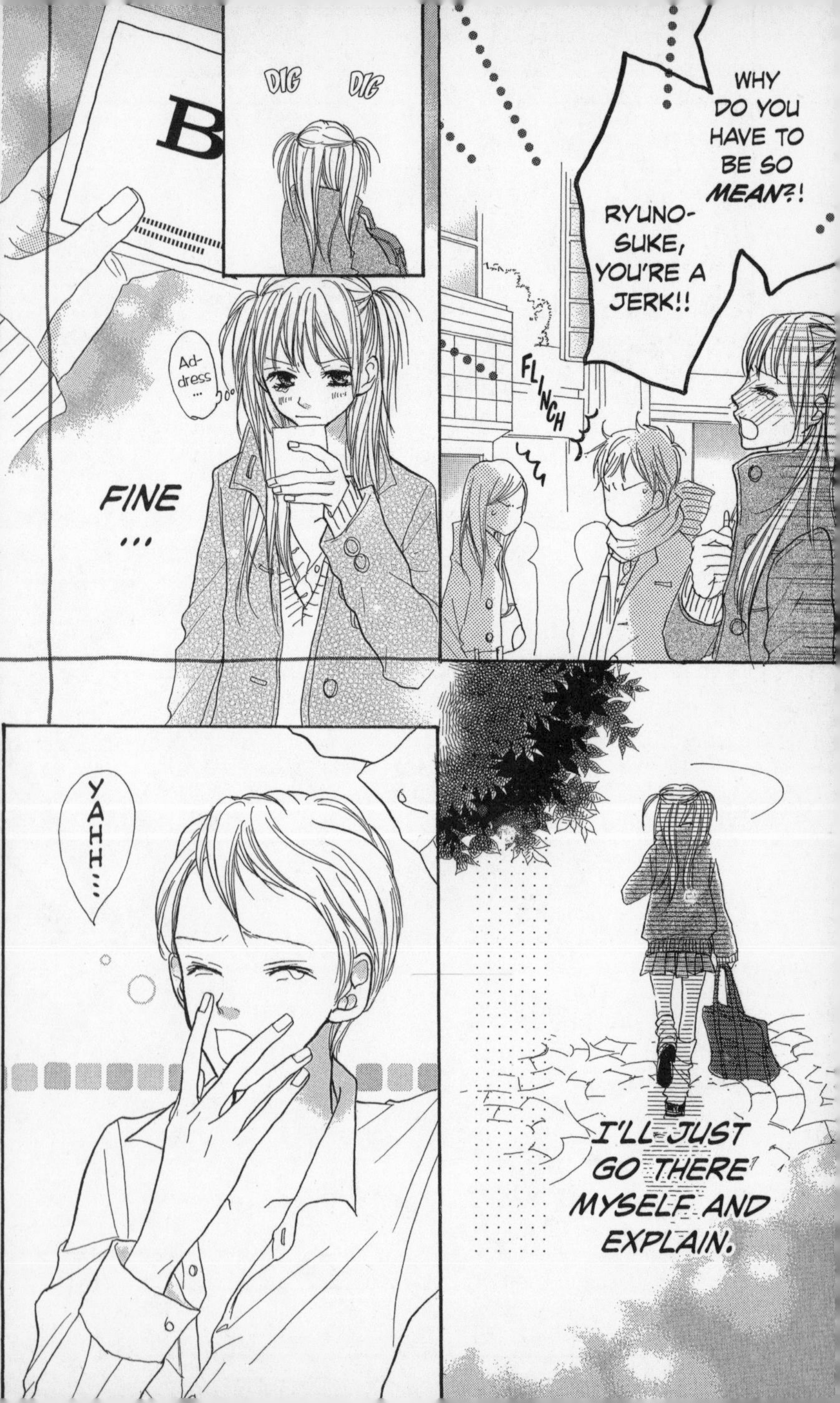
WHY DO YOU HAVE TO BE SO *MEAN*?!
RYUNO-SUKE, YOU'RE A JERK!!
FLINCH
DIG DIG
B
Ad-dress...
FINE...
I'LL JUST GO THERE MYSELF AND EXPLAIN.
YAHH...

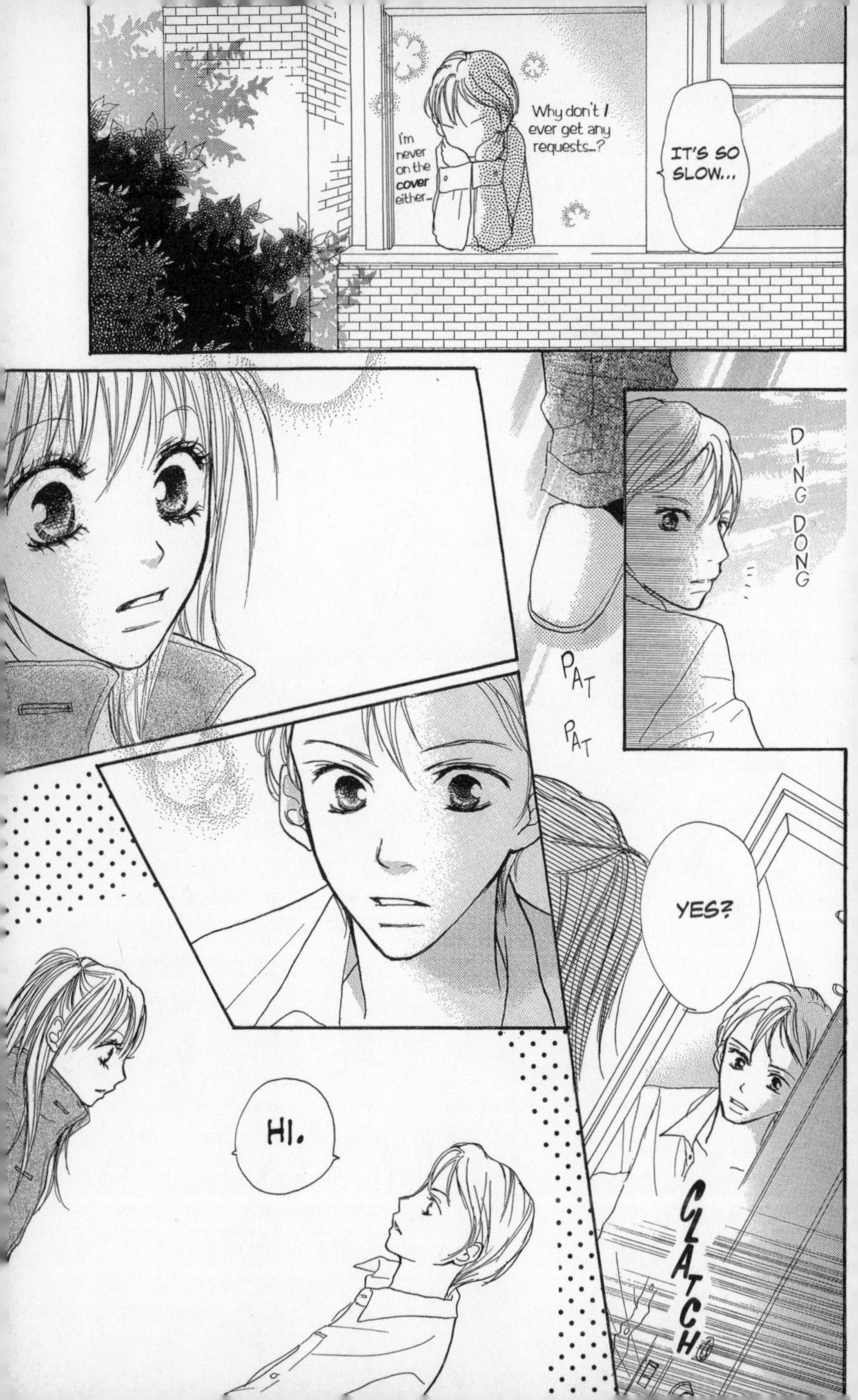
IT'S SO SLOW...
Why don't I ever get any requests...?
I'm never on the cover either...
DING DONG
PAT PAT
YES?
CLATCH
HI.

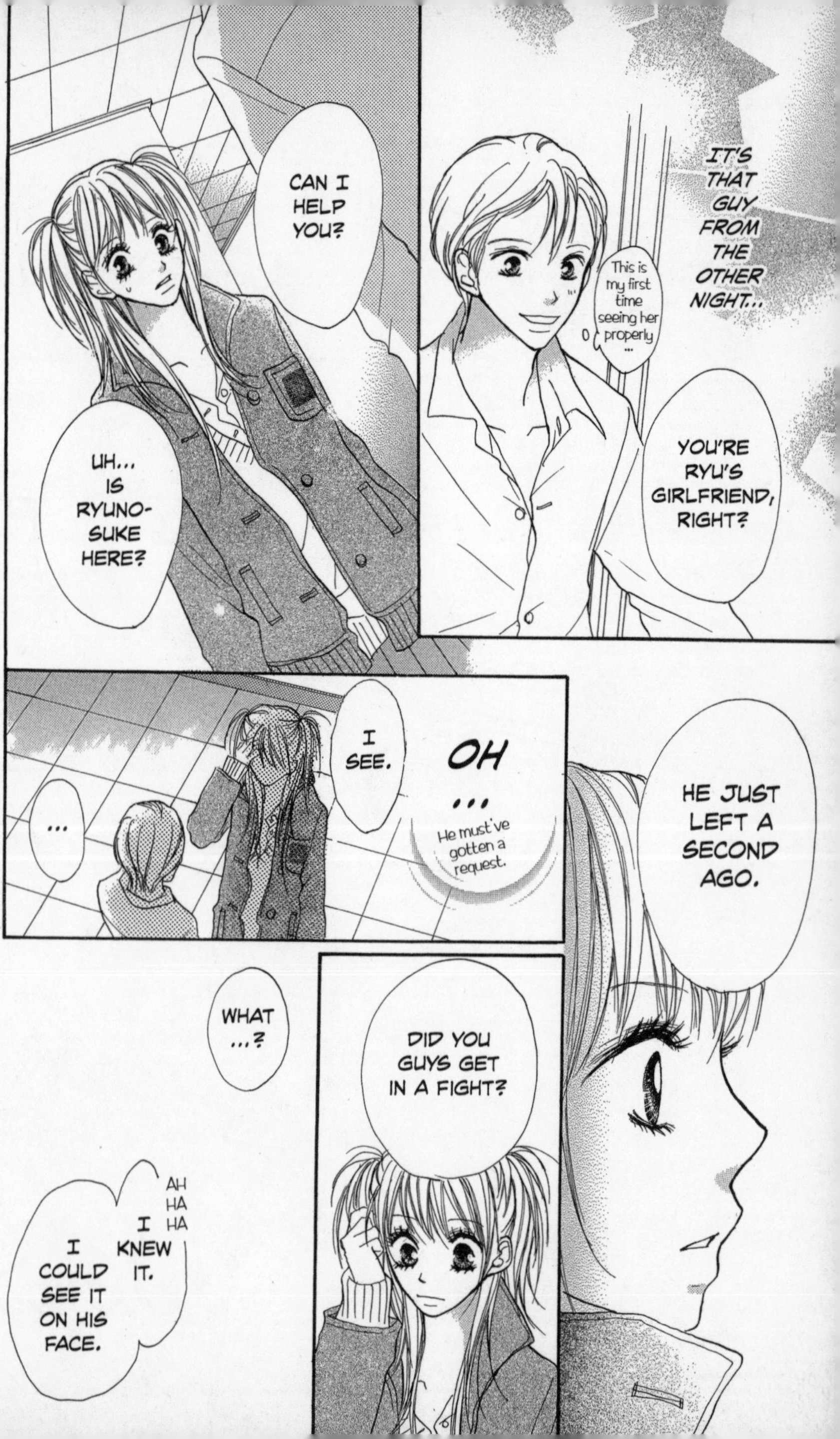
IT'S THAT GUY FROM THE OTHER NIGHT...
This is my first time seeing her properly...
YOU'RE RYU'S GIRLFRIEND, RIGHT?
CAN I HELP YOU?
UH... IS RYUNO-SUKE HERE?
HE JUST LEFT A SECOND AGO.
OH...
He must've gotten a request.
I SEE.
...
DID YOU GUYS GET IN A FIGHT?
WHAT...?
I KNEW IT.
AH HA HA
I COULD SEE IT ON HIS FACE.

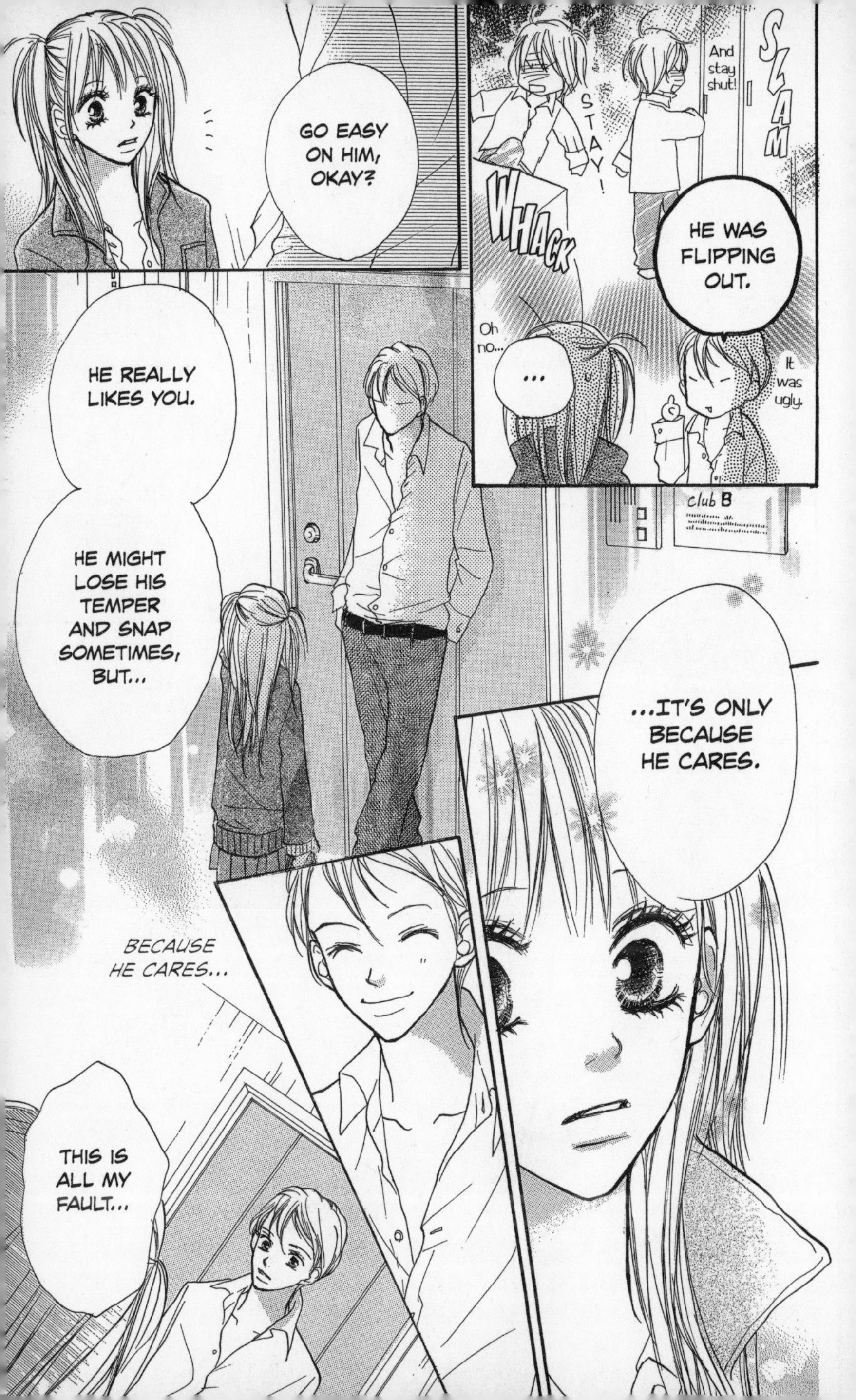
SLAM
And stay shut!
STAY!
WHACK
HE WAS FLIPPING OUT.
It was ugly.
Oh no...
...
GO EASY ON HIM, OKAY?
Club B
HE REALLY LIKES YOU.
HE MIGHT LOSE HIS TEMPER AND SNAP SOMETIMES, BUT...
...IT'S ONLY BECAUSE HE CARES.
BECAUSE HE CARES...
THIS IS ALL MY FAULT...

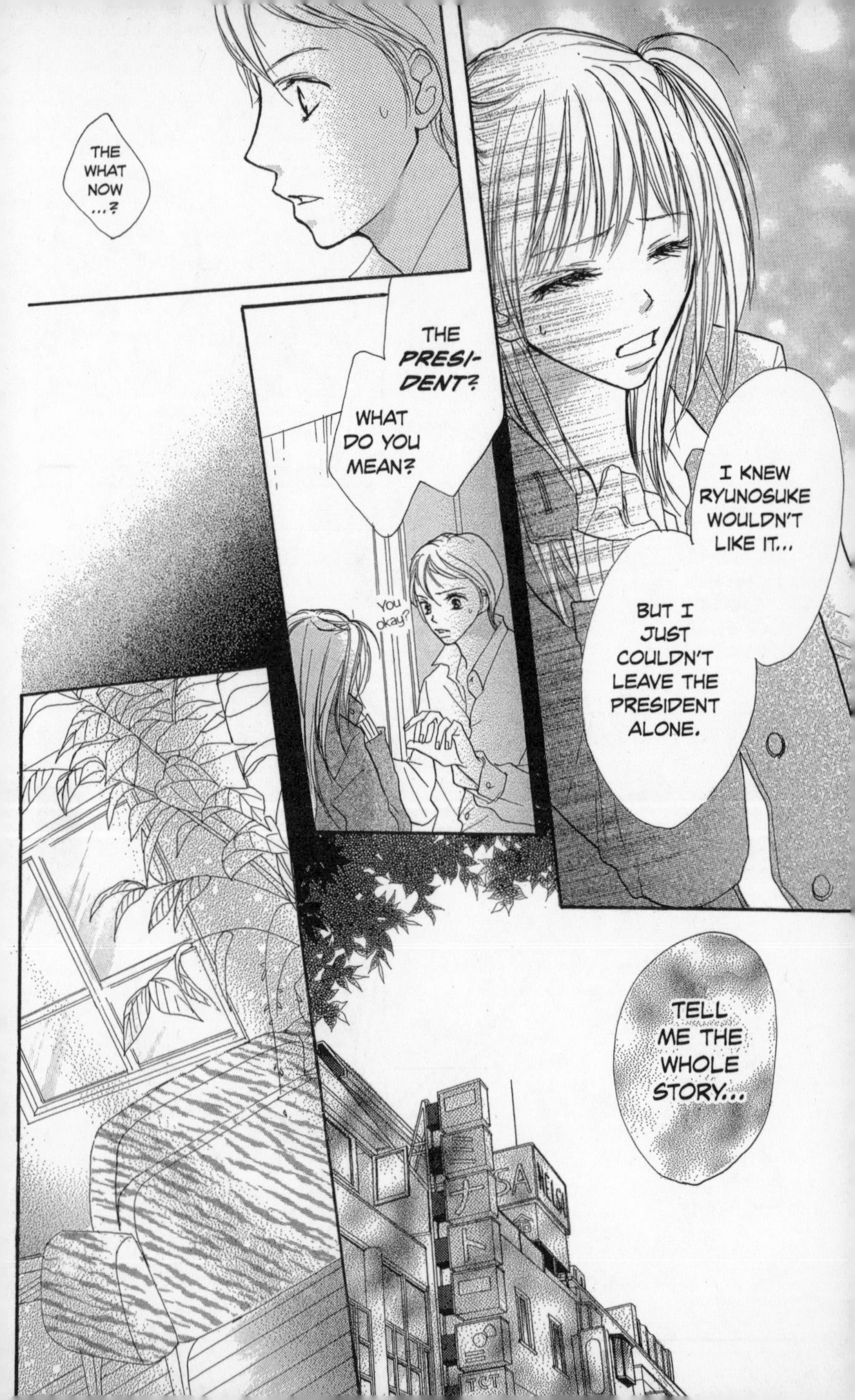
I KNEW RYUNOSUKE WOULDN'T LIKE IT...
BUT I JUST COULDN'T LEAVE THE PRESIDENT ALONE.
THE WHAT NOW ...?
THE *PRESI-DENT*?
WHAT DO YOU MEAN?
You okay?
TELL ME THE WHOLE STORY...

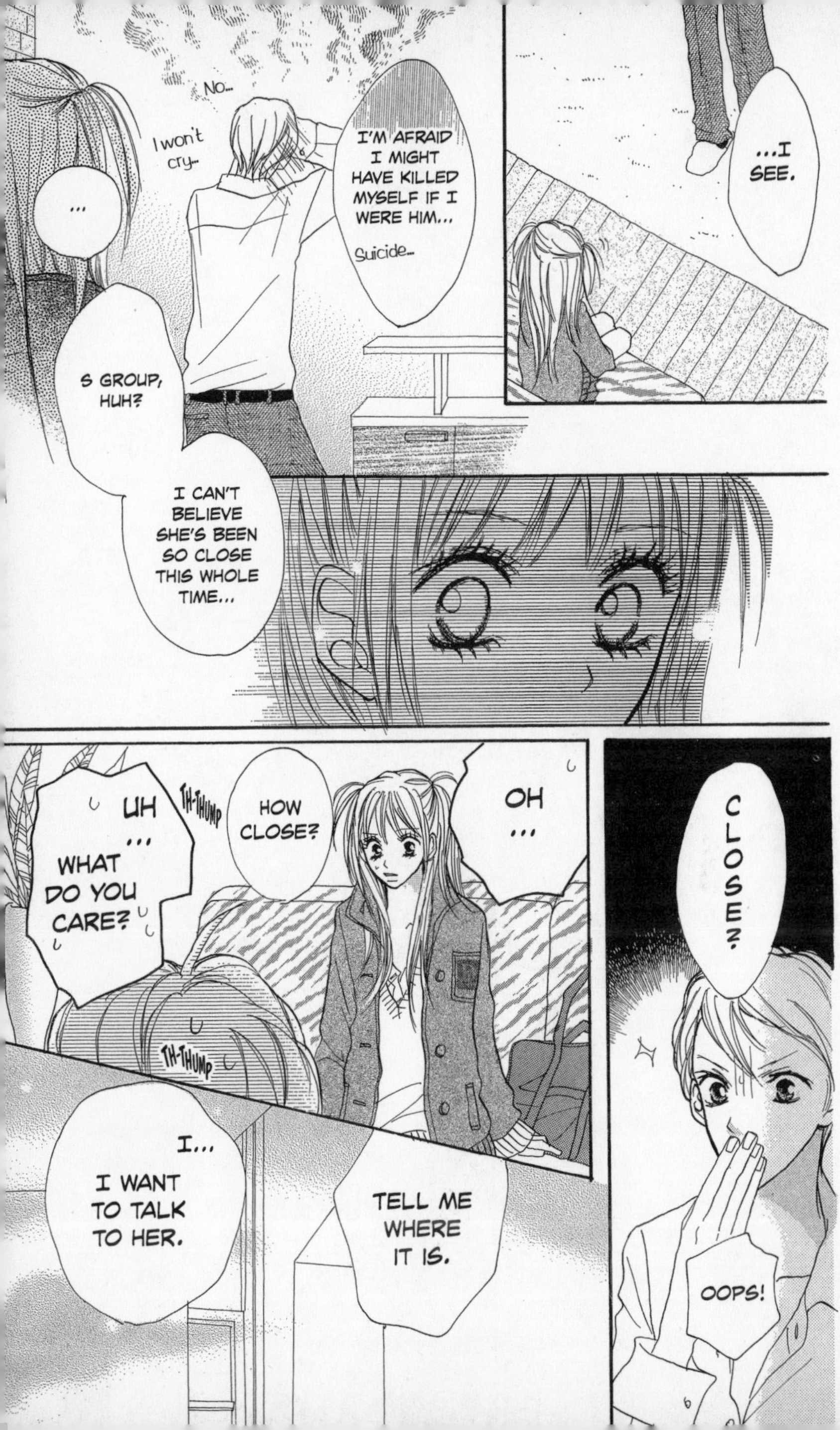
...I SEE.
I'M AFRAID I MIGHT HAVE KILLED MYSELF IF I WERE HIM...
Suicide...
No...
I won't cry...
...
S GROUP, HUH?
I CAN'T BELIEVE SHE'S BEEN SO CLOSE THIS WHOLE TIME...
CLOSE?
OOPS!
OH...
HOW CLOSE?
TH-THUMP
UH... WHAT DO YOU CARE?
TH-THUMP
TELL ME WHERE IT IS.
I... I WANT TO TALK TO HER.

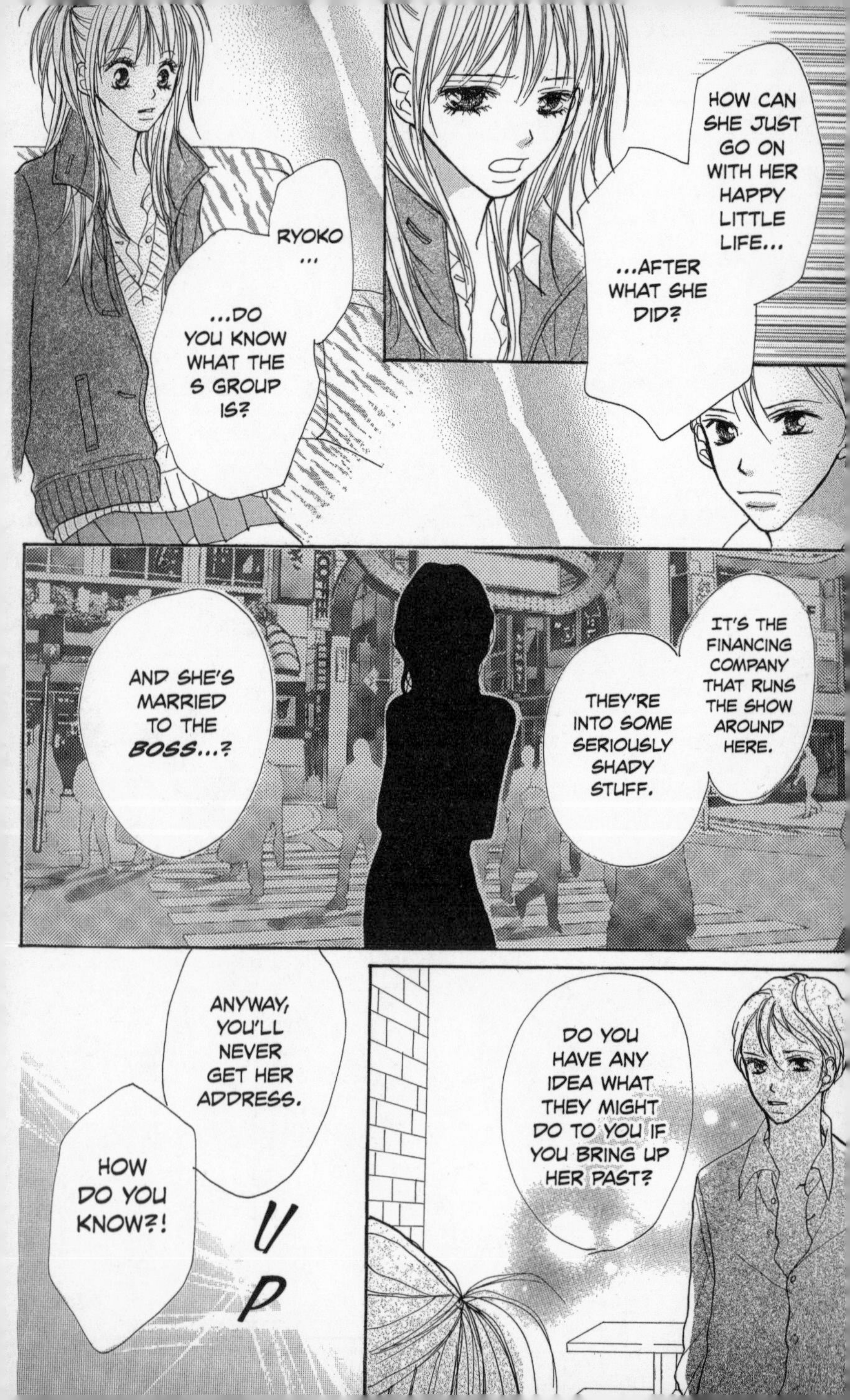
HOW CAN SHE JUST GO ON WITH HER HAPPY LITTLE LIFE...
...AFTER WHAT SHE DID?
RYOKO...
...DO YOU KNOW WHAT THE S GROUP IS?
IT'S THE FINANCING COMPANY THAT RUNS THE SHOW AROUND HERE.
THEY'RE INTO SOME SERIOUSLY SHADY STUFF.
AND SHE'S MARRIED TO THE *BOSS*...?
DO YOU HAVE ANY IDEA WHAT THEY MIGHT DO TO YOU IF YOU BRING UP HER PAST?
ANYWAY, YOU'LL NEVER GET HER ADDRESS.
HOW DO YOU KNOW?!
UP

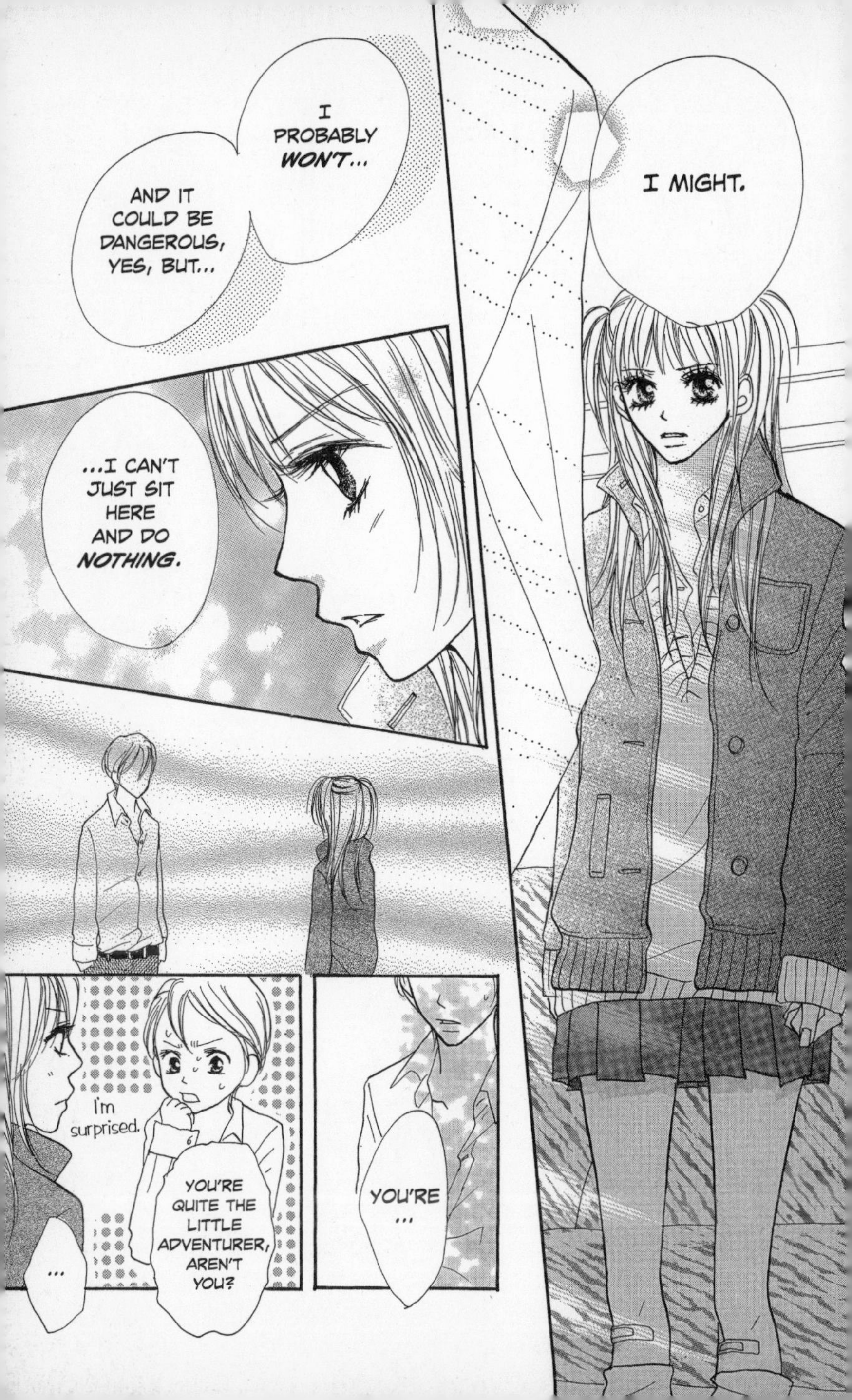
I MIGHT.
I PROBABLY WON'T...
AND IT COULD BE DANGEROUS, YES, BUT...
...I CAN'T JUST SIT HERE AND DO NOTHING.
YOU'RE...
I'm surprised.
YOU'RE QUITE THE LITTLE ADVENTURER, AREN'T YOU?
...

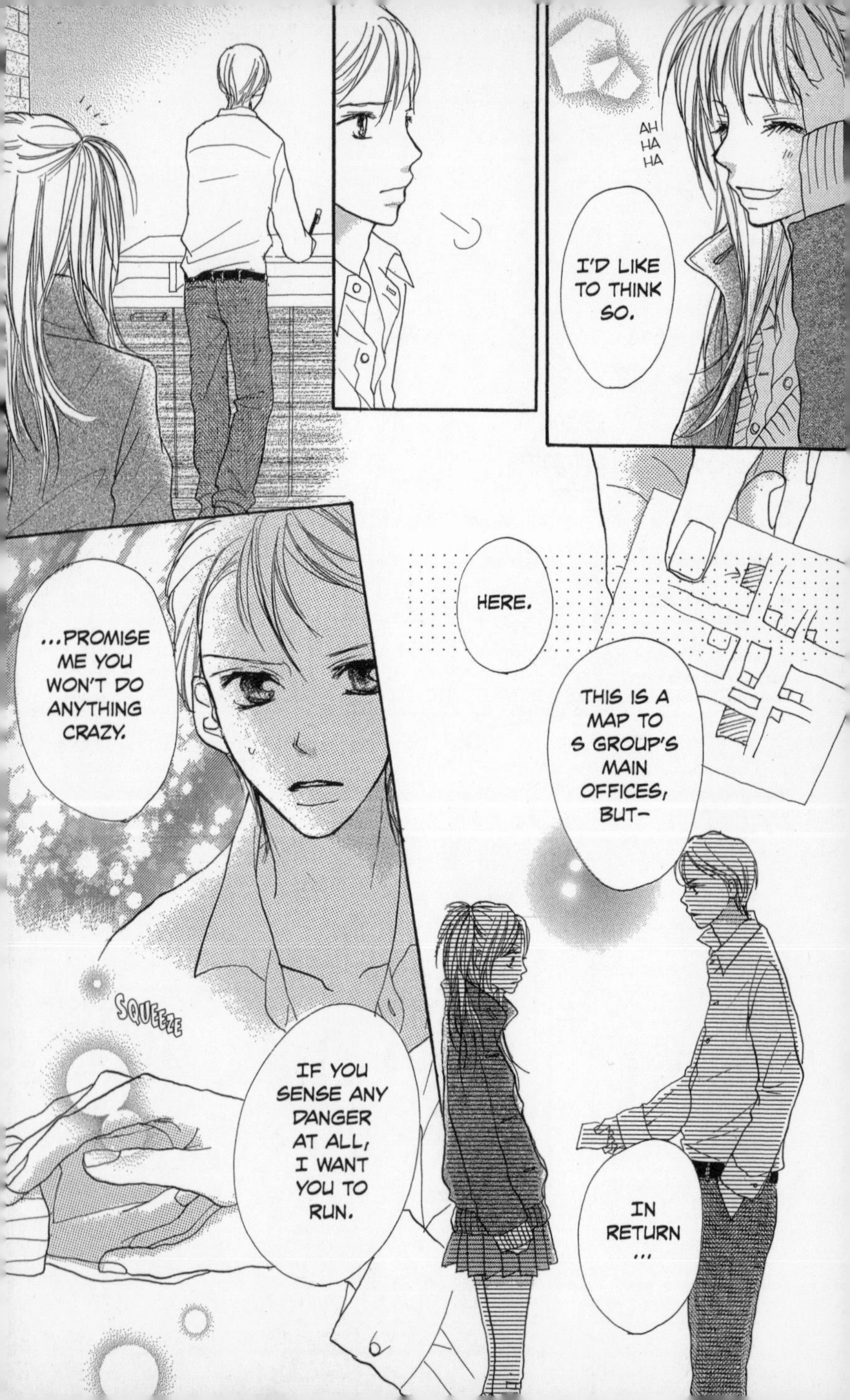
AH HA HA
I'D LIKE TO THINK SO.
HERE.
THIS IS A MAP TO S GROUP'S MAIN OFFICES, BUT-
IN RETURN ...
...PROMISE ME YOU WON'T DO ANYTHING CRAZY.
SQUEEZE
IF YOU SENSE ANY DANGER AT ALL, I WANT YOU TO RUN.

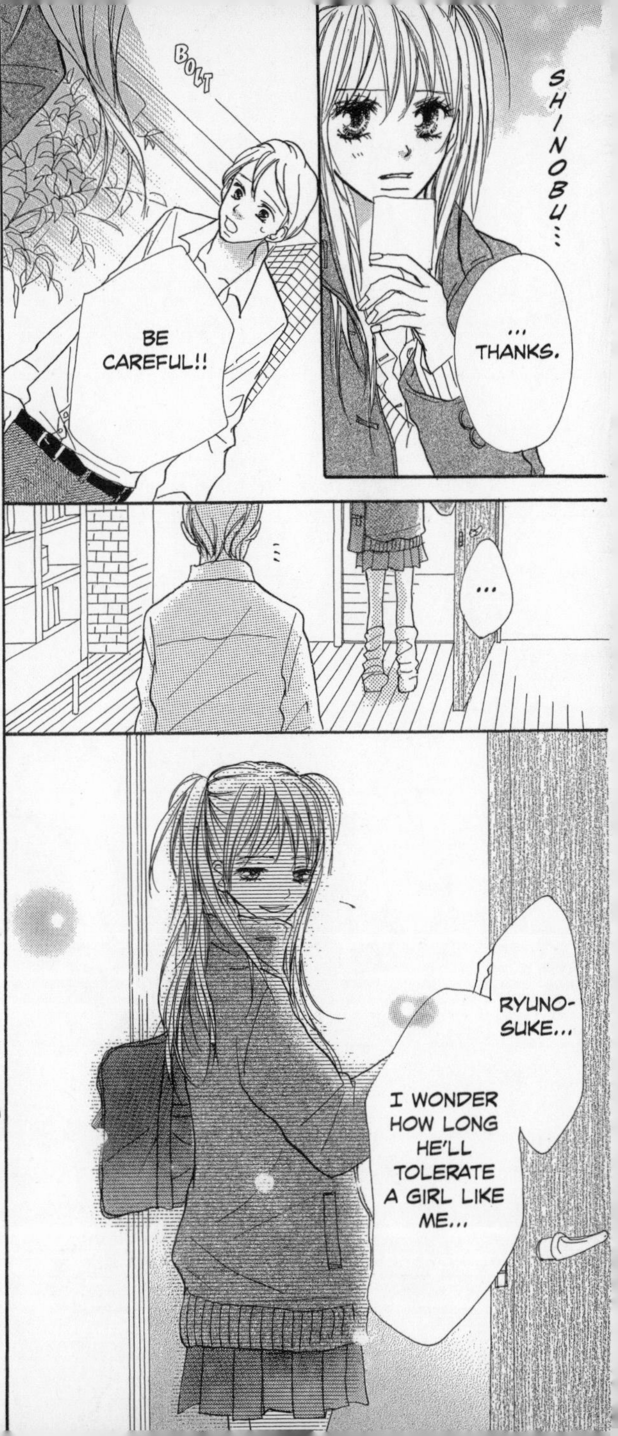
SHINOBU...
...THANKS.
BOLT
BE CAREFUL!!
...
RYUNOSUKE...
I WONDER HOW LONG HE'LL TOLERATE A GIRL LIKE ME...

③

Manga I'm into these days.

I found it... A manga series that grabbed hold of me and wouldn't let go: *Bobobo-bo Bo-bobo*!! (Stop reading if you don't know what I'm talking about!)

I first watched the anime and it really surprised me. It was Dengakuman's Hajike episode, of all things... I was totally lost and totally addicted. I even started collecting Hajike cards!! Now I'm pleased to report that when I'm feeling sad, I wipe my tears away with a Nu handkerchief!! My favorite characters are Don Patch and Tennosuke. Oh, and Sad Sack too! I guess I like them all.

• • • • • • • •

I also like *Naruto*, of course. What is it with me and *Shonen Jump*...? Shikamaru's my favorite!! Oh, and I like Akamaru too.

I force my cat to be like Akamaru...

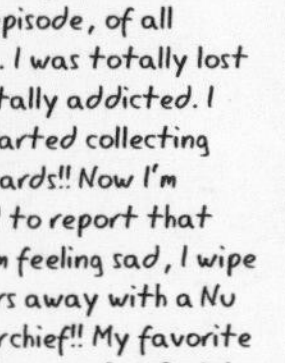
Good kitty, good kitty.
MEOW!

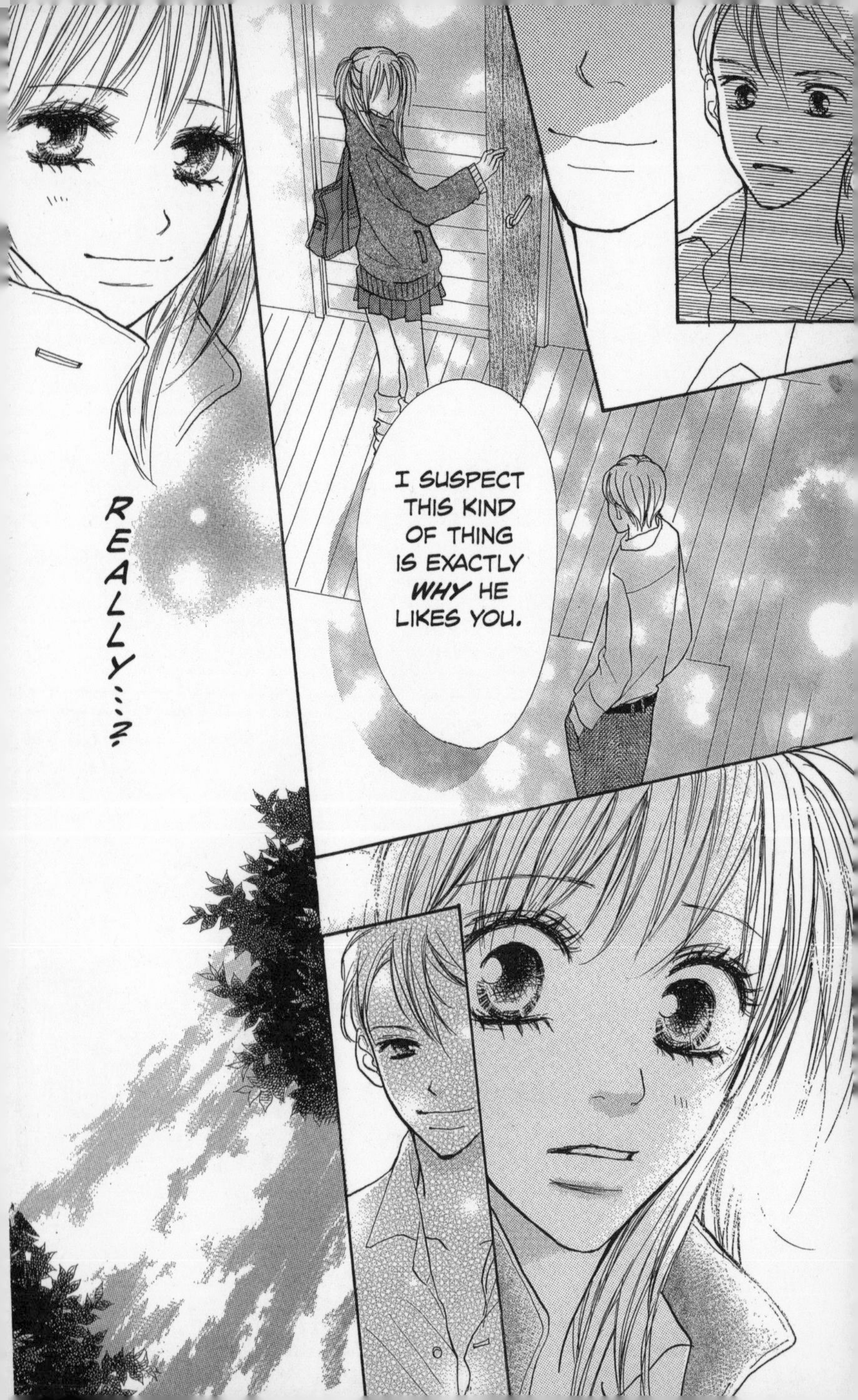
I SUSPECT THIS KIND OF THING IS EXACTLY WHY HE LIKES YOU.
REALLY...?

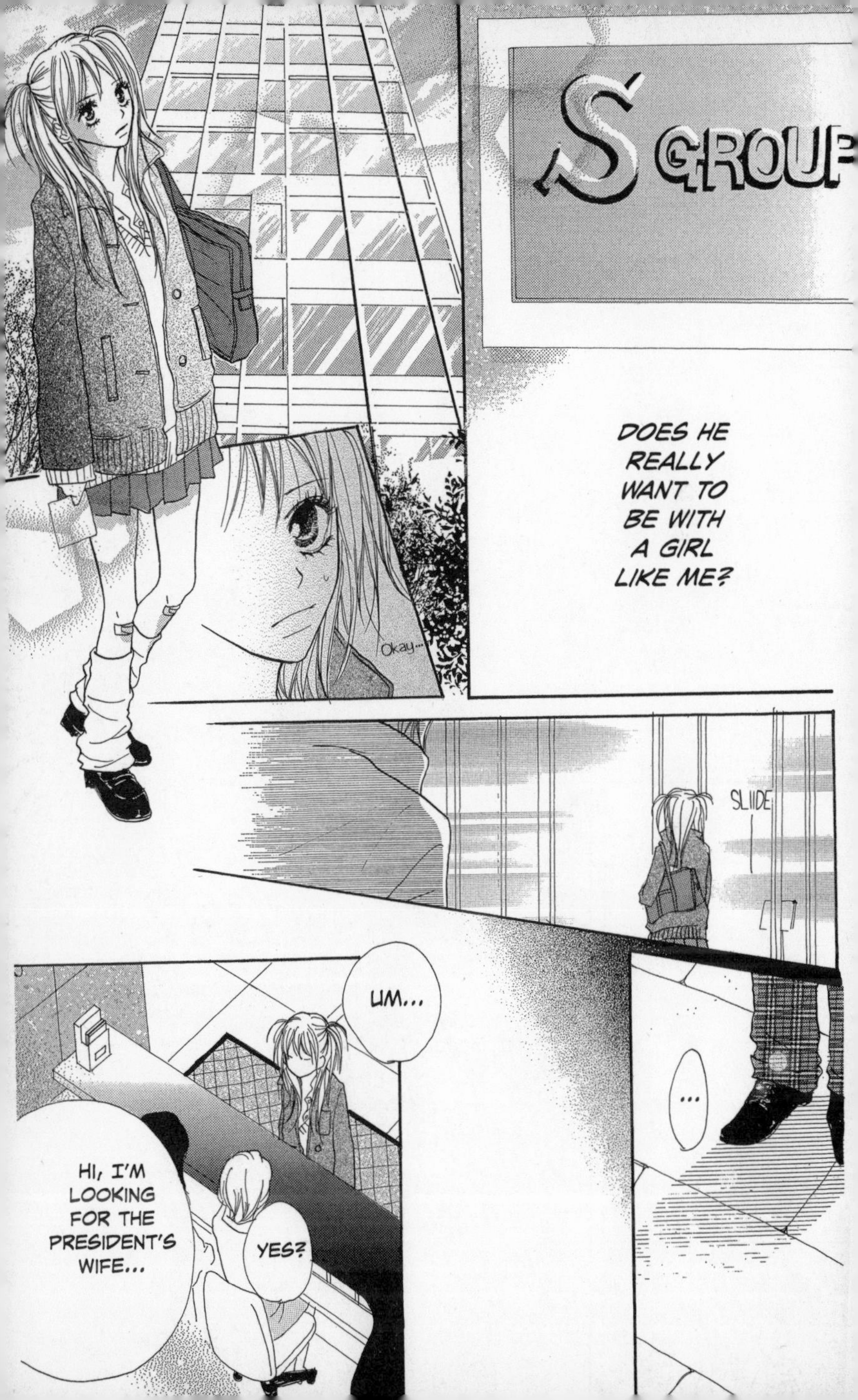
S GROUP
DOES HE REALLY WANT TO BE WITH A GIRL LIKE ME?
Okay...
SLIIDE
...
UM...
HI, I'M LOOKING FOR THE PRESIDENT'S WIFE...
YES?

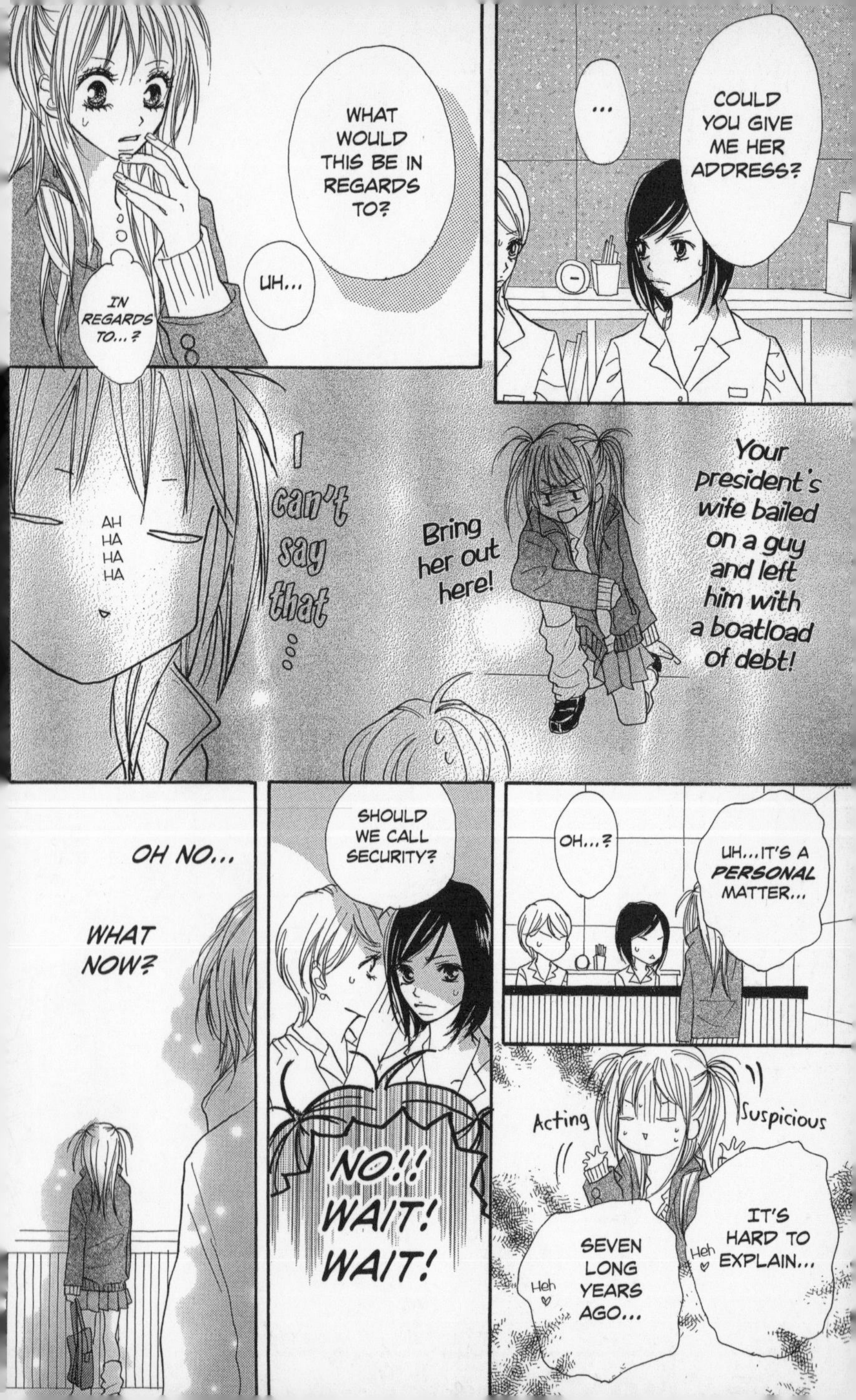
COULD YOU GIVE ME HER ADDRESS?
...
WHAT WOULD THIS BE IN REGARDS TO?
UH...
IN REGARDS TO...?
Your president's wife bailed on a guy and left him with a boatload of debt!
Bring her out here!
I can't say that...
AH HA HA HA
UH...IT'S A PERSONAL MATTER...
OH...?
Suspicious
IT'S HARD TO EXPLAIN...
Heh
Acting
SEVEN LONG YEARS AGO...
Heh
SHOULD WE CALL SECURITY?
NO!! WAIT! WAIT!
OH NO...
WHAT NOW?

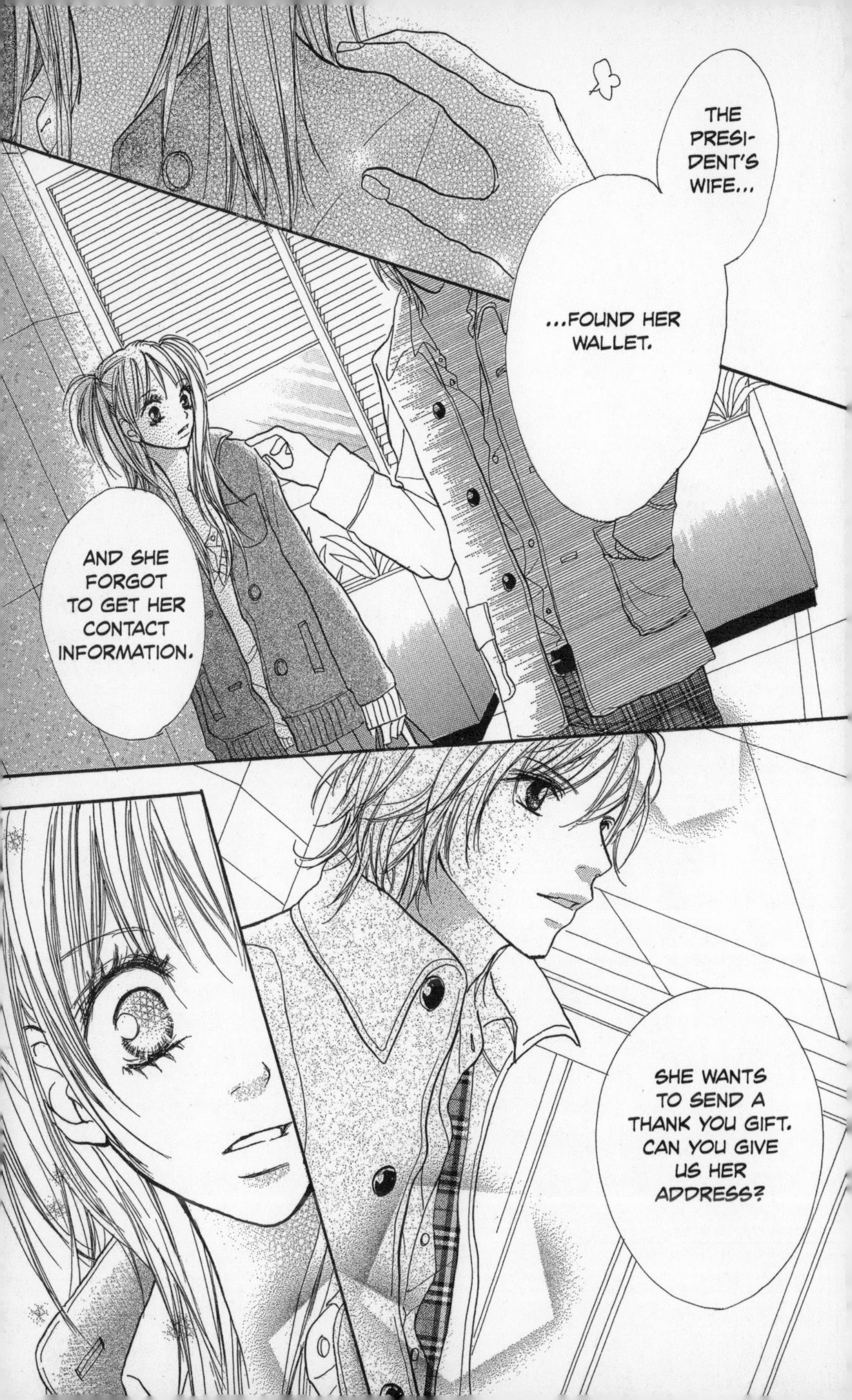
THE PRESI- DENT'S WIFE...
...FOUND HER WALLET.
AND SHE FORGOT TO GET HER CONTACT INFORMATION.
SHE WANTS TO SEND A THANK YOU GIFT. CAN YOU GIVE US HER ADDRESS?

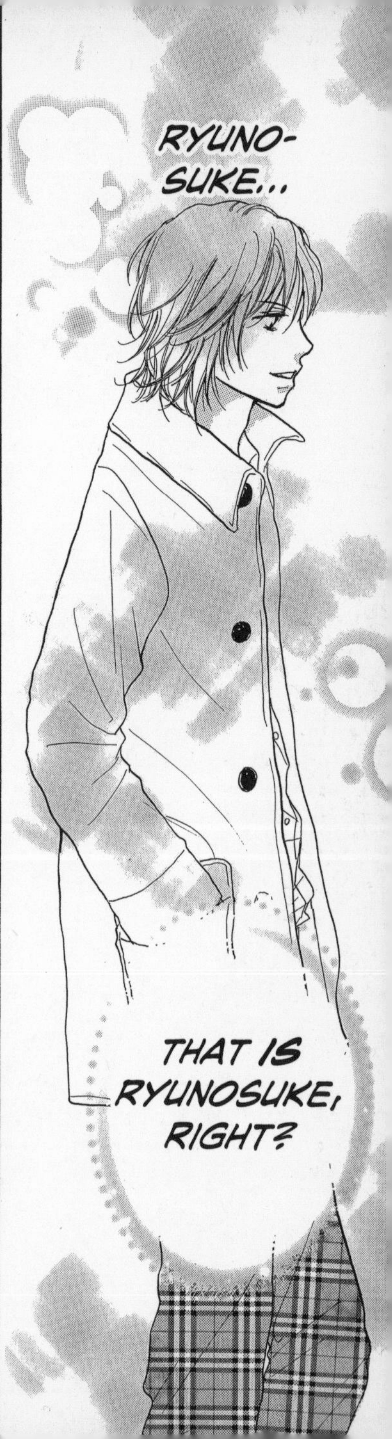
RYUNO-SUKE...
THAT IS RYUNOSUKE, RIGHT?

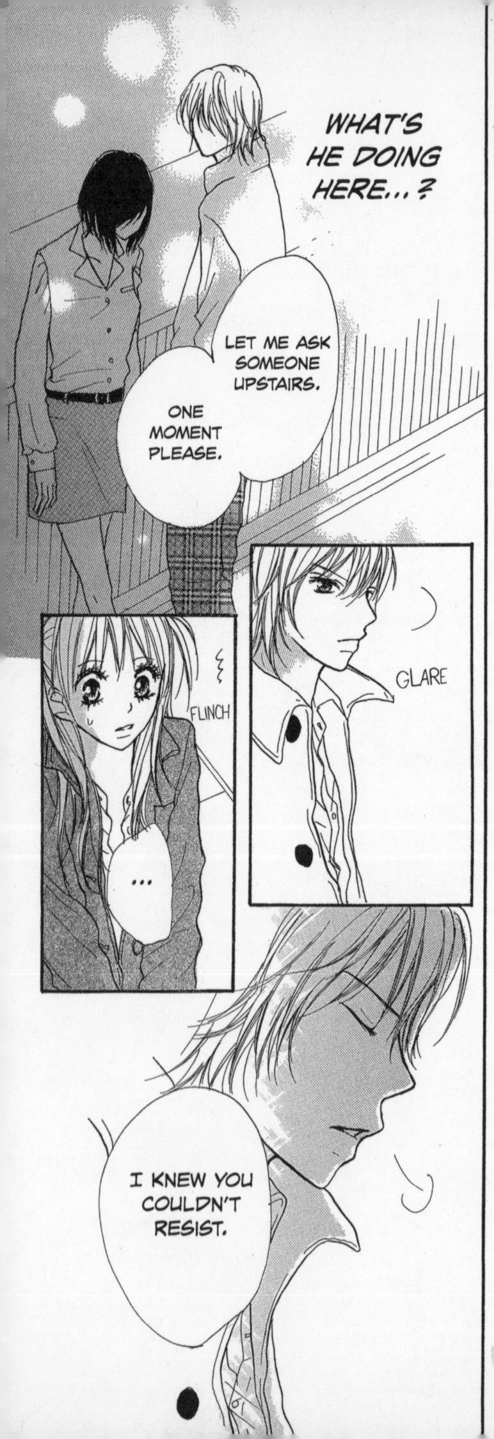
WHAT'S HE DOING HERE...?
LET ME ASK SOMEONE UPSTAIRS.
ONE MOMENT PLEASE.
GLARE
FLINCH
...
I KNEW YOU COULDN'T RESIST.

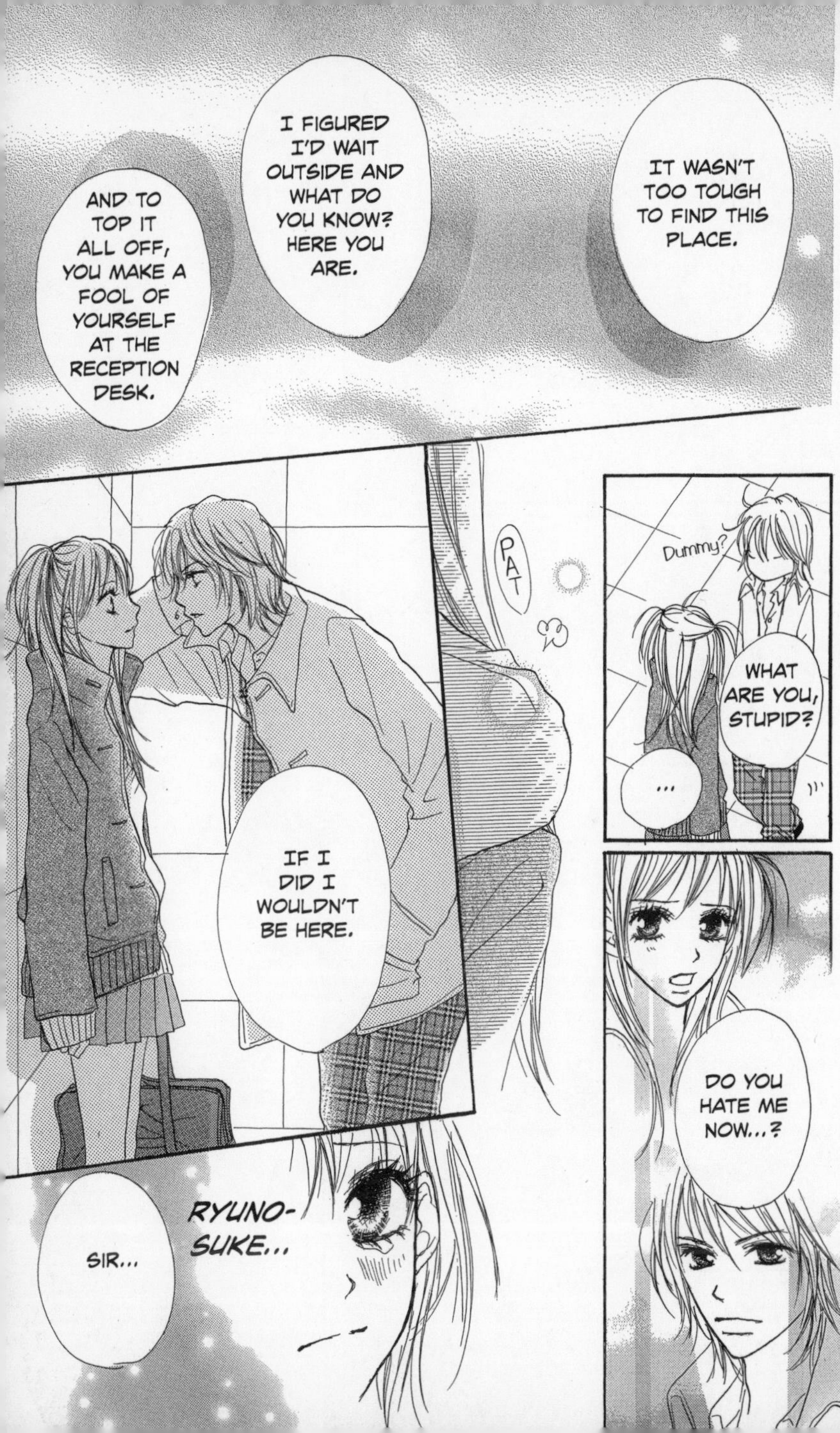
IT WASN'T TOO TOUGH TO FIND THIS PLACE.
I FIGURED I'D WAIT OUTSIDE AND WHAT DO YOU KNOW? HERE YOU ARE.
AND TO TOP IT ALL OFF, YOU MAKE A FOOL OF YOURSELF AT THE RECEPTION DESK.
Dummy?
WHAT ARE YOU, STUPID?
...
DO YOU HATE ME NOW...?
PAT
IF I DID I WOULDN'T BE HERE.
RYUNO-SUKE...
SIR...

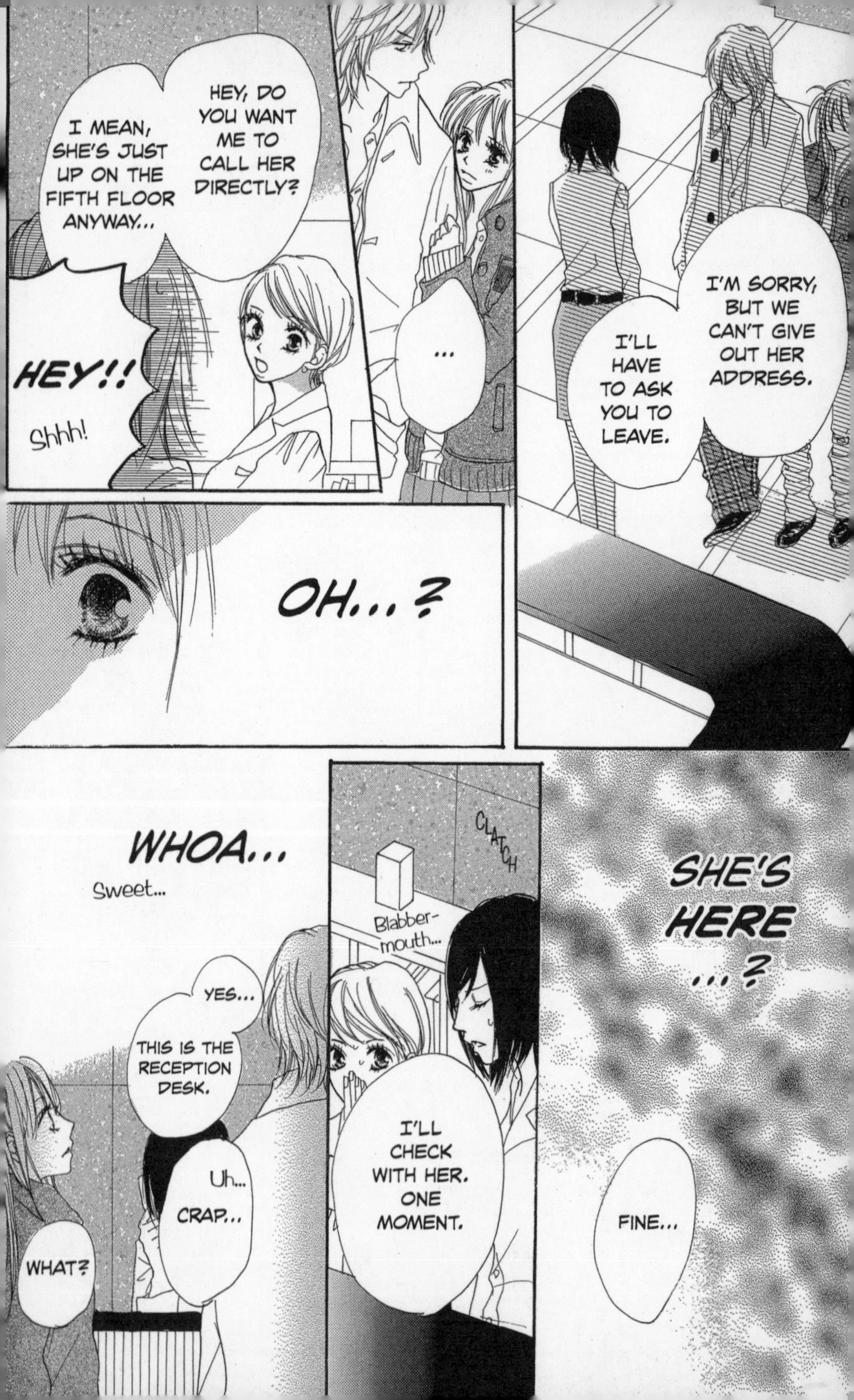
I'M SORRY, BUT WE CAN'T GIVE OUT HER ADDRESS.
I'LL HAVE TO ASK YOU TO LEAVE.
...
HEY, DO YOU WANT ME TO CALL HER DIRECTLY?
I MEAN, SHE'S JUST UP ON THE FIFTH FLOOR ANYWAY...
HEY!!
Shhh!
OH...?
SHE'S HERE...?
FINE...
CLATCH
Blabber-mouth...
I'LL CHECK WITH HER. ONE MOMENT.
WHOA...
Sweet...
YES...
THIS IS THE RECEPTION DESK.
Uh...
CRAP...
WHAT?

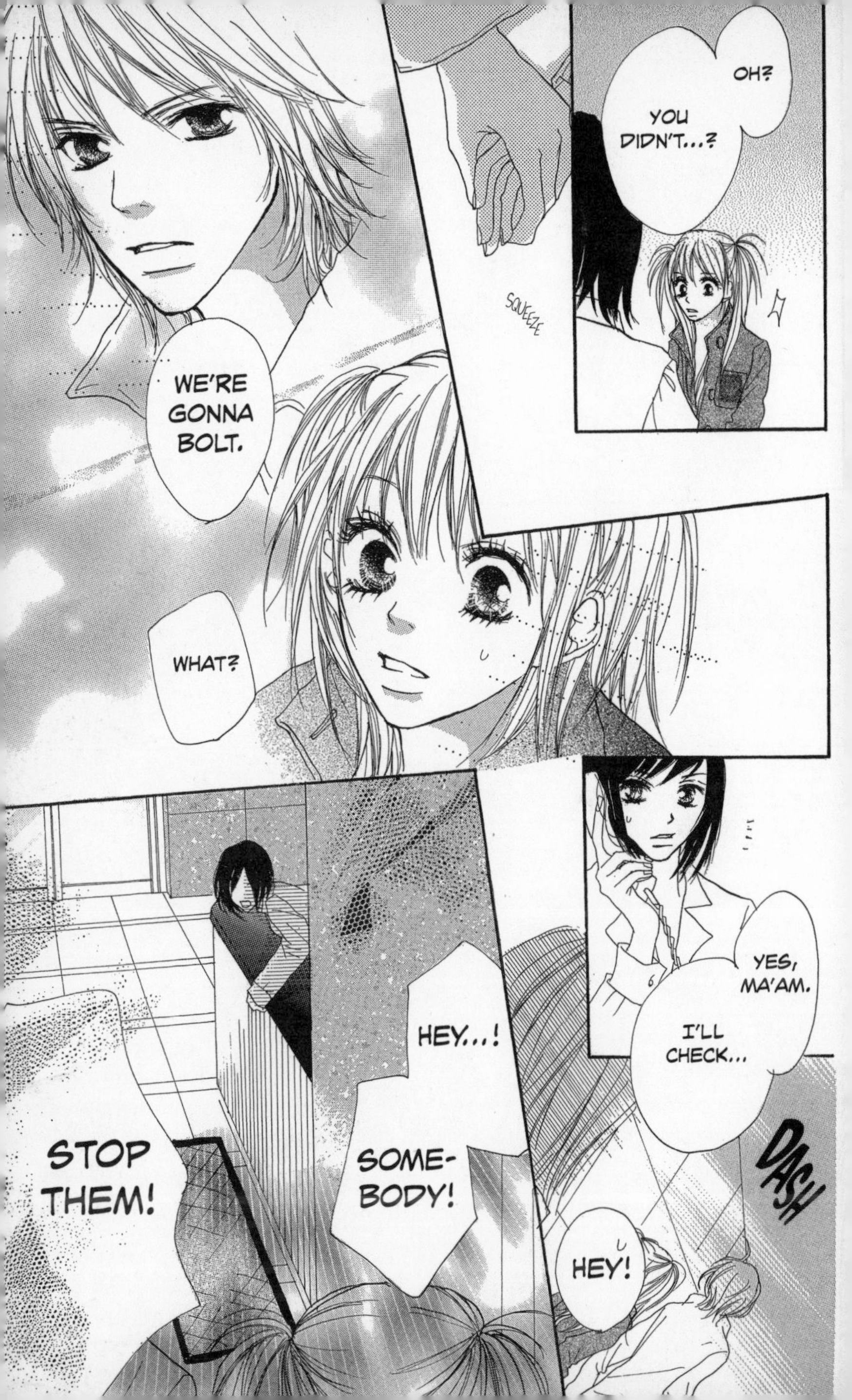
OH? YOU DIDN'T...?
SQUEEZE
WE'RE GONNA BOLT.
WHAT?
YES, MA'AM. I'LL CHECK...
DASH
HEY!
HEY...! SOMEBODY!
STOP THEM!

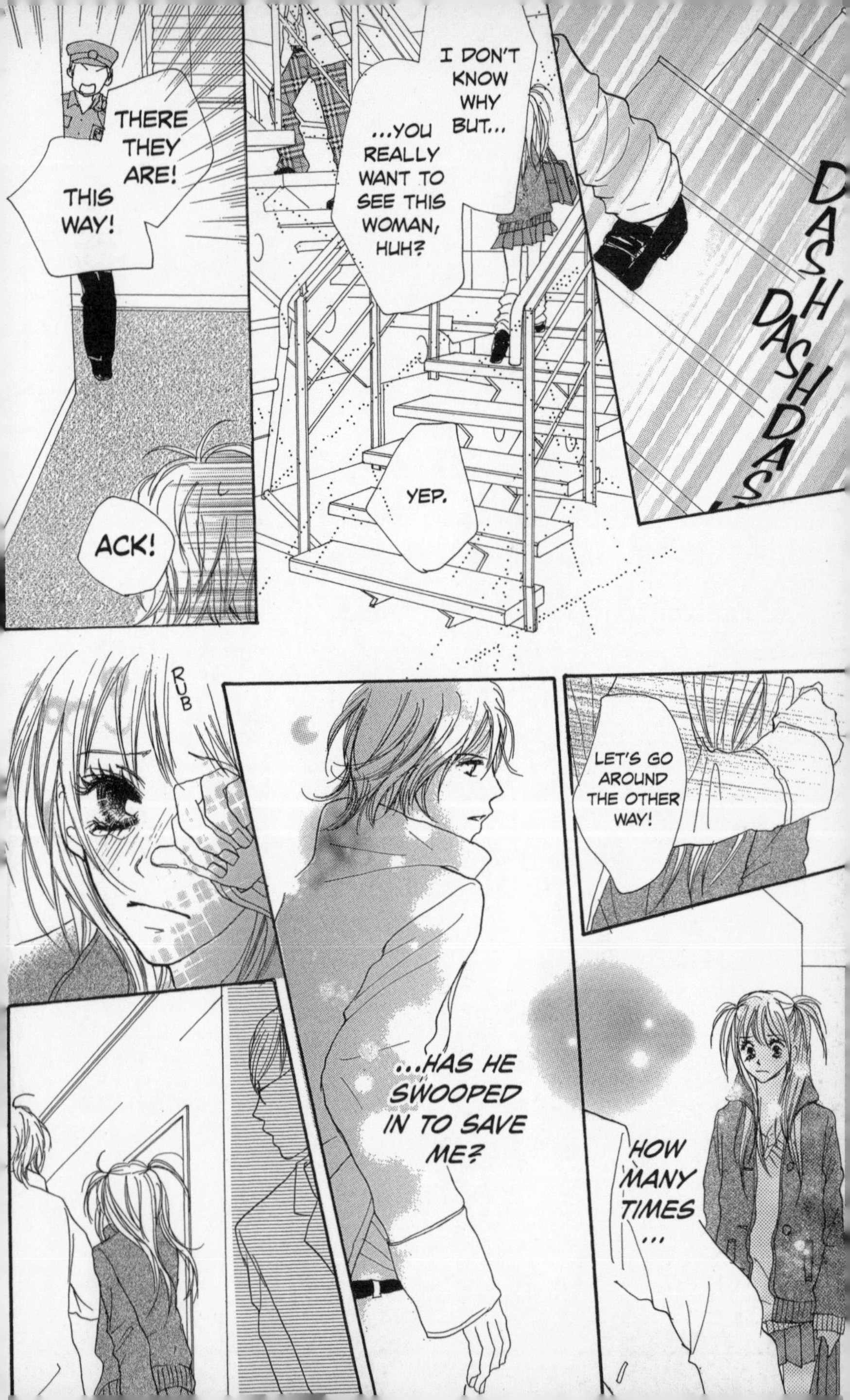
DASH DASH DASH DASH
I DON'T KNOW WHY BUT...
...YOU REALLY WANT TO SEE THIS WOMAN, HUH?
YEP.
THERE THEY ARE!
THIS WAY!
ACK!
LET'S GO AROUND THE OTHER WAY!
RUB
HOW MANY TIMES...
...HAS HE SWOOPED IN TO SAVE ME?

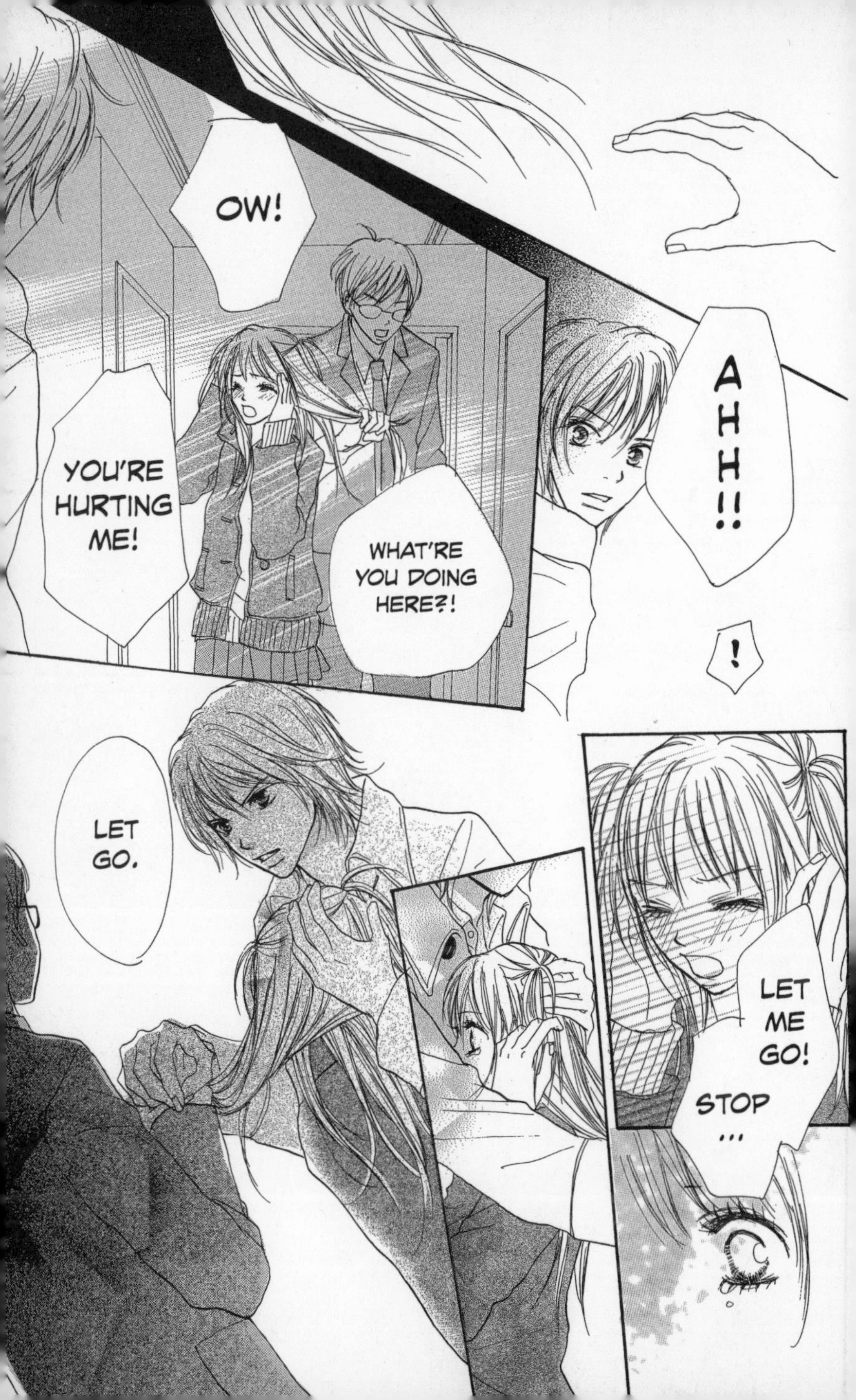
AHH!!
!
OW!
WHAT'RE YOU DOING HERE?!
YOU'RE HURTING ME!
LET ME GO!
STOP ...
LET GO.

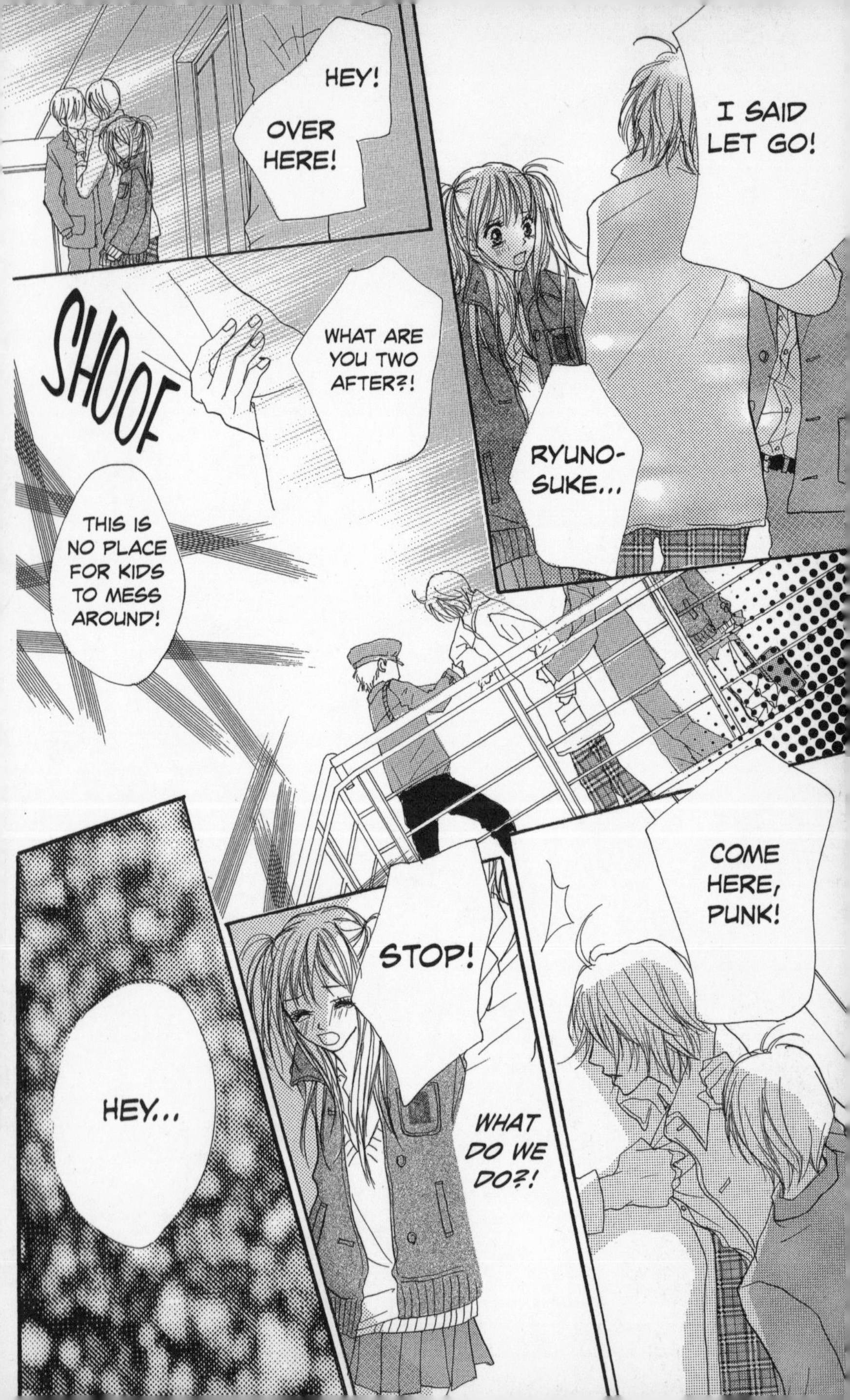
I SAID LET GO!
RYUNO-SUKE...
HEY!
OVER HERE!
WHAT ARE YOU TWO AFTER?!
SHOOF
THIS IS NO PLACE FOR KIDS TO MESS AROUND!
COME HERE, PUNK!
STOP!
WHAT DO WE DO?!
HEY...

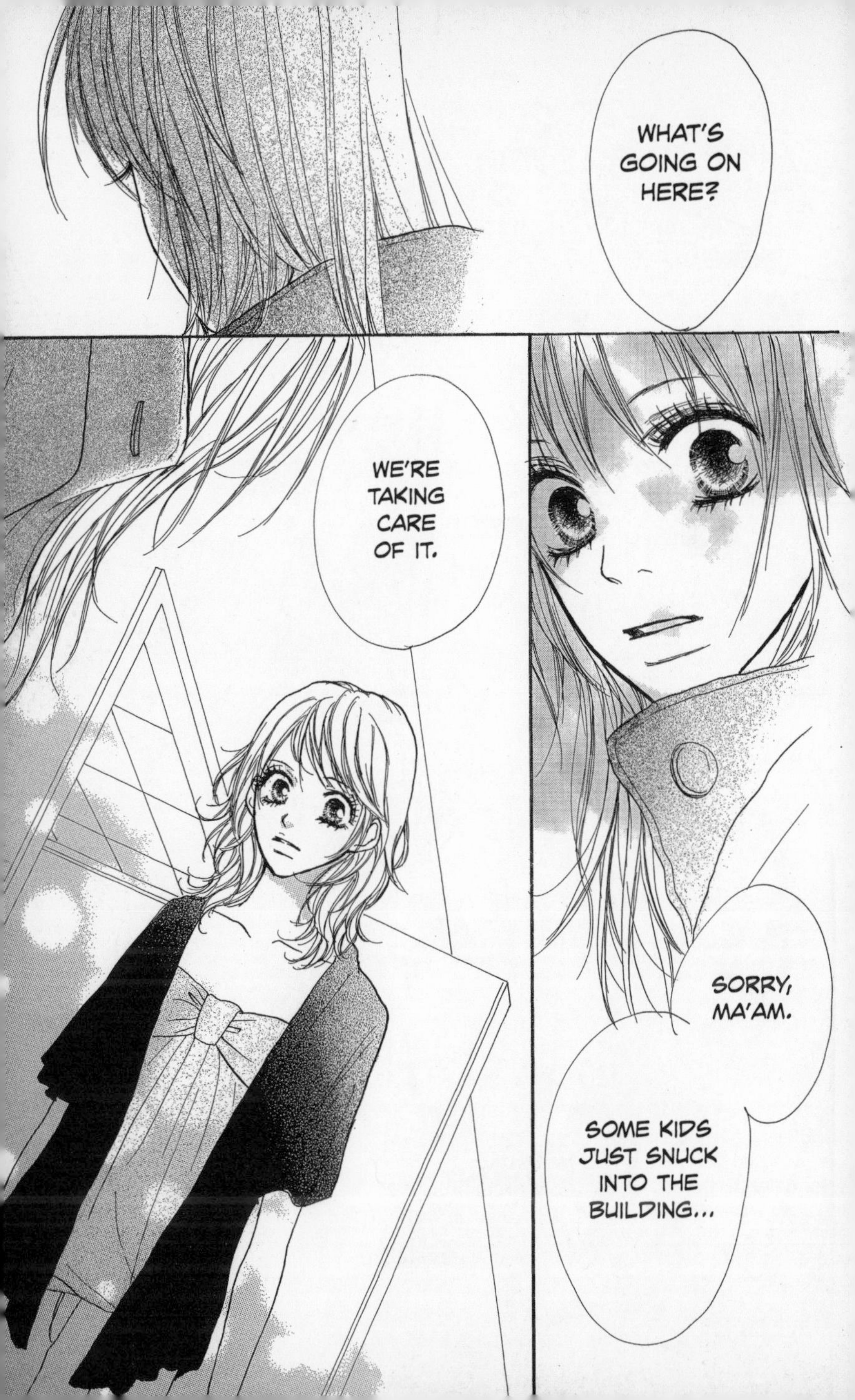
WHAT'S GOING ON HERE?
SORRY, MA'AM.
SOME KIDS JUST SNUCK INTO THE BUILDING...
WE'RE TAKING CARE OF IT.

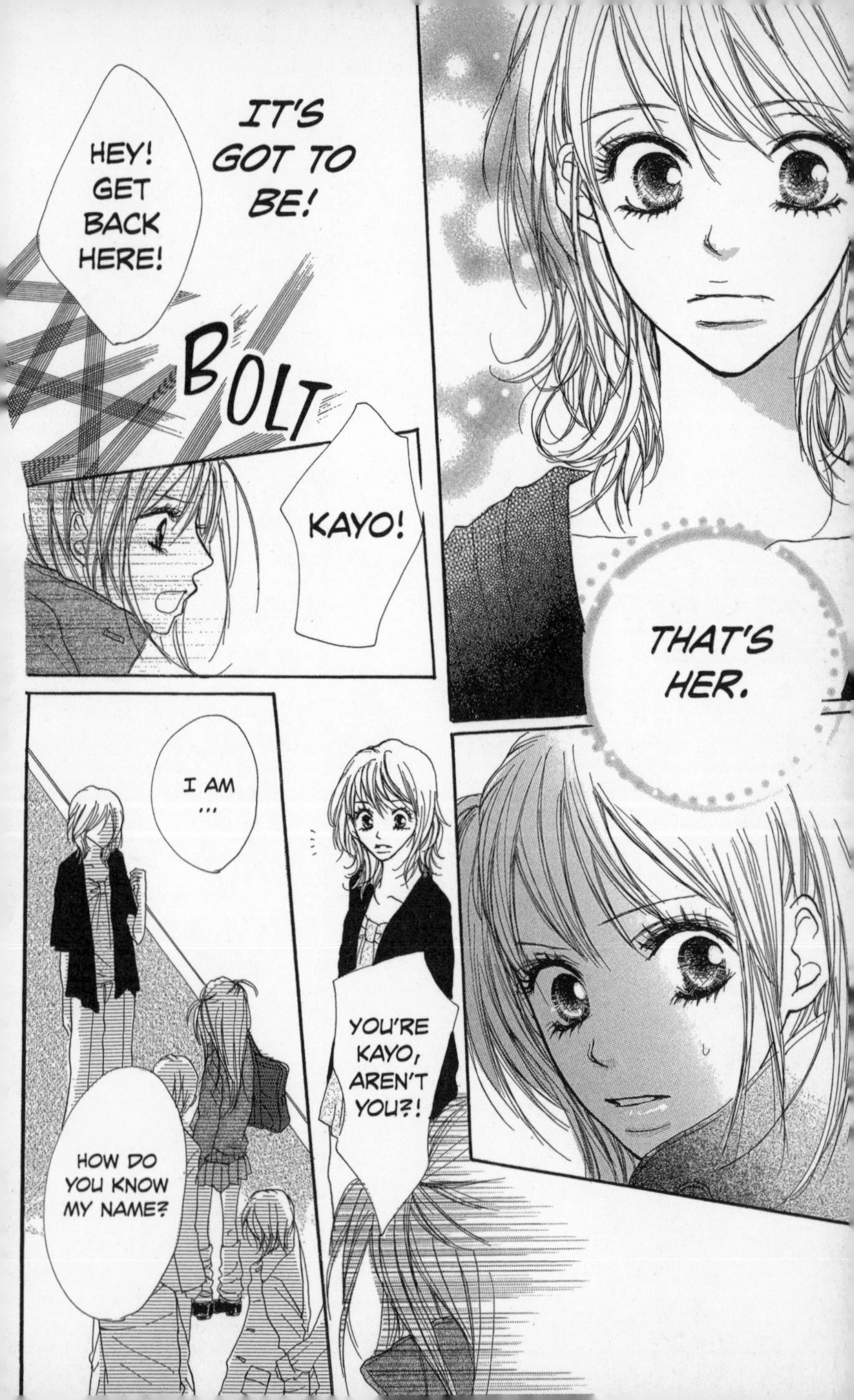
IT'S GOT TO BE!
HEY! GET BACK HERE!
BOLT
KAYO!
THAT'S HER.
YOU'RE KAYO, AREN'T YOU?!
I AM ...
HOW DO YOU KNOW MY NAME?

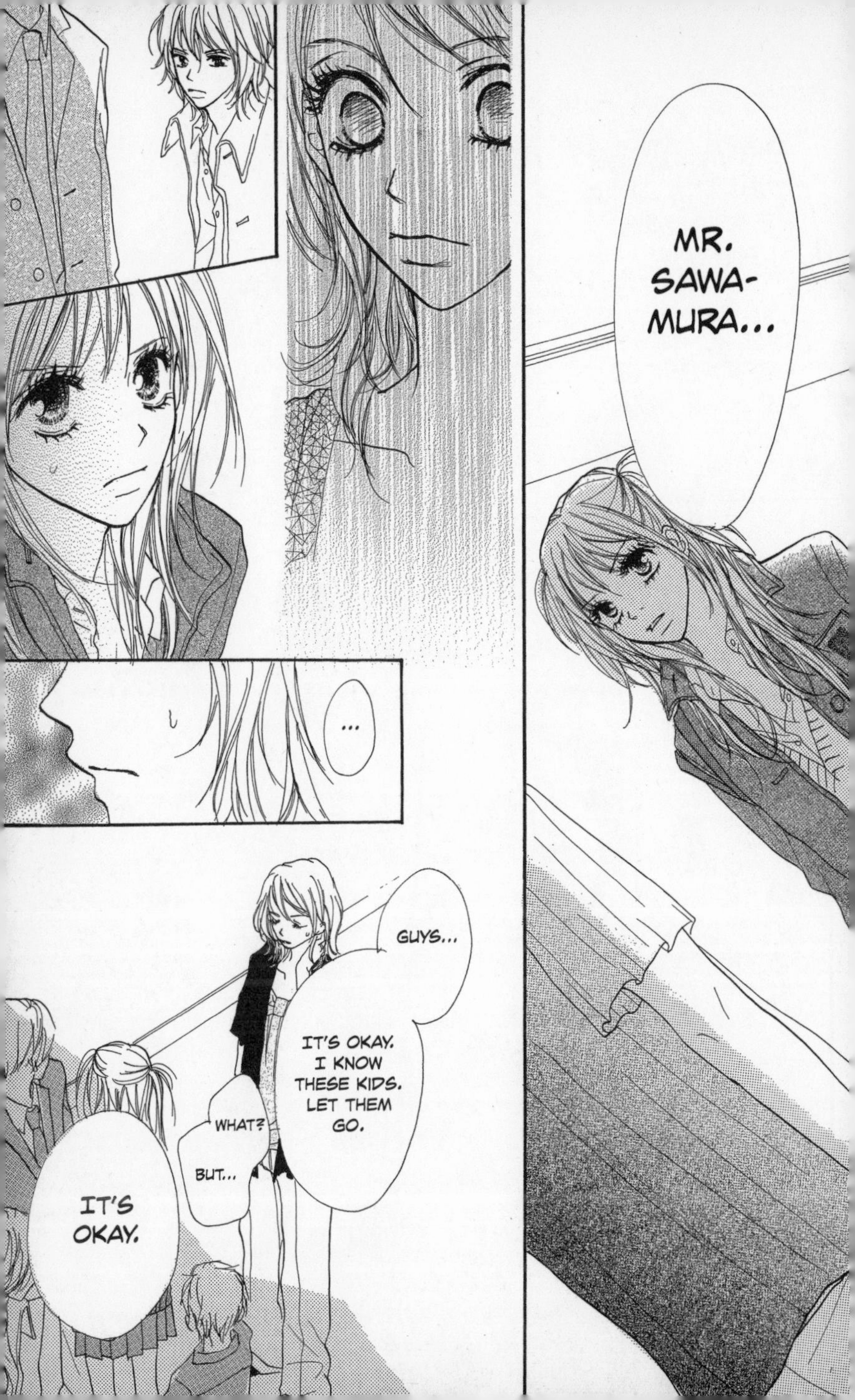
MR. SAWA-MURA...
...
GUYS...
IT'S OKAY. I KNOW THESE KIDS. LET THEM GO.
WHAT?
BUT...
IT'S OKAY.

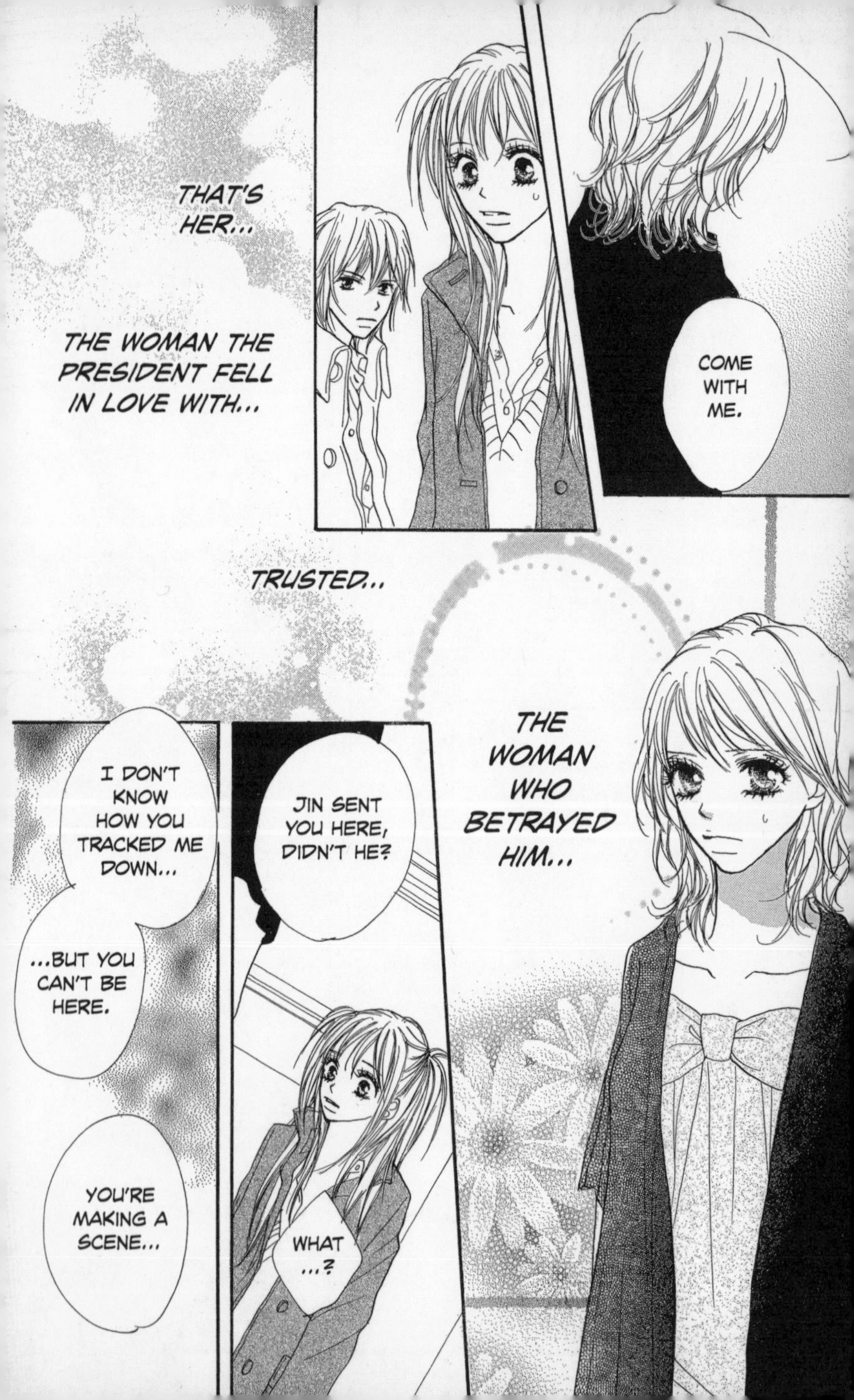

COME WITH ME.
THAT'S HER...
THE WOMAN THE PRESIDENT FELL IN LOVE WITH...
TRUSTED...
THE WOMAN WHO BETRAYED HIM...
JIN SENT YOU HERE, DIDN'T HE?
WHAT ...?
I DON'T KNOW HOW YOU TRACKED ME DOWN...
...BUT YOU CAN'T BE HERE.
YOU'RE MAKING A SCENE...

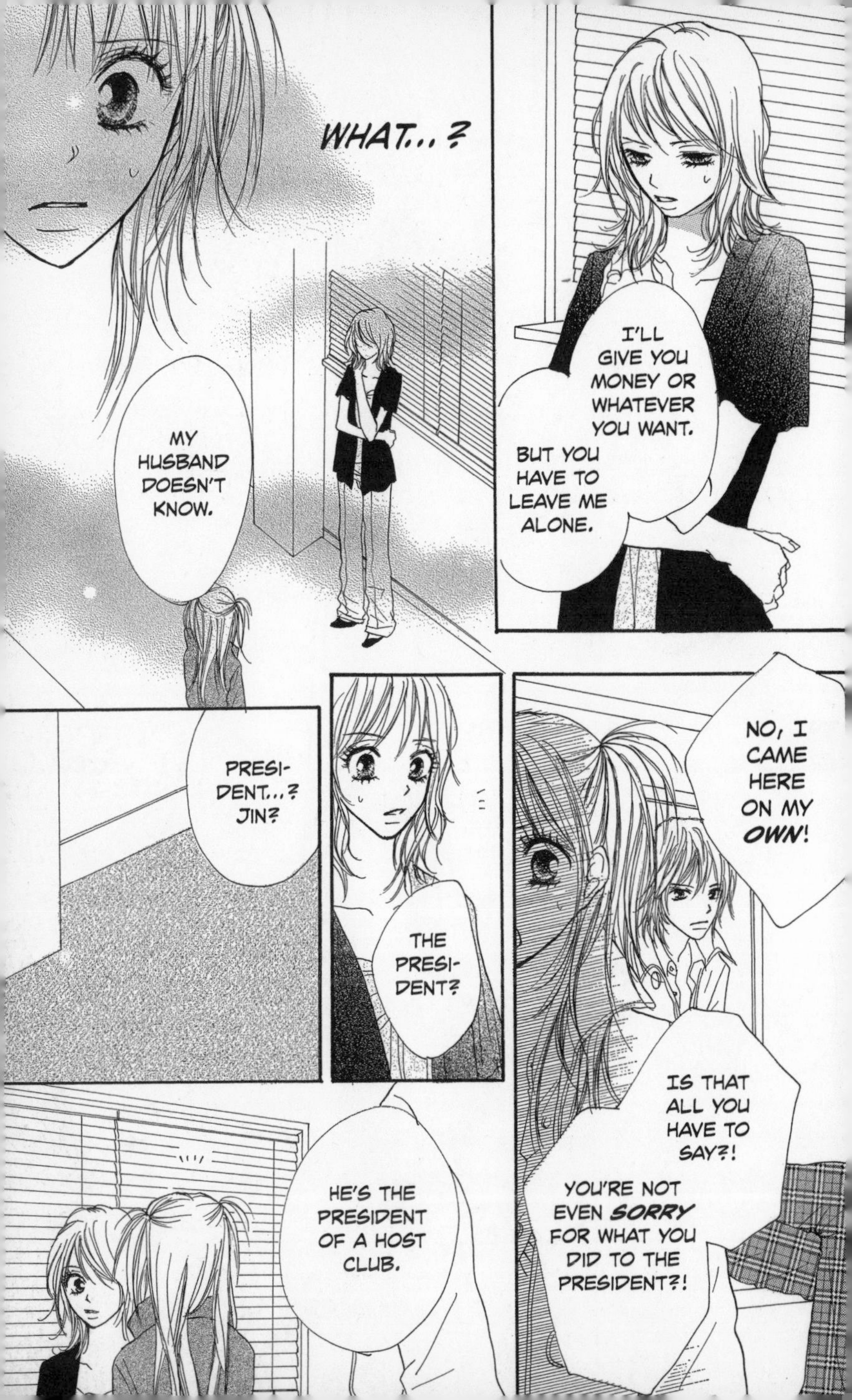
I'LL GIVE YOU MONEY OR WHATEVER YOU WANT.
BUT YOU HAVE TO LEAVE ME ALONE.
WHAT...?
MY HUSBAND DOESN'T KNOW.
NO, I CAME HERE ON MY *OWN*!
IS THAT ALL YOU HAVE TO SAY?!
YOU'RE NOT EVEN *SORRY* FOR WHAT YOU DID TO THE PRESIDENT?!
THE PRESI-DENT?
PRESI-DENT...? JIN?
HE'S THE PRESIDENT OF A HOST CLUB.

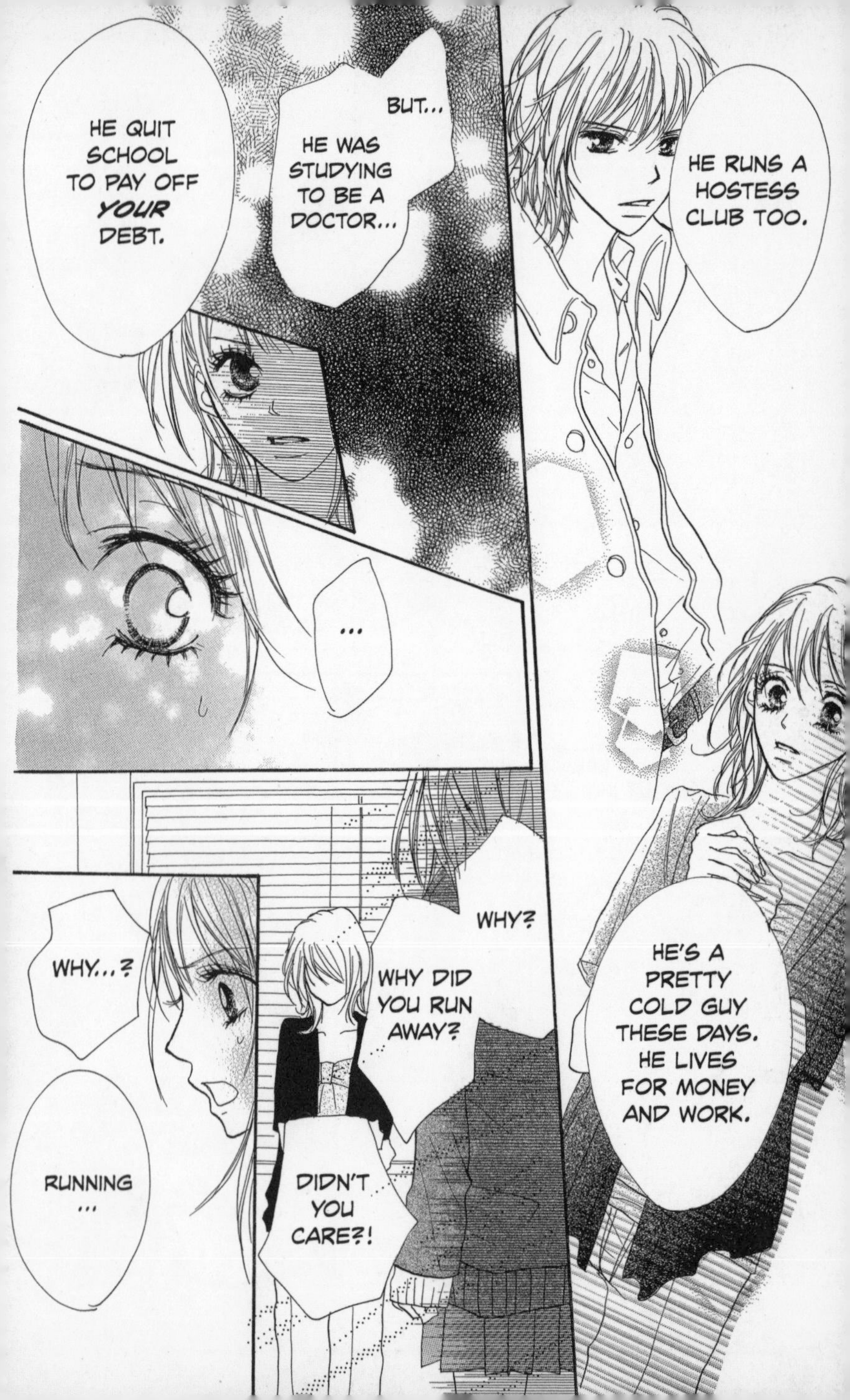
HE RUNS A HOSTESS CLUB TOO.
HE'S A PRETTY COLD GUY THESE DAYS. HE LIVES FOR MONEY AND WORK.
BUT... HE WAS STUDYING TO BE A DOCTOR...
HE QUIT SCHOOL TO PAY OFF *YOUR* DEBT.
...
WHY?
WHY DID YOU RUN AWAY?
DIDN'T YOU CARE?!
WHY...?
RUNNING ...

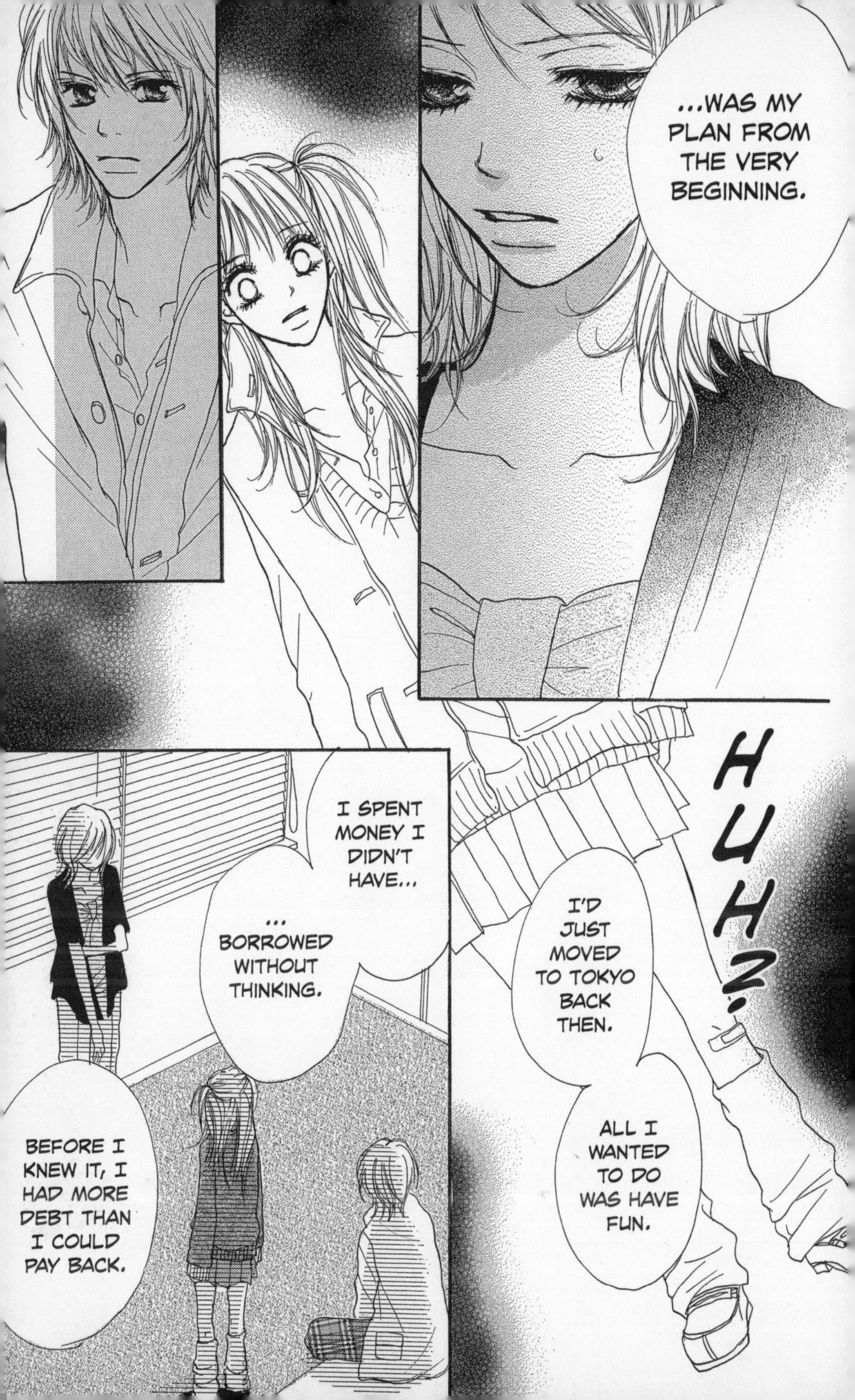
...WAS MY PLAN FROM THE VERY BEGINNING.
HUH?
I'D JUST MOVED TO TOKYO BACK THEN.
ALL I WANTED TO DO WAS HAVE FUN.
I SPENT MONEY I DIDN'T HAVE...
...BORROWED WITHOUT THINKING.
BEFORE I KNEW IT, I HAD MORE DEBT THAN I COULD PAY BACK.

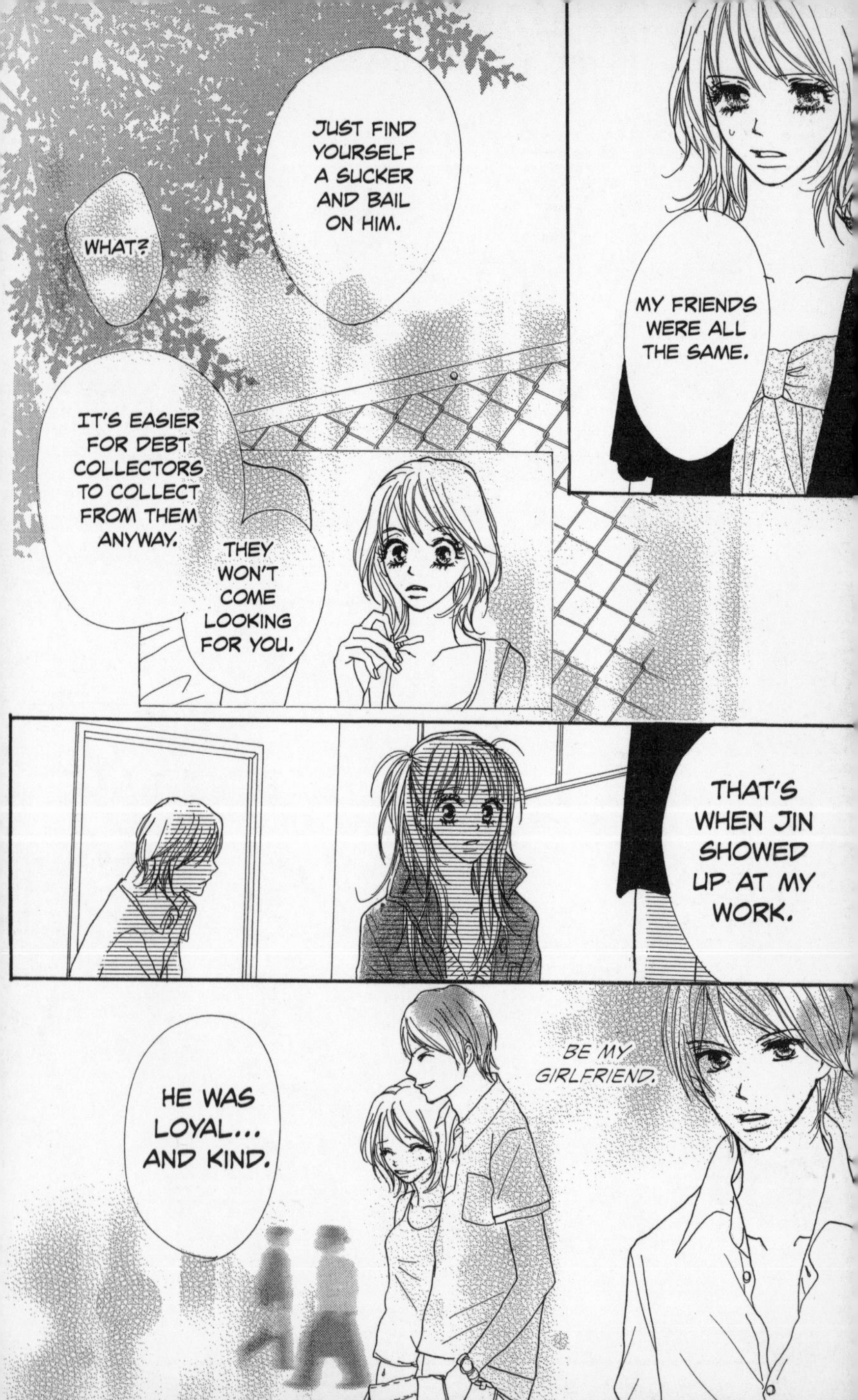
MY FRIENDS WERE ALL THE SAME.
JUST FIND YOURSELF A SUCKER AND BAIL ON HIM.
WHAT?
THEY WON'T COME LOOKING FOR YOU.
IT'S EASIER FOR DEBT COLLECTORS TO COLLECT FROM THEM ANYWAY.
THAT'S WHEN JIN SHOWED UP AT MY WORK.
BE MY GIRLFRIEND.
HE WAS LOYAL... AND KIND.

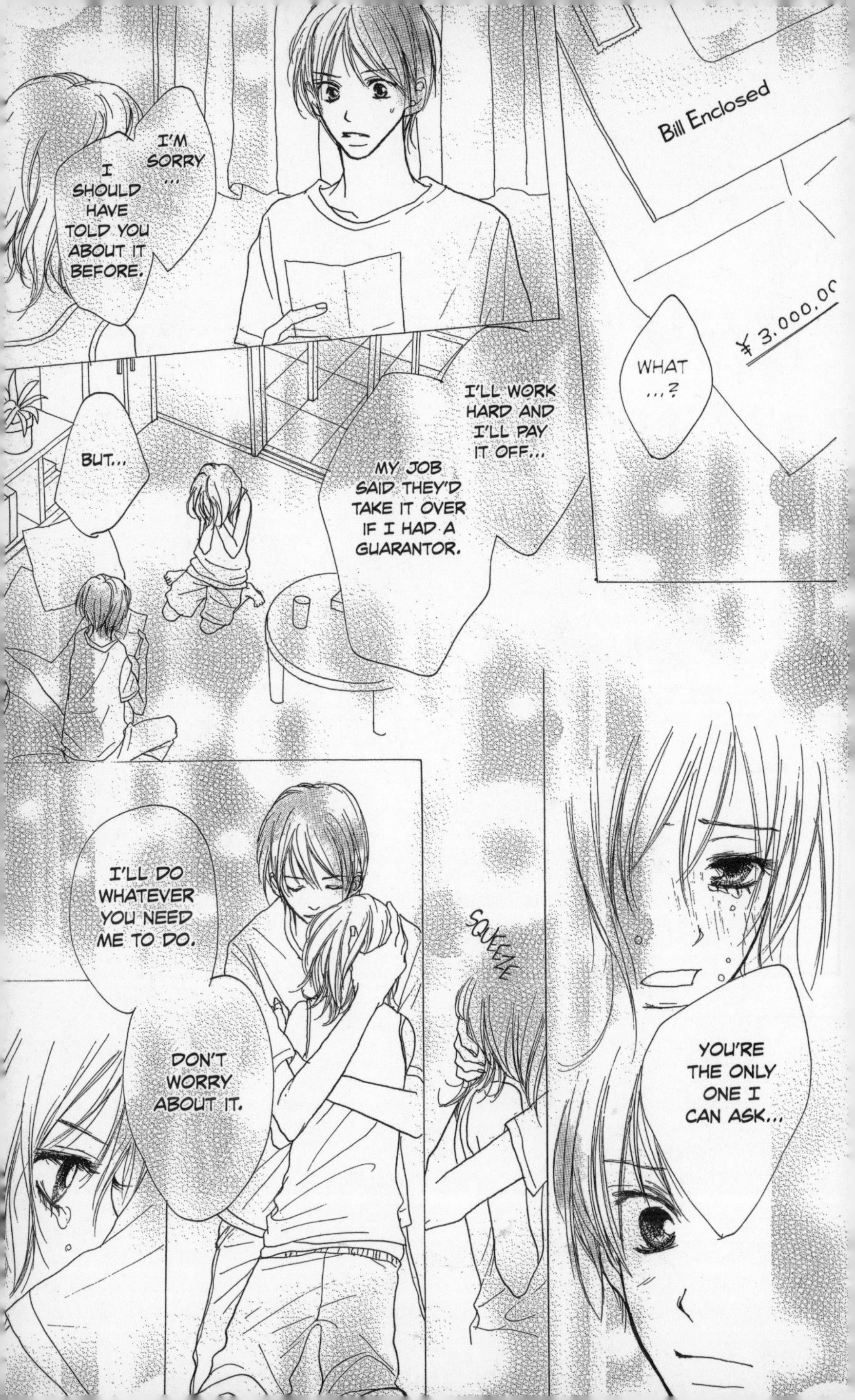
Bill Enclosed
¥3.000,00
WHAT ...?
I'M SORRY ...
I SHOULD HAVE TOLD YOU ABOUT IT BEFORE.
I'LL WORK HARD AND I'LL PAY IT OFF...
MY JOB SAID THEY'D TAKE IT OVER IF I HAD A GUARANTOR.
BUT...
YOU'RE THE ONLY ONE I CAN ASK...
SQUEEZE
I'LL DO WHATEVER YOU NEED ME TO DO.
DON'T WORRY ABOUT IT.

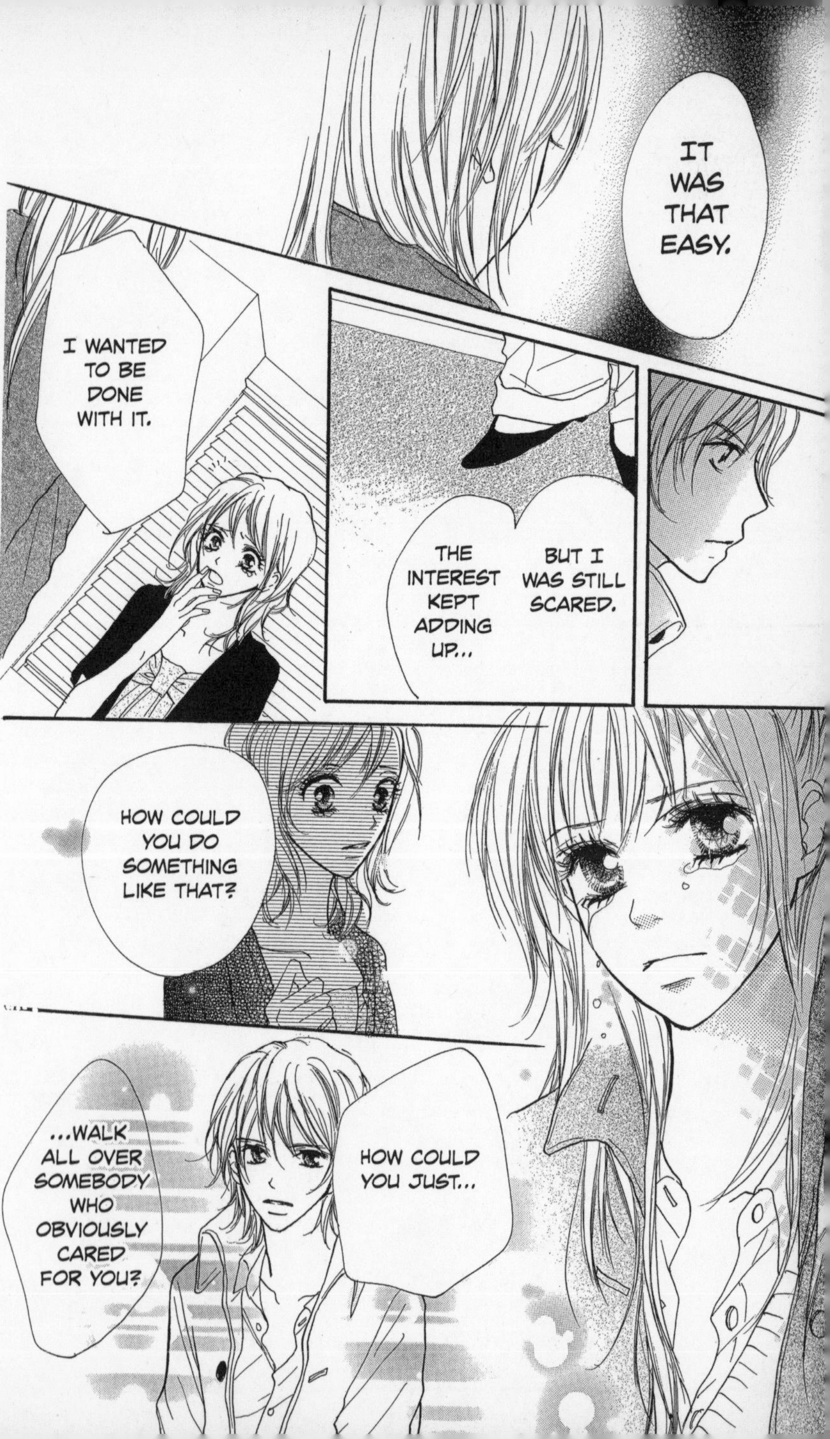
IT WAS THAT EASY.
BUT I WAS STILL SCARED.
THE INTEREST KEPT ADDING UP...
I WANTED TO BE DONE WITH IT.
HOW COULD YOU DO SOMETHING LIKE THAT?
HOW COULD YOU JUST...
...WALK ALL OVER SOMEBODY WHO OBVIOUSLY CARED FOR YOU?

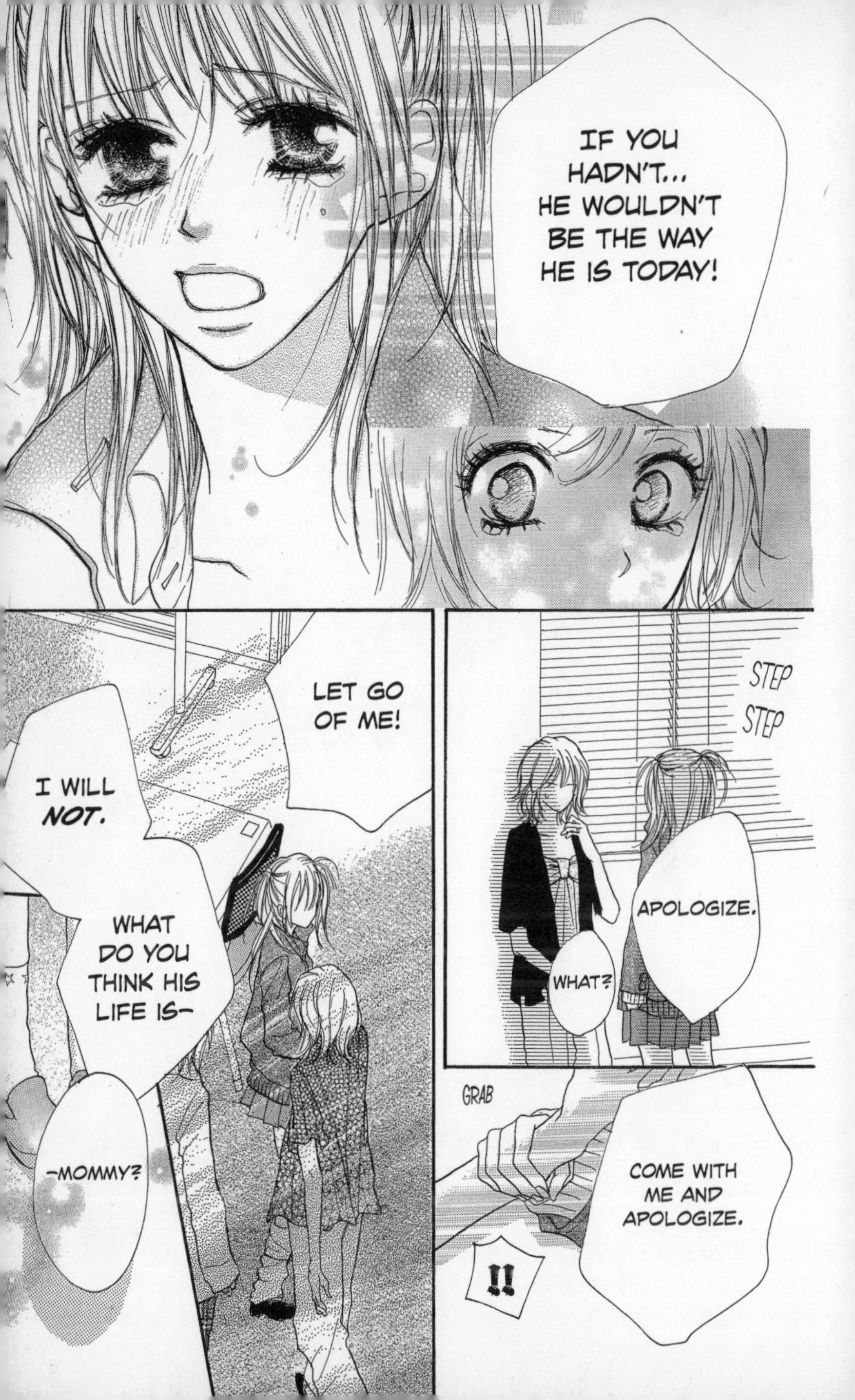
IF YOU HADN'T... HE WOULDN'T BE THE WAY HE IS TODAY!
STEP
STEP
APOLOGIZE.
WHAT?
GRAB
COME WITH ME AND APOLOGIZE.
!!
LET GO OF ME!
I WILL *NOT*.
WHAT DO YOU THINK HIS LIFE IS—
—MOMMY?

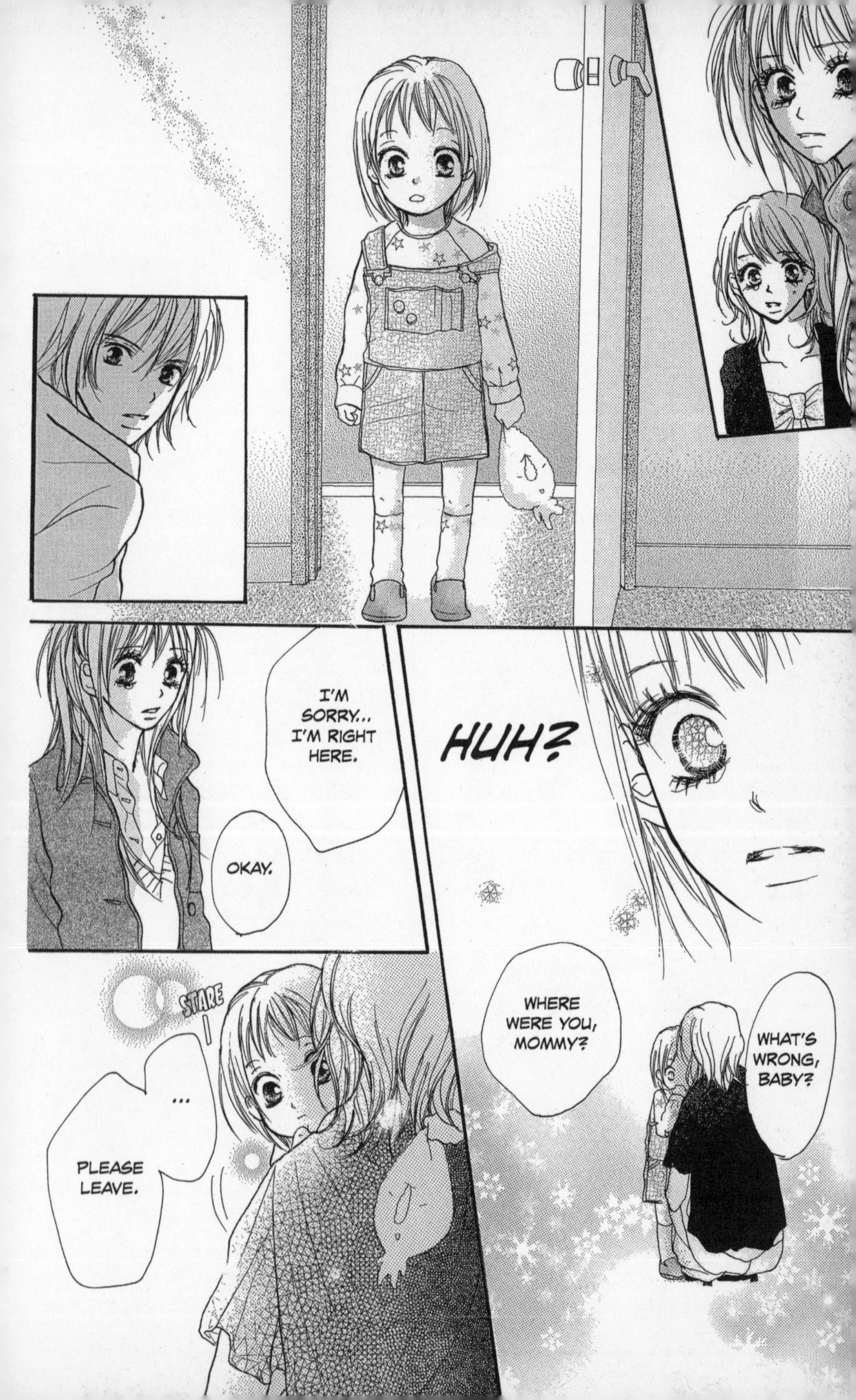
HUH?
I'M SORRY... I'M RIGHT HERE.
OKAY.
WHAT'S WRONG, BABY?
WHERE WERE YOU, MOMMY?
STARE
...
PLEASE LEAVE.

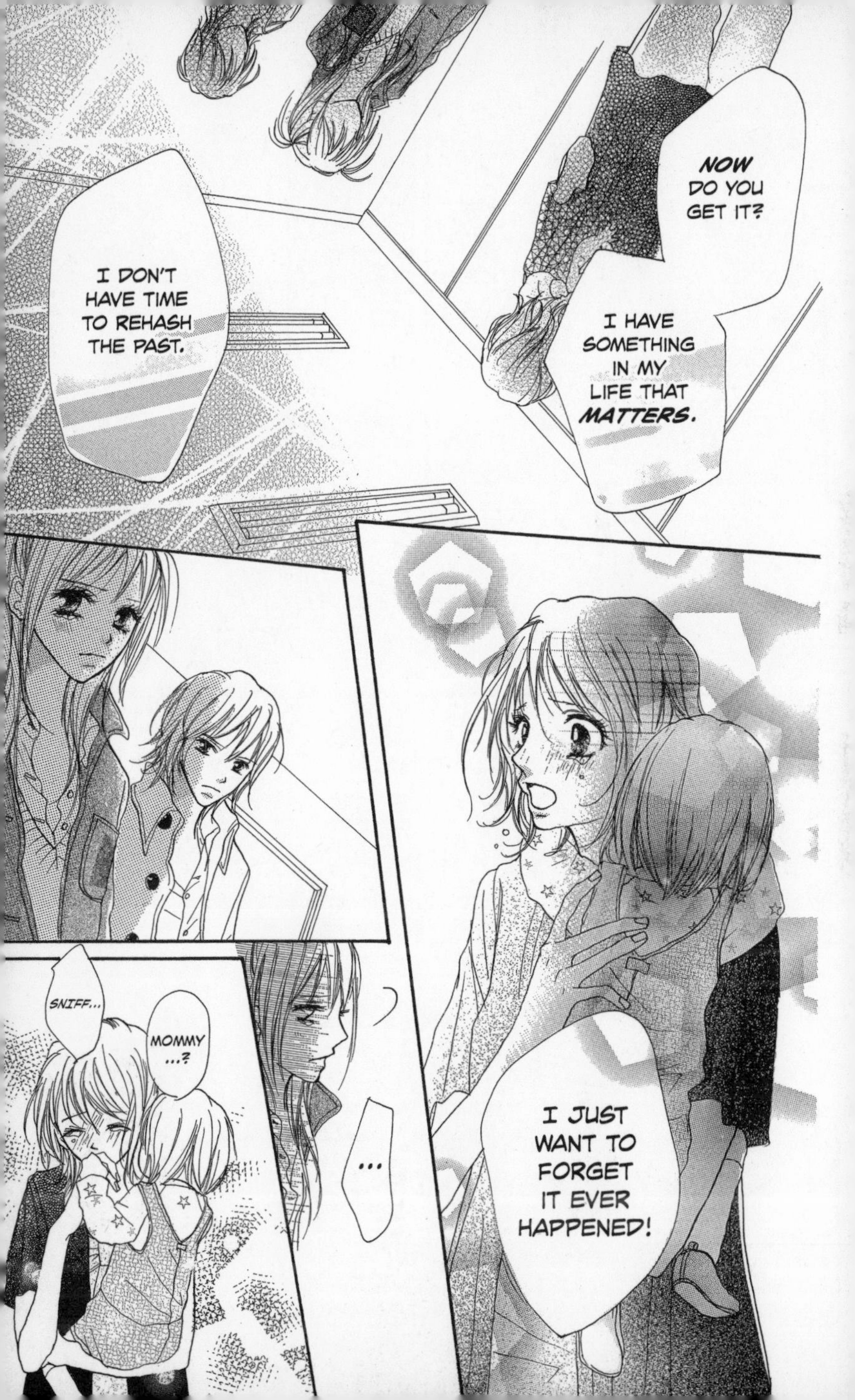
NOW DO YOU GET IT?
I HAVE SOMETHING IN MY LIFE THAT MATTERS.
I DON'T HAVE TIME TO REHASH THE PAST.
I JUST WANT TO FORGET IT EVER HAPPENED!
SNIFF...
MOMMY ...?
...

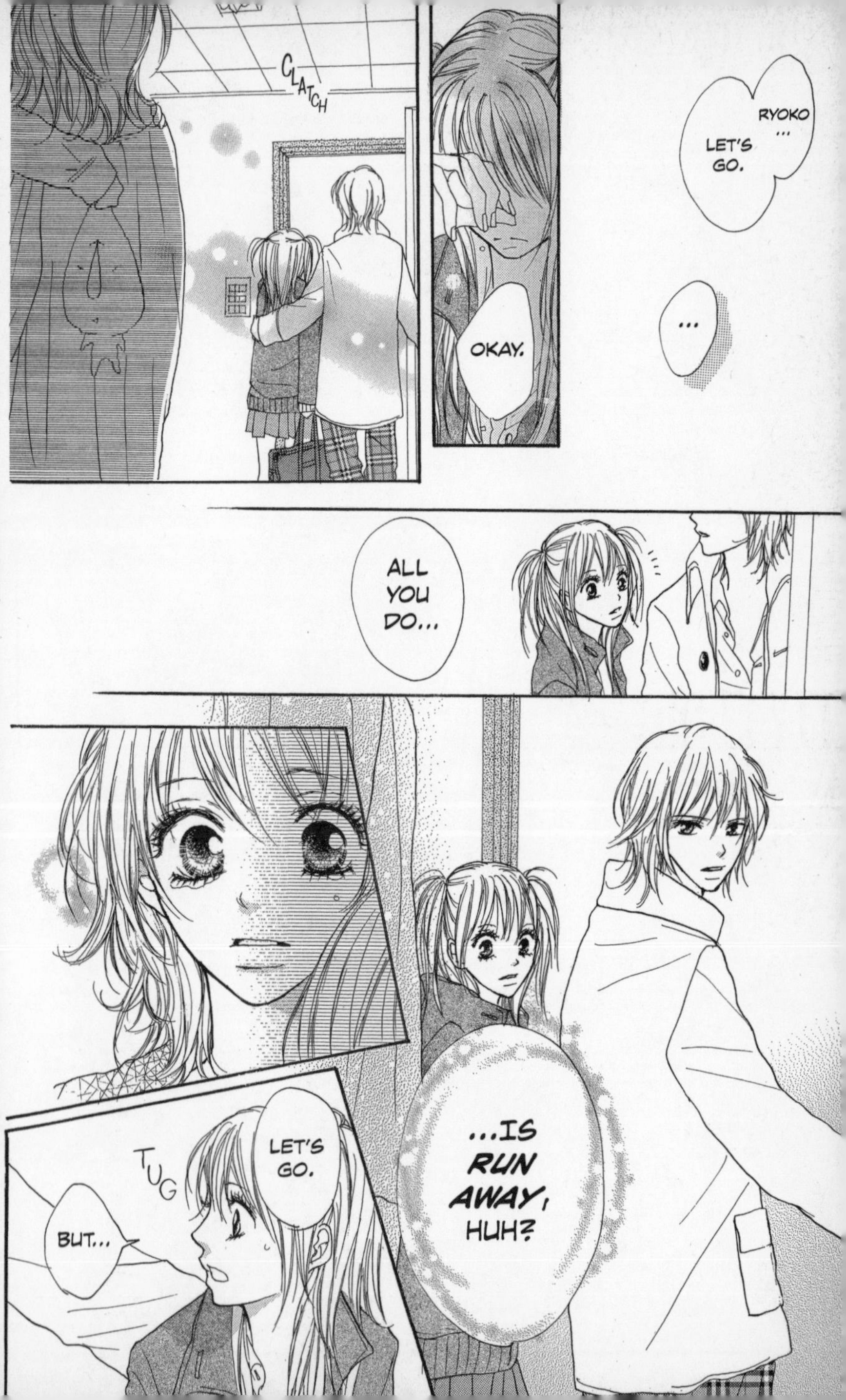
RYOKO... LET'S GO.
...
OKAY.
CLATCH
ALL YOU DO...
...IS RUN AWAY, HUH?
LET'S GO.
TUG
BUT...

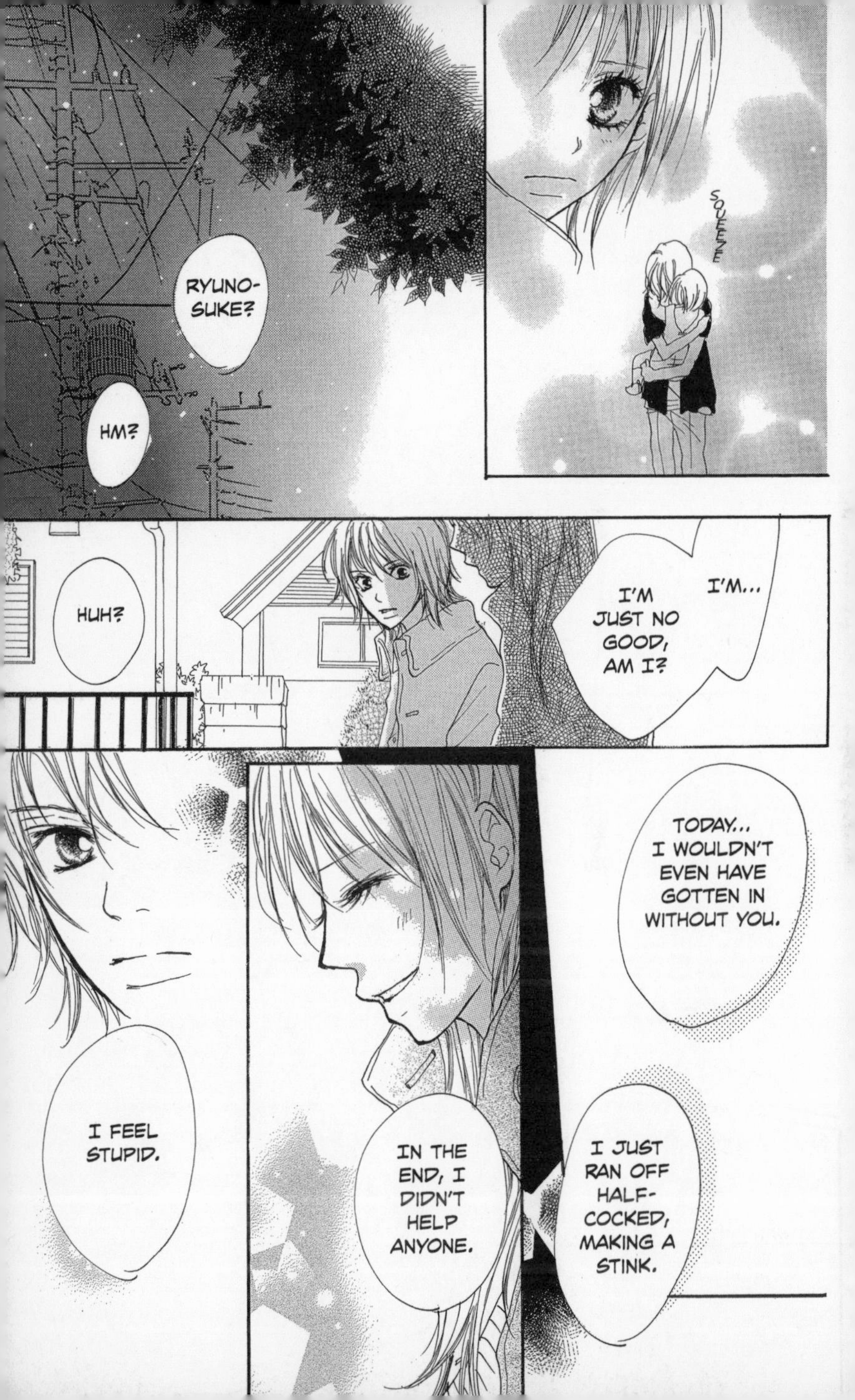
SQUEEZE
RYUNOSUKE?
HM?
I'M... I'M JUST NO GOOD, AM I?
HUH?
TODAY... I WOULDN'T EVEN HAVE GOTTEN IN WITHOUT YOU.
I JUST RAN OFF HALF-COCKED, MAKING A STINK.
IN THE END, I DIDN'T HELP ANYONE.
I FEEL STUPID.

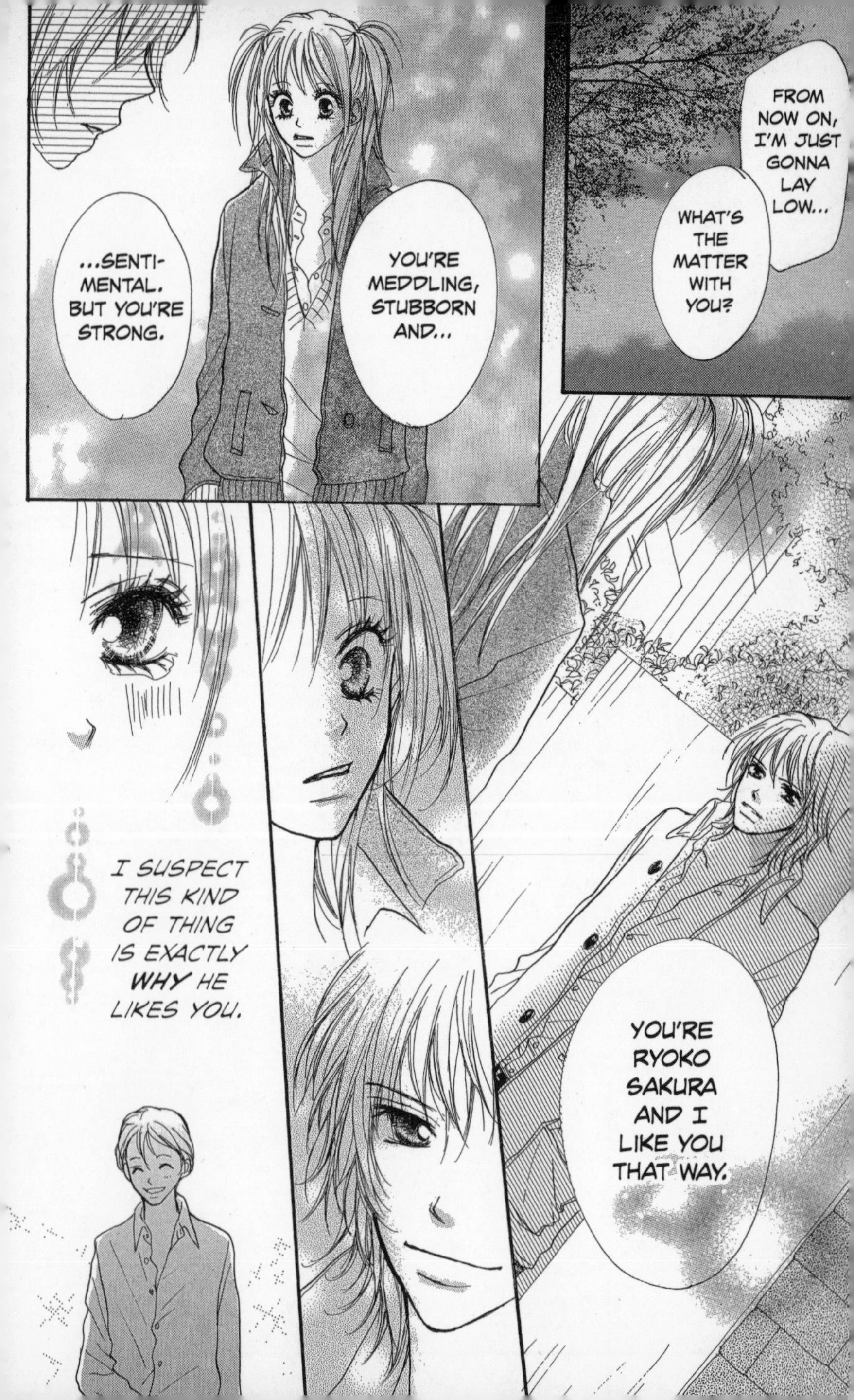
FROM NOW ON, I'M JUST GONNA LAY LOW...
WHAT'S THE MATTER WITH YOU?
YOU'RE MEDDLING, STUBBORN AND...
...SENTI-MENTAL. BUT YOU'RE STRONG.
YOU'RE RYOKO SAKURA AND I LIKE YOU THAT WAY.
I SUSPECT THIS KIND OF THING IS EXACTLY WHY HE LIKES YOU.

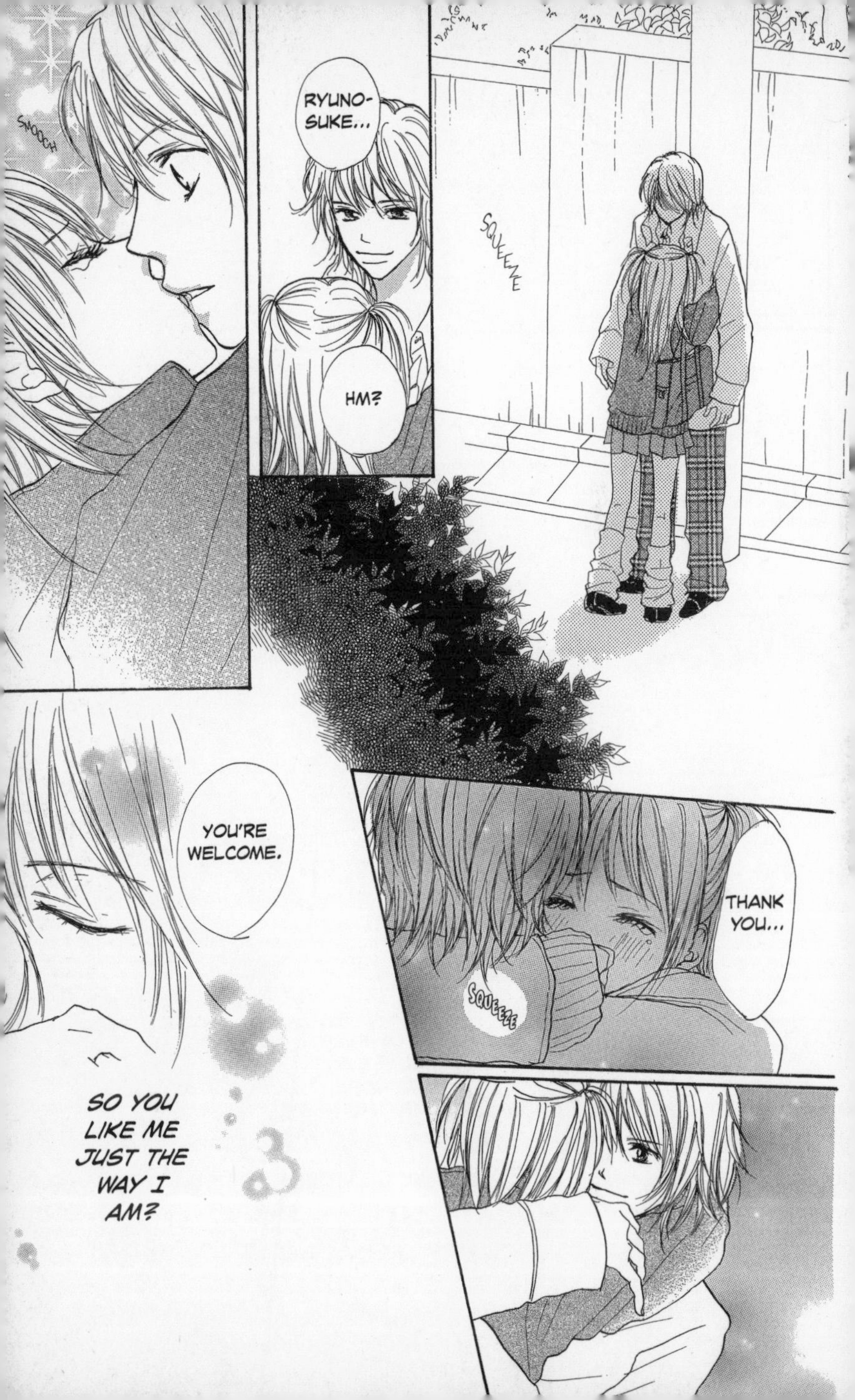
SQUEEZE
RYUNO-SUKE...
HM?
SMOOCH
THANK YOU...
SQUEEZE
YOU'RE WELCOME.
SO YOU LIKE ME JUST THE WAY I AM?

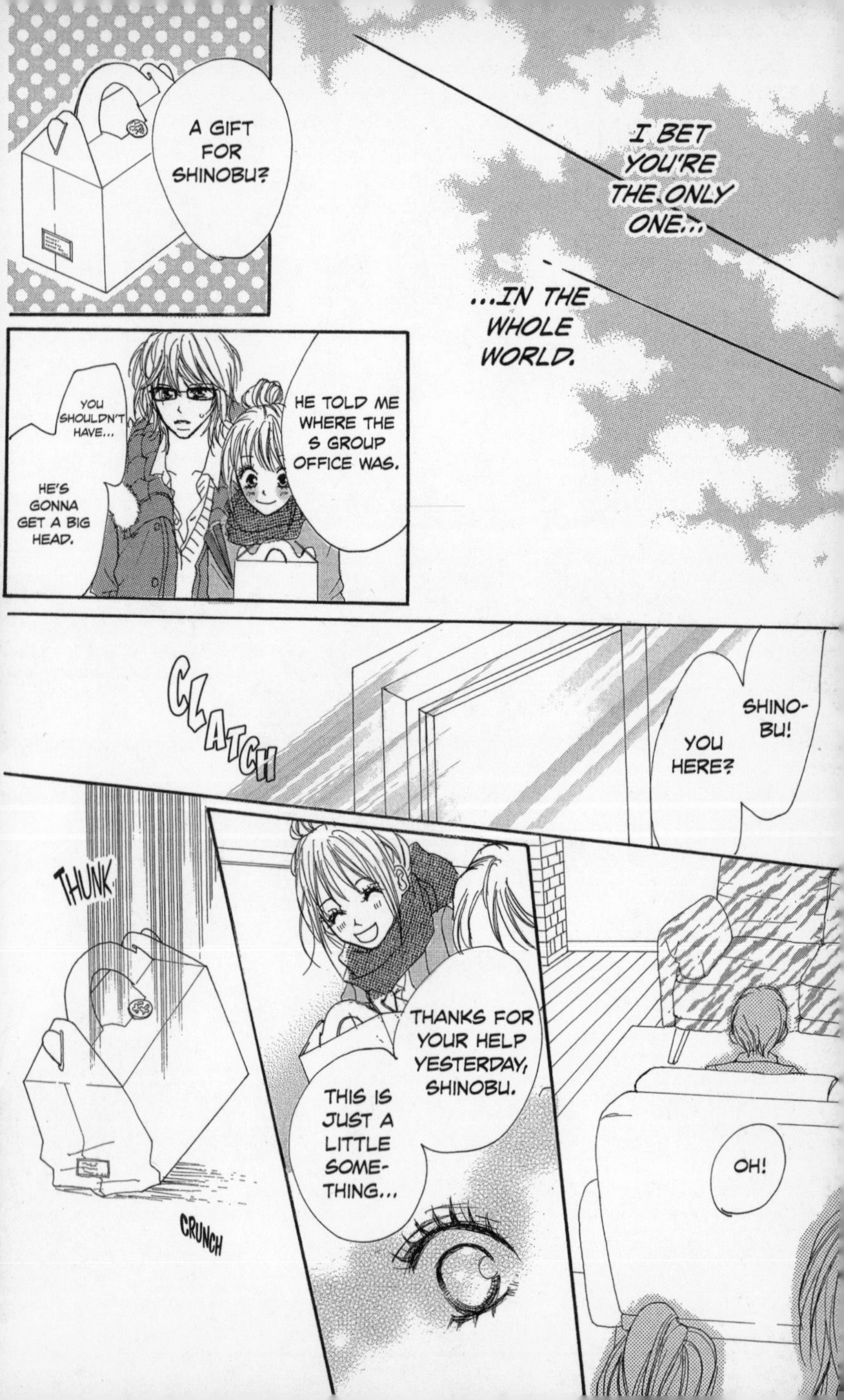
I BET YOU'RE THE ONLY ONE...
...IN THE WHOLE WORLD.
A GIFT FOR SHINOBU?
HE TOLD ME WHERE THE S GROUP OFFICE WAS.
YOU SHOULDN'T HAVE...
HE'S GONNA GET A BIG HEAD.
SHINO-BU!
YOU HERE?
CLATCH
OH!
THANKS FOR YOUR HELP YESTERDAY, SHINOBU.
THIS IS JUST A LITTLE SOME-THING...
THUNK
CRUNCH

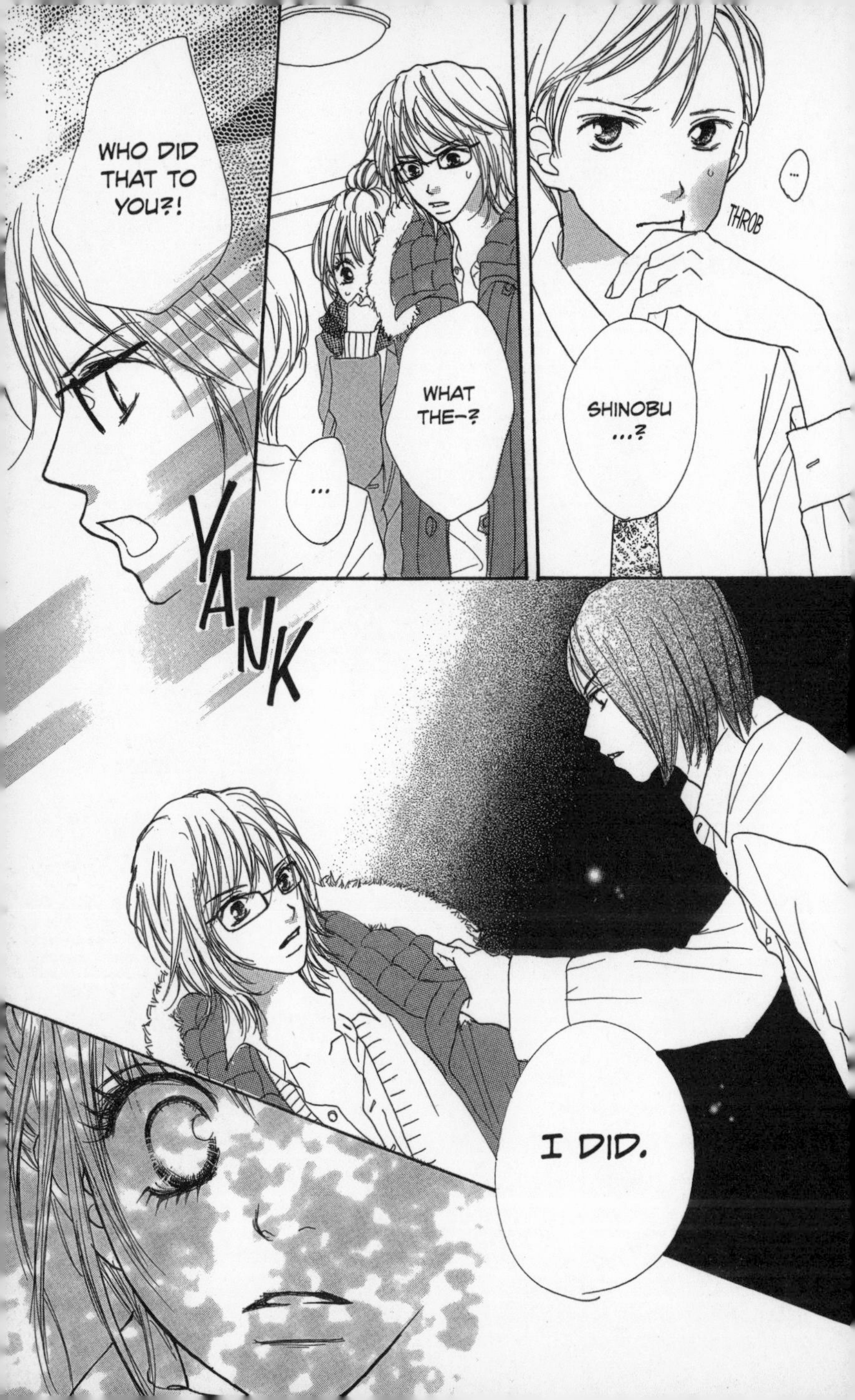
...
THROB
SHINOBU ...?
WHAT THE-?
...
WHO DID THAT TO YOU?!
YANK
I DID.

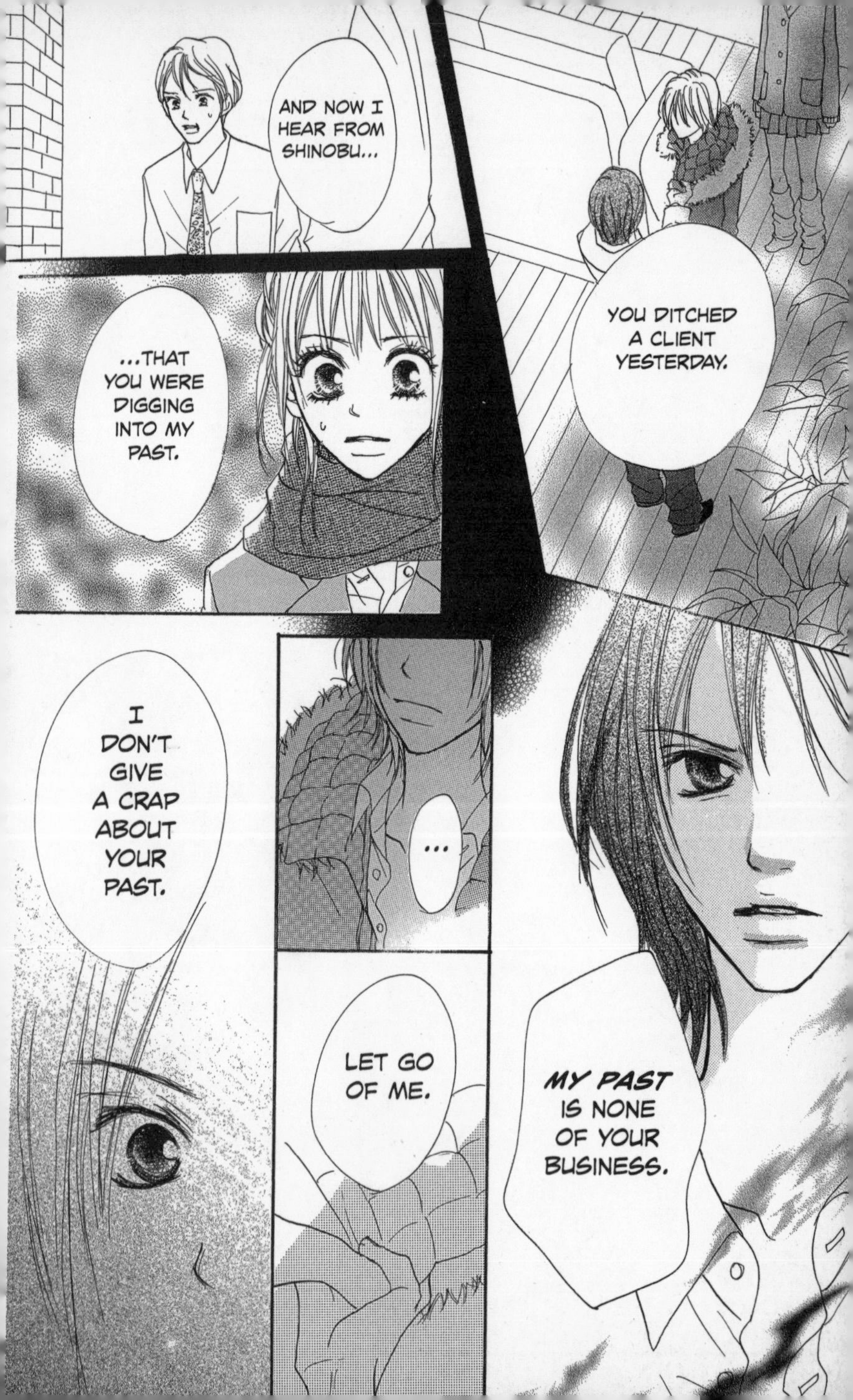
YOU DITCHED A CLIENT YESTERDAY.
AND NOW I HEAR FROM SHINOBU...
...THAT YOU WERE DIGGING INTO MY PAST.
MY PAST IS NONE OF YOUR BUSINESS.
...
LET GO OF ME.
I DON'T GIVE A CRAP ABOUT YOUR PAST.

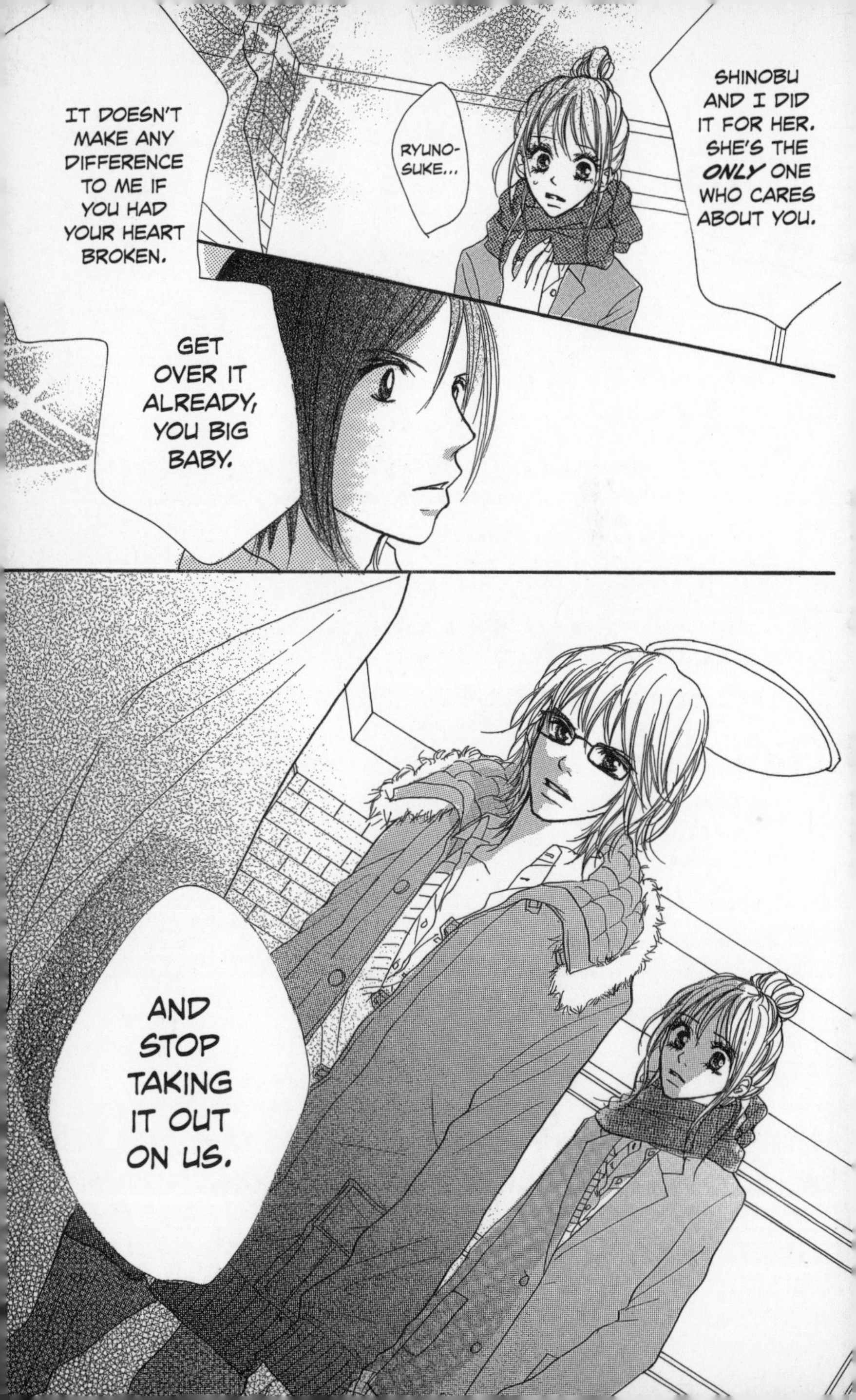
SHINOBU AND I DID IT FOR HER. SHE'S THE ***ONLY*** ONE WHO CARES ABOUT YOU.
RYUNO-SUKE...
IT DOESN'T MAKE ANY DIFFERENCE TO ME IF YOU HAD YOUR HEART BROKEN.
GET OVER IT ALREADY, YOU BIG BABY.
AND STOP TAKING IT OUT ON US.

Thank You For Your Letters

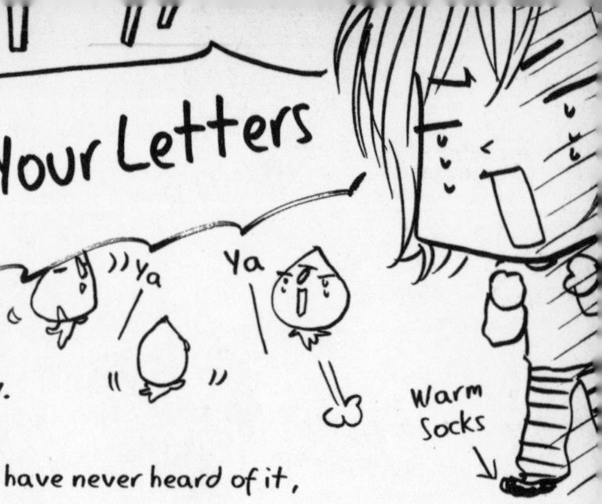
Ya
Ya
Warm Socks

I'd like to share a few.

■ Most of my friends say they have never heard of it, but I love *B.O.D.Y.*!

Great...thanks for telling me no one's heard of my book. Like I wasn't bummed out enough already... I'm just kidding, I'm kidding!!

□ Your manga is more dear to me than life itself.

I'm pretty sure that's not healthy...

■ I especially look forward to your sketch pages. Why are manga artists so weird?

...Me? Weird? Am I really?

□ When my store was sold out of Volume 2, I almost went on a rampage!

Calm down!!! That's not your bookseller's fault! I should work harder so they'll stock more of my books!

One of you read in Volume 2 that I liked Umagon and you sent me a *Zatch Bell* doll! I can't express how grateful I am to have received so many happy, fun letters!! Keep 'em coming!! Please forgive me for not being able to respond to them all...

Address

Ao Mimori, B.O.D.Y. Office
c/o Viz Media, LLC
PO Box 77010
San Francisco, CA 94107

Ao Mimori

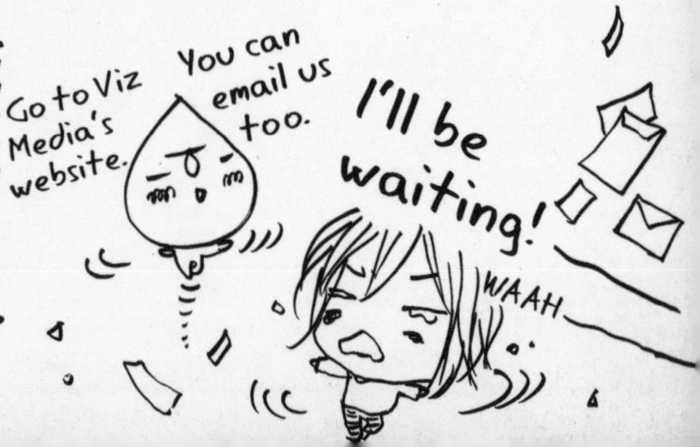
Go to Viz Media's website.
You can email us too.
I'll be waiting!
WAAH

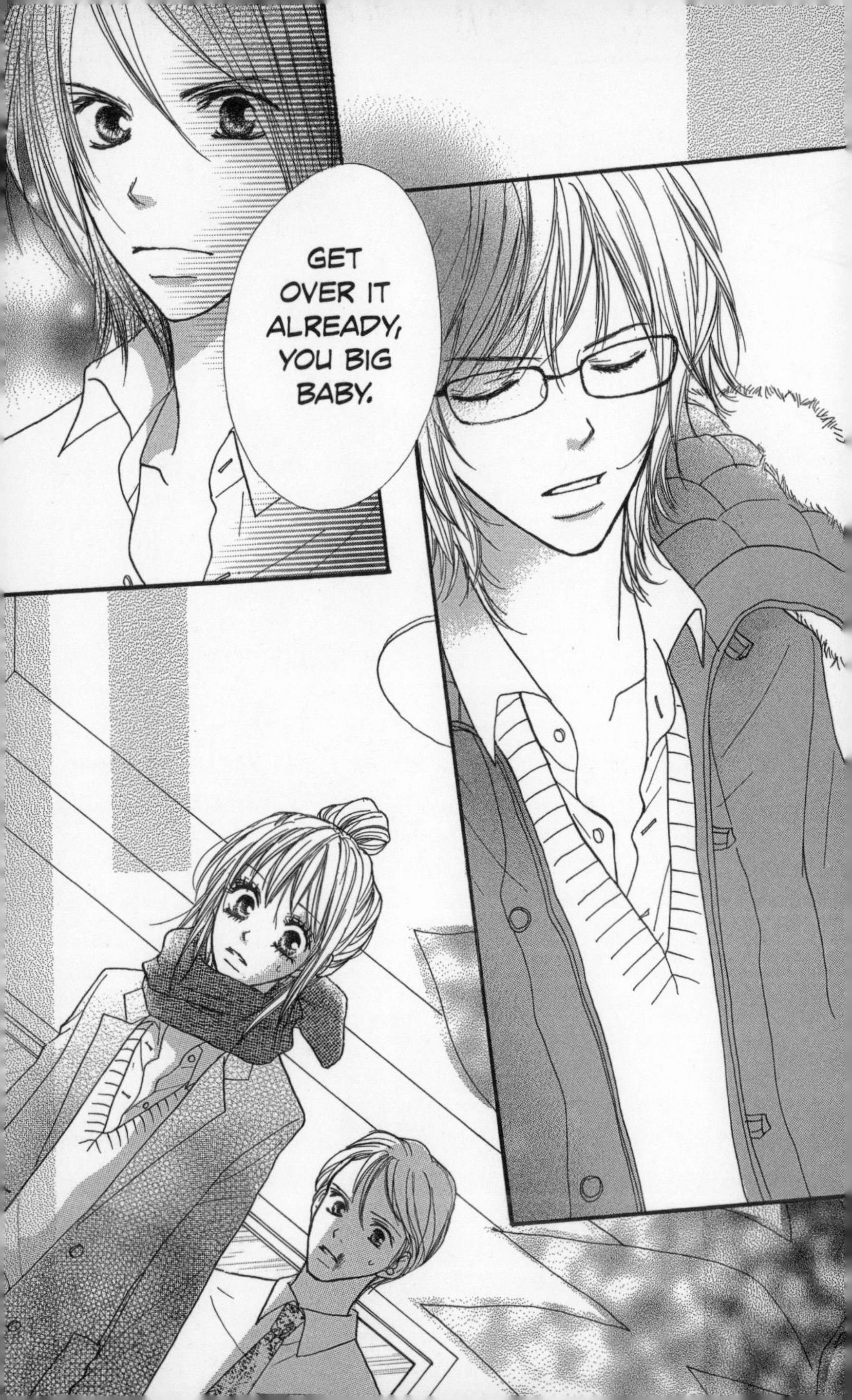
GET OVER IT ALREADY, YOU BIG BABY.

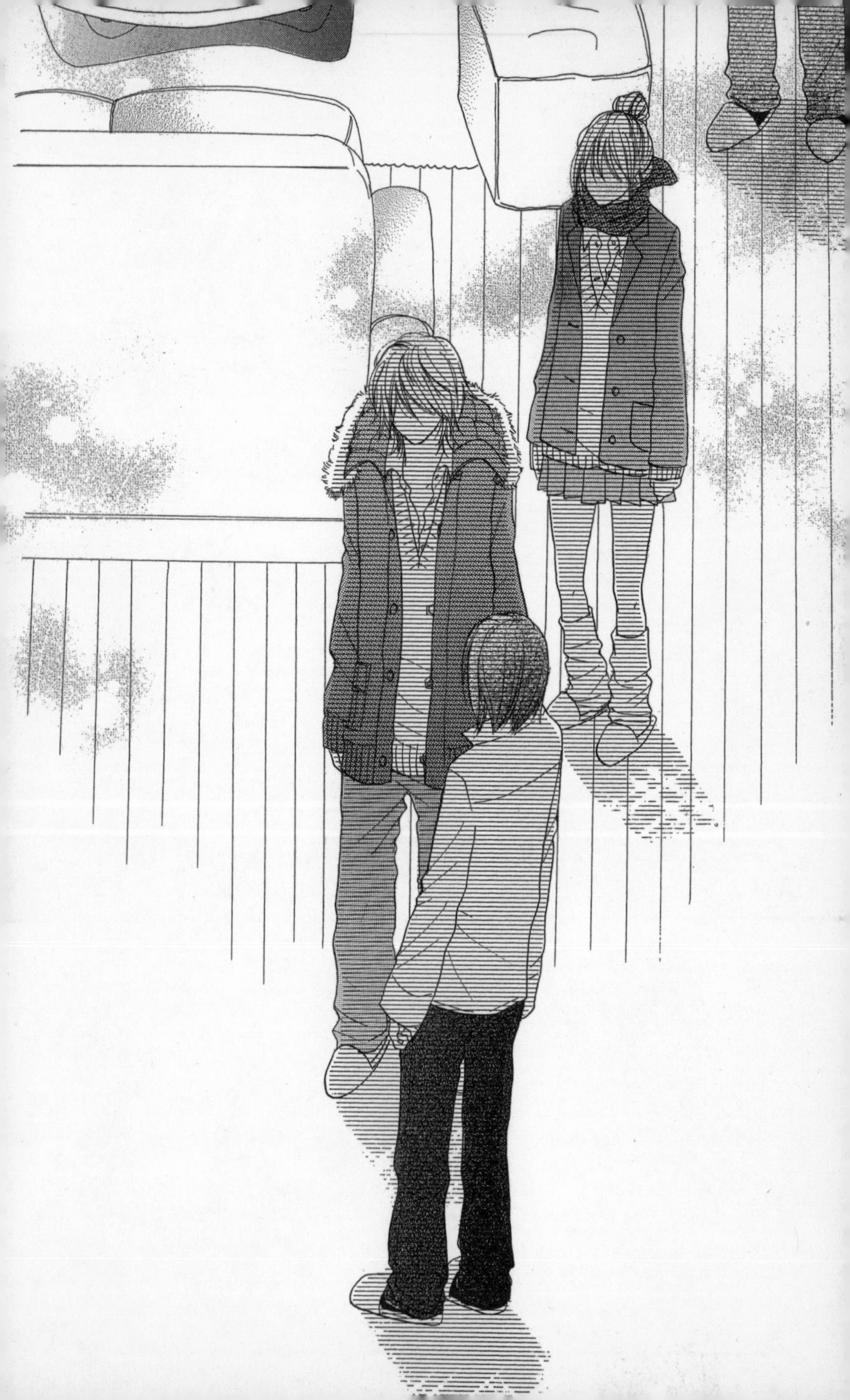

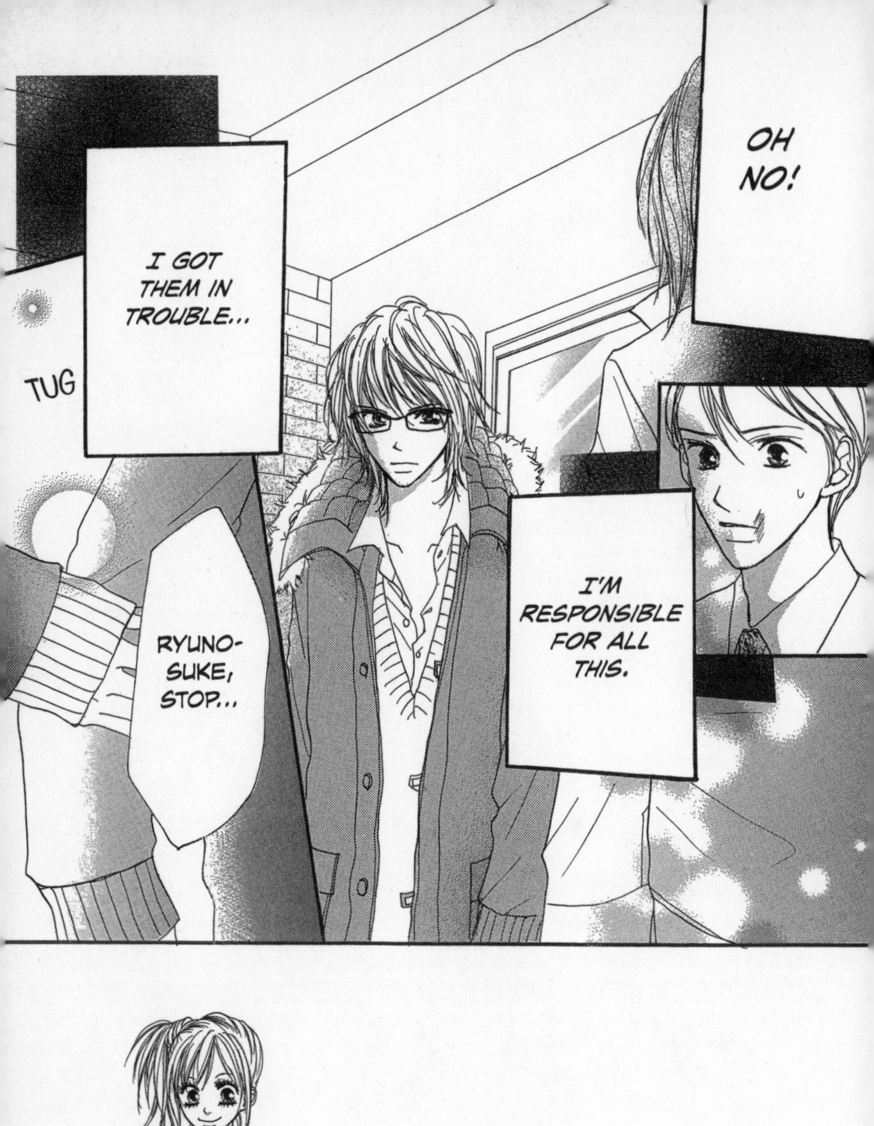
OH NO!
I GOT THEM IN TROUBLE...
I'M RESPONSIBLE FOR ALL THIS.
TUG
RYUNO-SUKE, STOP...

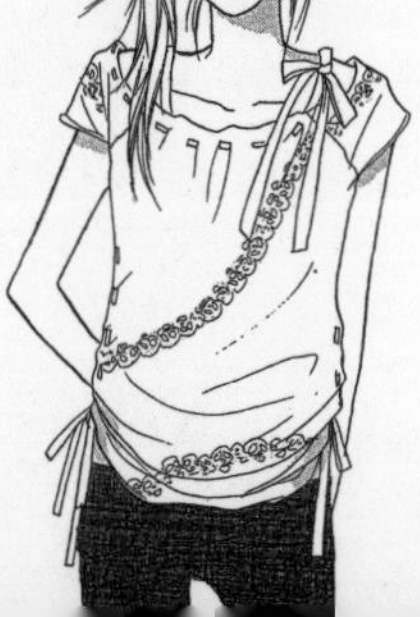

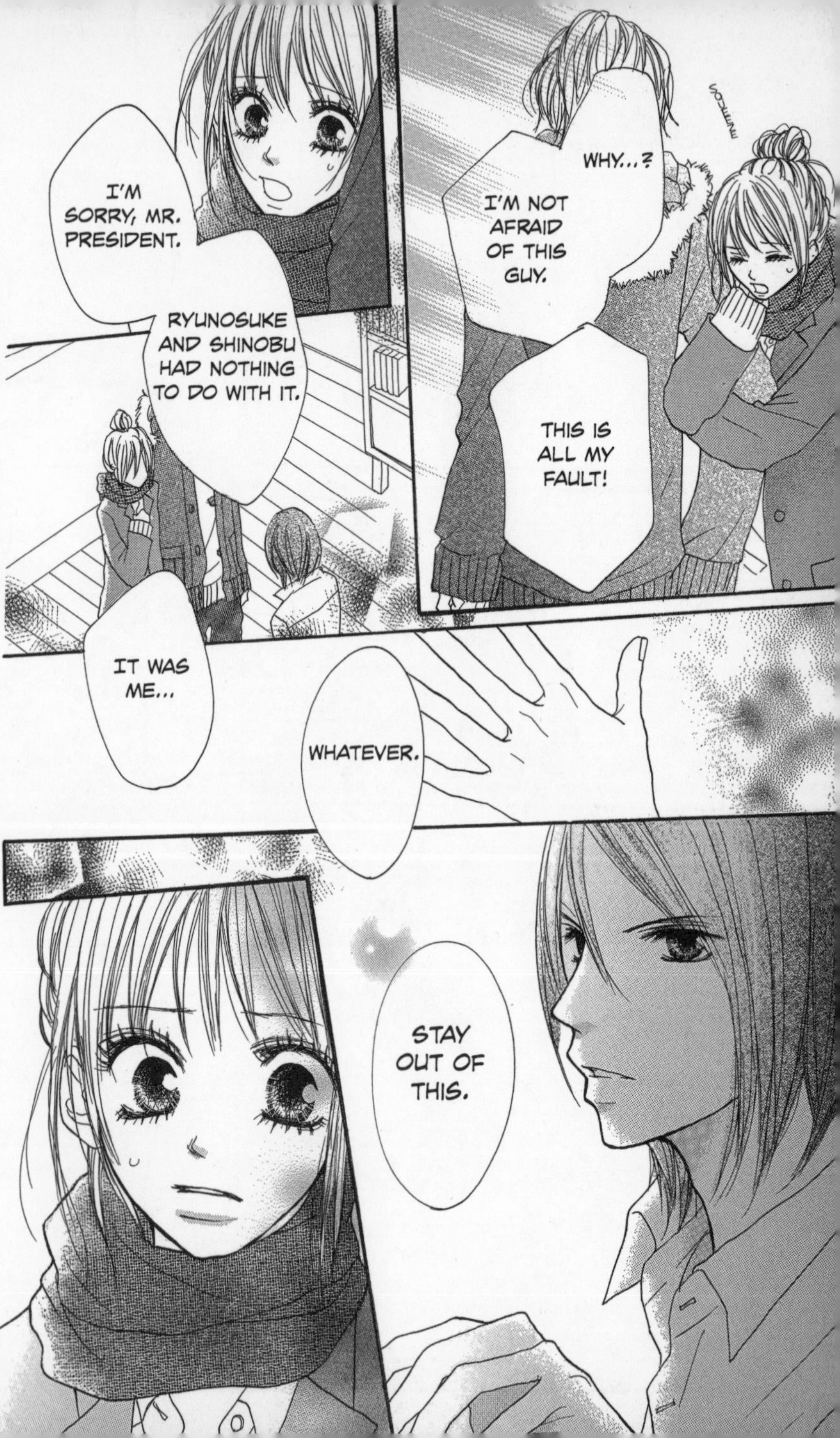
SQUEEZE
WHY...?
I'M NOT AFRAID OF THIS GUY.
THIS IS ALL MY FAULT!
I'M SORRY, MR. PRESIDENT.
RYUNOSUKE AND SHINOBU HAD NOTHING TO DO WITH IT.
IT WAS ME...
WHATEVER.
STAY OUT OF THIS.

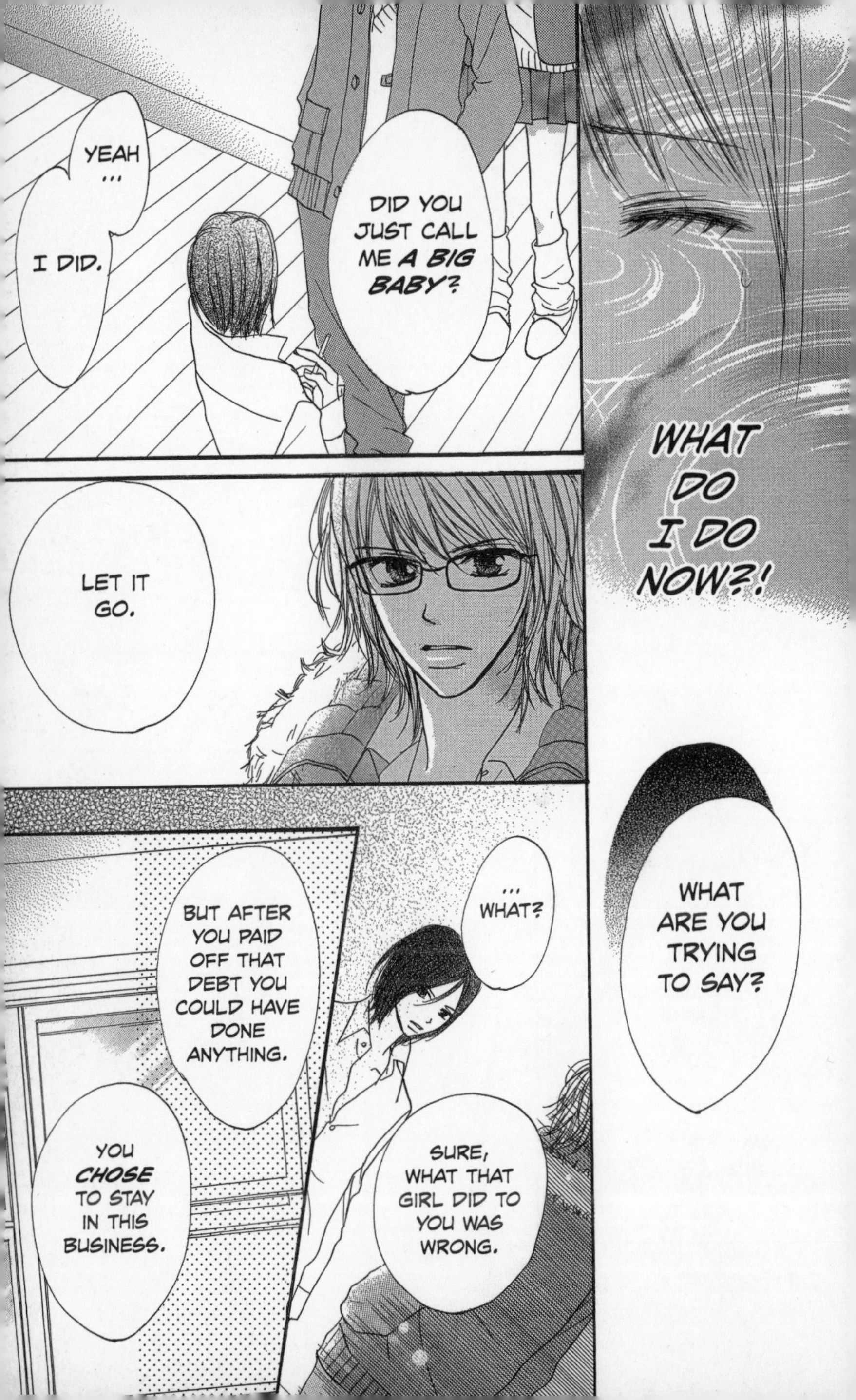

WHAT DO I DO NOW?!
DID YOU JUST CALL ME *A BIG BABY*?
YEAH... I DID.
LET IT GO.
WHAT ARE YOU TRYING TO SAY?
...WHAT?
SURE, WHAT THAT GIRL DID TO YOU WAS WRONG.
BUT AFTER YOU PAID OFF THAT DEBT YOU COULD HAVE DONE ANYTHING.
YOU *CHOSE* TO STAY IN THIS BUSINESS.

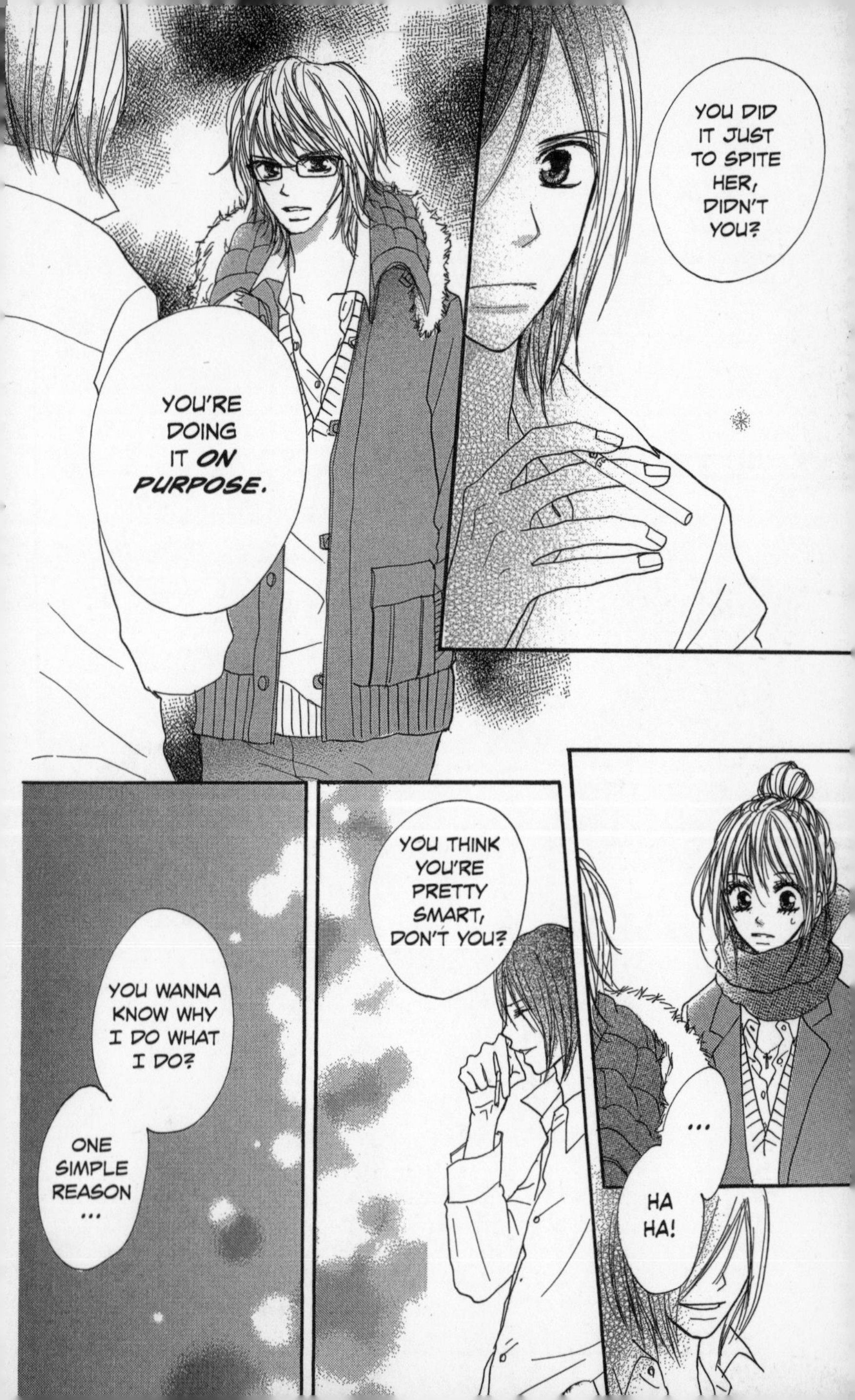
YOU DID IT JUST TO SPITE HER, DIDN'T YOU?
YOU'RE DOING IT *ON PURPOSE.*
...
HA HA!
YOU THINK YOU'RE PRETTY SMART, DON'T YOU?
YOU WANNA KNOW WHY I DO WHAT I DO?
ONE SIMPLE REASON...

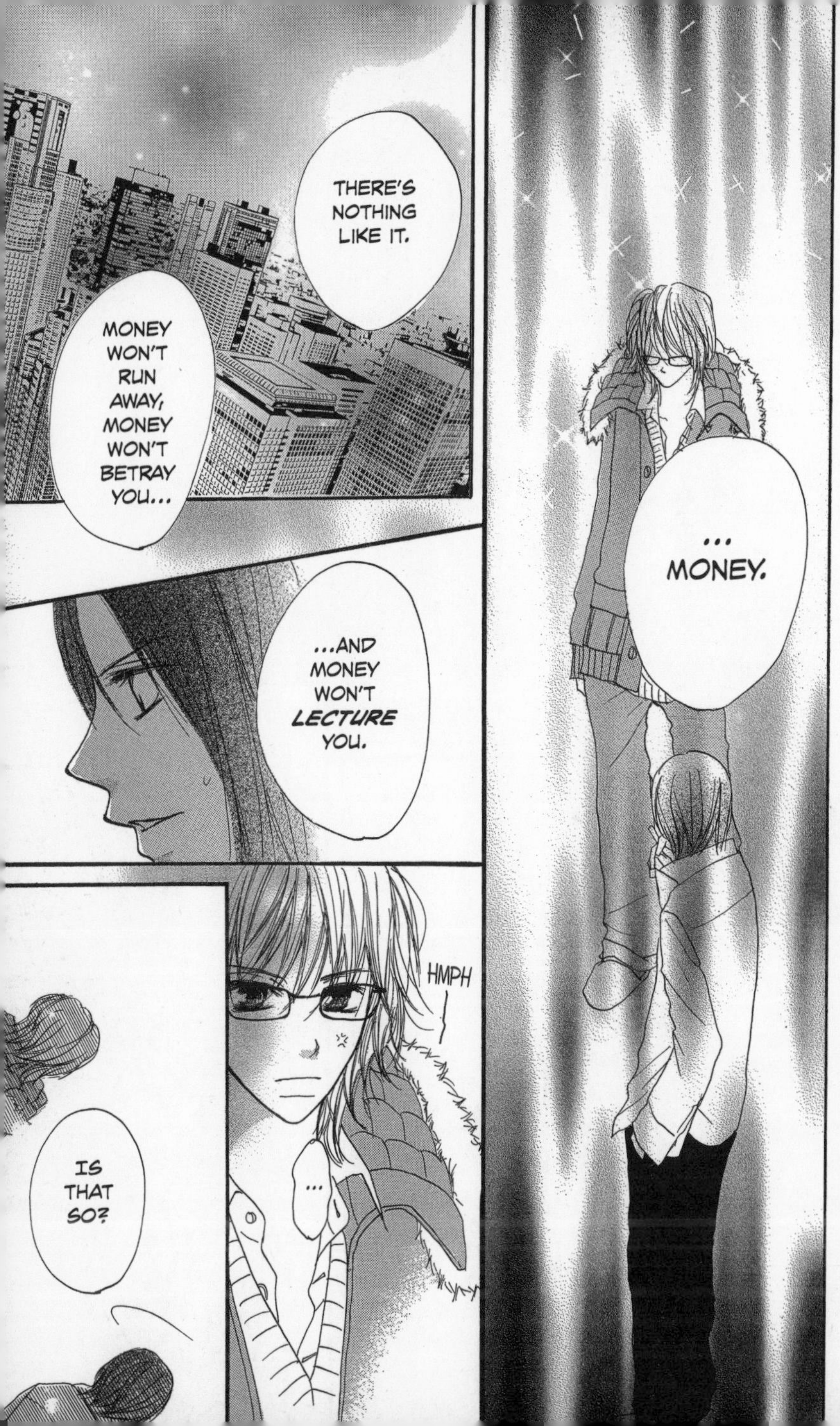

... MONEY.
THERE'S NOTHING LIKE IT.
MONEY WON'T RUN AWAY, MONEY WON'T BETRAY YOU...
...AND MONEY WON'T *LECTURE* YOU.
HMPH
...
IS THAT SO?

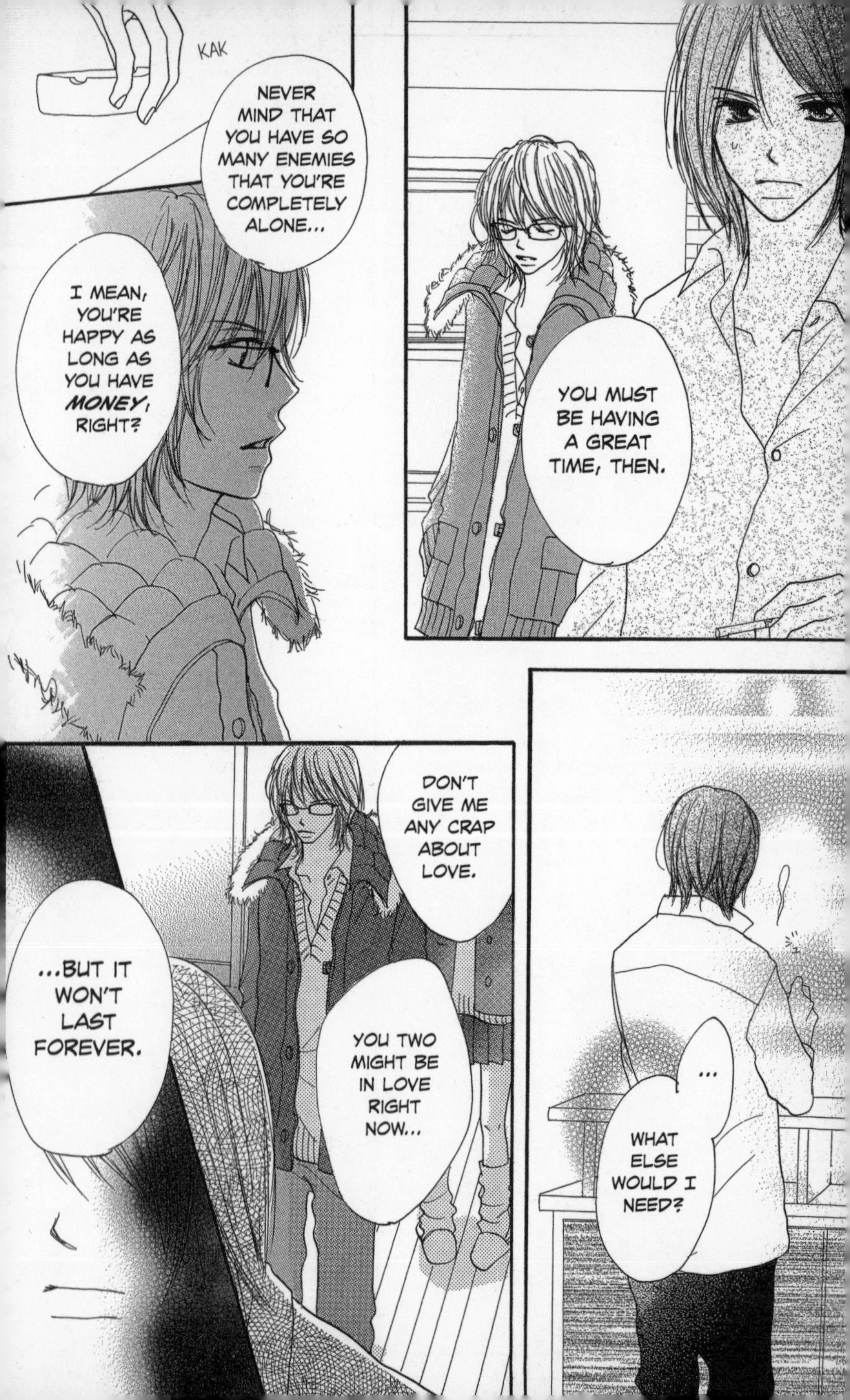
YOU MUST BE HAVING A GREAT TIME, THEN.
KAK
NEVER MIND THAT YOU HAVE SO MANY ENEMIES THAT YOU'RE COMPLETELY ALONE...
I MEAN, YOU'RE HAPPY AS LONG AS YOU HAVE *MONEY*, RIGHT?
...
WHAT ELSE WOULD I NEED?
DON'T GIVE ME ANY CRAP ABOUT LOVE.
YOU TWO MIGHT BE IN LOVE RIGHT NOW...
...BUT IT WON'T LAST FOREVER.

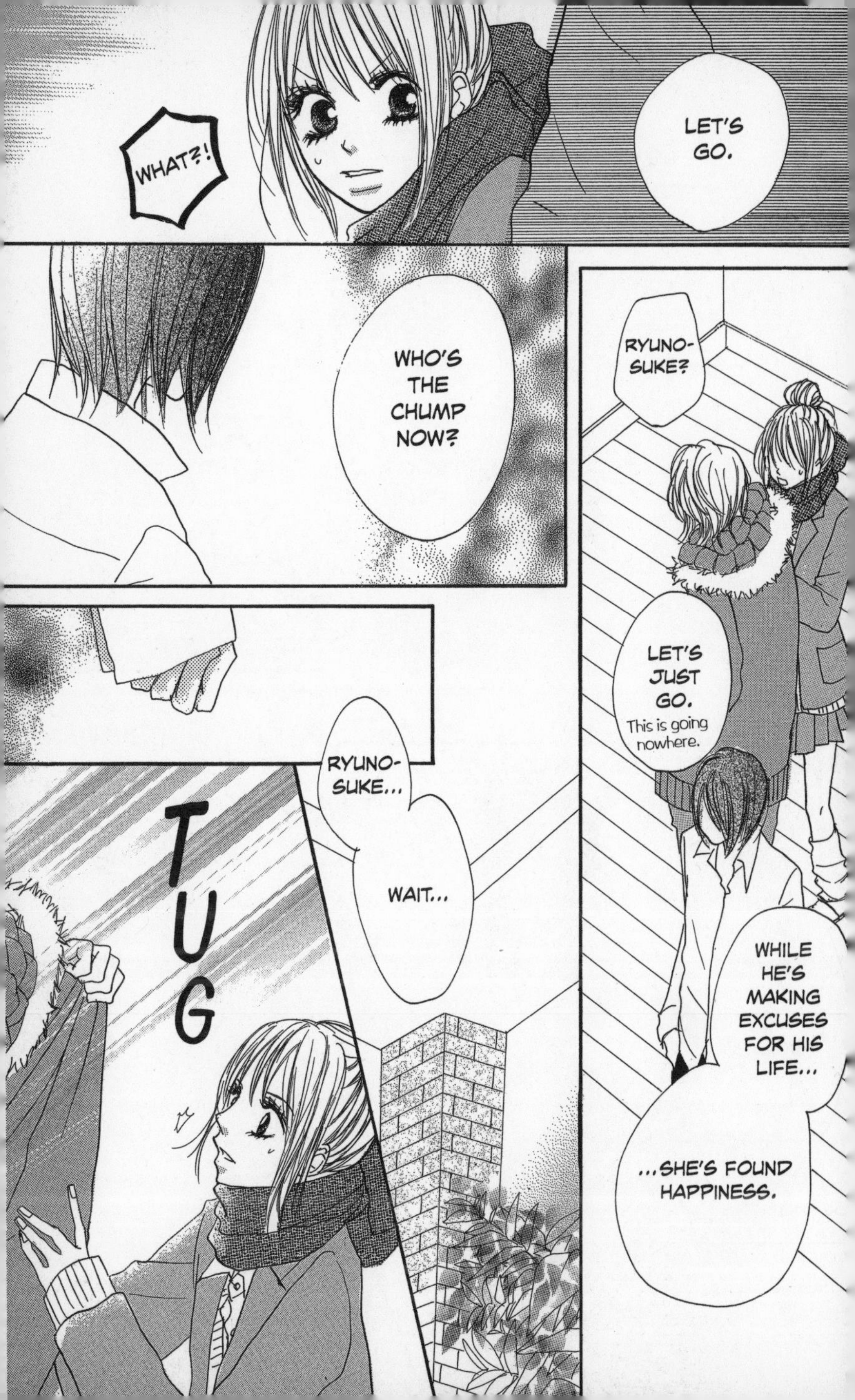
LET'S GO.
WHAT?!
RYUNO-SUKE?
LET'S JUST GO.
This is going nowhere.
WHILE HE'S MAKING EXCUSES FOR HIS LIFE...
...SHE'S FOUND HAPPINESS.
WHO'S THE CHUMP NOW?
RYUNO-SUKE...
WAIT...
TUG

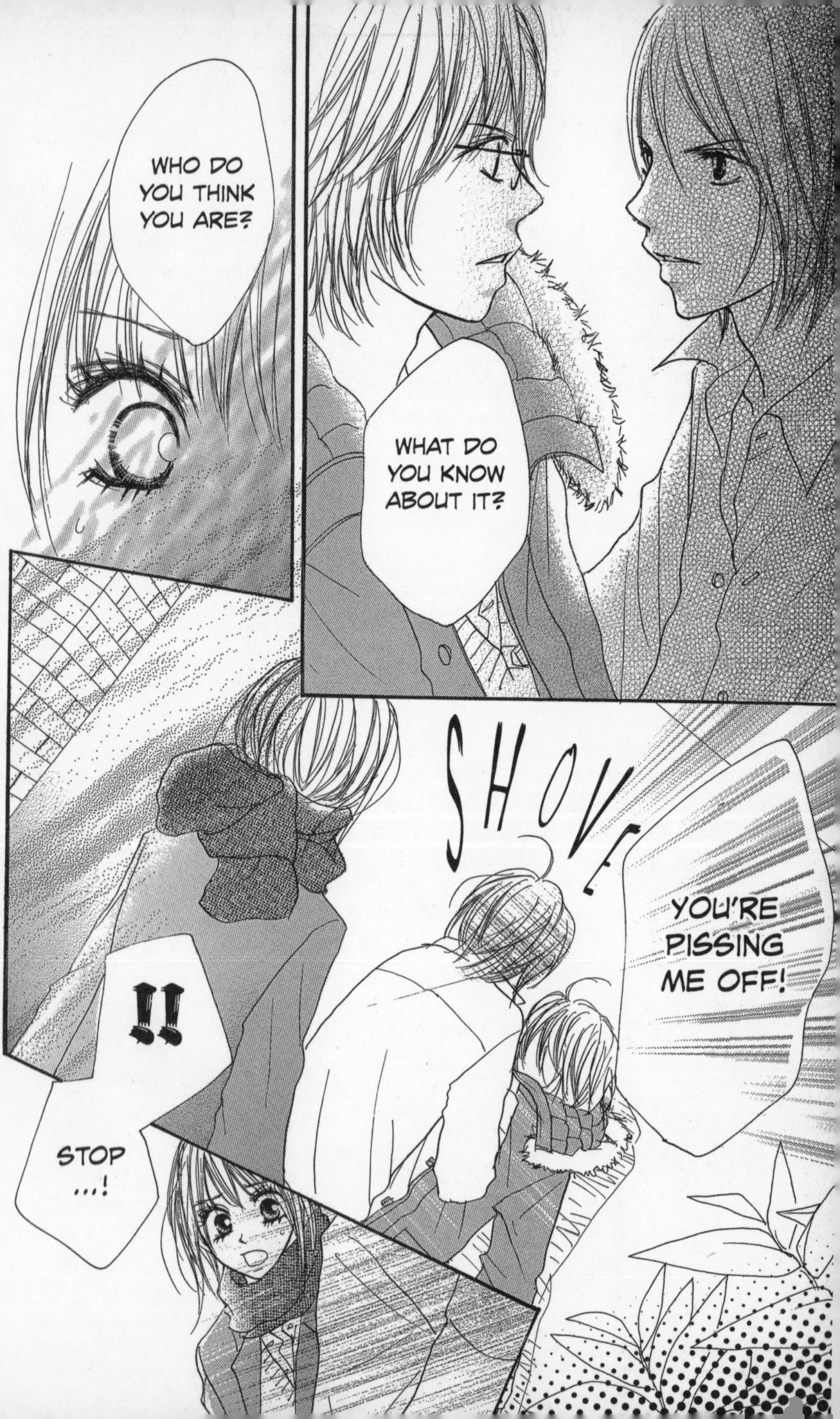
WHAT DO YOU KNOW ABOUT IT?
WHO DO YOU THINK YOU ARE?
SHOVE
YOU'RE PISSING ME OFF!
!!
STOP ...!

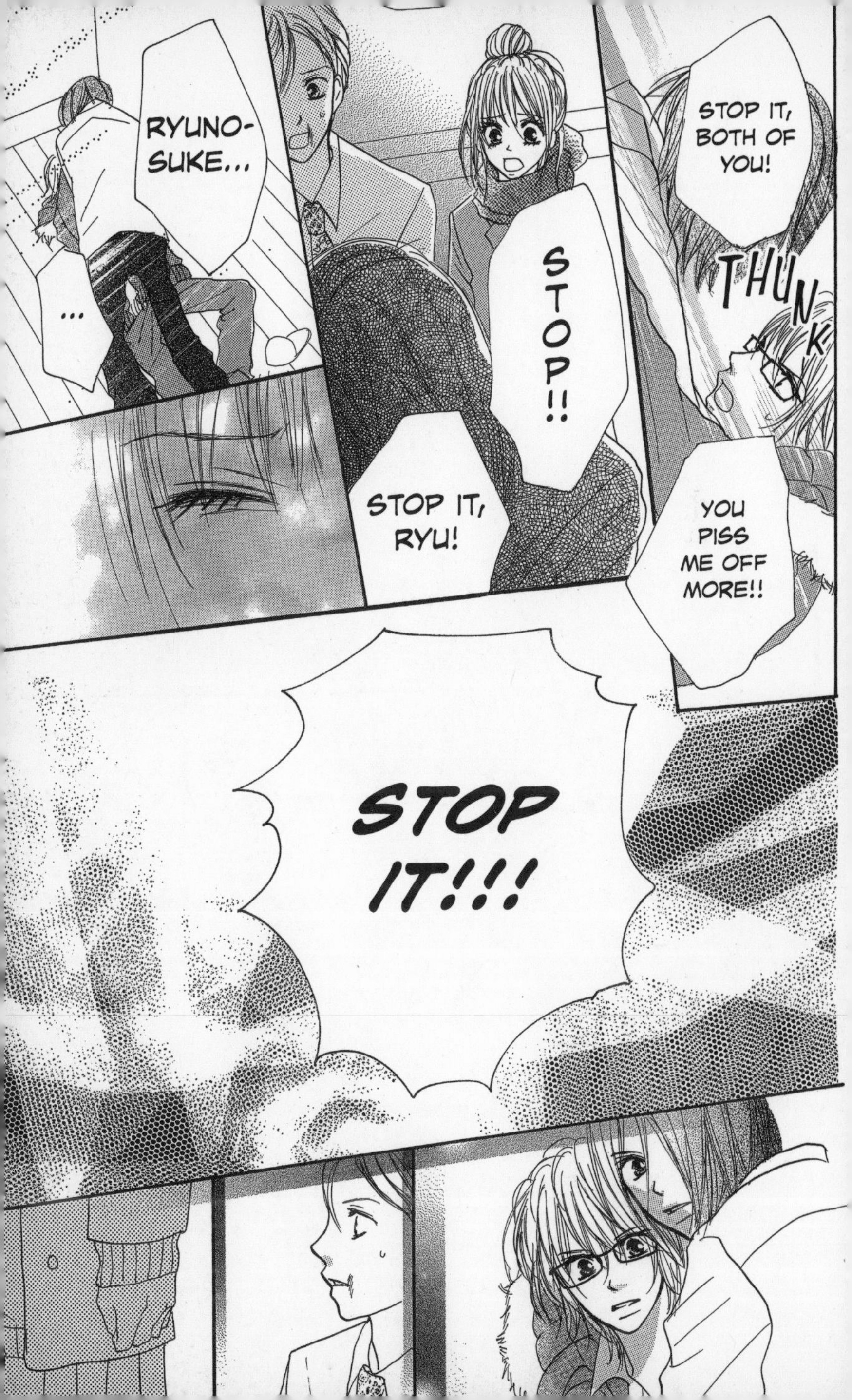
STOP IT, BOTH OF YOU!
THUNK
YOU PISS ME OFF MORE!!
STOP!!
STOP IT, RYU!
RYUNO-SUKE...
...
STOP IT!!!

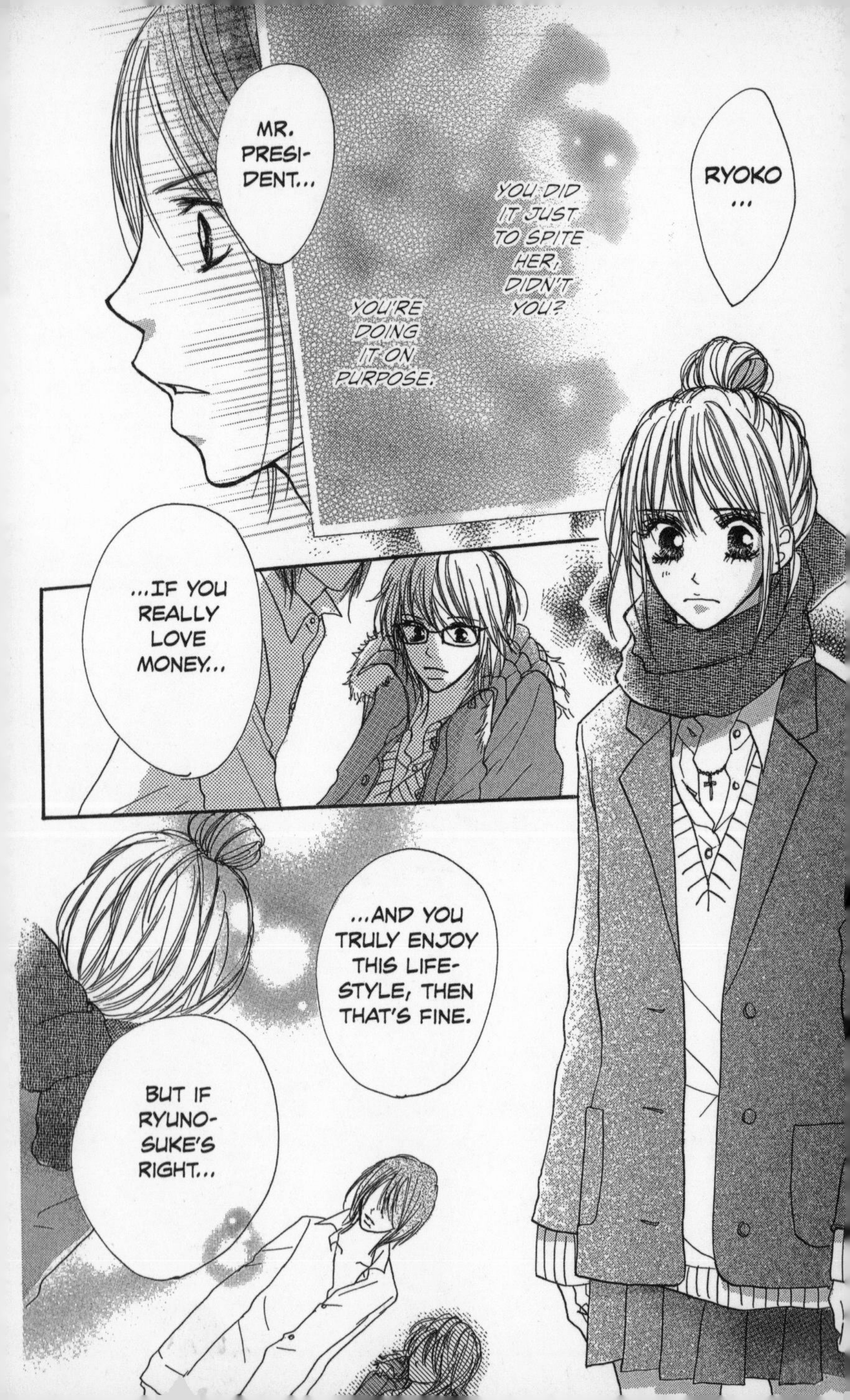
RYOKO...
YOU DID IT JUST TO SPITE HER, DIDN'T YOU?
YOU'RE DOING IT ON PURPOSE.
MR. PRESI-DENT...
...IF YOU REALLY LOVE MONEY...
...AND YOU TRULY ENJOY THIS LIFE-STYLE, THEN THAT'S FINE.
BUT IF RYUNO-SUKE'S RIGHT...

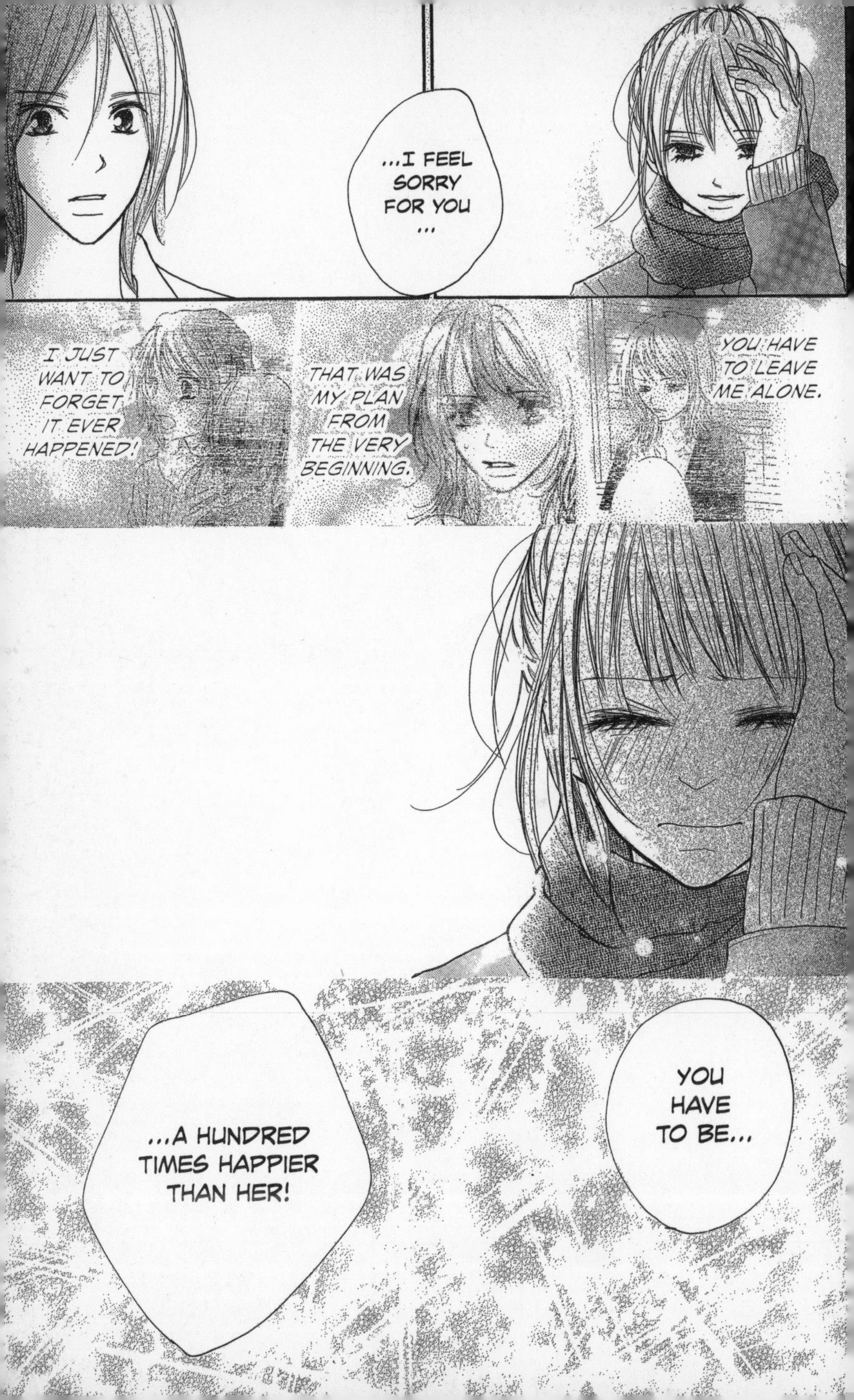
...I FEEL SORRY FOR YOU ...
YOU HAVE TO LEAVE ME ALONE.
THAT WAS MY PLAN FROM THE VERY BEGINNING.
I JUST WANT TO FORGET IT EVER HAPPENED!
YOU HAVE TO BE...
...A HUNDRED TIMES HAPPIER THAN HER!

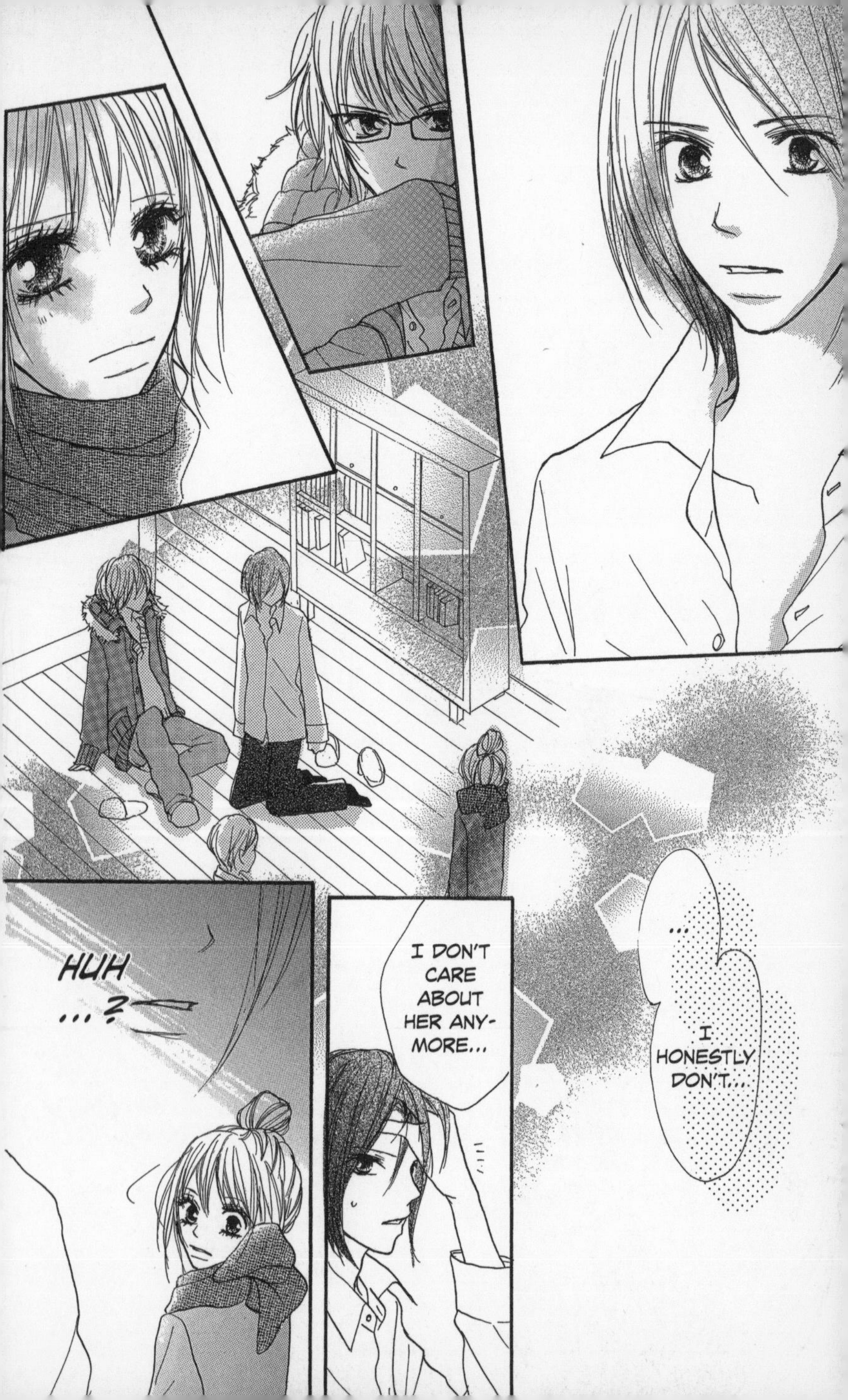
...
I HONESTLY DON'T...
I DON'T CARE ABOUT HER ANYMORE...
HUH ...?

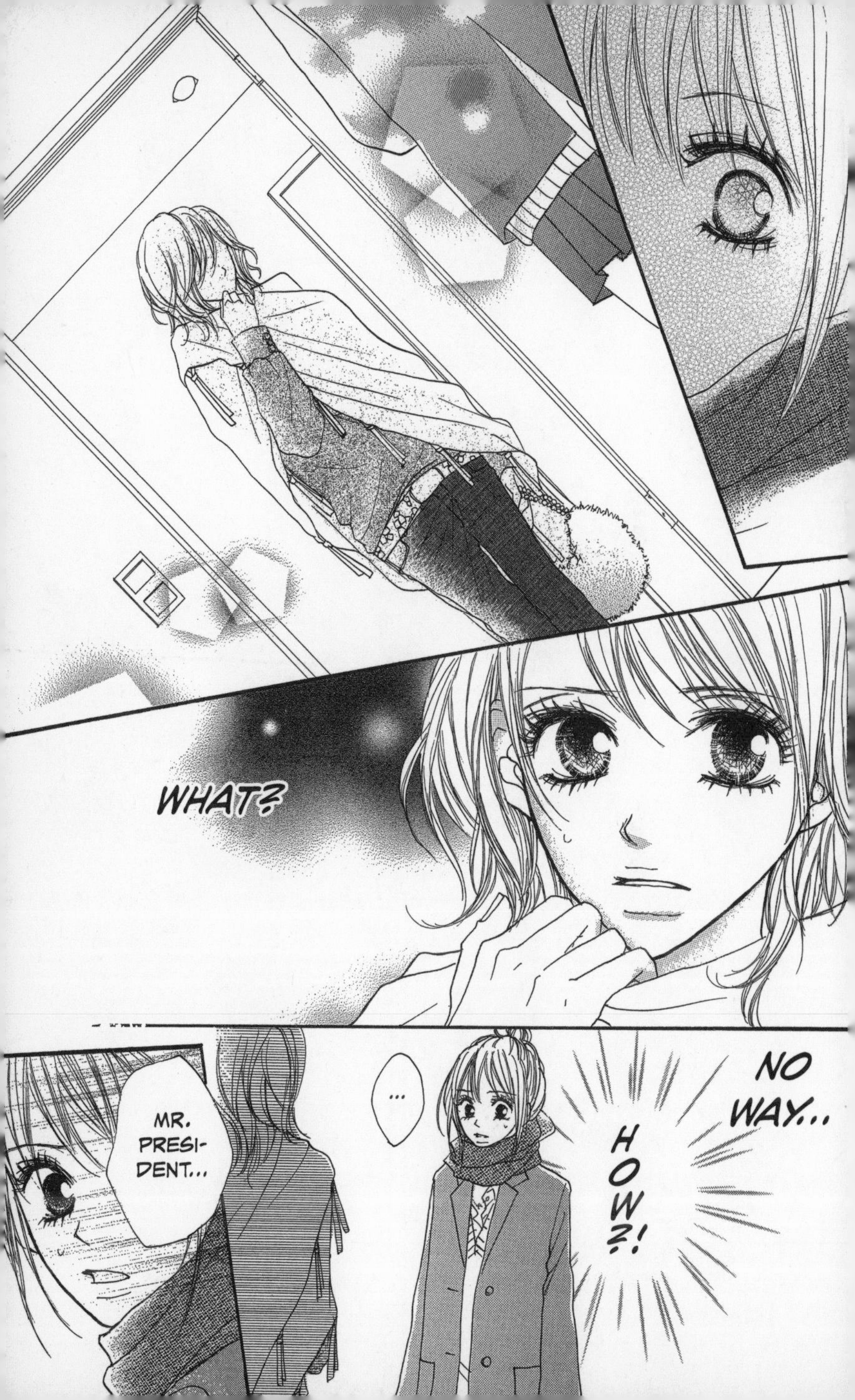
WHAT?
NO WAY...
HOW?!
...
MR. PRESIDENT...

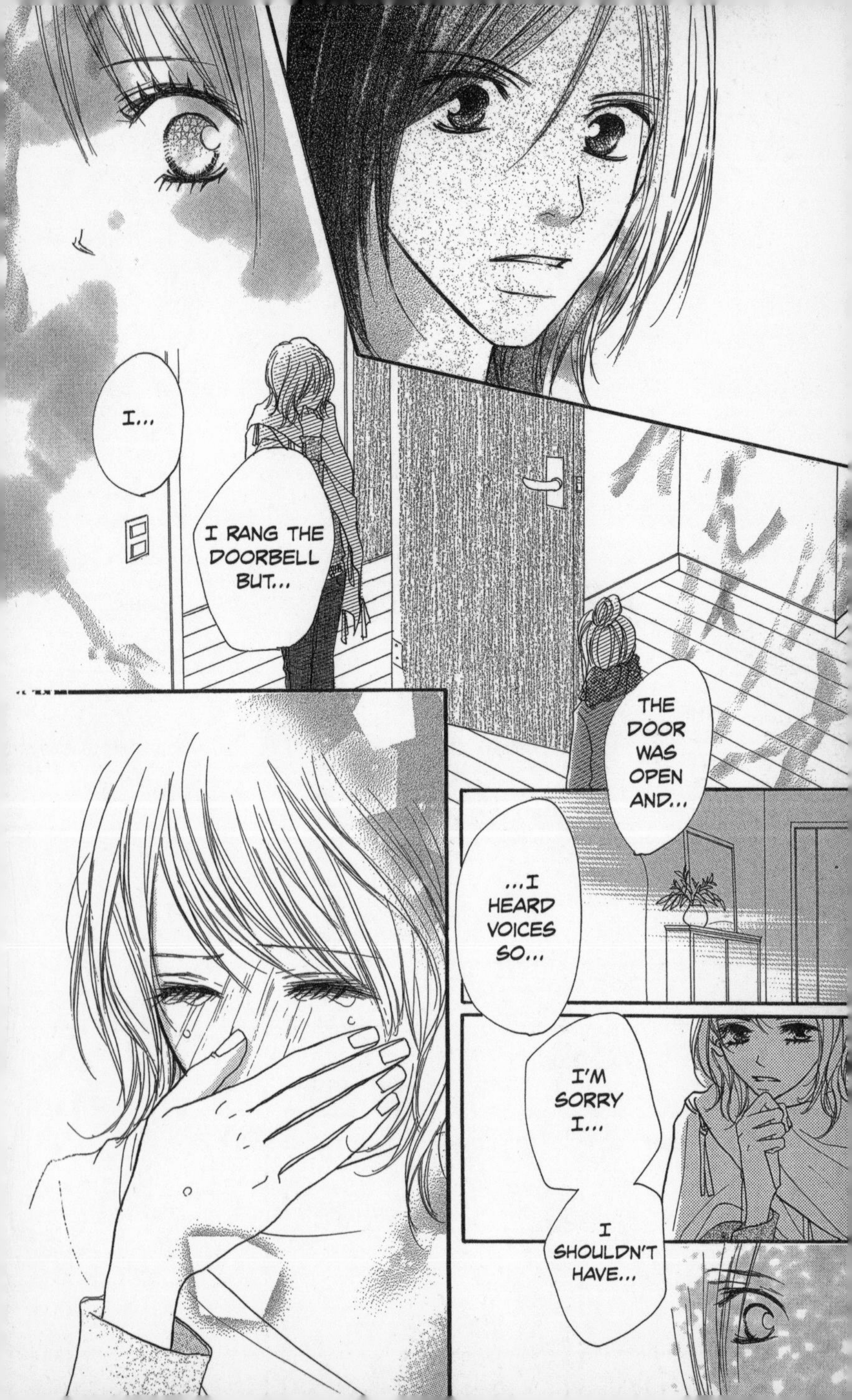
I...
I RANG THE DOORBELL BUT...
THE DOOR WAS OPEN AND...
...I HEARD VOICES SO...
I'M SORRY I...
I SHOULDN'T HAVE...

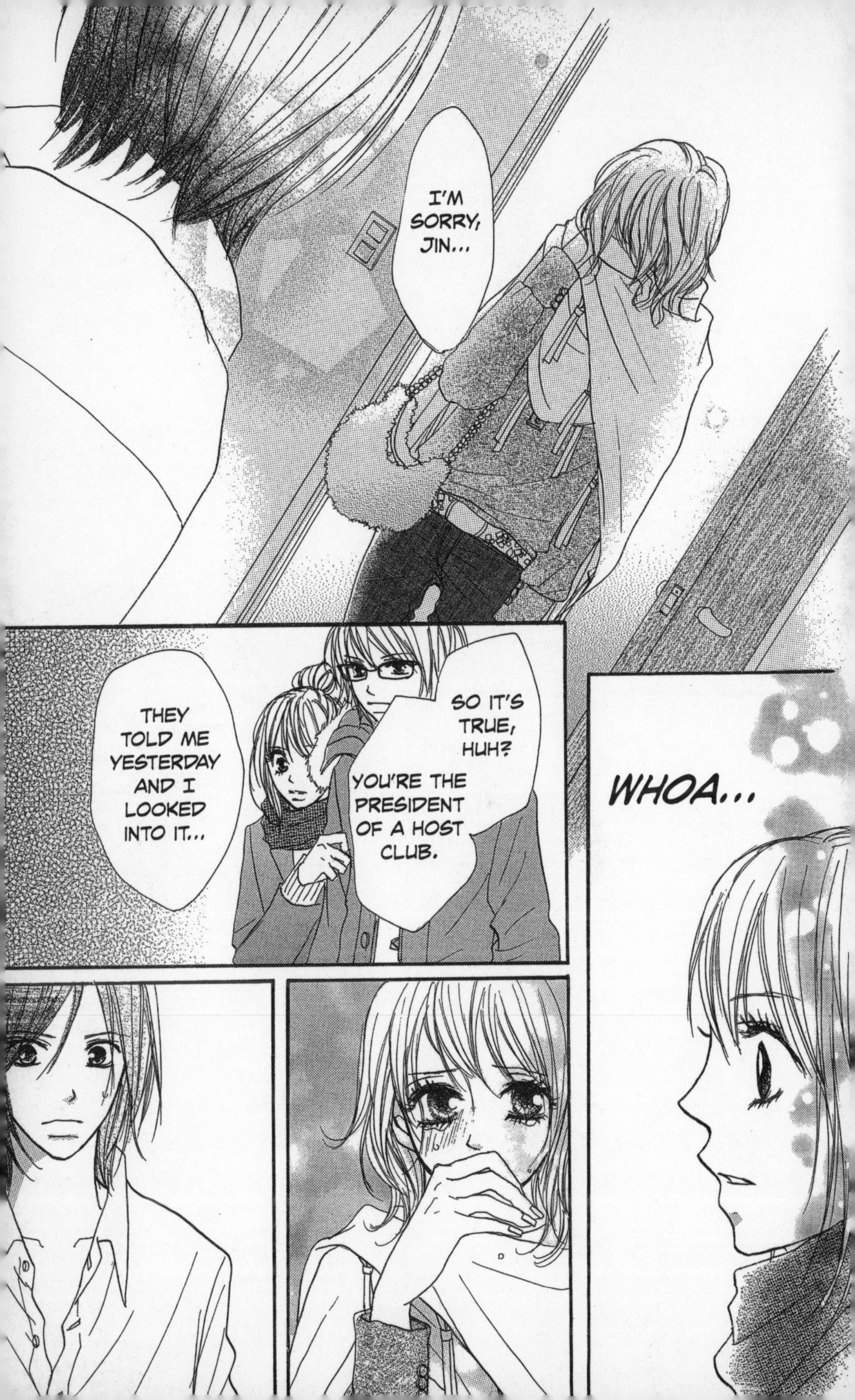
I'M SORRY, JIN...
WHOA...
SO IT'S TRUE, HUH?
YOU'RE THE PRESIDENT OF A HOST CLUB.
THEY TOLD ME YESTERDAY AND I LOOKED INTO IT...

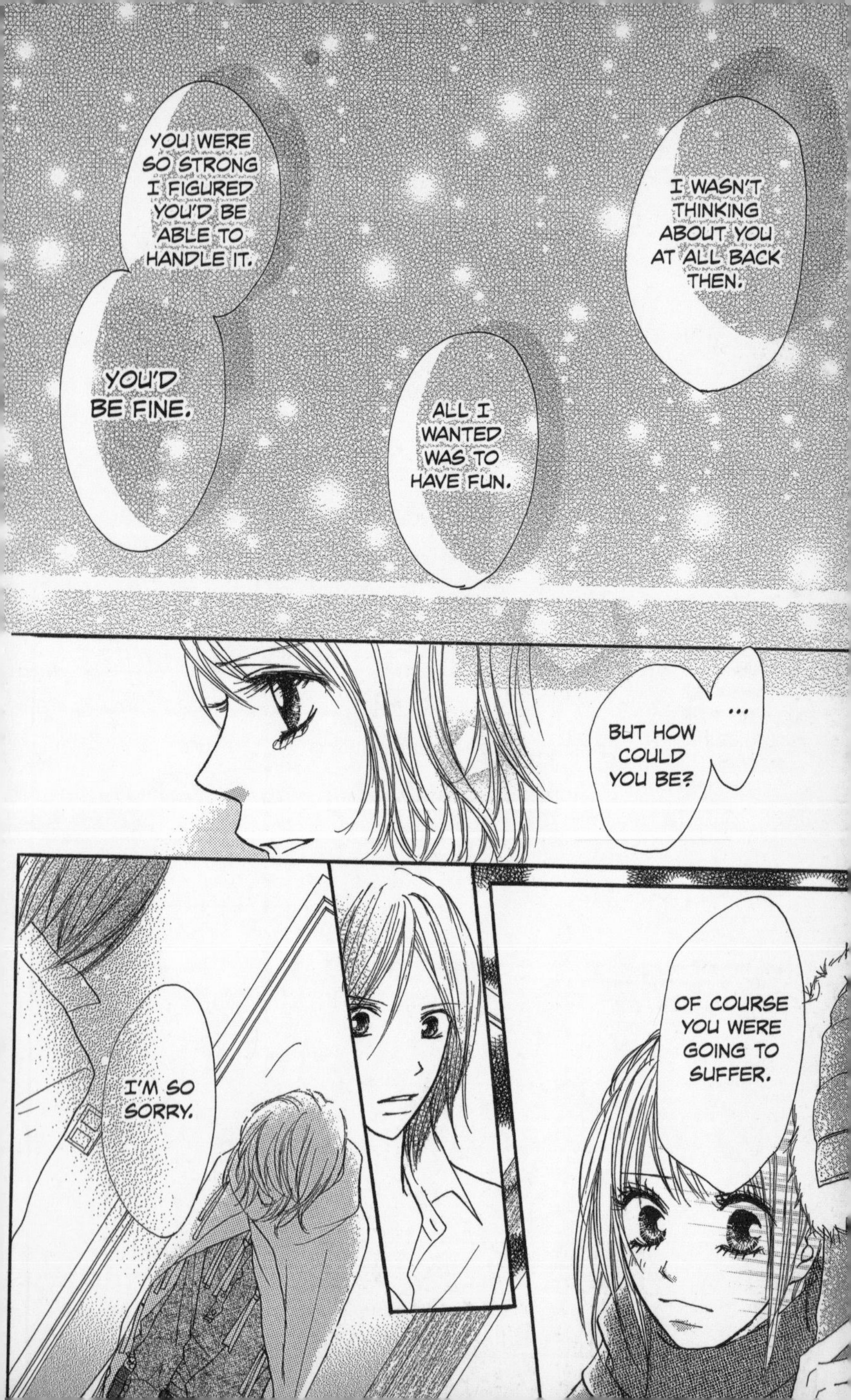
I WASN'T THINKING ABOUT YOU AT ALL BACK THEN.
ALL I WANTED WAS TO HAVE FUN.
YOU WERE SO STRONG I FIGURED YOU'D BE ABLE TO HANDLE IT.
YOU'D BE FINE.
... BUT HOW COULD YOU BE?
OF COURSE YOU WERE GOING TO SUFFER.
I'M SO SORRY.

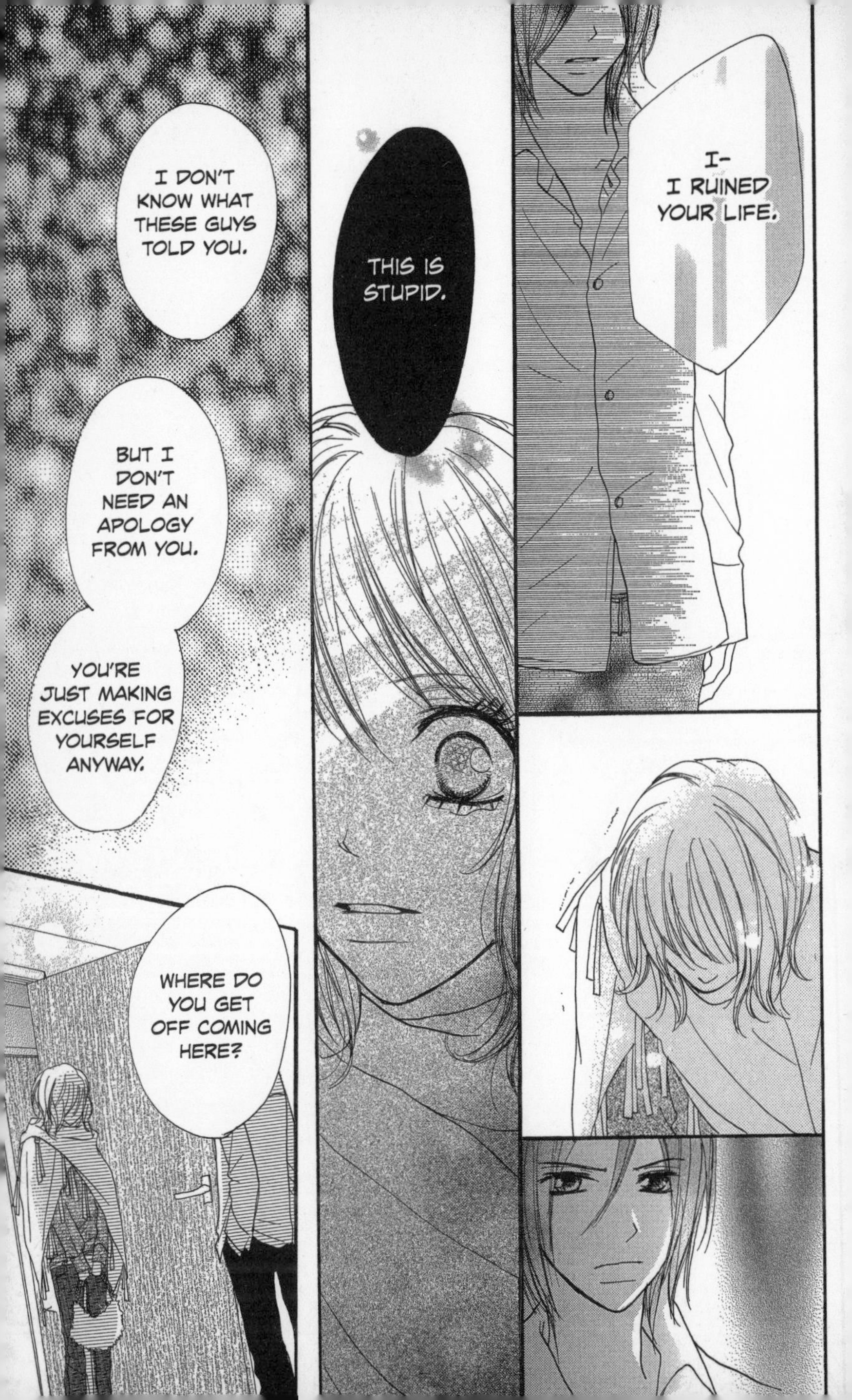
I- I RUINED YOUR LIFE.
THIS IS STUPID.
I DON'T KNOW WHAT THESE GUYS TOLD YOU.
BUT I DON'T NEED AN APOLOGY FROM YOU.
YOU'RE JUST MAKING EXCUSES FOR YOURSELF ANYWAY.
WHERE DO YOU GET OFF COMING HERE?

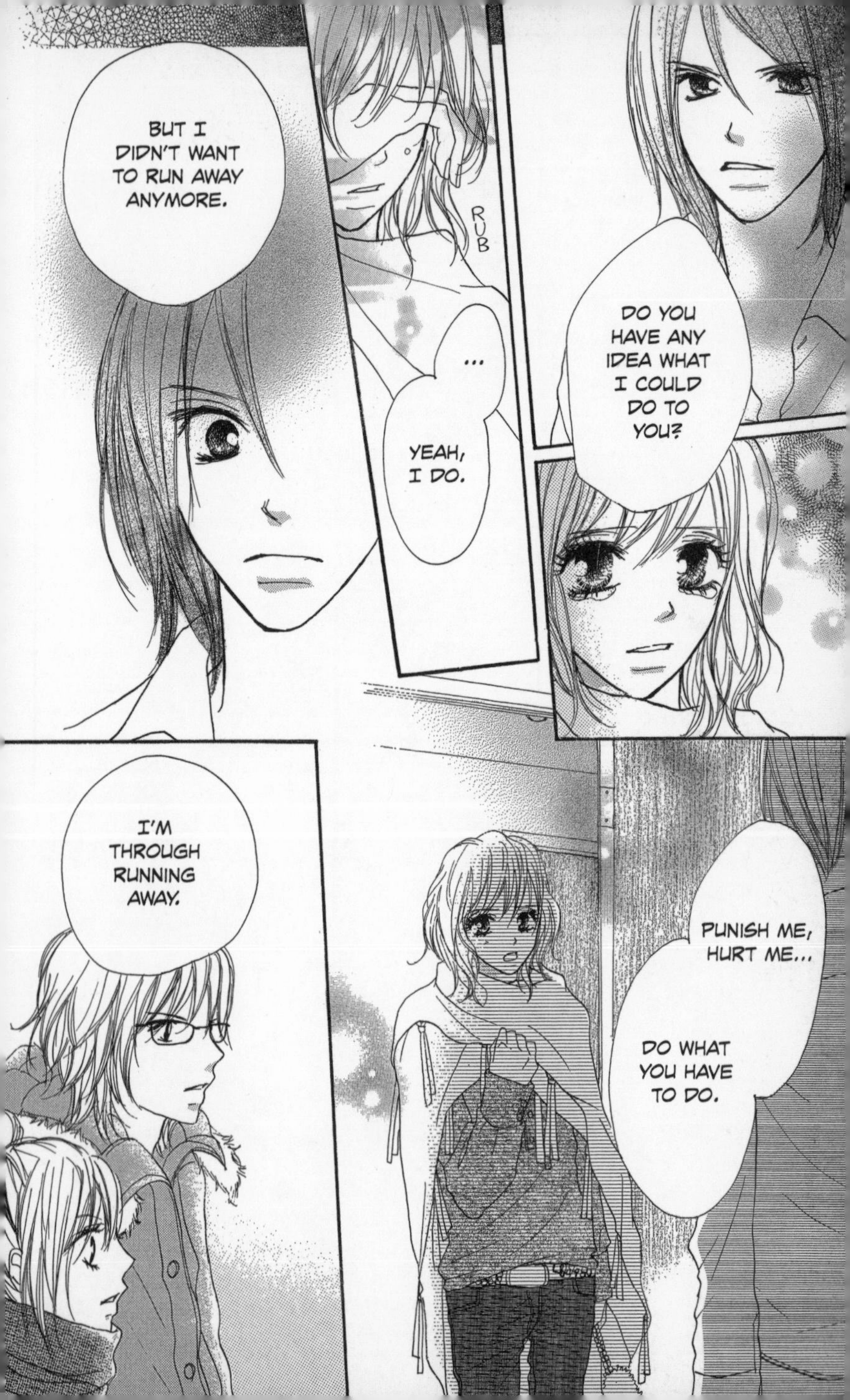
DO YOU HAVE ANY IDEA WHAT I COULD DO TO YOU?
RUB
...
YEAH, I DO.
BUT I DIDN'T WANT TO RUN AWAY ANYMORE.
PUNISH ME, HURT ME...
DO WHAT YOU HAVE TO DO.
I'M THROUGH RUNNING AWAY.

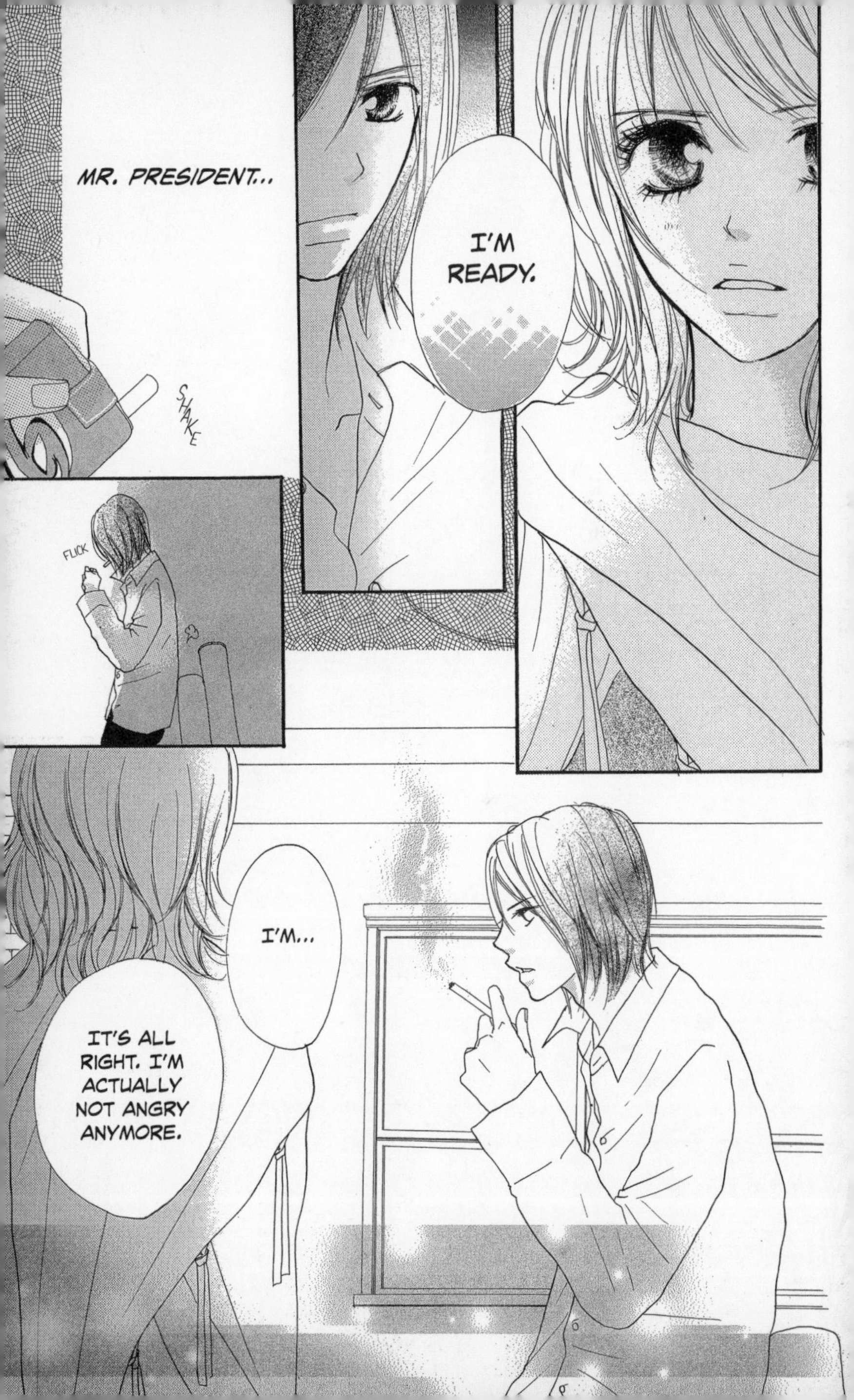
I'M READY.
MR. PRESIDENT...
SHAKE
FLICK
I'M...
IT'S ALL RIGHT. I'M ACTUALLY NOT ANGRY ANYMORE.

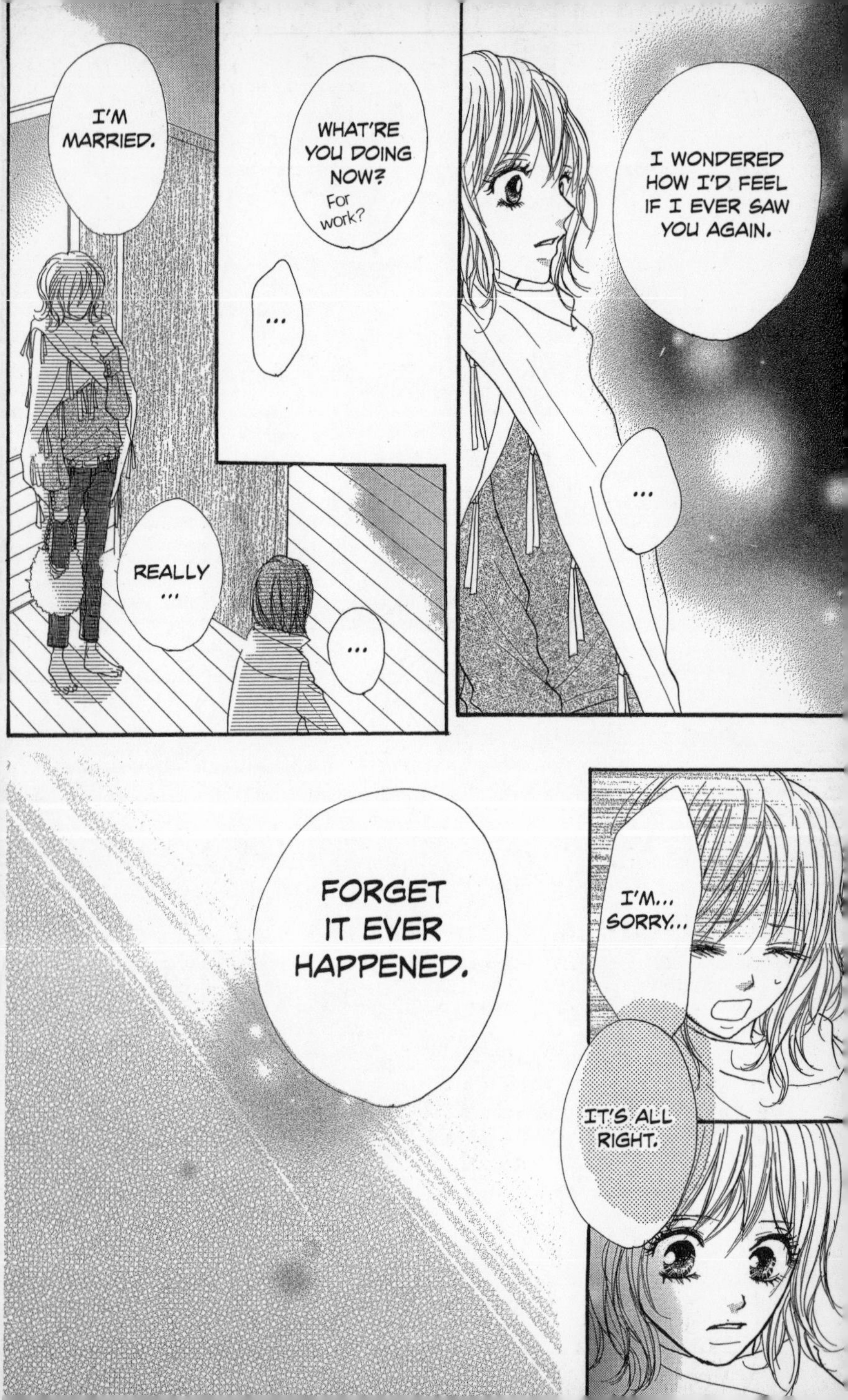
I WONDERED HOW I'D FEEL IF I EVER SAW YOU AGAIN.
...
WHAT'RE YOU DOING NOW?
For work?
...
I'M MARRIED.
...
REALLY ...
I'M... SORRY...
IT'S ALL RIGHT.
FORGET IT EVER HAPPENED.

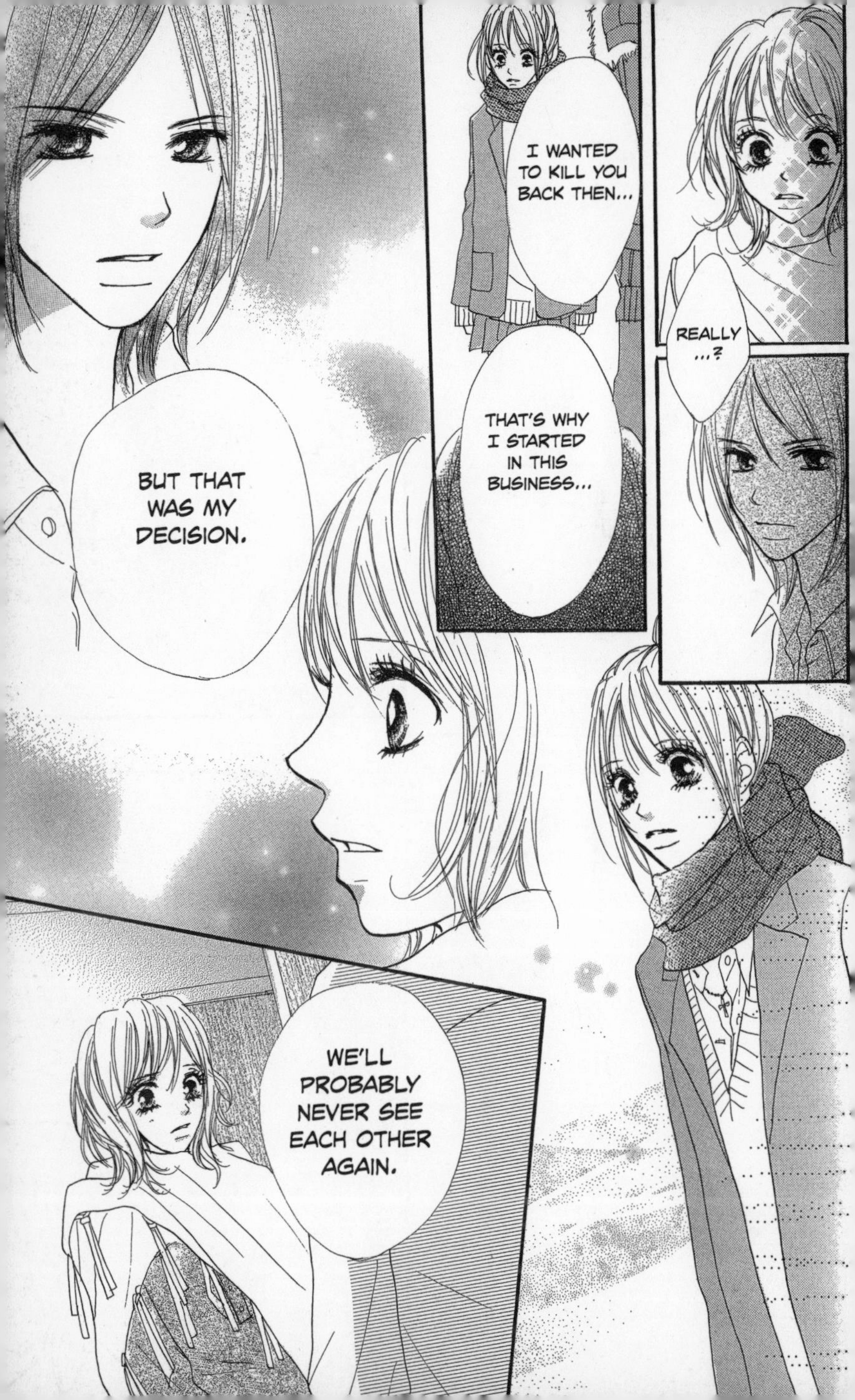
REALLY ...?
I WANTED TO KILL YOU BACK THEN...
THAT'S WHY I STARTED IN THIS BUSINESS...
BUT THAT WAS MY DECISION.
WE'LL PROBABLY NEVER SEE EACH OTHER AGAIN.

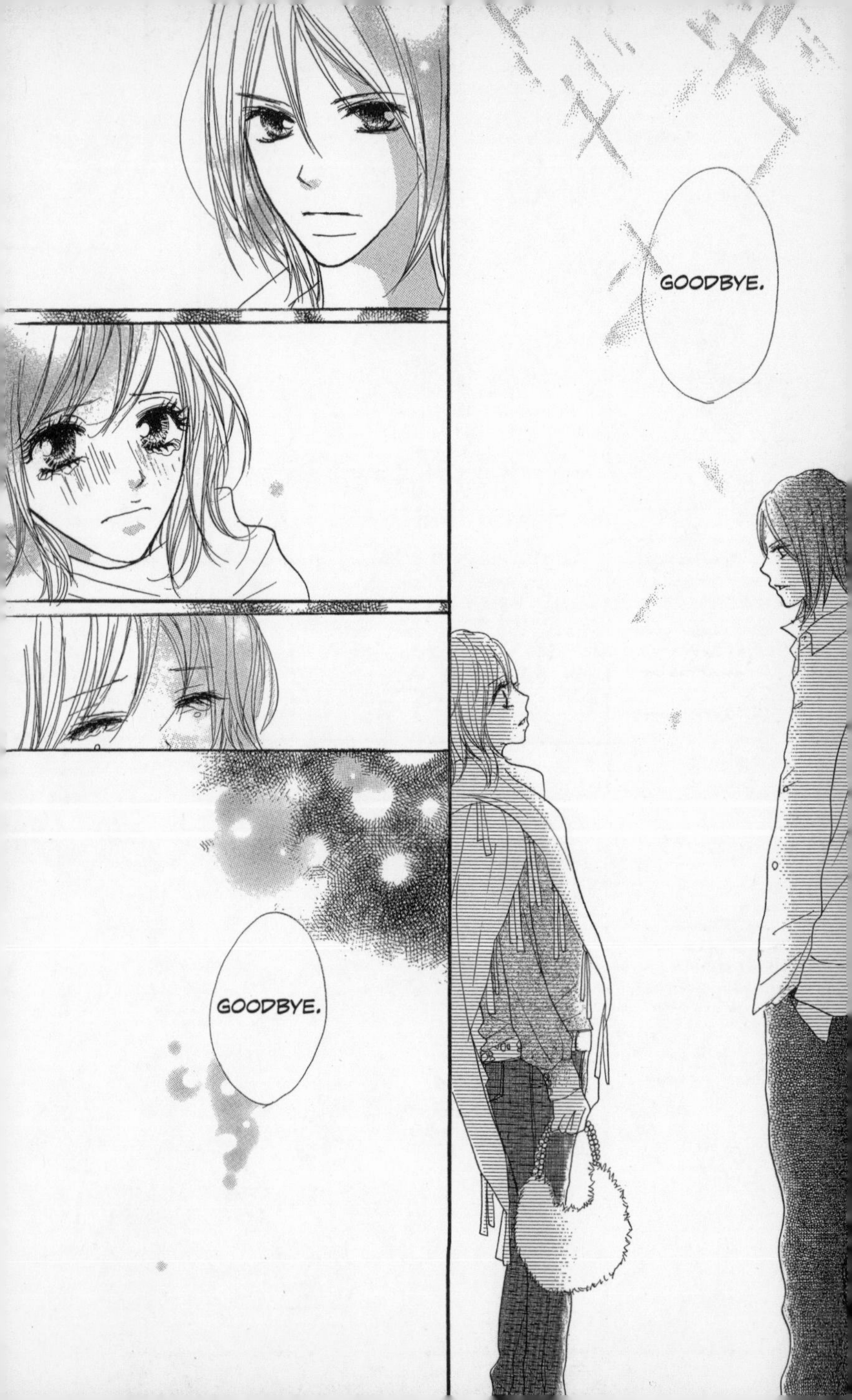
GOODBYE.
GOODBYE.

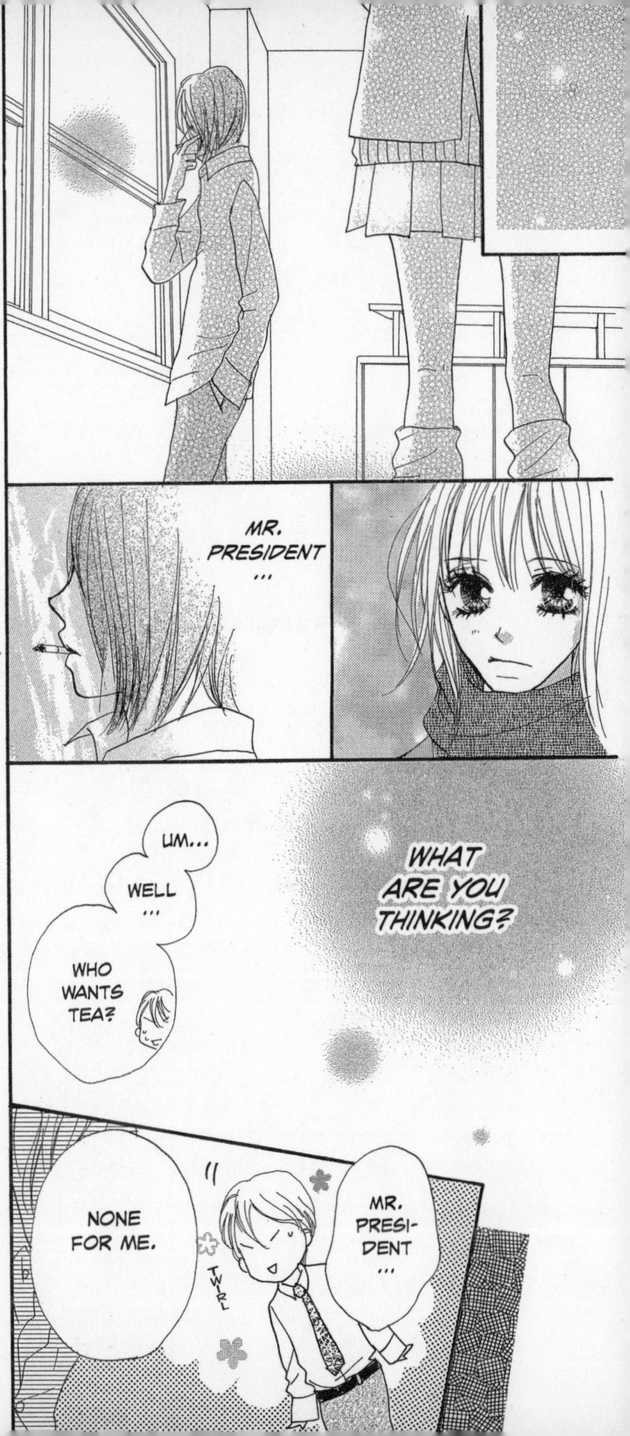
MR. PRESIDENT ...
WHAT ARE YOU THINKING?
UM... WELL ... WHO WANTS TEA?
MR. PRESI-DENT ...
TWIRL
NONE FOR ME.

4 ← About Him.

I got a letter asking 'What is that water-drop looking thing?' If I may explain, he was a character I used to draw in my notebooks when I was in high school. Two or three other girls used to draw him, but none of them draw him anymore so I have a monopoly. Smirk.

If I recall correctly, he used to be about this long.

On test papers:

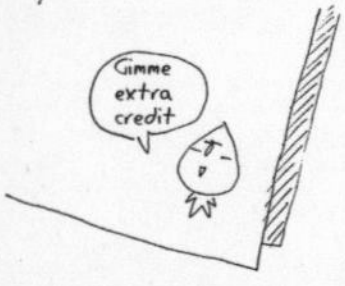
Gimme extra credit

My teachers would just blow me off, though. There's actually a trick to drawing him. He can't be too cute, he has to be a little off. Anyway, I'm glad you like him!

Thank you.
Thank you.

END

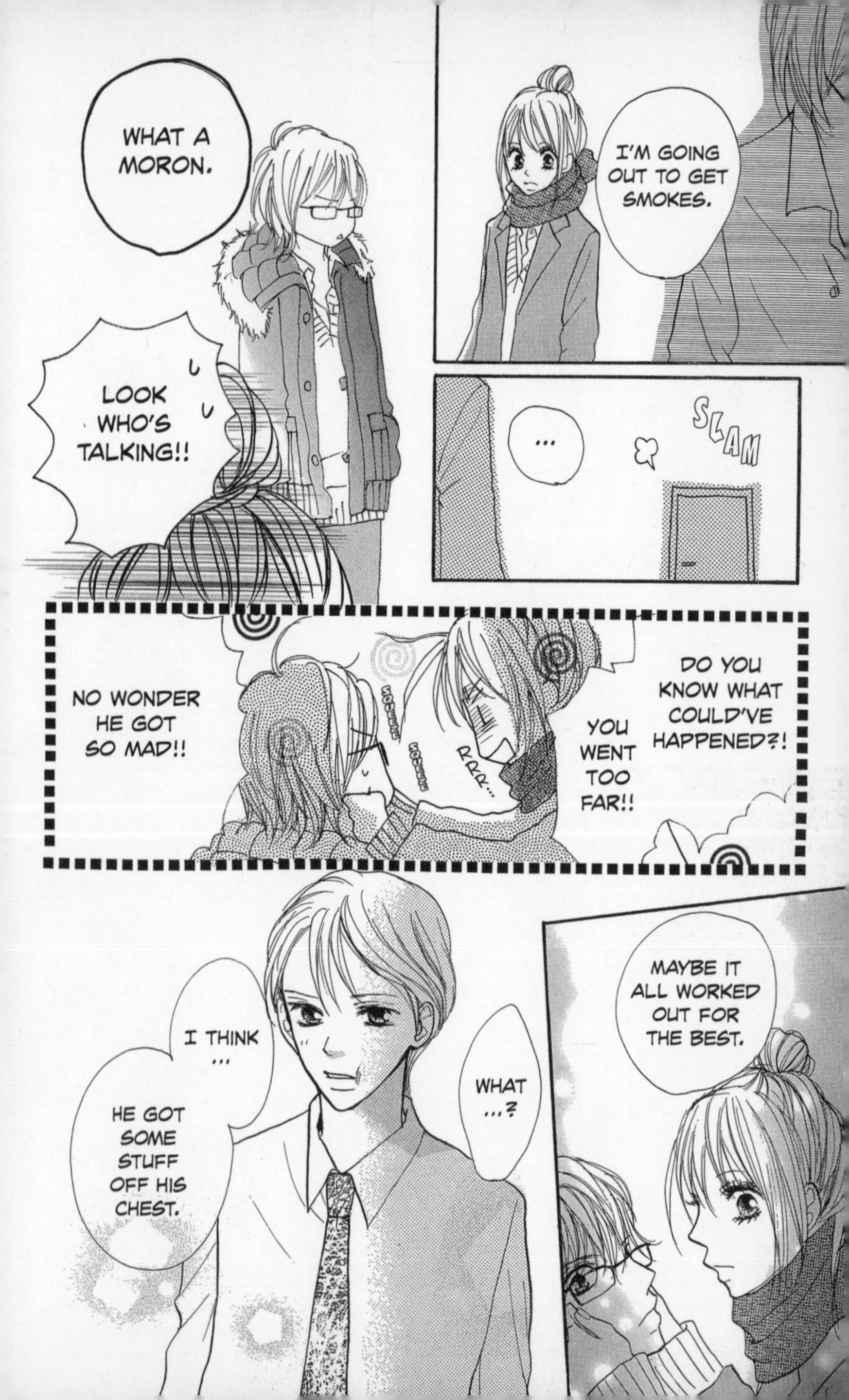
I'M GOING OUT TO GET SMOKES.
...
SLAM
WHAT A MORON.
LOOK WHO'S TALKING!!
DO YOU KNOW WHAT COULD'VE HAPPENED?!
YOU WENT TOO FAR!!
RRR...
NO WONDER HE GOT SO MAD!!
MAYBE IT ALL WORKED OUT FOR THE BEST.
WHAT ...?
I THINK ...
HE GOT SOME STUFF OFF HIS CHEST.

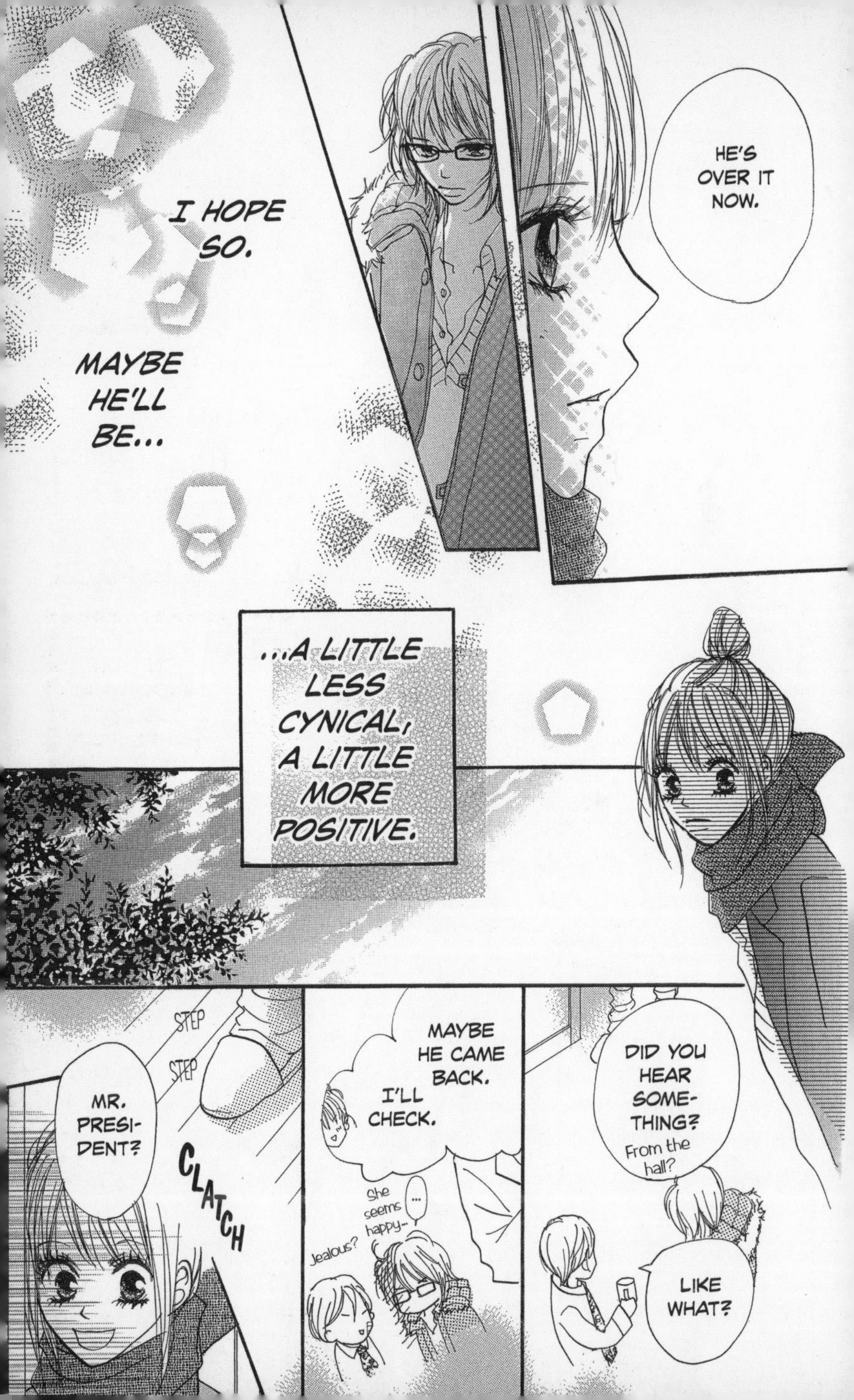
HE'S OVER IT NOW.
I HOPE SO.
MAYBE HE'LL BE...
...A LITTLE LESS CYNICAL, A LITTLE MORE POSITIVE.
DID YOU HEAR SOMETHING? From the hall?
LIKE WHAT?
MAYBE HE CAME BACK.
I'LL CHECK.
...
She seems happy...
Jealous?
STEP
STEP
MR. PRESIDENT?
CLATCH

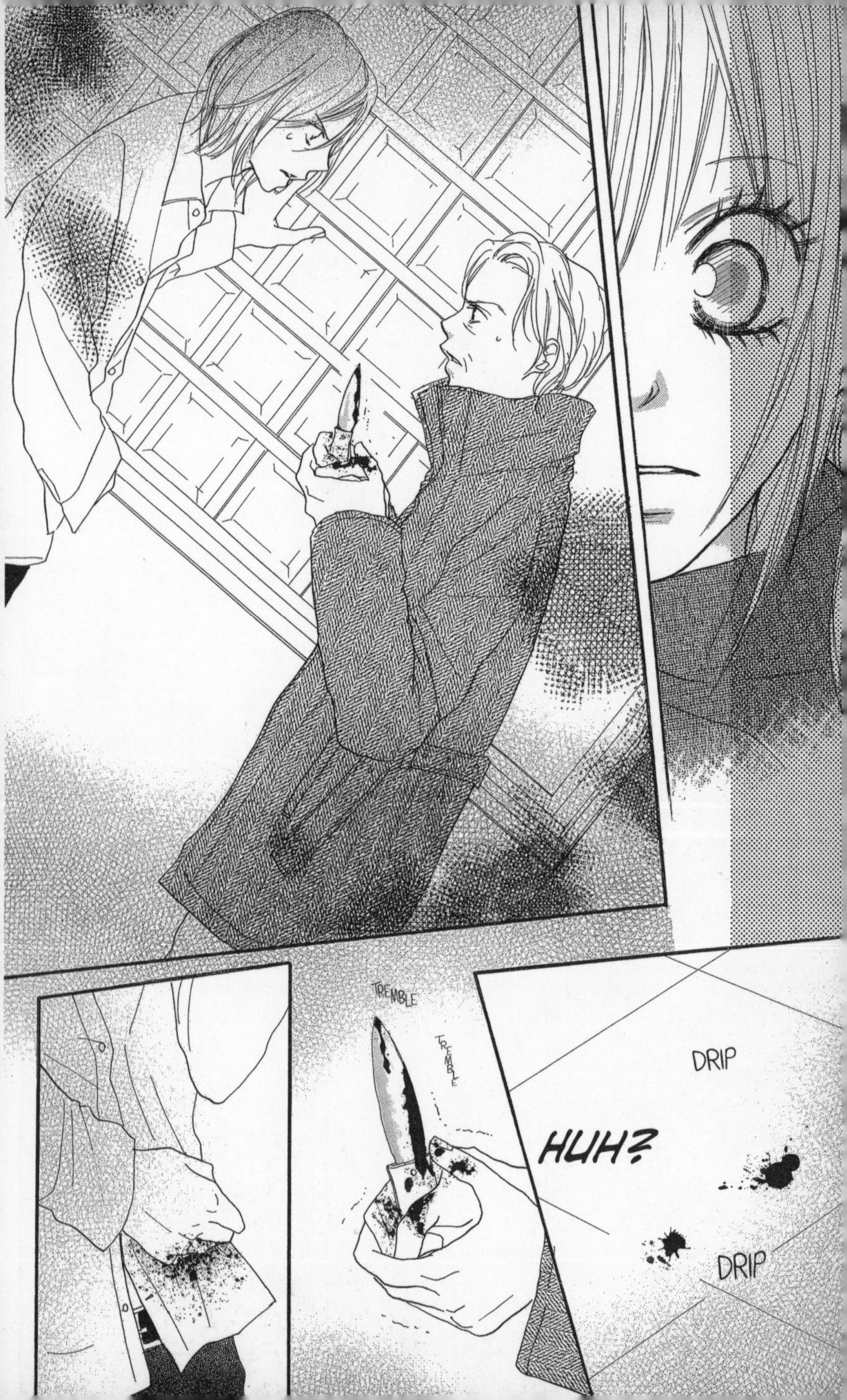
DRIP
HUH?
DRIP
TREMBLE
TREMBLE

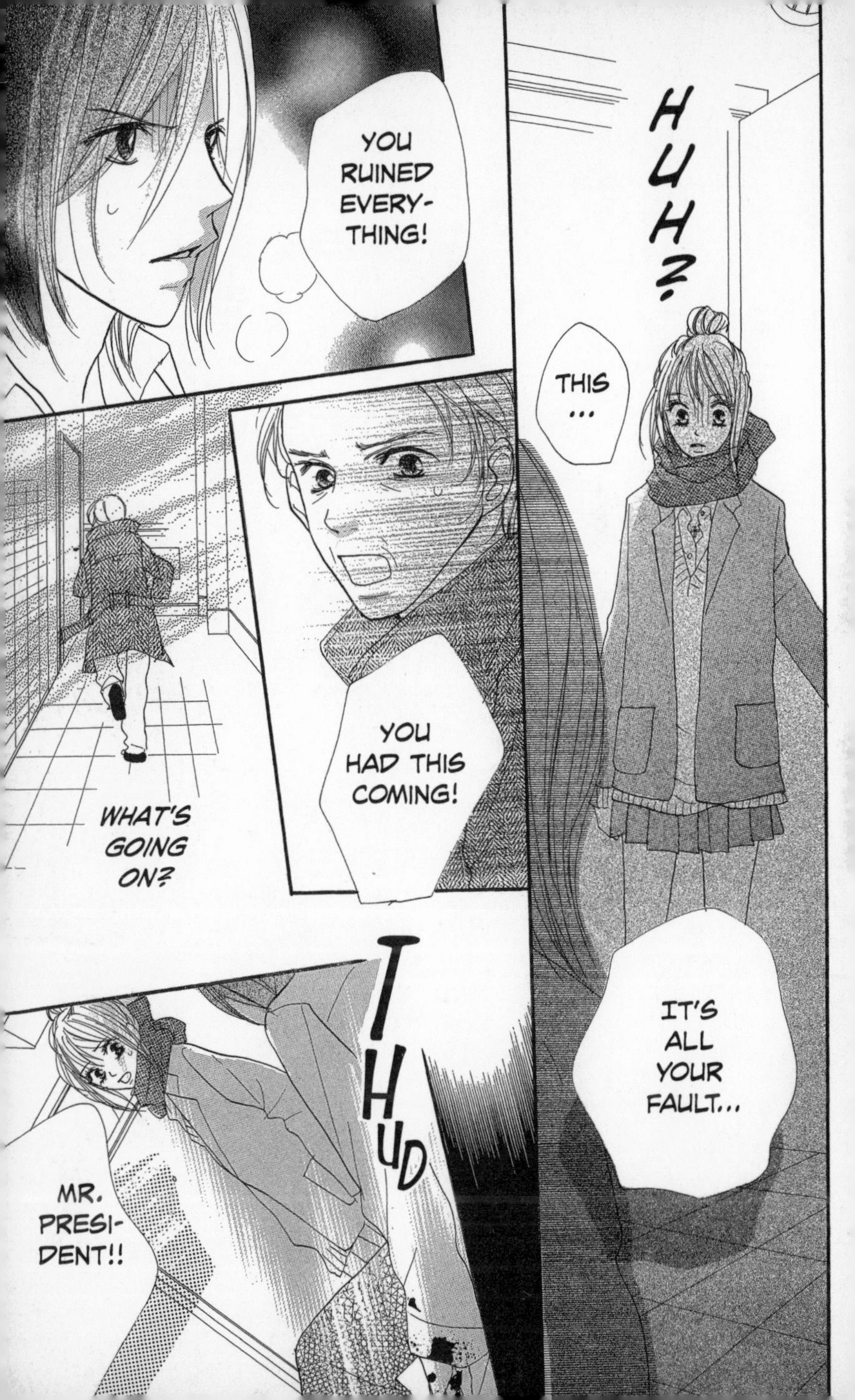
HUH?
THIS...
IT'S ALL YOUR FAULT...
YOU RUINED EVERYTHING!
YOU HAD THIS COMING!
WHAT'S GOING ON?
THUD
MR. PRESIDENT!!

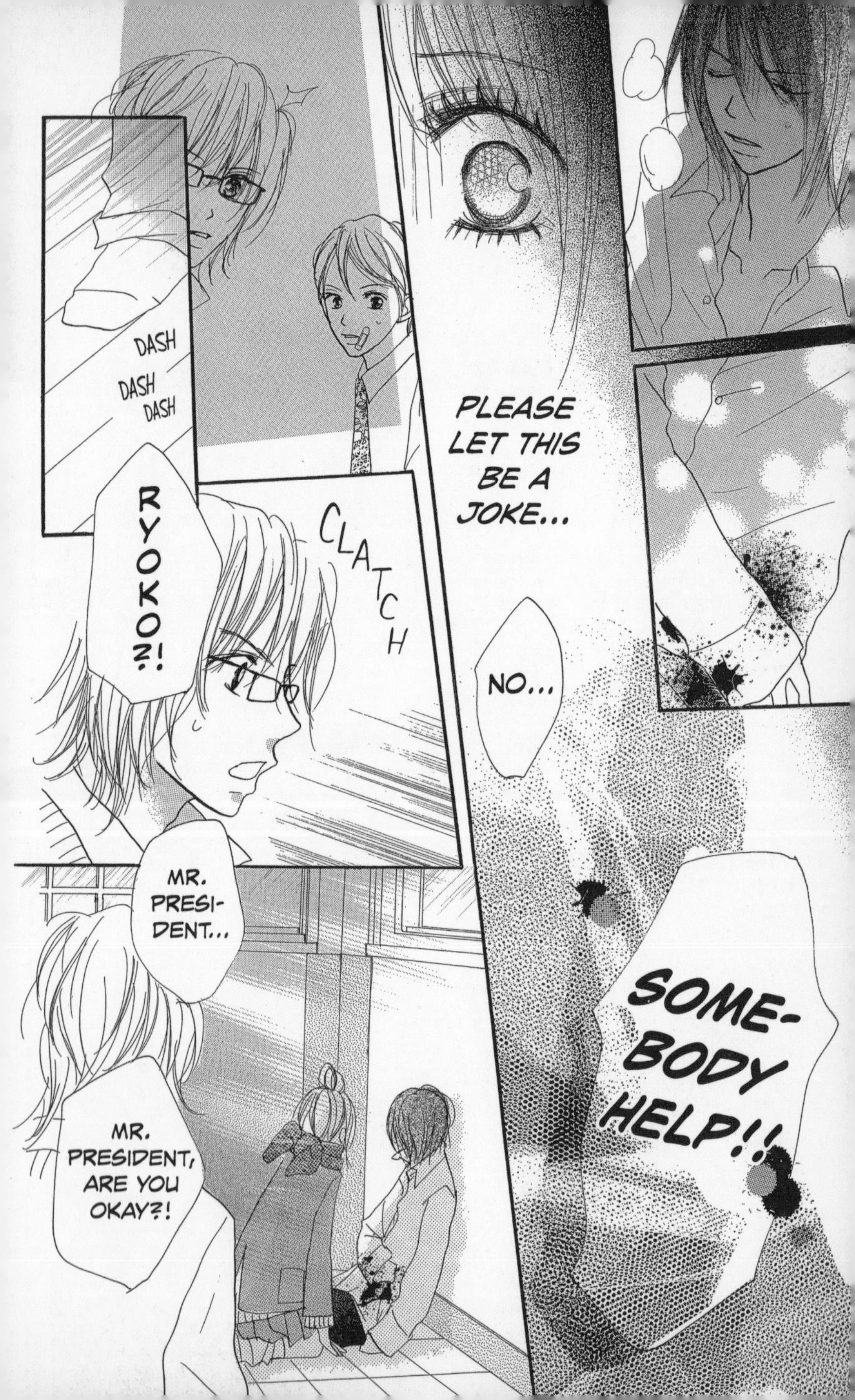
PLEASE LET THIS BE A JOKE...
NO...
SOME-BODY HELP!!
DASH
DASH
DASH
RYOKO?!
CLATCH
MR. PRESI-DENT...
MR. PRESIDENT, ARE YOU OKAY?!

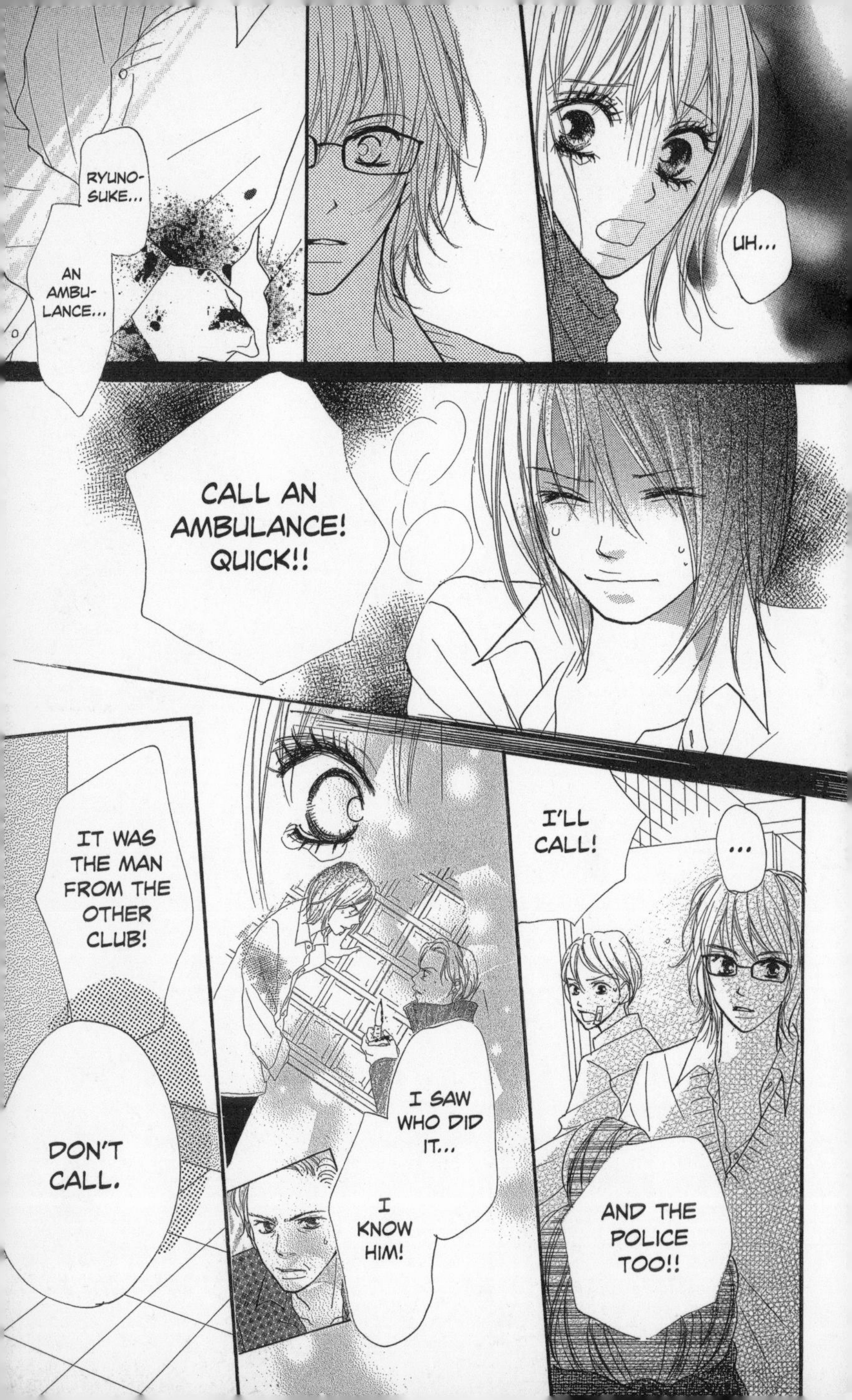
UH...
RYUNO-SUKE...
AN AMBU-LANCE...
CALL AN AMBULANCE! QUICK!!
I'LL CALL!
...
AND THE POLICE TOO!!
I SAW WHO DID IT...
I KNOW HIM!
IT WAS THE MAN FROM THE OTHER CLUB!
DON'T CALL.

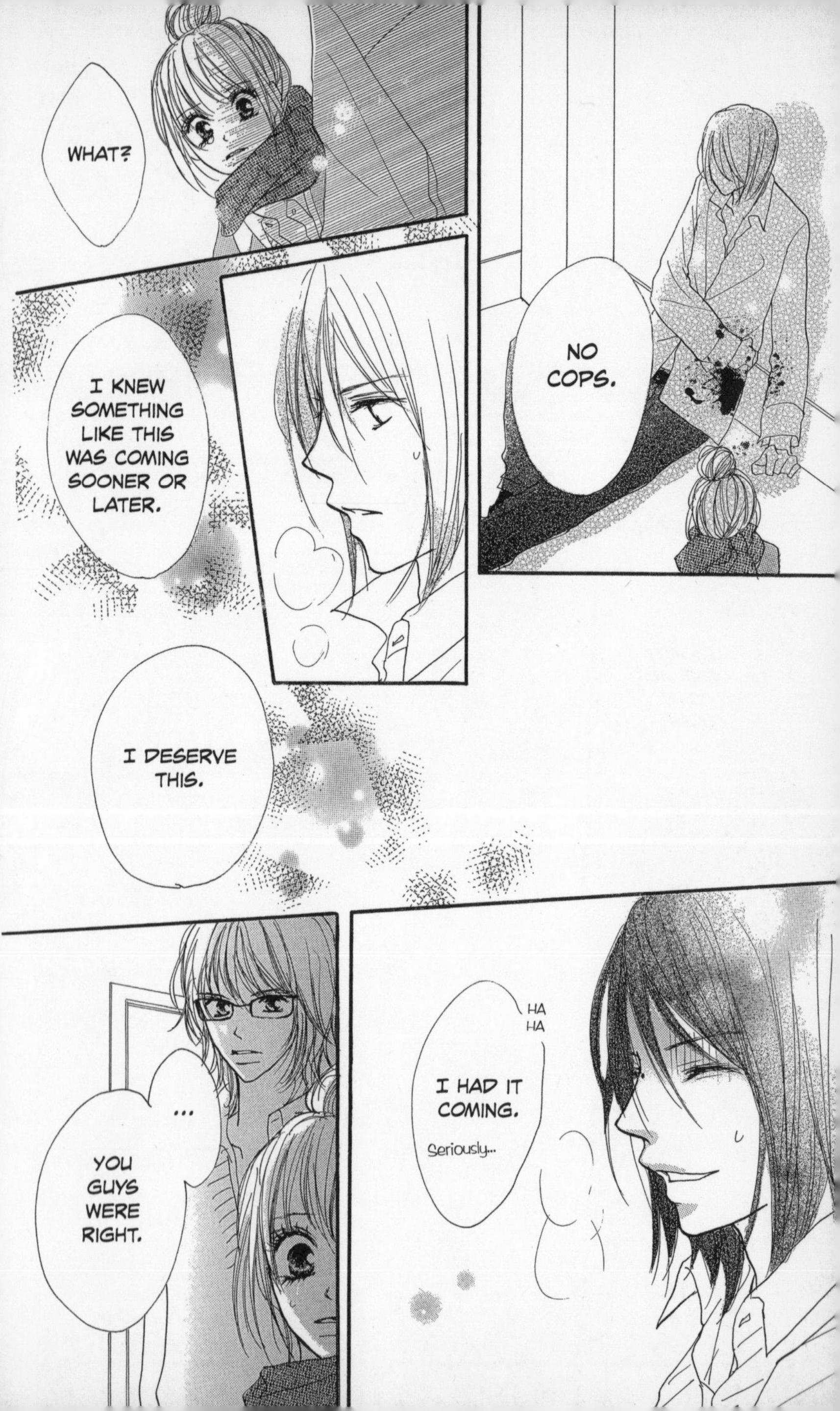
NO COPS.
WHAT?
I KNEW SOMETHING LIKE THIS WAS COMING SOONER OR LATER.
I DESERVE THIS.
HA HA
I HAD IT COMING.
Seriously...
...
YOU GUYS WERE RIGHT.

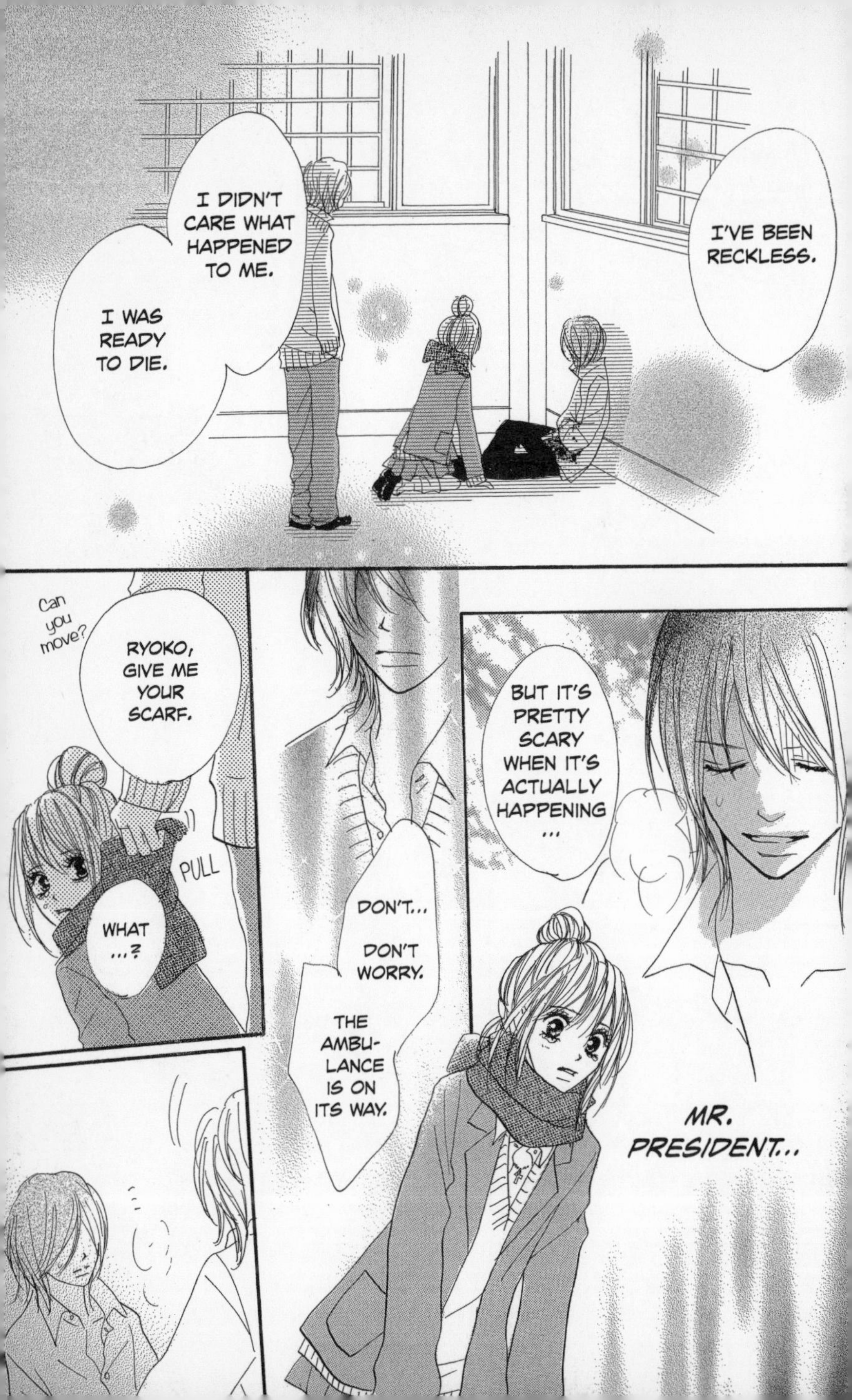
I'VE BEEN RECKLESS.
I DIDN'T CARE WHAT HAPPENED TO ME.
I WAS READY TO DIE.
BUT IT'S PRETTY SCARY WHEN IT'S ACTUALLY HAPPENING...
MR. PRESIDENT...
DON'T...
DON'T WORRY.
THE AMBULANCE IS ON ITS WAY.
Can you move?
RYOKO, GIVE ME YOUR SCARF.
PULL
WHAT...?

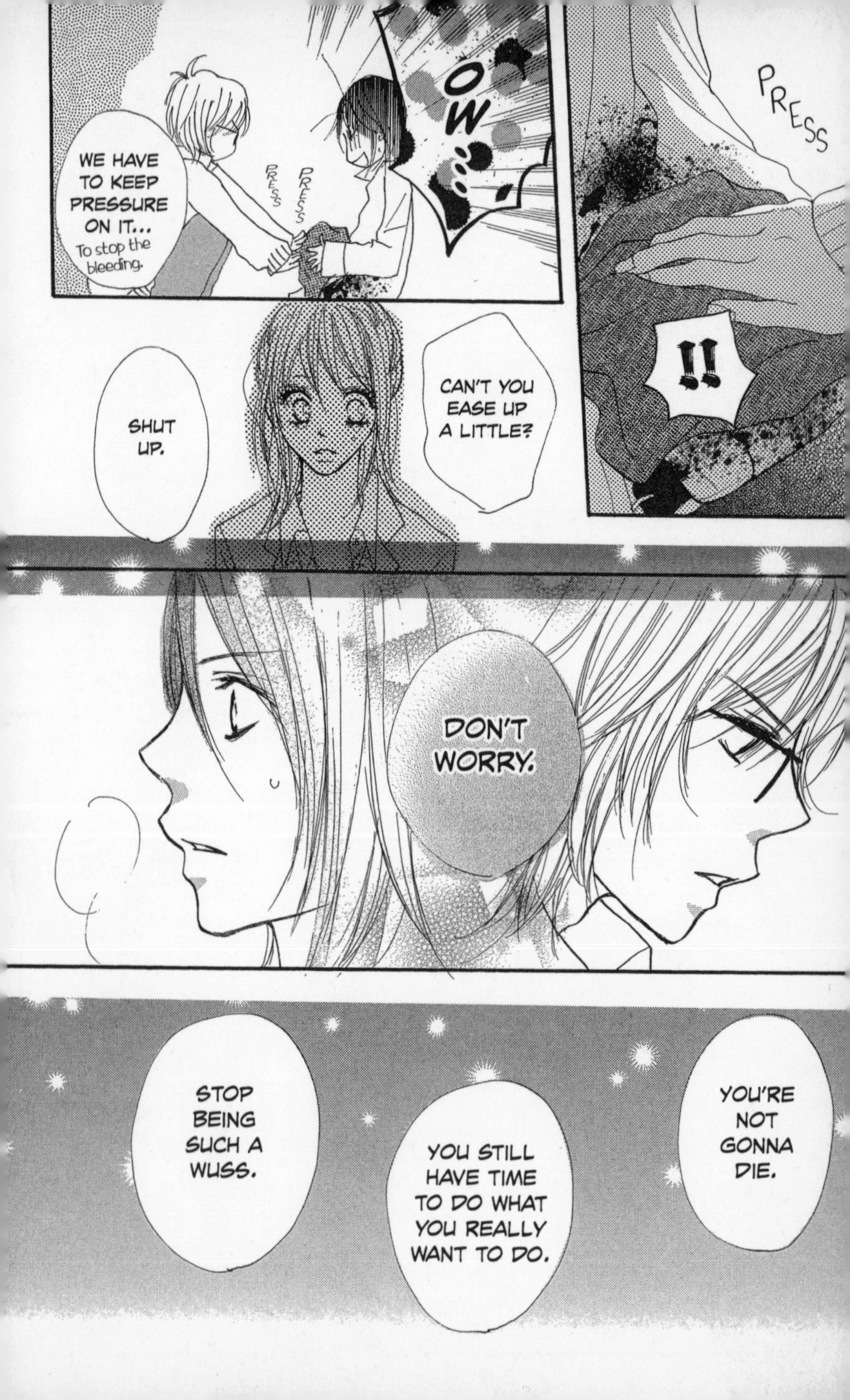
PRESS
!!
OW...
PRESS PRESS
WE HAVE TO KEEP PRESSURE ON IT... To stop the bleeding.
CAN'T YOU EASE UP A LITTLE?
SHUT UP.
DON'T WORRY.
YOU'RE NOT GONNA DIE.
YOU STILL HAVE TIME TO DO WHAT YOU REALLY WANT TO DO.
STOP BEING SUCH A WUSS.

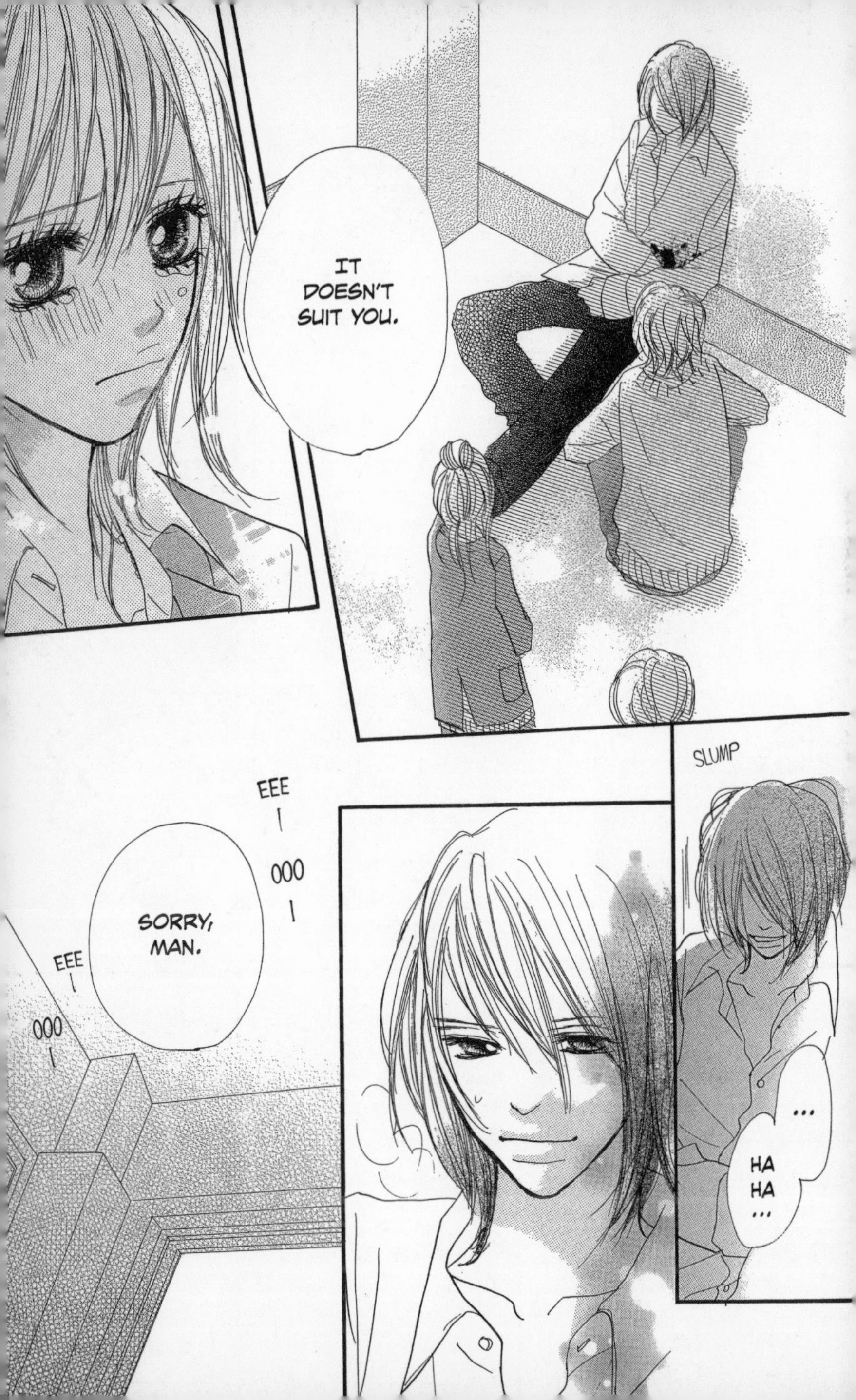
IT DOESN'T SUIT YOU.
SLUMP
... HA HA ...
EEE—OOO—
SORRY, MAN.
EEE—OOO—

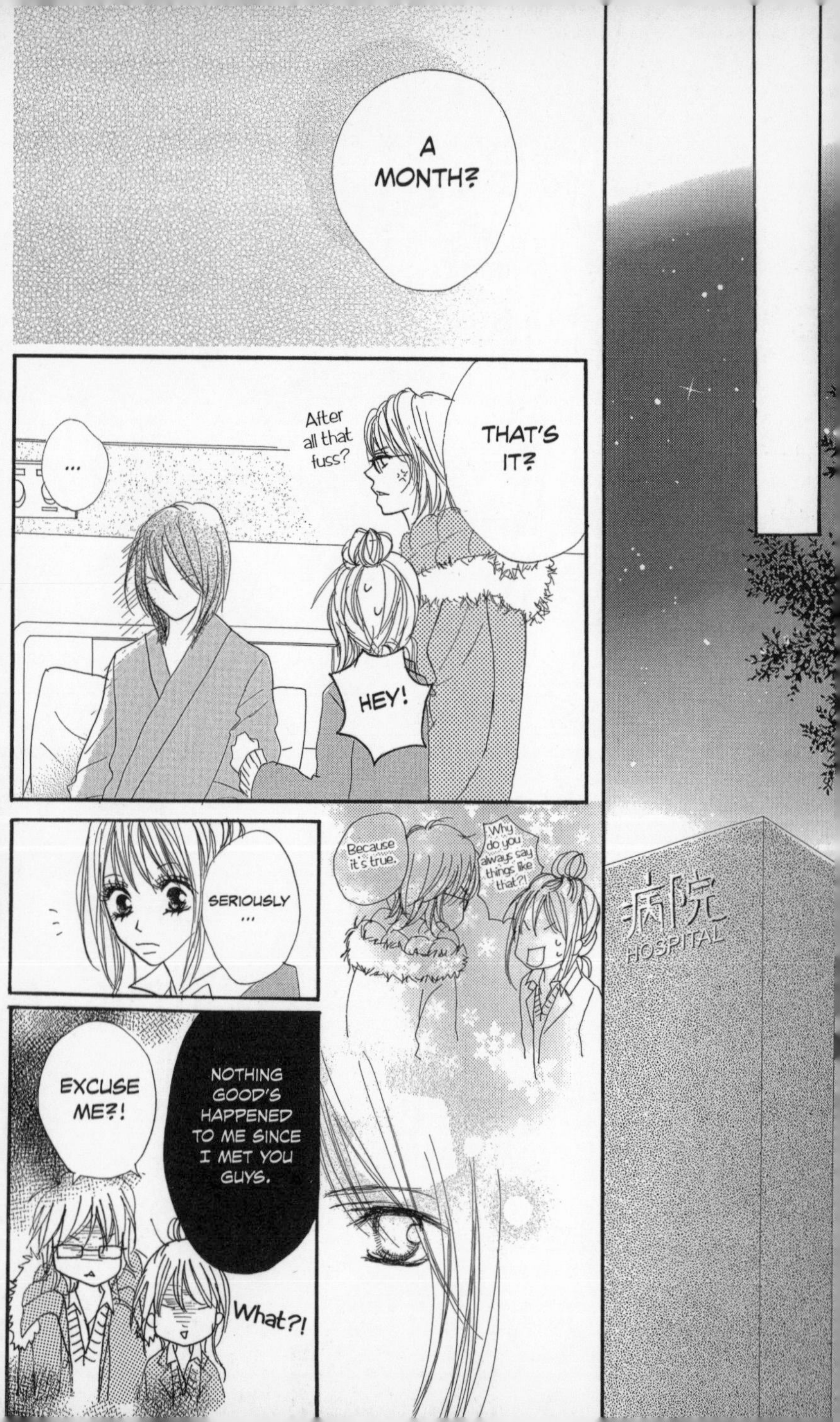
病院
HOSPITAL
A MONTH?
THAT'S IT?
After all that fuss?
...
HEY!
Why do you always say things like that?!
Because it's true.
SERIOUSLY...
NOTHING GOOD'S HAPPENED TO ME SINCE I MET YOU GUYS.
EXCUSE ME?!
What?!

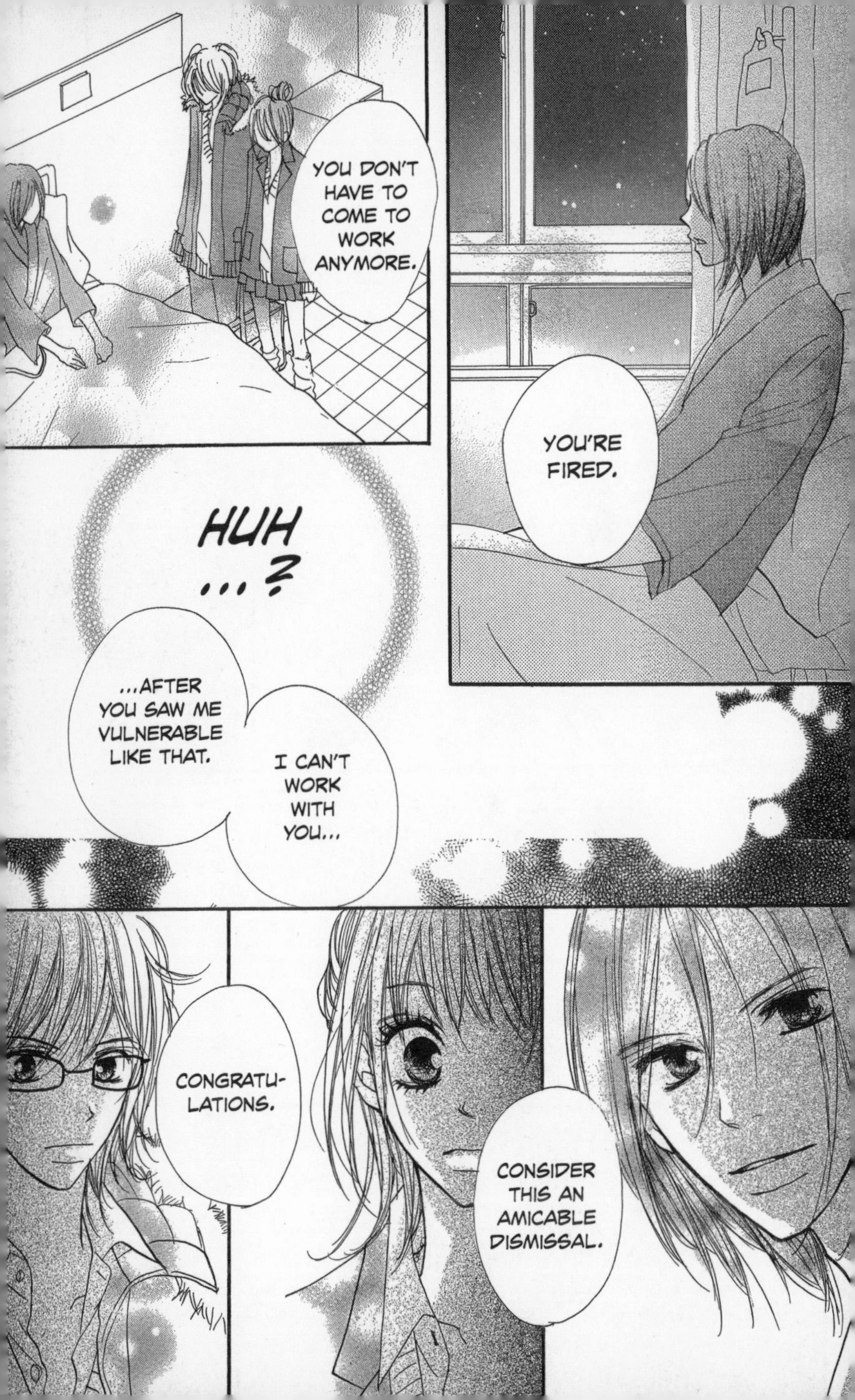
YOU'RE FIRED.
YOU DON'T HAVE TO COME TO WORK ANYMORE.
HUH ...?
I CAN'T WORK WITH YOU...
...AFTER YOU SAW ME VULNERABLE LIKE THAT.
CONSIDER THIS AN AMICABLE DISMISSAL.
CONGRATULATIONS.

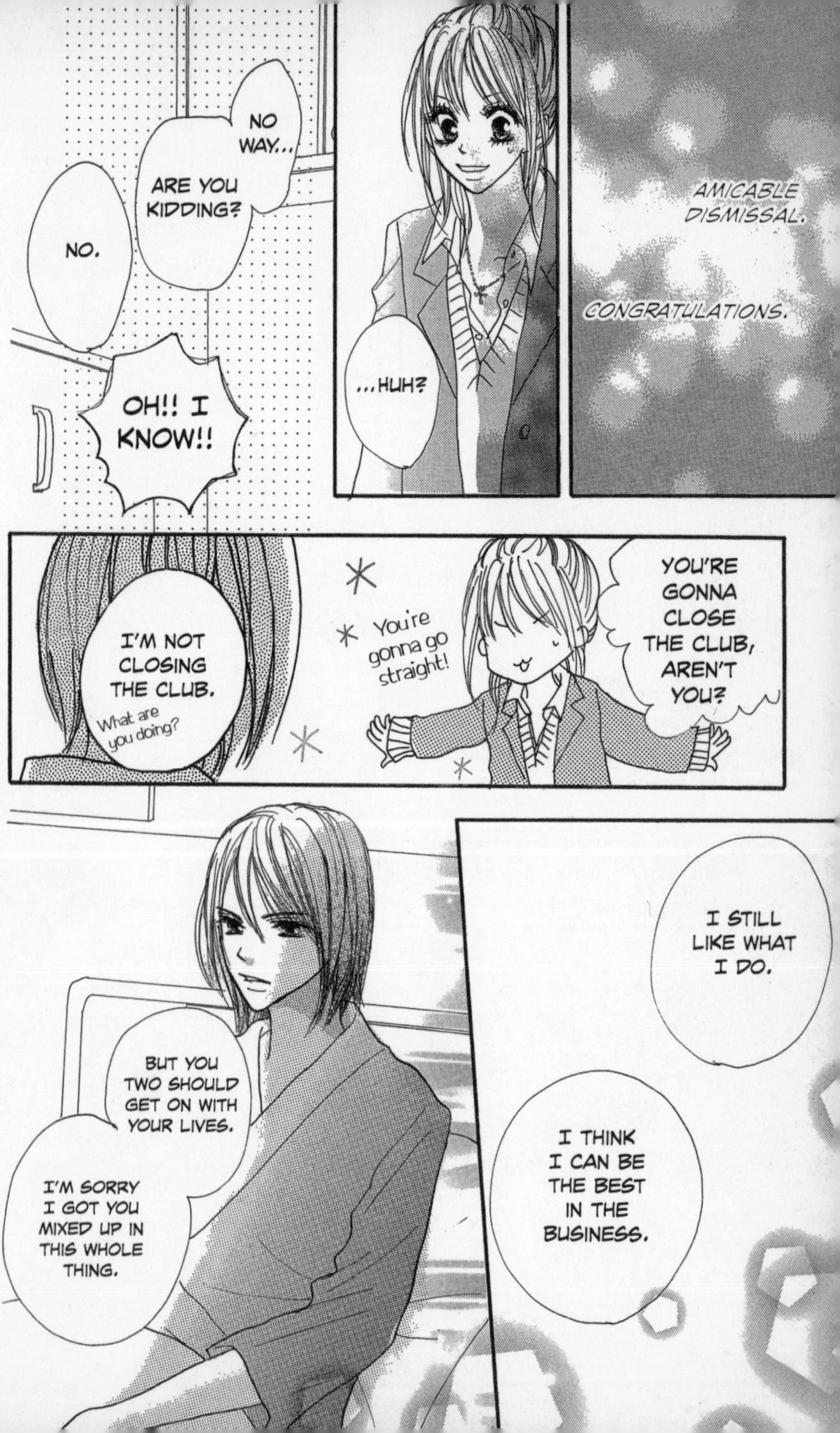
AMICABLE DISMISSAL.
CONGRATULATIONS.
...HUH?
NO WAY...
ARE YOU KIDDING?
NO.
OH!! I KNOW!!
YOU'RE GONNA CLOSE THE CLUB, AREN'T YOU?
You're gonna go straight!
I'M NOT CLOSING THE CLUB.
What are you doing?
I STILL LIKE WHAT I DO.
I THINK I CAN BE THE BEST IN THE BUSINESS.
BUT YOU TWO SHOULD GET ON WITH YOUR LIVES.
I'M SORRY I GOT YOU MIXED UP IN THIS WHOLE THING.

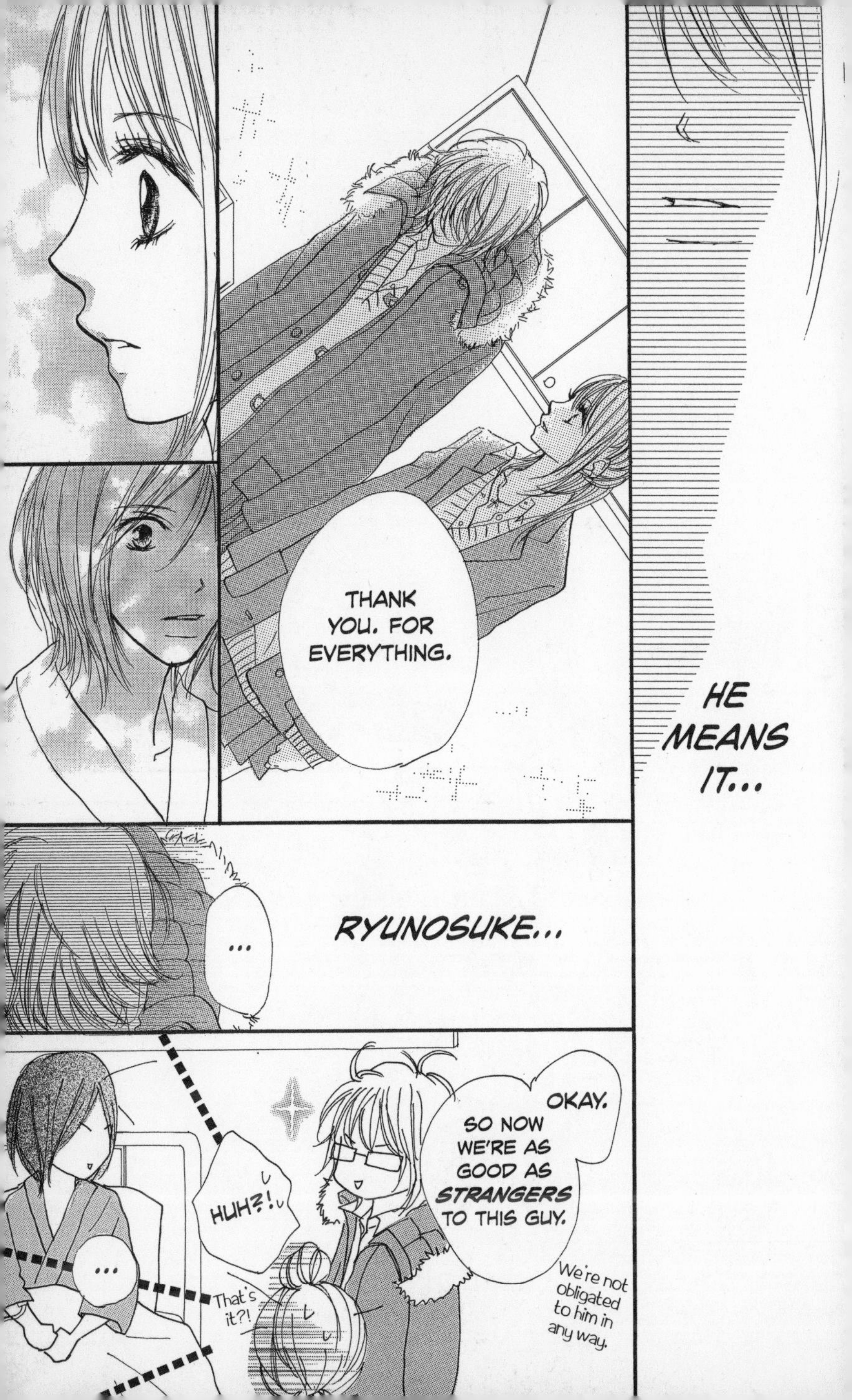
HE MEANS IT...
THANK YOU. FOR EVERYTHING.
RYUNOSUKE...
...
OKAY. SO NOW WE'RE AS GOOD AS STRANGERS TO THIS GUY.
We're not obligated to him in any way.
HUH?!
That's it?!
...

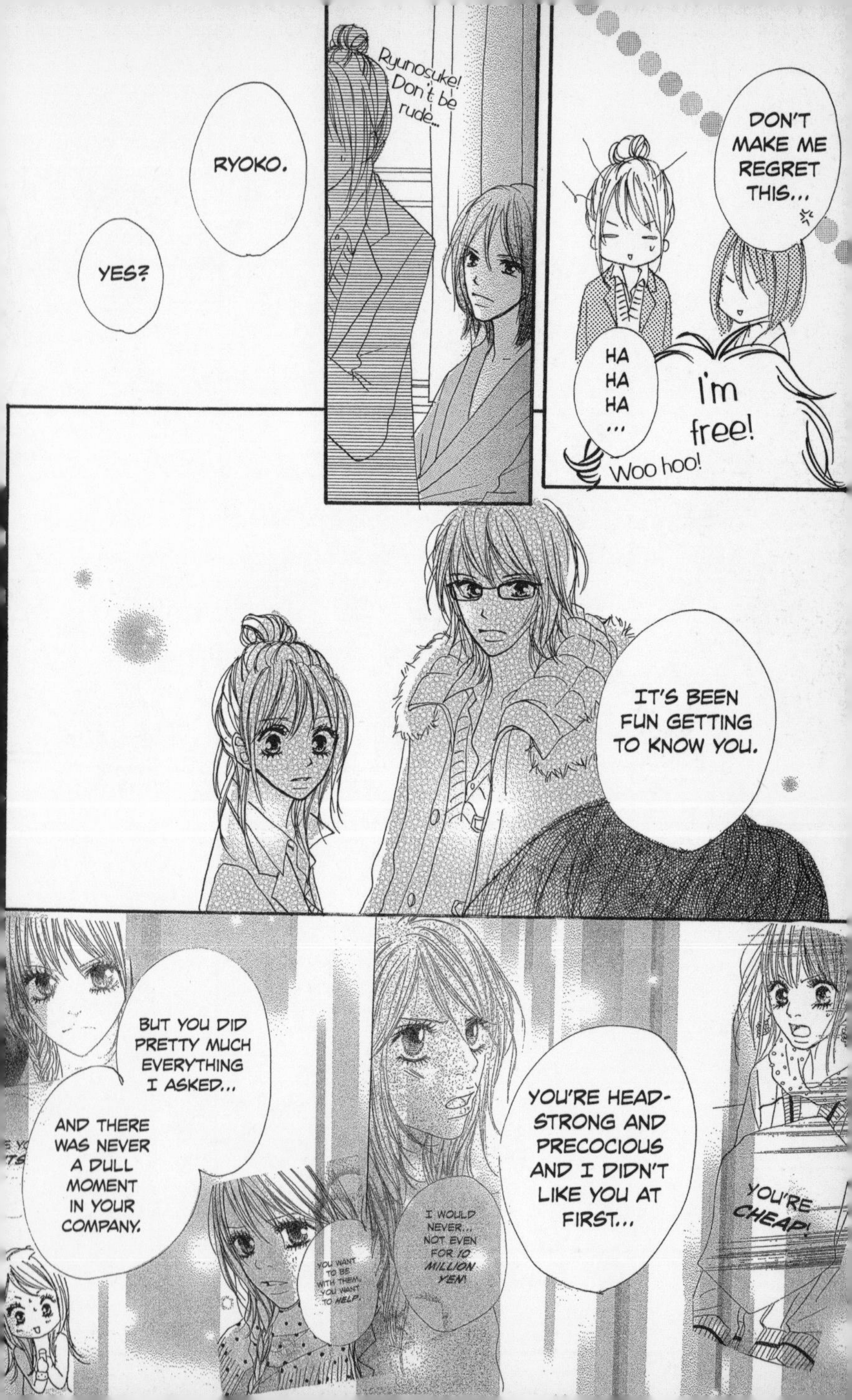
DON'T MAKE ME REGRET THIS...
I'm free!
HA HA HA ...
Woo hoo!
Ryunosuke! Don't be rude...
RYOKO.
YES?
IT'S BEEN FUN GETTING TO KNOW YOU.
YOU'RE CHEAP!
YOU'RE HEAD-STRONG AND PRECOCIOUS AND I DIDN'T LIKE YOU AT FIRST...
I WOULD NEVER... NOT EVEN FOR 10 MILLION YEN!
YOU WANT TO BE WITH THEM. YOU WANT TO HELP.
BUT YOU DID PRETTY MUCH EVERYTHING I ASKED...
AND THERE WAS NEVER A DULL MOMENT IN YOUR COMPANY.

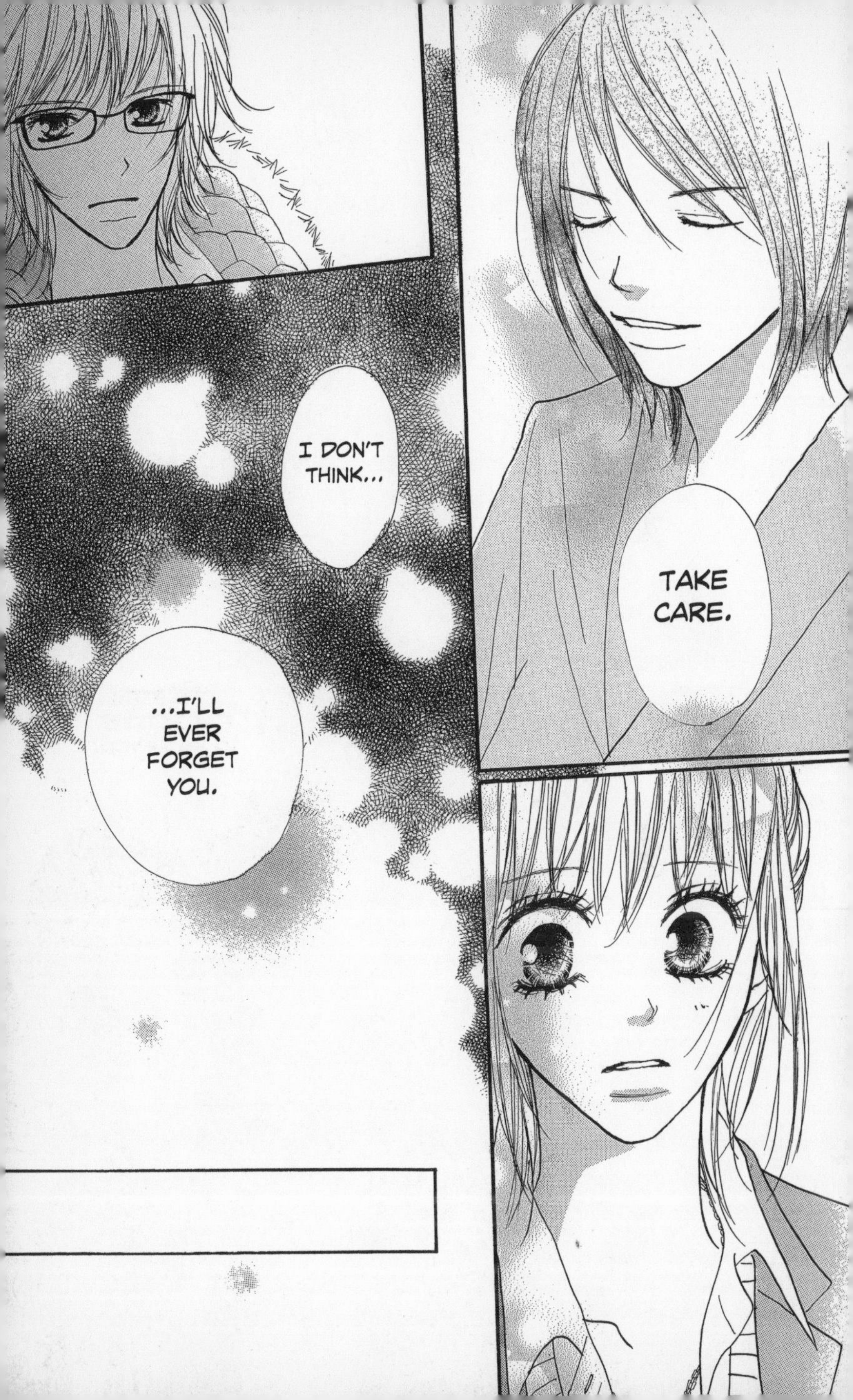
TAKE CARE.
I DON'T THINK...
...I'LL EVER FORGET YOU.

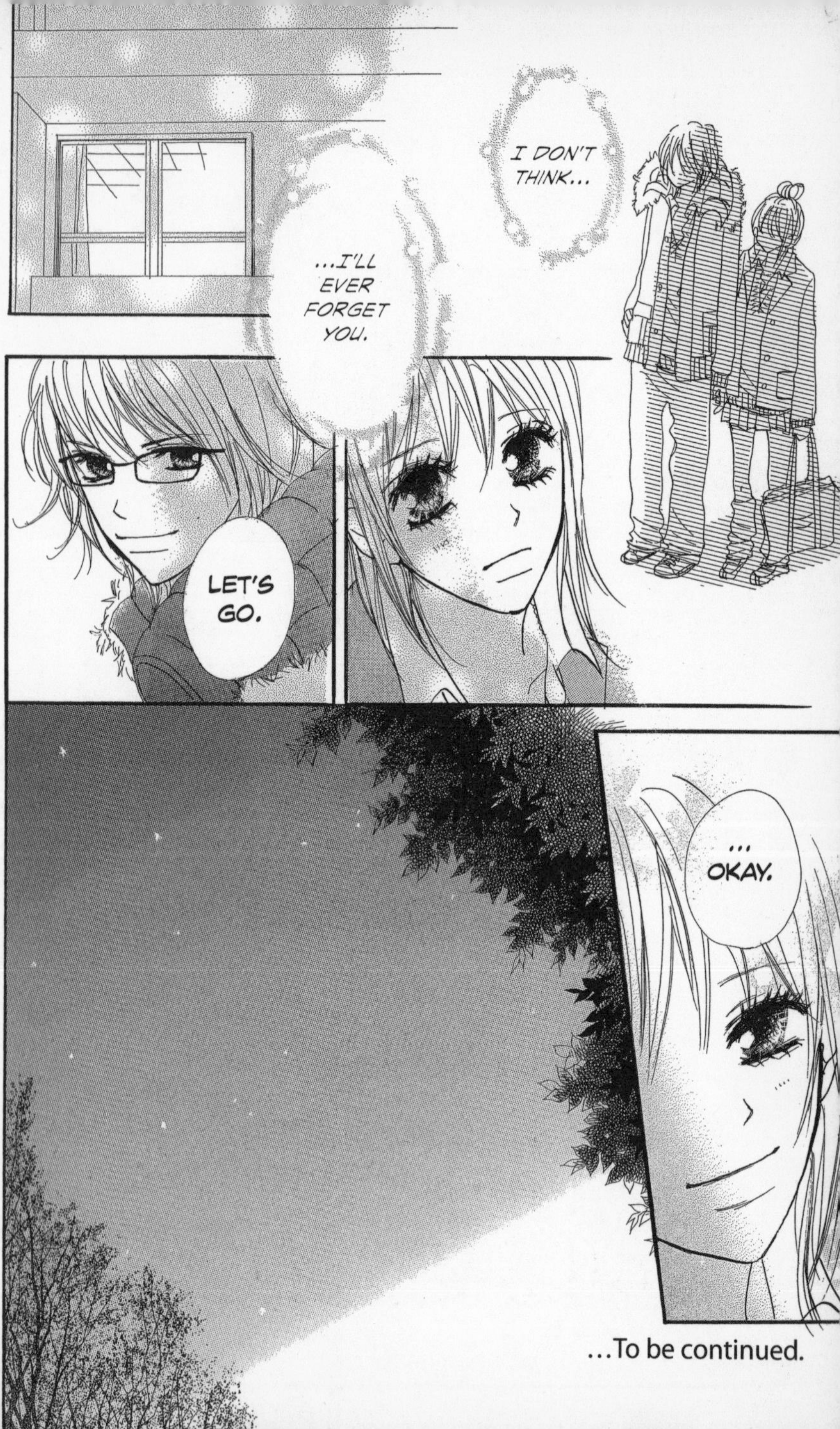
I DON'T THINK...
...I'LL EVER FORGET YOU.
LET'S GO.
... OKAY.

…To be continued.

C-95
RYUNOSUKE FUJI
HEIGHT 177
WEIGHT 63
BLOOD O
$ 50,0000
C-94
RYOKO SAKURA
HEIGHT 159
WEIGHT
NYAH NYAH
BLOOD A
$ —0
C-93
JIN SAWAMURA
HEIGHT 175
WEIGHT 59
BLOOD A
$ 20,0000

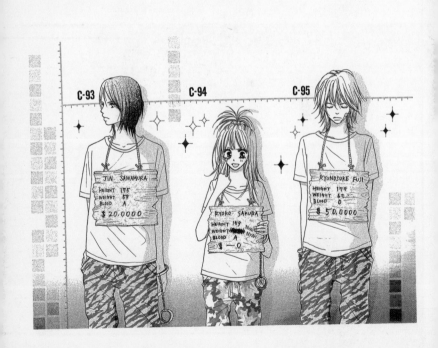

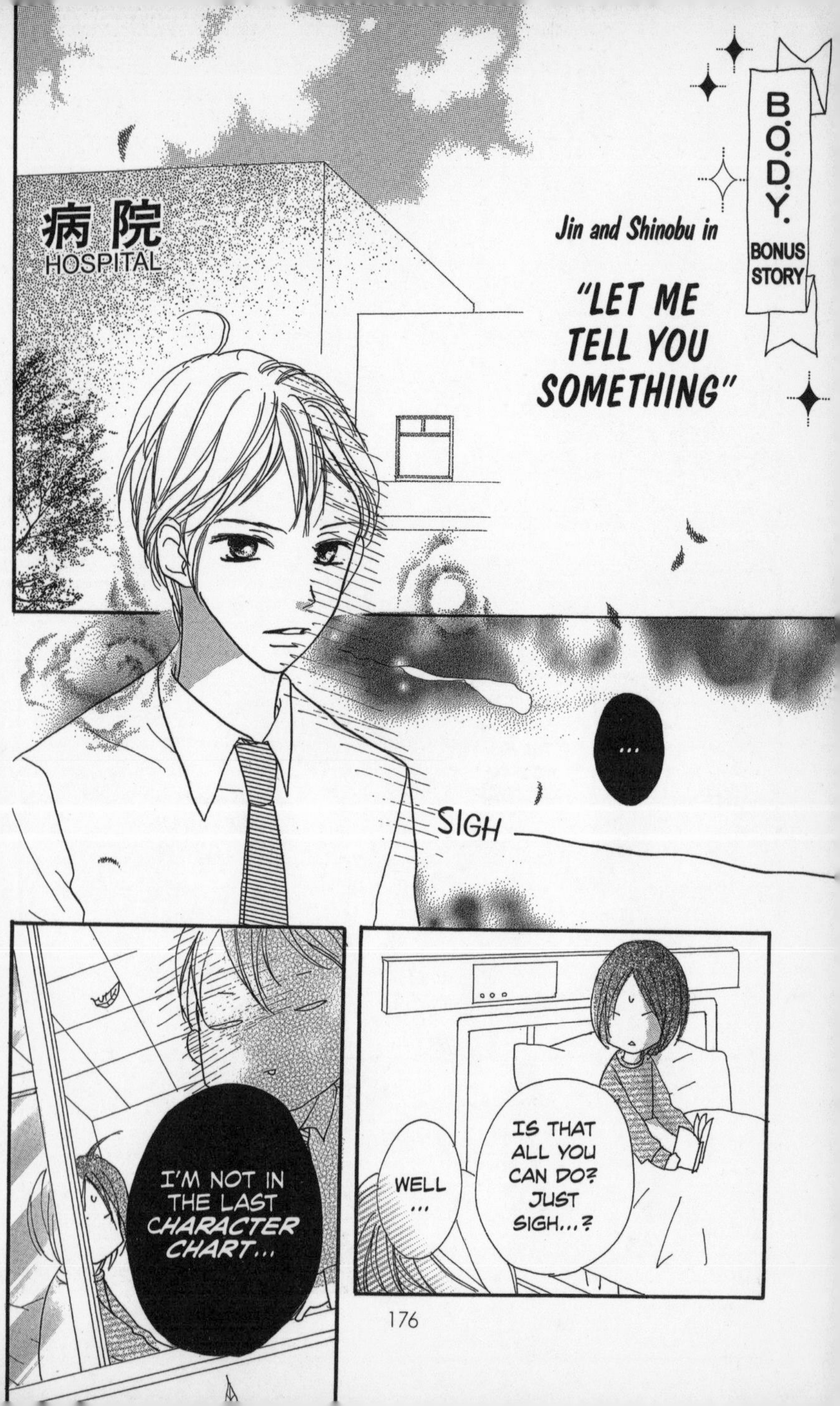
B.O.D.Y.
BONUS STORY
Jin and Shinobu in
"LET ME TELL YOU SOMETHING"
病院
HOSPITAL
...
SIGH
IS THAT ALL YOU CAN DO? JUST SIGH...?
WELL ...
I'M NOT IN THE LAST CHARACTER CHART...

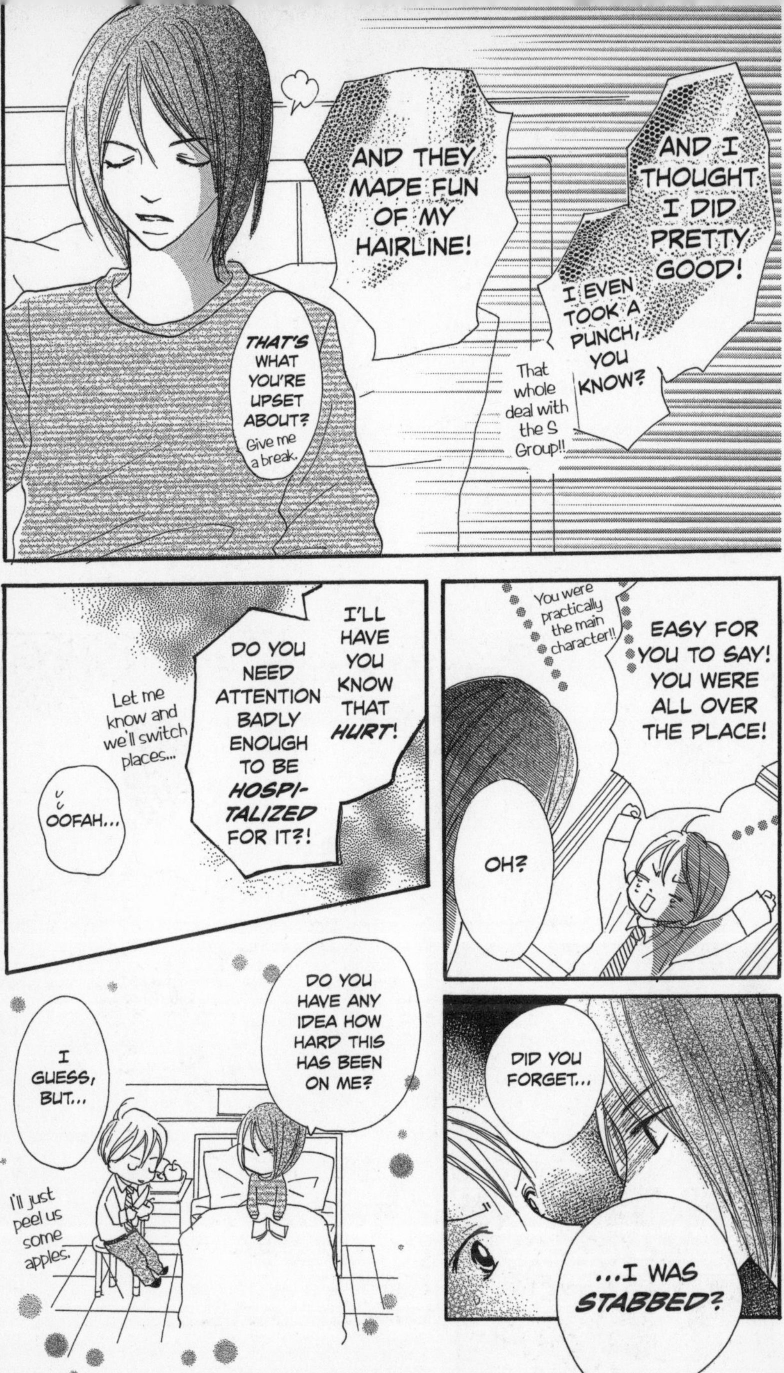
AND I THOUGHT I DID PRETTY GOOD!
I EVEN TOOK A PUNCH, YOU KNOW?
That whole deal with the S Group!!
AND THEY MADE FUN OF MY HAIRLINE!
THAT'S WHAT YOU'RE UPSET ABOUT?
Give me a break.
You were practically the main character!!
EASY FOR YOU TO SAY! YOU WERE ALL OVER THE PLACE!
OH?
I'LL HAVE YOU KNOW THAT HURT!
DO YOU NEED ATTENTION BADLY ENOUGH TO BE HOSPITALIZED FOR IT?!
Let me know and we'll switch places...
OOFAH...
DID YOU FORGET...
...I WAS STABBED?
DO YOU HAVE ANY IDEA HOW HARD THIS HAS BEEN ON ME?
I GUESS, BUT...
I'll just peel us some apples.

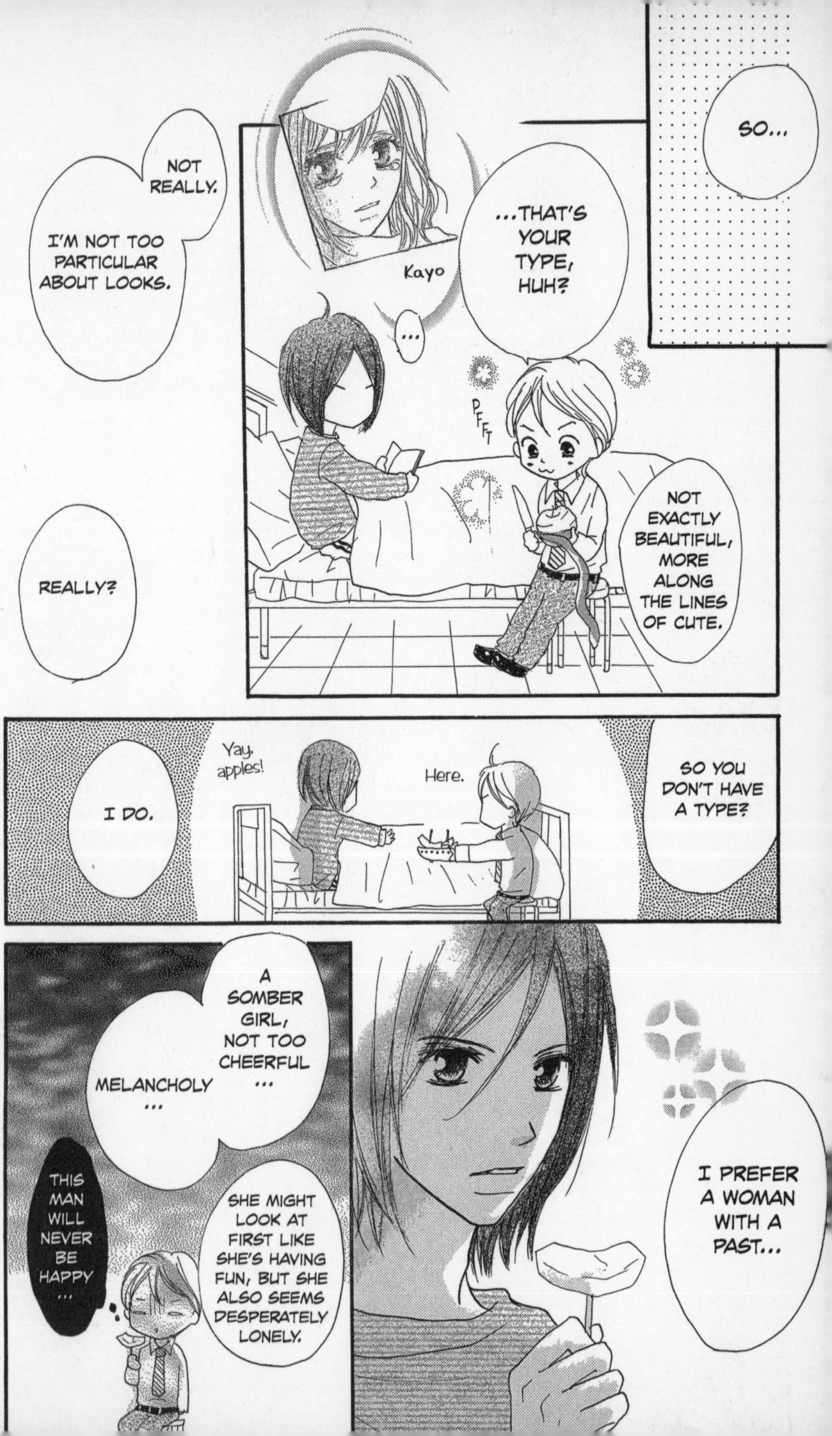
SO...
...THAT'S YOUR TYPE, HUH?
Kayo
...
PFFFT
NOT EXACTLY BEAUTIFUL, MORE ALONG THE LINES OF CUTE.
NOT REALLY.
I'M NOT TOO PARTICULAR ABOUT LOOKS.
REALLY?
SO YOU DON'T HAVE A TYPE?
Here.
Yay, apples!
I DO.
I PREFER A WOMAN WITH A PAST...
A SOMBER GIRL, NOT TOO CHEERFUL...
MELANCHOLY...
SHE MIGHT LOOK AT FIRST LIKE SHE'S HAVING FUN, BUT SHE ALSO SEEMS DESPERATELY LONELY.
THIS MAN WILL NEVER BE HAPPY...

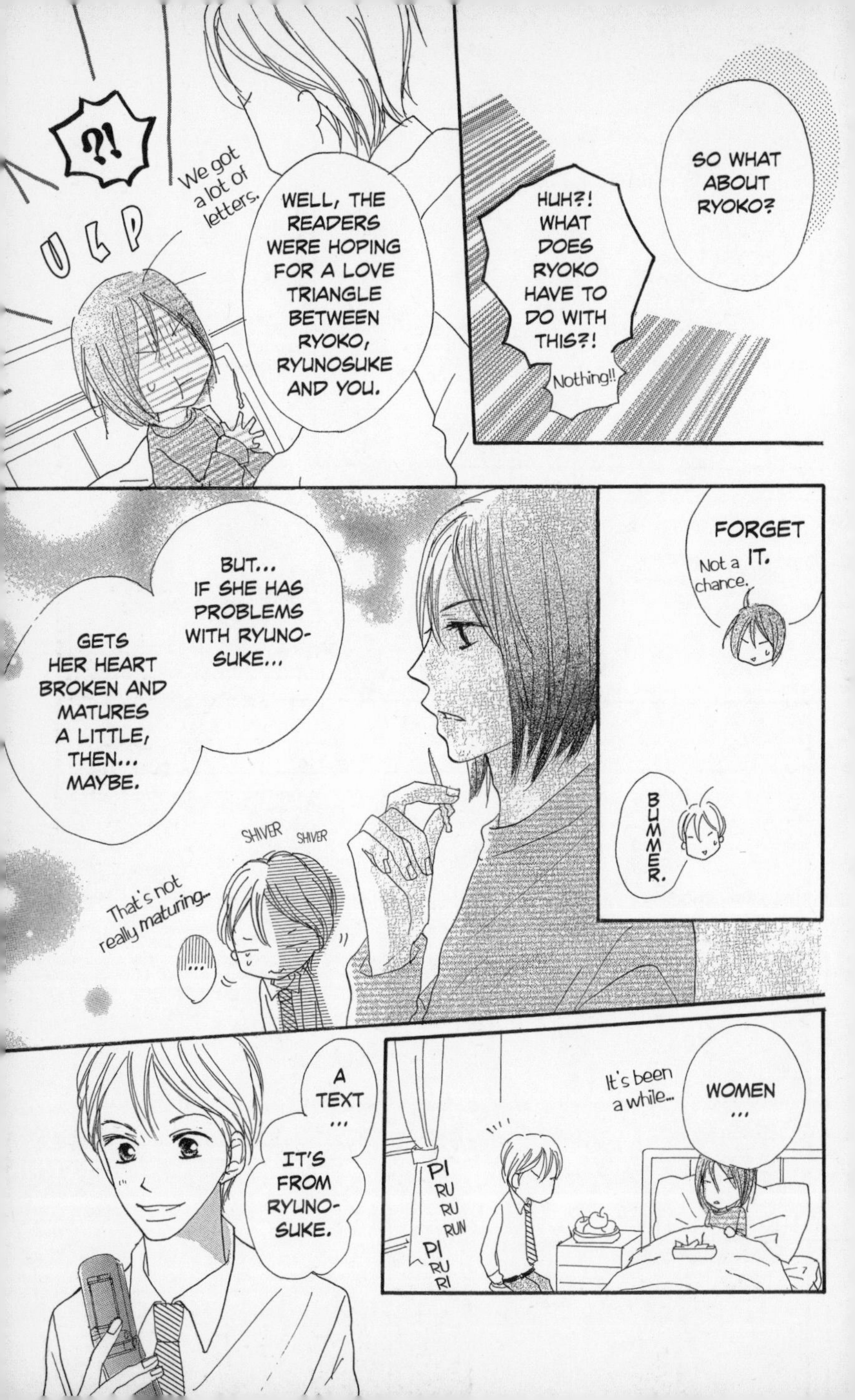
SO WHAT ABOUT RYOKO?
HUH?! WHAT DOES RYOKO HAVE TO DO WITH THIS?!
Nothing!!
?!
WELL, THE READERS WERE HOPING FOR A LOVE TRIANGLE BETWEEN RYOKO, RYUNOSUKE AND YOU.
We got a lot of letters.
ULP
FORGET IT.
Not a chance.
BUMMER.
BUT... IF SHE HAS PROBLEMS WITH RYUNO-SUKE...
GETS HER HEART BROKEN AND MATURES A LITTLE, THEN... MAYBE.
SHIVER SHIVER
That's not really maturing..
...
WOMEN...
It's been a while...
PI RU RU RUN
PI RU RI
A TEXT...
IT'S FROM RYUNO-SUKE.

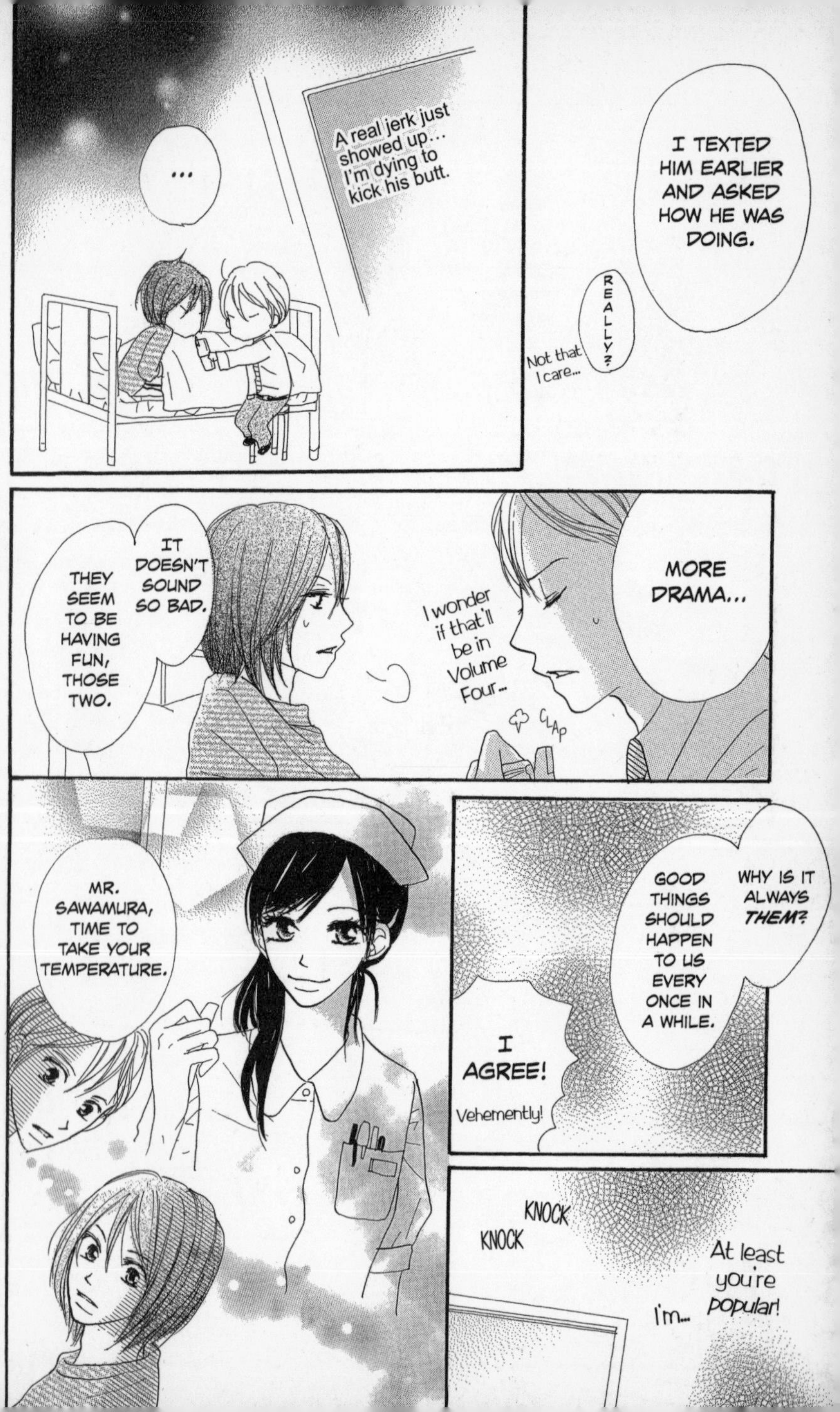
I TEXTED HIM EARLIER AND ASKED HOW HE WAS DOING.
REALLY?
Not that I care...
A real jerk just showed up... I'm dying to kick his butt.
...
MORE DRAMA...
I wonder if that'll be in Volume Four...
CLAP
IT DOESN'T SOUND SO BAD.
THEY SEEM TO BE HAVING FUN, THOSE TWO.
WHY IS IT ALWAYS *THEM*?
GOOD THINGS SHOULD HAPPEN TO US EVERY ONCE IN A WHILE.
I AGREE!
Vehemently!
At least you're popular!
I'm...
KNOCK
KNOCK
MR. SAWAMURA, TIME TO TAKE YOUR TEMPERATURE.

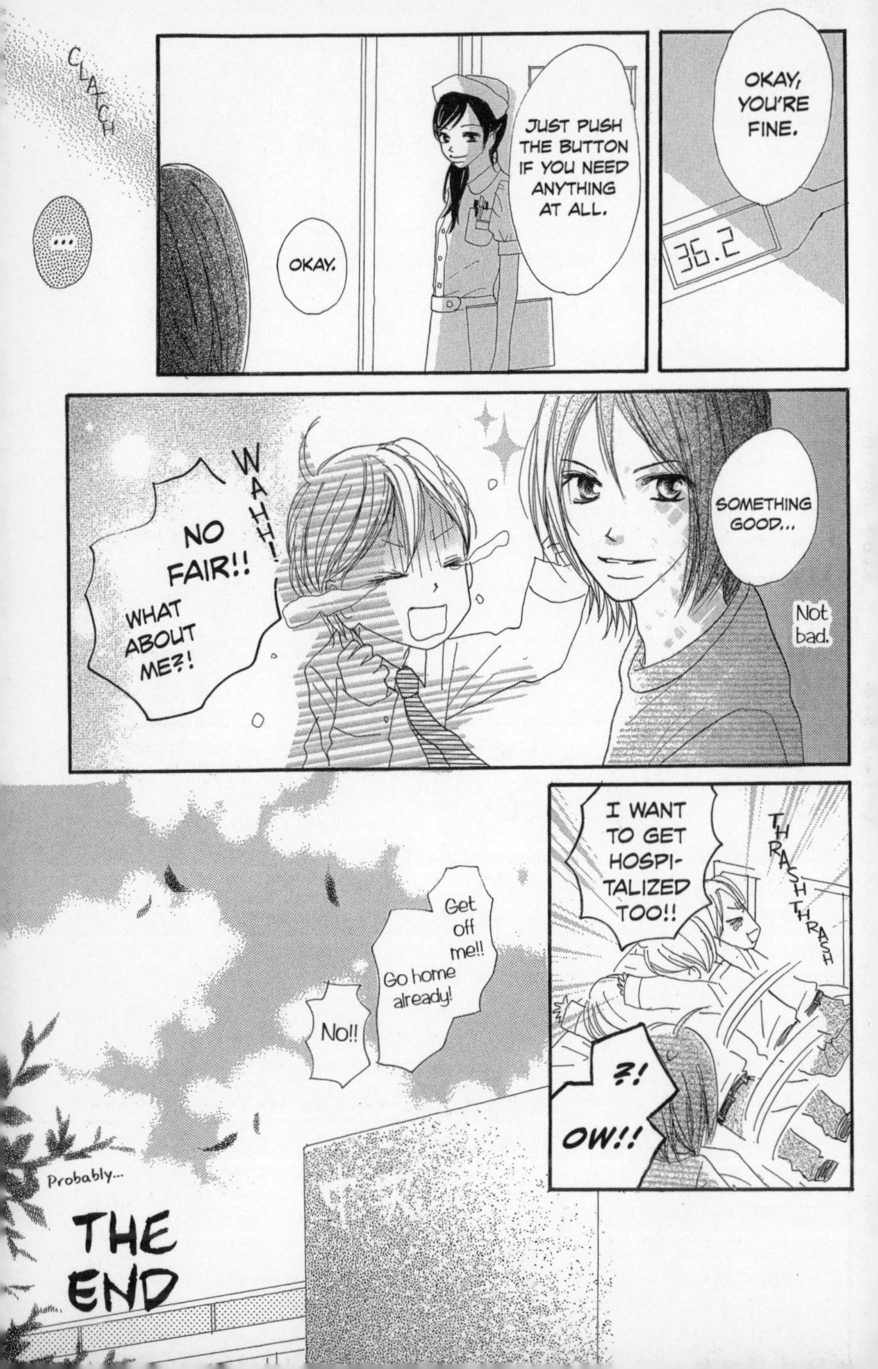
OKAY, YOU'RE FINE.
36.2
JUST PUSH THE BUTTON IF YOU NEED ANYTHING AT ALL.
OKAY.
CLATCH
...
SOMETHING GOOD...
Not bad.
WAHH!
NO FAIR!! WHAT ABOUT ME?!
I WANT TO GET HOSPI-TALIZED TOO!!
THRASH THRASH
?!
OW!!
Get off me!!
Go home already!
No!!
Probably...
THE END

Well, what did you think?

FLUTTER FLUTTER

Thank you for sticking around!! I guarantee some new developments in the next episode... I mean, the next volume. We're going to find out a little more about their school life... Are these kids really making time to study during all this?

- Helpers!

  As you all know—

  Natsume Hirose, Mastu Kotô

  HA HA

  Uh...

  Thank you, thank you!

  ← Perfunctory

  Show more respect!

- The person who gave me a great gift after something good happened to me this year—

  Mari Fujimura

  Deep bow

  Thank you———!!

- The person who deals with all my work related kvetching—

  Karuho Shiina

  Karuho

  Loves Ryoko Yamagishi's ← HU NO ANJI

  Kuku...

  You shoulda seen Kasuga's face!

  This joke's been going on for three months now...

  Like the C.F.Y. bag

  CRAZY FOR YOU

  ← Tattered from so much use!

  And the C.F.Y. mug

  Thank you—!!

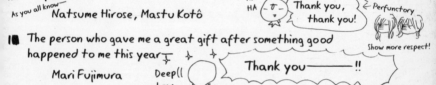

- And you—the reader!!

  Thank you———!!

HA HA

Well then—

Thank you!!

I'll see you in Volume 4! ♡

12/13/2004

Ao Mimori

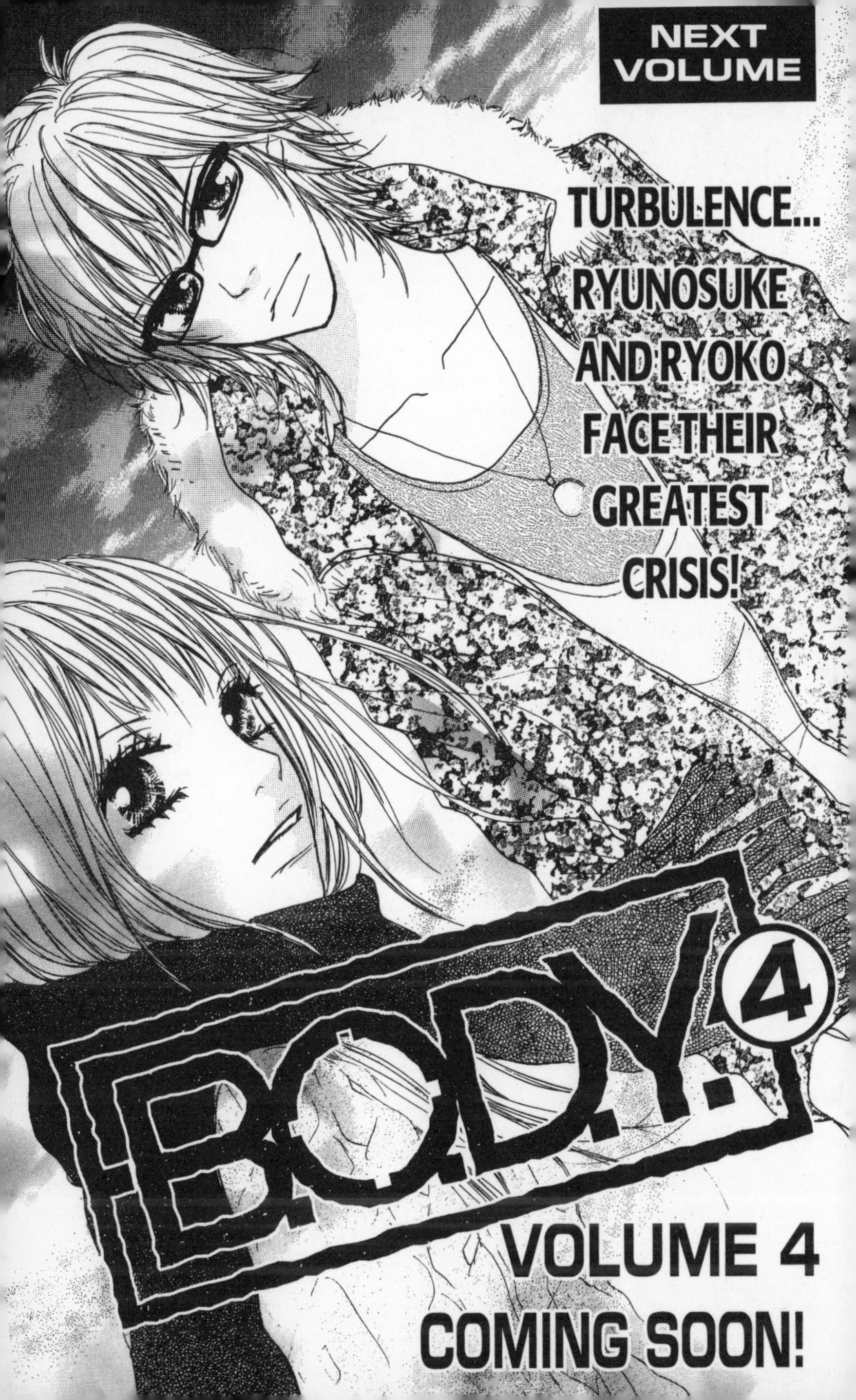
NEXT VOLUME
TURBULENCE...
RYUNOSUKE AND RYOKO FACE THEIR GREATEST CRISIS!
B.O.D.Y. 4
VOLUME 4 COMING SOON!

B.O.D.Y. Language

Page 41, Author's Note: Natsume Hirose
Shojo manga artist whose works include *Kimi wa Candy* (You Are Candy), *Honto no Koi wo Ageru Ne* (I'll Give You My True Heart) and *Koigokoro Part 2*.

Page 83, panel 3: your seal
In Japan, personal seals, or hanko, are traditionally used to prove identity on official documents. Nowadays, people can often use either a seal or a signature.

Page 99, Author's Note: *Bobobo-bo Bo-bobo*
A slapstick action/comedy manga by Yoshio Sawai, published in English by VIZ Media. Both *Bobobo-bo Bo-bobo* and *Naruto* first appeared in Japan in *Weekly Shonen Jump* magazine.

Page 182, Author's Note: Ryoko Yamagishi
A classic shojo manga artist whose most famous works include *Arabesque*, about a Russian ballerina, and *Hi Izuru Tokoro no Tenshi* (Heaven's Son in the Land of the Rising Sun).

Nine volumes...

TUP TUP TUP TUP

Author's Commentary

How do I stop being sleepy?
Do I just have to sleep it off?
I don't know any other way,
so I sleep late even when I've
got a big deadline coming up.
Only because there's no other
way, mind you...

Ao Mimori began creating manga during her junior year of college, and
her work debuted when she was only 23. *B.O.D.Y.*, her third series, was
first published in *Bessatsu Margaret* in 2003 and is also available in
Japanese as an audio CD. Her other work includes *Sonnano Koi Jyanai*
(That's Not Love), *Anta Nanka Iranai* (I Don't Need You), *Dakishimetaiyo
Motto* (I Want to Hold You More), *I LOVE YOU* and *Kamisama no Iu Toori*
(As the God of Death Dictates).

B.O.D.Y. VOL 3
The Shojo Beat Manga Edition

STORY & ART BY
AO MIMORI

English Adaptation/Kelly Sue DeConnick
Translation/Joe Yamazaki
Touch-up Art & Lettering/James Gaubatz
Design/Izumi Hirayama
Editor/Shaenon K. Garrity

Editor in Chief, Books/Alvin Lu
Editor in Chief, Magazines/Marc Weidenbaum
VP, Publishing Licensing/Rika Inouye
VP, Sales and Product Marketing/Gonzalo Ferreyra
VP, Creative/Linda Espinosa
Publisher/Hyoe Narita

B.O.D.Y. © 2003 by Ao Mimori
All rights reserved.
First published in Japan in 2003 by SHUEISHA Inc., Tokyo.
English translation rights arranged by SHUEISHA Inc.
The stories, characters and incidents mentioned in this
publication are entirely fictional.

Printed in Canada

Published by VIZ Media, LLC
P.O. Box 77010
San Francisco, CA 94107

Shojo Beat Manga Edition
10 9 8 7 6 5 4 3 2 1
First printing, November 2008

www.viz.com

store.viz.com

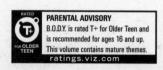

PARENTAL ADVISORY
B.O.D.Y. is rated T+ for Older Teen and
is recommended for ages 16 and up.
This volume contains mature themes.
ratings.viz.com

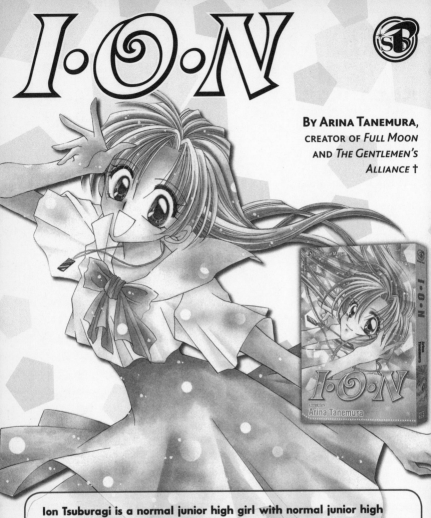

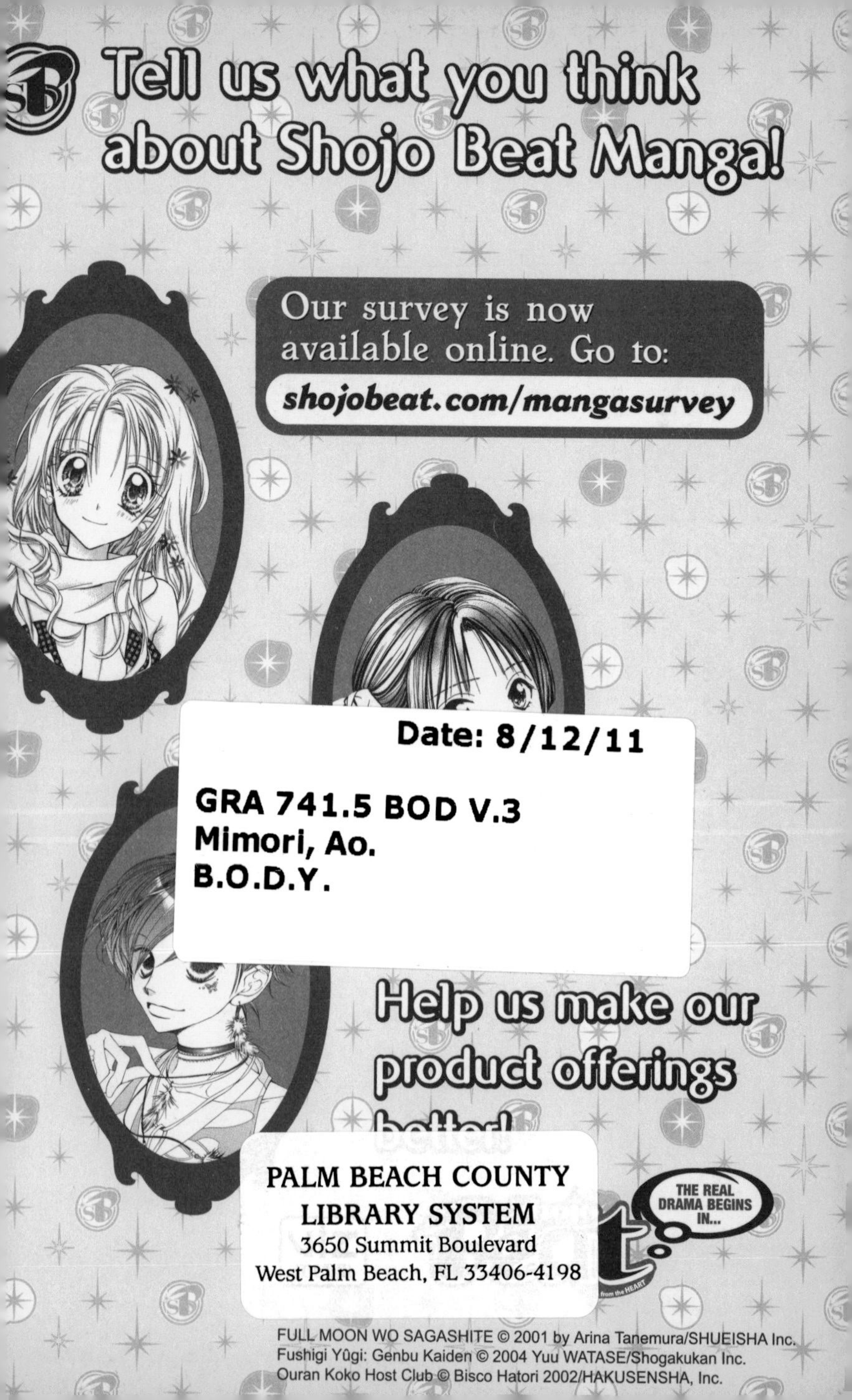
Tell us what you think about Shojo Beat Manga!
Our survey is now available online. Go to:
shojobeat.com/mangasurvey
Help us make our product offerings better!
THE REAL DRAMA BEGINS IN...
FULL MOON WO SAGASHITE © 2001 by Arina Tanemura/SHUEISHA Inc.
Fushigi Yûgi: Genbu Kaiden © 2004 Yuu WATASE/Shogakukan Inc.
Ouran Koko Host Club © Bisco Hatori 2002/HAKUSENSHA, Inc.